LIBRARY OF HEBREW BIBLE/
OLD TESTAMENT STUDIES

432

Formerly Journal for the Study of the Old Testament Supplement Series

RHETORIC AND SOCIAL JUSTICE
IN ISAIAH

Mark Gray

t&t clark

NEW YORK • LONDON

Copyright © 2006 by Mark Gray

T & T Clark International, 80 Maiden Lane, New York, NY 10038

T & T Clark International, The Tower Building, 11 York Road, London SE1 7NX

T & T Clark International is a Continuum imprint.

Library of Congress Cataloging-in-Publication Data
Gray, Mark, 1960-
Rhetoric and social justice in Isaiah / Mark Gray.
    p. cm. -- (Library of Hebrew Bible/Old Testament studies ; 432)
Includes bibliographical references and index.
ISBN 0-567-02761-9 (hardcover)
1. Bible. O.T. Isaiah--Language, style. 2. Social justice--Biblical teaching. 3. God--Righteousness--Biblical teaching. I. Title. II. Series.
 BS1515.6.J8G73 2006
 224'.1066--dc22
                        2006001138

Printed in the United States of America

    06 07 08 09 10   10 9 8 7 6 5 4 3 2 1

CONTENTS

ACKNOWLEDGMENTS

I would like to thank Dr James McKeown for the kindly, competent, and professional manner in which he undertook the supervision of this work as it existed as a thesis and guided it with attentive care to completion. Focused on the text, we became colleagues and friends, intrigued by the interpretative possibilities in the book of Isaiah and its continued significance for our world. I would also like to thank my friends, the late Professor J. Severino Croatto and Professor Kathleen M. O'Connor, who read a draft of the manuscript in its entirety, and whose greatly appreciated encouragement added to the momentum to get the work finished. In addition, Professor Walter Brueggemann, whose work I first read by oil lamp in Africa, has been immensely generous in his support and friendship: his approach to the world of the text has greatly influenced my own. Finally, I would like to thank my dear friend, Reverend Hsu T'ien Hsien, a minister of the Presbyterian Church in Taiwan, a former Amnesty International prisoner of conscience and past moderator of his denomination, who first introduced me to the importance of social justice in the Old Testament.

On a more practical but nonetheless important front, I would like to acknowledge and thank the St. Luke's College Foundation, the Dr Williams's Trust, the Presbyterian Association Foundation, and the Ministerial Development Programme of the Presbyterian Church in Ireland, each of which provided financial support at different times during the course of the research which eventually resulted in this book. Glad thanks are also due to my friend and colleague John Turnbull, who edited and advised in the final form of this work. Of course, all remaining shortcomings and mistakes are my own.

Although academic in nature, this study has also been shaped by my journey of life and faith, especially the experience of having lived and worked in the African country of Malawi. The late, great Archbishop Trevor Huddleston writes movingly of "the witchery of Africa: the way it lays its hold upon your heart and will not let you go. There are many exiles from Africa, whose hearts are still there, and will always be."[1]

1. Trevor Huddleston, *Naught for Your Comfort* (Glasgow: Collins, 1956), 13.

This I find to be poignantly so. Malawi was and is among the poorest countries in the world, and this in itself directs attention to the importance of the primal necessities of life: to bread, clothing, shelter, welcome, community, justice—to the Isa 58 agenda.

In this shaping of life and faith, my heartfelt thanks go to my parents, Margaret and Hugh Gray, who had the grace to let me go and experience the world from a different perspective; to Betsy, whom I met on the journey; and to our children, Nathan, Hannah, and Rose, who at this stage of their development at any rate are neither too abstract nor academic. In their insistence on immediacy in response to need they remind us of the need for action now to create a more just, compassionate world for all of God's children.

This book is dedicated to Betsy, who lives toward the day when the tear will be wiped from every eye, in a world without violence.

ABBREVIATIONS

BDB	Francis Brown, S.R. Driver and Charles A. Briggs. *A Hebrew and English Lexicon of the Old Testament*. Oxford: Clarendon Press, 1907
AB	Anchor Bible
ABR	*Australian Biblical Review*
AnBib	Analecta biblica
ASTI	*Annual of the Swedish Theological Institute*
BAR	*Biblical Archaeology Review*
BASOR	*Bulletin of the American Schools of Oriental Research*
BAT	Die Botschaft des Alten Testaments
BETL	Bibliotheca ephemeridum theologicarum lovaniensium
BibInt	*Biblical Interpretation*
BST	The Bible Speaks Today
BTB	*Biblical Theology Bulletin*
BZAW	Beihefte zur Zeitschrift für die alttestamentliche Wissenschaft
CB	Cultura biblica
CBQ	Catholic Biblical Quarterly
ET	English translation
ExpTim	*Expository Times*
FTL	Forum theologiae linguisticae
HTR	*Harvard Theological Review*
HUCA	*Hebrew Union College Annual*
IB	*Interpreter's Bible*. Edited by G. A. Buttrick et al. 12 vols. New York, 1951–57
Int	*Interpretation*
ITC	International Theological Commentary
JAAR	*Journal of the American Academy of Religion*
JBL	*Journal of Biblical Literature*
JBQ	*Jewish Bible Quarterly*
JNES	*Journal of Near Eastern Studies*
JQR	*Jewish Quarterly Review*
JSOT	*Journal for the Study of the Old Testament*
JSOTSup	Journal for the Study of the Old Testament: Supplement Series
KAT	Kommentar zum Alten Testament
KHC	Kurzer Hand-Commentar zum Alten Testament
KuD	*Kerygma und Dogma*
LCBI	Literary Currents in Biblical Interpretation
NCB	New Century Bible

NEB	*New English Bible*
NGTT	*Nederduitse gereformeerde teologiese tydskrif*
NIBCOT	New International Biblical Commentary on the Old Testament
NICOT	New International Commentary on the Old Testament
NIV	New International Version
NLV	New Living Translation
NRSV	New Revised Standard Version
OBT	Overtures to Biblical Theology
OTG	Old Testament Guides
OTL	Old Testament Library
PMLA	*Proceedings of the Modern Language Association*
SBLDS	Society of Biblical Literature Dissertation Series
SBS	Stuttgarter Bibelstudien
TLZ	*Theologische Literaturzeitung*
TQ	*Theologische Quartalschrift*
TynBul	*Tyndale Bulletin*
USQR	*Union Seminary Quarterly Review*
VT	*Vetus Testamentum*
VTSup	Vetus Testamentum Supplements
WBC	Word Biblical Commentary
ZAW	*Zeitschrift für die alttestamentliche Wissenschaft*
ZBK	Zürcher Bibelkommentare
ZTK	*Zeitschrift für Theologie und Kirche*

Introduction

THE BOOK OF ISAIAH:
A TEXT-BASED METHOD FOR A LITERARY READING

1. *"Only the Text"*

D. H. Lawrence advises, "Never trust the artist. Trust the tale."[1] He continues that "the proper function of a critic is to save the tale from the artist who created it."[2] In this characteristically forthright assessment, attention is effectively directed away from the artist–author and refocused on the tale–text as of central importance in literary-aesthetic evaluation. The role of the critic-reader is explicitly recognized, specifically in suspicious opposition to the artist, who for Lawrence "is usually a damned liar."[3] Again, the work of art, rather than the intention or mind of the artist, is emphasized as the locus of what Lawrence calls "truth."[4] Thus, although Lawrence does not propose the redundancy or, more extremely, the death of the concept of author,[5] his opinions can legitimately be located in a tendency of thought which eventuates in such positions.[6]

1. D. H. Lawrence, *Studies in Classic American Literature* (London: Penguin, 1971 [1923]), 8. The subheading is from Samuel Beckett, speaking of the Odéon production of *Waiting for Godot* in 1960; quoted in Deirdre Bair, *Samuel Beckett: A Biography* (London: Picador/Pan, 1980), 433. The full quotation reads, "The best possible play is one in which there are no actors, only the text. I'm trying to find a way to write one."
2. Lawrence, *Studies in Classic American Literature*, 8.
3. Ibid.
4. Ibid. He asserts, "Art-speech is the only truth. An artist is usually a damned liar, but his art, if it be art, will tell you the truth of his day."
5. As an author himself, perhaps a degree of self-interest is at work here, acting as a disincentive to Lawrence taking this step.
6. For a helpful introduction to this area, see Roger Lundin, "Interpreting Orphans: Hermeneutics in the Cartesian Tradition," in *The Promise of Hermeneutics* (ed. Roger Lundin, Clarence Walhout, and Anthony C. Thiselton; Grand Rapids: Eerdmans; Cambridge: Paternoster, 1999), 1–64. More succinctly and provocatively, Valentine Cunningham claims that "the characteristic heroes of modernism are Oedipus and his clones—father-killers and mother-fuckers" (*In the Reading Gaol: Postmodernity, Texts, and History* [Oxford: Blackwell, 1994], 377). See also

Moreover, the work of art begins to gain independence from the artist in the way integrity and worth are found in the work itself, while the person who produced it is associated with mendacity. Effectually, the work has taken on a life of its own beyond the control of the hand that initially shaped it.[7]

Cunningham aptly observes that "it is as impossible for us to imagine a text without an author, or a busy pen or paintbrush without some hand holding it, as it is for a text of any kind to exist without some text-making hand."[8] However, as access to the author (or Author) of literary works is neither unmediated nor unproblematical, attention becomes focused on the text in conjunction with readers as the arena in which meaning is forged.[9] Furthermore, the death, in a very literal sense, of the "author" or "authors" of the book of Isaiah[10] accentuates justification for

William K. Wimsatt Jr. and Monroe C. Beardsley, *The Verbal Icon: Studies in the Meaning of Poetry* (London: Methuen, 1970 [1954]), 5; Pierre Macherey, *A Theory of Literary Production* (trans. Geoffrey Wall; London: Routledge & Kegan Paul, 1978), 7; Michael Foucault, *Language, Counter-Memory, Practice: Selected Essays and Interviews* (ed. and with an introduction by Donald F. Bouchard; trans. Donald F. Bouchard and Sherry Simon; Oxford: Blackwell, 1977), 120. On the death of the Author, see Jean-François Lyotard, *The Differend: Phrases in Dispute* (trans. Georges Van Den Abbeele; Manchester: Manchester University Press, 1988), 83; Roland Barthes, *The Semiotic Challenge* (trans. Richard Howard; Oxford: Blackwell, 1988), 242. Interestingly, Lawrence (*Studies in Classic American Literature*, 9), in the course of a sort of proto-deconstructionist handling of the founding and still-powerful myth that the Pilgrim Fathers went to America "in search of freedom," prefigures this thinking by asserting that instead they came to get "away from everything," driven by "a black revulsion from Europe, from the old authority of Europe, from kings and bishops and popes. And more" (p. 11). Ultimately, Lawrence suggests, the Pilgrim Fathers wanted "no kings, no bishops maybe. Even *no God Almighty*" (emphasis added).

7. Paul Ricoeur, *A Ricoeur Reader: Reflection and Imagination* (ed. Mario Valdés; New York: Harvester-Wheatsheaf, 1991), 89.

8. Cunningham, *In the Reading Gaol*, 30.

9. This focus on text substantially renders immaterial theological implications and questions associated with Death of the Author thinking at one end of the spectrum, and philosophically based attempts to reinstate the divine Author at the other; on which, see Nicholas Wolterstorff, *Divine Discourse: Philosophical Reflections on the Claim that God Speaks* (Cambridge: Cambridge University Press, 1993).

10. Since Bernhard Duhm, *Das Buch Jesaia* (5th ed.; Göttingen: Vandenhoeck & Ruprecht, 1968 [1892]), the predominant school of critical thought has argued for three or perhaps two authors/redactors; recently, Ronald E. Clements ("Isaiah: A Book without an Ending," *JSOT* 97 [2002]: 109–26 [118]) has interestingly suggested the need for a "Fourth Isaiah" who is "fundamental to making sense of the book as a finished whole."

concentrating on the text itself, especially in a literary reading. As Ricoeur argues, "[I]t is when the author is dead that the relation to the book becomes complete and, as it were, intact. The author can no longer respond; it only remains to read his work."[11] In what follows, the attention devoted to literary theory explicates the methodology employed and consequently sustains this text-based reading of the book of Isaiah.

2. *The Revival of Rhetoric*

This turn toward the text has taken place and been assisted by a revival in rhetoric,[12] viewed not merely as the ornamental embellishment of the core thesis of a text,[13] but, rather, as constitutive of reality.[14] In effect, the process has involved the expansion of what is understood by rhetoric through the proposal of different and sometimes competing definitions,[15] which, despite long-standing perils and pitfalls,[16] may be said to share the underlying aim of attempting to reclaim rhetoric as a theoretical category suitable for use in the modern literary world.[17]

11. Ricoeur, *A Ricoeur Reader*, 45.

12. See Thomas Conley, *Rhetoric in the European Tradition* (White Plains, N.Y.: Longman, 1990); Winifred Bryan Horner, *The Present State of Scholarship in Historical and Contemporary Rhetoric* (Columbia: University of Missouri Press, 1990); Steven Mailloux, *Rhetorical Power* (Ithaca, N.Y.: Cornell University Press, 1989); Brian Vickers, *In Defence of Rhetoric* (Oxford: Clarendon, 1988).

13. James Barr writes "that rhetoric is *despised*" (*The Concept of Biblical Theology: An Old Testament Perspective* [London: SCM Press, 1999], 547 [emphasis in original]) because ultimately "there is nothing behind it." Suspicion of rhetoric has a long history, as Susan A. Handelman observes (*The Slayers of Moses: The Emergence of Rabbinic Interpretation in Modern Literary Theory* [Albany, N.Y.: SUNY Press, 1982], 15).

14. See Robert L. Scott, "On Viewing Rhetoric as Epistemic," *Central States Speech Journal* 18 (1967): 9–17.

15. See B. L. Brock and Robert L. Scott, *Methods of Rhetorical Criticism: A Twentieth-Century Perspective* (2d rev. ed.; Detroit: Wayne State University Press, 1980); also, Heinrich Plett, *Einführung in die rhetorische Textanalyse* (3d ed.; Hamburg: Buske, 1975); idem, *Rhetorik der Affekte: Englische Wirkungsästhetik im Zeitalter der Renaissance* (Tübingen: Niemeyer, 1975); Bruce Bashford, "The Rhetorical Method in Literary Criticism," *Philosophy and Rhetoric* 9 (1976): 133–46.

16. See Loren D. Reid, "The Perils of Rhetoric Criticism," *The Quarterly Journal of Speech* 30 (1944): 416–22; also, M. O. Sillars, "Persistent Problems in Rhetorical Criticism," in *Rhetoric and Communication: Studies in the University of Illinois Tradition* (ed. J. Blankenship and H. G. Stelzner; Urbana: University of Illinois Press, 1976), 69–88.

17. See Terry Eagleton, *Literary Theory: An Introduction* (Minneapolis: University of Minnesota Press, 1983), 205–6.

For some, the idea that rhetoric may be defined, in summary, "as the means by which a text establishes and manages its relationship to its audience in order to achieve a particular effect,"[18] could be the pretext for the reinstatement of the idea of authorial intention,[19] especially in light of the explication that while auditors/readers are free to interpret the language of discourse in any way they wish, "the speaker or author attempts to constrain that freedom and direct interpretation by giving the audience cues and indicators as to how he or she means the discourse to function for them."[20] This, however, would be to claim too much, and perhaps the most accurate assessment is that evidence from the text itself assists in constituting an implied author,[21] not as the determiner or guarantor of one intended meaning, but as a necessary component in a communicative act.[22] The text—and the tale it tells—is in this way maintained as more important than the teller, a search for whom would be futile.

Furthermore, it may be argued that interpretation is always to some extent a function of the subjectivity of the reader. As Aichele observes:

> Neither the attempt to re-create the original reception of the text by its first readers nor the search for an originating intentionality nor the reconstruction of a series of actual events "behind" the text can determine its proper meaning. Historical reconstructions of the past are always undertaken from the point of view of the present, and they are therefore themselves inevitably intertextual and thus ideological.[23]

Linking this point specifically to a concern with rhetoric, the writers of the Bible and Culture Collective, reacting against limiting "the role of the critic to releasing the rhetorical power of the ancient text,"[24] argue that what is missing in this approach is an

> awareness that the power of the text includes the reader as part of the text. When the reader reconstructs the text's rhetorical situation, its interests and contextualization, she does so out of a rhetorical situation of her own,

---

18.   Dale Patrick and Allen Scult, *Rhetoric and Biblical Interpretation* (JSOTSup 82; Sheffield: Almond, 1990), 12.

19.   On which see E. D. Hirsch Jr., *Validity in Interpretation* (New Haven: Yale University Press, 1967).

20.   Patrick and Scult, *Rhetoric and Biblical Interpretation*, 15.

21.   See Wayne C. Booth, *The Rhetoric of Fiction* (2d ed.; Chicago: University of Chicago Press, 1983).

22.   See George Aichele, *Sign, Text, Scripture: Semiotics and the Bible* (Interventions 1; Sheffield: Sheffield Academic Press, 1997), 31.

23.   Ibid., 114–15.

24.   George Aichele et al., *The Postmodern Bible: The Bible and Culture Collective* (New Haven: Yale University Press, 1995), 163.

her own interests and contextualization. The new rhetorical criticism emphasizes that rhetorical power is present in a text not just once, when it is first uttered or written, but also for future readers in their own rhetorical situation.[25]

All of this underscores that reader orientation is an integral aspect of the rhetorical situation.[26]

In studying the rhetoric of the Hebrew Bible, two main approaches may be identified. One approach applies an external frame of rhetorical reference—usually categories drawn from classical Greek rhetoric—to the text.[27] The second approach follows the contours of the text itself, largely basing its analysis on features internal to the world of the text.[28] In this study the latter approach will predominate, for "[t]o the extent to which one can recover ancient Israelite models, those models should direct any attempts to understand the literary artistry of particular biblical texts."[29] Further, my approach takes place in the awareness that to be adequate to modern usage, the concept of rhetoric must retain a close tie to its traditional emphasis on *"verbal expression"*; be understood as constitutive of how truth is mediated and discovered; be linked "with the creation of meaning and the domain of *hermeneutics"*; be viewed "as *a factor in social discourse and societal formation"*; and be conceived, in keeping with the connection of thought and emotions, as a "prime motivating force for action."[30]

---

25. Ibid., 163–64.

26. This phrase may be traced to Lloyd F. Bitzer, "The Rhetorical Situation," *Philosophy and Rhetoric* 1 (1968): 1–14; developing Bitzer's work, see Alan Brinton, "Situation in the Theory of Rhetoric," *Philosophy and Rhetoric* 14 (1981): 234–48.

27. E.g. Phyllis Trible, *Rhetorical Criticism: Context, Method, and the Book of Jonah* (Minneapolis: Fortress, 1994); Yehoshua Gitay, *Isaiah and his Audience: The Structure and Meaning of Isaiah 1–12* (Assen: Van Gorcum, 1991); idem, *Prophecy and Persuasion* (FTL 14; Bonn: Linguistica Biblica, 1981). Patrick and Scult, *Rhetoric and Biblical Interpretation*, blend classical rhetoric with more modern reader-response strategies.

28. See Roland Meynet, *Rhetorical Analysis: An Introduction to Biblical Rhetoric* (JSOTSup 256; Sheffield: Sheffield Academic Press, 1998). See also Ronald C. Katz, *The Structure of Ancient Arguments: Rhetoric and its Near Eastern Origin* (New York: Shapolsky/Steinmatzky, 1977); Isaac Rabinowitz, "Pre-modern Jewish Study of Rhetoric: An Introductory Bibliography," *Rhetorica* 3 (1985): 137–44.

29. Duane F. Watson and Alan J. Hauser, *Rhetorical Criticism and the Bible: A Comprehensive Bibliography with Notes on History and Method* (Biblical Interpretation 4; Leiden: Brill, 1994), 7.

30. Aichele et al., *Postmodern Bible*, 159–61 (emphasis in original).

3. *Dimensions of Rhetorical Analysis*

At the heart of what this book conceives as a rhetorical method lies a close-reading technique focusing on words within an identified passage, both collectively for their shape, pattern, and structure in a literary context, and individually for the resonance they have primarily in the work as a whole, but also intertextually within the canon of the Hebrew Bible.[31] Part of this technique will be concerned with key words or phrases, not exclusively as "integrating devices" that bond and help delimit rhetorical units,[32] but as much for the contribution they make to the explication of a theme, which will be that of social justice.[33]

This idea of close reading may profitably be aligned with Aichele's concept of the literal as opposed to the spiritual sense of translation.[34] The former "stays close to the physical dimension of the text," regarding "the ambiguity and multiplicity of meanings that the text makes possible not as imperfections but as inevitabilities, resulting from the text's inherent *resistance* to meaning." The latter "expects the text to yield a clear, coherent meaning. Ambiguity in the text is an imperfection, to be removed by the careful reader."[35] He concludes that "a literal translation will leave more reading options than will a spiritual translation, which by its very nature seeks to clarify the source text."[36]

So, detailed attention to the text is the first order of business for rhetorical criticism, generating interpretative possibility and thereby opening the way for fresh theological insights to be drawn. Theology is a contingent, second-order matter, dependent on literary analysis, rather than the predetermined *regula fidei* restrictively reigning in interpretation.[37] As

---

31. For a collection of essays, each of which pursues an emphasis on verbal artistry, see David J. A. Clines, David M. Gunn, and Alan J. Hauser, eds., *Art and Meaning: Rhetoric in Biblical Literature* (JSOTSup 19; Sheffield: JSOT Press, 1982).

32. Watson and Hauser, *Rhetorical Criticism of the Bible*, 9.

33. Ibid., 9. See also H. Van Dyke Parunak, "Transitional Techniques in the Bible," *JBL* 102 (1983): 525–48; idem, "Oral Typesetting: Some Uses of Biblical Structure," *Biblica* 62 (1981): 153–68.

34. Aichele, *Sign, Text, Scripture*, 41–49; see also Handelman, *Slayers of Moses*, 15–21, 54–55, 84–107, 116–20, 163–68, on different dimensions of what she calls the Letter vs. Spirit dichotomy.

35. Aichele, *Sign, Text, Scripture*, 48 (emphasis in original).

36. Ibid., 55.

37. Note how Herbert N. Schneidau ("Biblical Narrative and Modern Consciousness," in *The Bible and the Narrative Tradition* [ed. Frank McConnell; New York and Oxford: Oxford University Press, 1986], 132–50) stresses that narrative is the essence of the Bible, not doctrinal propositions.

Barr correctly remarks, "[T]he Bible is not in itself a work of doctrine or of theology."[38] Rather, on account of its essentially literary character, the Bible "represents a range and variety of viewpoints that no doctrinal position has ever been able to incorporate or to represent."[39]

Further supporting the concept of texts being polyvalent and, in addition, containing a surplus of meaning,[40] Ricoeur perceives that "[w]hat the work of reading reveals is not only a lack of determinacy but also an excess of meaning," which leads him to conclude that "the text thus appears, by turns, both lacking and excessive in relation to reading."[41] This textual quality is magnified in longer works, such as the book of Isaiah. It is further accentuated when those works, as is the case for large sections of the Isaianic corpus, are composed of poetry, which is by nature richly imagistic and densely allusive, and therefore able to sustain a range of interpretations construed through observation of poetic detail and technique.[42] Discussing the intrinsically symbolic nature of biblical language, Ricoeur argues that "symbols give rise to an endless exegesis"[43] and that therefore the biblical text in its metaphorical dimensions "is infinite and incapable of exhausting the innovative meaning."[44] This is especially true of a work like the book of Isaiah, which, replete with

38. James Barr, *The Scope and Authority of the Bible* (London: Xpress Reprints, SCM Bookroom, 1993), 121.

39. Ibid., 122; for a similar assessment, see Patrick and Scult, *Rhetoric and Biblical Interpretation*, 137–38.

40. Note how Shelley ("A Defence of Poetry," in *Peacock's Four Ages of Poetry, Shelley's Defence of Poetry, Browning's Essay on Shelley* [ed. H. F. B. Brett-Smith; Oxford: Blackwell, 1972], 23–59) contends that "A great poem is a fountain for ever overflowing with the waters of wisdom and delight" (p. 48); and, further, that "the most glorious poetry that has ever been communicated to the world is probably but a shadow of the original conceptions of the poet" (p. 54).

41. Ricoeur, *A Ricoeur Reader*, 401.

42. For a justification of viewing prophetic works as also poetic, see Stephen A. Geller, "Were the Prophets Poets?," *Prooftexts* 3 (1983): 211–21; Robert Carroll, "Poets Not Prophets," *JSOT* 27 (1983): 25–31. See also Michael Brennan Dick, "Prophetic *Poiesis* and the Verbal Icon," *CBQ* 46 (1984): 226–46, who argues that even as the prophets were criticizing idol-making, they were ironically honing their own literary skill.

43. Paul Ricoeur, *Interpretation Theory: Discourse and the Surplus of Meaning* (Fort Worth, Tex.: Texas Christian University Press, 1976), 57.

44. Ibid., 52; or as Brueggemann ("Biblical Authority: A Personal Reflection," in *Struggling with Scripture* [ed. Walter Brueggemann, William C. Placher, and Brian K. Blount; Louisville, Ky.: Westminster John Knox, 2002], 5–31 [17]) puts it, "Interpretation is not the reiteration of the text. It is rather the movement of the text beyond itself in fresh ways."

metaphor and rich in symbol, lends itself to being understood as an open text.[45]

While it may be admitted that the Isaianic corpus is not a narrative as conventionally conceived, it does contain an implied narrative thread,[46] as through the twists and turns of prophetic warning, human recalcitrance, divine punishment and promise, it presses toward the idealized future of Isa 65:17–25, which is itself prefigured from as early as Isa 2:1–4. Therefore issues of narratology[47] can be understood to play a part undergirding the rhetoric of the work. Finally, therefore, this study is canonical in the way it probes how the rhetoric of specific passages contributes to the rhetoric of the entire book with regard to its presentation of the theme of social justice.[48]

Another important literary-rhetorical device is characterization,[49] especially that of Yahweh, whose voice and personality dominate and determine so much of Isaianic discourse. Accepting the divine "as a literary creation . . . Yahweh should not be given the preferential treatment we would accord a real deity. Rather, his actions, character and intentions too must be placed under critical scrutiny *as a part of the text* if we are to do justice" to a literary reading.[50] In particular, I assess whether God is the suitably complex, ambiguous, yet unified and judicious character proposed by John Watts,[51] or the considerably more unreliable and

45. Contra Edgar W. Conrad, "Yehoshua Gitay: 'What is *He* Doing?,'" *JSOT* 27 (2002): 237–41, who regards the Bible as "a closed text" employing "codes that the addressee is expected to understand for communication to take place."

46. See Norman K. Gottwald, "Tragedy and Comedy in the Latter Prophets," *Semeia* 32 (1984): 83–96.

47. See Mieke Bal, *Narratology: Introduction to the Theory of Narrative* (trans. Christine von Boheemen; Toronto: University of Toronto Press, 1985).

48. See Watson and Hauser, *Rhetorical Criticism of the Bible*, 9; Aichele et al., *Postmodern Bible*, 165. Noting how Robert Carroll ("Clio and Canons: In Search of a Cultural Poetics of the Hebrew Bible," *BibInt* 5, no. 4 [1997]: 300–23) insists rightly that there are several different canons, this research, for reasons of delimitation, accepts the Masoretic text of the scroll of Isaiah as a suitable study; further, it agrees, with John Barton (*Reading the Old Testament: Method in Biblical Study* [2d ed.; London: Darton, Longman & Todd, 1996], 96–101), that Childs's proposals regarding the canon show close affinity with literary methodology, and is therefore content to present itself as a literary-canonical study.

49. See Donald Davie, "Personification," *Essays in Criticism* 31, no. 2 (1981): 91–104, for the centrality of personification as a literary trope.

50. Andrew Davies, *Double Standards in Isaiah: Re-evaluating Prophetic Ethics and Divine Justice* (Leiden: Brill, 2000), 11 (emphasis in original).

51. John D. W. Watts, "The Characterization of Yahweh in the Vision of Isaiah," *Review and Expositor* 83 (1986): 439–50.

disturbing figure envisaged by Peter Miscall.[52] On the basis of this assessment, in connection with the Isaianic theme of exclusive trust in God, the extent to which humanity might be posited as a legitimate source of social justice is explored. Despite significant claims to the contrary, if the divine character can reasonably be demonstrated to be tainted by unjustness, then a role for humanity in the search for justice may yet be considered.

Related to this discussion, mention may also be made of one of the master literary-rhetorical tropes, irony. If it is accepted that irony arises in the discrepancy between the *expected* and the *actual*,[53] then the failure of the glowing promises of Isa 40–55 and elsewhere to materialize in the way described raises the possibility of reading Isaiah as more implicitly ironical than has been commonly assumed,[54] with all of the attendant interpretative options, such as, to name only one, viewing this as potentially undermining confidence in God's trustworthiness.[55]

The employment of these dimensions of rhetorical criticism, rooted in a close reading of the text that is observant of recurring patterns in discourse or action, including the repeated use of images, metaphors, arguments, structural arrangements, and configurations of language,[56] aims at a strong, "full-bodied encounter with the Biblical text,"[57] in this case the text of the book of Isaiah as it speaks of matters of justice.

---

52. Peter D. Miscall, "Isaiah: Dreams and Nightmares, Fantasy and Horror," *Journal of the Fantastic in the Arts* 8 (1997): 151–69.

53. In line with the definition of Douglas C. Muecke, *Irony* (London: Methuen, 1970); for his classification of types of irony, see idem, *The Compass of Irony* (London: Methuen, 1969).

54. See Edwin M. Good, *Irony in the Old Testament* (Philadelphia: Westminster, 1965); more generally, see also Wayne C. Booth, *A Rhetoric of Irony* (Chicago: University of Chicago Press, 1975).

55. Charles S. Glicksberg (*The Ironic Vision in Modern Literature* [The Hague: Martinus Nijhoff, 1969]) posits irony as contributing to a sense of humankind being lost in a world without meaning, which might, for some, be one of the consequences of a loss of trust in God; for an appraisal of this work and Muecke's *The Compass of Irony*, see Norman Knox, "On the Classification of Irony," *Modern Philology* 70 (1972): 53–62.

56. See Karlyn Kohrs Campbell and Kathleen Hall Jamieson, eds., *Form and Genre: Shaping Rhetorical Action* (Falls Church, Va.: Speech Communication Association, 1976).

57. Patrick and Scult, *Rhetoric and Biblical Interpretation*, 18. See also Walter Brueggemann, "Five Strong Readings of the Book of Isaiah," in *The Bible in Human Society: Essays in Honour of John Rogerson* (ed. M. D. Carroll R, D. J. A. Clines, and P. R. Davies; JSOTSup 200, Sheffield: Sheffield Academic, 1995), 87–104.

4. *Before the (Deconstructive) Flood:*
Reading with the Grain

An accusation directed against rhetorical criticism is that it "can too easily be harnessed to an ideologically conservative program of reaffirming classical texts and values"[58] by effectually encouraging the acceptance of their claims through the demonstration of the apparent success of their persuasive strategies.[59] Clines describes this as reading "from right to left," his metaphor for "adopting the ideology inscribed in the text."[60] An adequate response to this is usually formulated as some form of deconstructive reading against the grain.[61]

While there is merit in this approach, it is perhaps advisable initially to read closely *with* the grain to illuminate aspects of the text that may be overlooked in theologically driven readings keen to elicit the "point." These theologically driven readings may be impatient with the text's awkward detail and insufficiently sensitive to what may be the struggle, inscribed in the rhetoric, in arriving at the point. Effectively, a text, in part and whole, may be more broodingly tensive, more a dramatic play of light and shade than an interested summary of its conclusions can ever reveal. Awareness of this could significantly alter how the text is understood.

Within this study, an appreciation of how difficult it may be to trust Yahweh could lead to a greater understanding of those unable to cede that trust easily. Related to this point, the puncturing of the buoyant, exaggerated rhetoric of Isa 49:8–13 (especially v. 13, with its singing mountains!) by Zion lamenting glumly, "The Lord has forsaken me, the Lord has forgotten me" (v. 14), is the occasion for a more urgent reply from Yahweh in a changed, more serious, rhetorical register (vv. 15–16): if God can take seriously these dissenting voices inscribed in the text, then perhaps readers should too.[62]

58. Aichele et al., *Postmodern Bible*, 166.
59. Ibid., 182.
60. David J. A. Clines, *Interested Parties: The Ideology of Writers and Readers of the Hebrew Bible* (JSOTSup 205; Sheffield: Sheffield Academic Press, 1995), 26.
61. In a sense, Clines's whole book is a demonstration of different aspects of this approach applied to a variety of texts from across the canon.
62. Aichele et al., *Postmodern Bible*, 179–81, makes a similar point with regard to the New Testament; the observation (Jon L. Berquist, *Judaism in Persia's Shadow: A Social and Historical Approach* [Minneapolis: Fortress, 1995], 79) that Isa 56–66 is remarkable for the way "that it *preserves* the losing voices in the struggle" (emphasis in original) further directs attention to them for the role they play in the rhetorical situation.

Furthermore, a focus on the contours of the rhetoric within the Isaianic corpus might lead not to an immediate acceptance of claims made but to a wondering about such claims on the basis of what has already been encountered as part of the reading process. This may develop into a more aggressive questioning, but is rooted in reading with the grain. Unequivocal assertions that "the Lord is a God of justice" (30:18),[63] made even more difficult for some to resist or deny when placed in the mouth of the divine in first person direct speech (61:8), may be undermined by what is portrayed and logically implied elsewhere.[64] This is all part of the rich complexity of the rhetorical fabric of the book of Isaiah into which the reader is drawn.[65]

Amplifying this idea, Handelman argues that characteristically the Hebrew Bible

> points not outwards towards images and forms, but inwards towards itself, its own network of relations, of verbal and temporal ambiguities. It calls for its own decipherment, not for a movement away from itself towards vision or abstraction; the word leads inwards into itself, not outwards towards the "thing." What is required is that one "listen" to or read it more intently.[66]

This attitude reinforces the validity of first reading with the grain of the text. It also respects the text[67] and does not seek to conform it to prior dogmatic assumptions.[68]

---

63. The *Guardian Weekly* (11–17 July 2002) reports how at the trial of an al-Qaida suspect, the accused, using terminology similar to the Bible, concludes his rejection of the charges brought against him by asserting that "He [God] is justice." And who would simply accept this at face value?

64. The God who claims to "hate robbery and iniquity" in 61:8 is implicated in seizing loot and snatching plunder in 10:6; the God who promises "an everlasting covenant" in 61:8 is the God who effectively broke an earlier one in 54:7; similarly, taking the news media as a body of text, repeated claims following 11 September 2001 that the U.S. is a bastion of justice and democracy do not automatically have to be acceded to, but can be juxtaposed with evidence that the Bush administration has worked to subvert the democratically elected government in Venezuela, and is in league with patently undemocratic Saudi Arabia and Pakistan.

65. As to a labyrinth, one might say with Peter D. Miscall, "Isaiah: The Labyrinth of Images," *Semeia* 54 (1991): 103–21.

66. Handelman, *Slayers of Moses*, 31.

67. Recently, Kevin J. Vanhoozer (*Is there a Meaning in this Text: The Bible, the Reader, and the Morality of Literary Knowledge* [Leicester: Apollos, 2001]) has sought to defend texts from the acids of postmodernity while at the same time taking postmodern questions seriously; it may be suggested that texts also need to be defended from the distortions of fundamentalism.

5. *The Necessary Reader*

A risk of reading too credulously with the grain is that "from a purely rhetorical perspective, the reader is, finally, the prey and the victim of the strategy worked out by the implied author."[69] There is a need for real readers who assert themselves against the ideology of the text as they negotiate "between the signals provided by the text and the synthetic activity of reading."[70] To accomplish this, the necessary reader is conceived as one who embraces "reading not simply as consumption but as productive activity, the making of meaning, in which one is guided by the text one reads, of course, but not simply manipulated by it."[71] This approach, thus, does not foster "an attitude of reverence before texts," but an engaged attitude which is "scrupulous to understand, alert to probe for blind spots and hidden agendas, and, finally, critical, questioning, skeptical."[72] Following this rubric, "we move from a submission to textual authority in reading, through a sharing of textual power in interpretation, toward an assertion of power through opposition in criticism."[73] The purpose of "the move from *interpretation* to *criticism* is not simply a destructive negation, however, not a mere rejection of ideas and values proposed by a text. It is a differentiation of the subjectivity of the critic from that of the author, an assertion of *another* textual power against that of the primary text."[74]

---

68. James Packer, "Hermeneutics and Biblical Authority," in *Solid Ground: Twenty-five Years of Evangelical Theology* (ed. Carl R. Trueman, Tony J. Gray, and Craig L. Blomberg; Leicester: Apollos, 2000), 137–54, comes perilously close, in the fashion of interpretation of the apostolic age, to making all texts speak of Jesus. Note, too, how R. S. Sugirtharajah (*The Bible and the Third World: Precolonial, Colonial, and Postcolonial Encounters* [Cambridge: Cambridge University Press, 2001], 240) observes that liberation hermeneutics are also "overtly Christocentric." The title *Disciplining Hermeneutics: Interpretation in Christian Perspective* (ed. Roger Lundin; Grand Rapids: Eerdmans; Leicester: Apollos, 1997) not only has a Miss Jean Brodie ring about it, as if supposedly unruly approaches to texts need a firm headmistress-figure to sort them out, but also implicitly lays claim to be *the* authentic Christian viewpoint on the topic. It is as if refusal to be subjected to such discipline in hermeneutical matters places one outside true Christian interpretation.
69. Ricoeur, *A Ricoeur Reader*, 398.
70. Ibid., 402–3.
71. Robert Scholes, *Textual Power: Literary Theory and the Teaching of English* (New Haven: Yale University Press, 1985), 8.
72. Ibid., 16.
73. Ibid., 39.
74. Ibid., 40 (emphasis in original).

6. *Poststructuralism: Text, Deconstruction, World*

As part of the wider configuration of postmodernism, poststructuralism, perhaps especially in its deconstructive aspect, is the object of suspicion from a variety of viewpoints.[75] It is, however, too significant a phenomenon to simply discount.[76] It too has a role to play in the interpretative process, even in relation to theological texts.[77] In particular, despite a trend to use deconstruction as a pretext for endlessly playful, dilettantish interpretation,[78] deconstruction too advocates close reading of texts in the context of the normative constraints of logic in order "to locate the symptomatic stress-points—the moments of *aporia* or logical tension—where such thinking meets its limit."[79] These features point to dimensions of texts that are ultimately irremediably ambiguous, indeterminate, or undecidable, and that consequently militate against closure. A close-reading strategy is thus endorsed, but in such a way that precludes "unicity"[80] or the search for singular meaning.[81]

75. E.g., see Gerald Graff, *Literature against Itself: Literary Ideas in Modern Society* (Chicago: University of Chicago Press, 1979); Jürgen Habermas, *The Philosophical Discourse of Modernity: Twelve Lectures* (trans. Frederick Lawrence; Cambridge, Mass.: Polity, 1987); John M. Ellis, *Against Deconstruction* (Princeton: Princeton University Press, 1989); David Hirsch, *The Deconstruction of Literature: Criticism after Auschwitz* (Providence, R.I.: Brown University Press, 1991).

76. As Fredric Jameson ("The Politics of Theory: Ideological Positions in the Postmodernism Debate," in *Modern Criticism and Theory: A Reader* [ed. David Lodge; London: Longman, 1988], 373–83 [381]) puts it, "[W]e are *within* the culture of postmodernism to the point where its facile repudiation is as impossible as any equally facile celebration of it is complacent and corrupt" (emphasis in original).

77. See Mark C. Taylor, *Erring: A Postmodern A/theology* (Chicago: University of Chicago Press, 1984); idem, *Altarity* (Chicago: University of Chicago Press, 1987); Kevin Hart, *The Trespass of the Sign: Deconstruction, Theology, and Philosophy* (Cambridge: Cambridge University Press, 1989); Graham Ward, *Barth, Derrida, and the Language of Theology* (Cambridge: Cambridge University Press, 1995); John D. Caputo, *The Prayers and Tears of Jacques Derrida: Religion without Religion* (Bloomington: Indiana University Press, 1997); Catherine Pitstock, *After Writing: On the Liturgical Consummation of Philosophy* (Oxford: Blackwell, 1998). Christopher Norris (*Deconstruction* [rev. ed.; London: Routledge, 2002], 175) notes that "such readings tend to pass over those passages in 'early' Derrida where he emphatically denies that deconstruction is in any sense a version of negative theology."

78. Norris, *Deconstruction*, 125, 162; Cunningham, *In the Reading Gaol*, 37.

79. Norris, *Deconstruction*, 163.

80. Jean-François Lyotard, *The Postmodern Condition: A Report on Knowledge* (trans. Geoff Bennington and Brian Massumi; Theory and History of Literature 10; Minneapolis: University of Minnesota Press, 1999), 12.

81. In the literary field specifically, see Macherey, *Theory of Literary Production*.

Related to this point, it may be argued that in certain regards the book of Isaiah lends itself to aspects of poststructuralist interpretative theory. Once claims that God is incomparable, beyond all human comprehension, and inaccessible are expressed in writing, God becomes enmeshed in that web of semiotic signification in which every signified is itself a signifier.[82] Consequently, a sense of endless deferral is created so that it is possible to conclude (and perhaps impossible not to conclude) "that Isaiah's ending is still 'unfulfilled,'" since what is depicted "remains a visionary goal."[83] In this system, the idea of a "transcendental signified," or God, "which in and of itself, in its essence, would refer to no signifier, would exceed the chain of signs, and would no longer itself function as a signifier," becomes unattainable because it posits "thinking a *concept signified in and of itself*, a concept simply present for thought, independent of a relationship to language."[84]

This also impinges on the Isaianic theme of presence and absence, for in the context of explaining the sign as "deferred presence," Derrida argues that "the signified concept is never present in and of itself, in a sufficient presence that would refer only to itself."[85] Instead, governed by the idea of *différance* as the primal mechanism for structuring and demarcating differences, a sign is defined as a trace, which is neither a presence nor an absence, but in all cases, "the trace of a trace."[86] In this frame of reference, God is textually mediated through an interconnection of traces. Since ultimately no interpreter has unmediated access to the "God's-eye" view of the text, this understanding should engender a sense of hermeneutical humility, with the recognition "that there is no transcendental ground, no Archimedian standpoint beyond all argumentation, beyond all rhetoric, from which truth-claims can be adjudicated."[87] All interpretation is contingent. Moreover, the postmodern insistence that the dichotomy

82. As Cunningham (*In the Reading Gaol*, 402) observes, "Biblical logocentricity is already deconstructionist."

83. Clements, "Isaiah: Book without an Ending," 124.

84. Jacques Derrida, *Positions* (trans. Alan Bass; Chicago: University of Chicago Press, 1981), 19–20; see also idem, *Of Grammatology* (trans. Gayatri Chakravorty Spivack; Baltimore: The Johns Hopkins University Press, 1976), 14–15; idem, *Speech and Phenomena* (trans. David B. Allison; Evanston, Ill.: Northwestern University Press, 1973), 129–60.

85. Jacques Derrida, *Margins of Philosophy* (trans. Alan Bass; Chicago: University of Chicago Press, 1982), 11.

86. Geoffrey Bennington and Jacques Derrida, eds., *Jacques Derrida* (Chicago: University of Chicago Press, 1993), 75, which goes on, "No element is anywhere present (nor simply absent), there are only traces."

87. Steven Mailloux, *Reception Histories: Rhetoric, Pragmatism, and American Cultural Politics* (Ithaca, N.Y.: Cornell University Press, 1998), 57.

between fact and value is a chimera not only undermines purported scientific objectivity, but encourages the role of imagination and creativity in the interpretative enterprise.[88] Even though at times cutting in his criticism of the postmodern phenomenon, Cunningham yet validates its importance for interpretation, arguing that "deconstruction is not some awful spectre to be banished if possible from the Table of the Lord. Theology needs the reminders of deconstruction as much as deconstruction depends on theology's."[89]

However, the emphasis on textuality contained in the now famous phrase *il n' y a pas de hors-texte*[90] has in certain quarters eventuated in stasis, a "deconstructive paralysis, a permanent state of equivocation."[91] It is acceptable to decenter and destabilize texts, but not to use this as the basis for reconfiguring relationships of power inscribed in text and world (or world as text) for the purpose of liberation.[92] By hermetically sealing texts off from the world,[93] and the harsh reality of existence for so many

88.   See Lyotard, *Postmodern Condition*, 60, 52; Garrett Green, *Theology, Hermeneutics, and Imagination: The Crisis of Interpretation at the End of Modernity* (Cambridge: Cambridge University Press, 2000), 16, 187–206. Douglas Groothuis (*Truth Decay: Defending Christianity against the Challenges of Postmodernism* [Downers Grove, Ill.: InterVarsity, 2000]) comes very close to identifying the gospel with a foundationalist objectivism by correlating Christianity with the methods of modernity, though it should be noted that prior to the emergence of postmodernism, conservatives were not as receptive to modernity. See also in this discussion Elisabeth Schüssler Fiorenza, *Rhetoric and Ethic: The Politics of Biblical Studies* (Minneapolis: Fortress, 1999), 31–55; Daniel Patte, *Ethics of Biblical Interpretation: A Reevaluation* (Louisville, Ky.: Westminster John Knox, 1995). On the role of imagination, see Brueggemann, "Biblical Authority," 16–23.

89.   Cunningham, *In the Reading Gaol*, 402.

90.   Derrida, *Of Grammatology*, 158; though note how Cunningham (*In the Reading Gaol*, 25), in connection with the use to which *il n' y a pas de hors-texte* has been derivatively put, observes that "rebutting in this particular matter is just one aspect of Derrida's increasing impatience with much of the American deconstructionist thinking done in his name since the sixties." On how (mis)translation and amendment has assisted in distorting Derrida's thought, see Cunningham, *In the Reading Gaol*, 56–59 and 381–86.

91.   Scholes, *Textual Power*, 7; Catherine Belsey, "Literature, History, Politics," in Lodge, ed., *Modern Criticism and Theory*, 400–10 (402); see also Eagleton, *Literary Theory*, 146.

92.   See Terry Eagleton, "Capitalism, Modernism, and Postmodernism," in Lodge, ed., *Modern Criticism and Theory*, 385–98 (395); Sugirtharajah, *Bible and the Third World*, 265–66; Norman K. Gottwald and Richard A. Horsley, eds., *The Bible and Liberation: Political and Social Hermeneutics* (rev. ed.; Maryknoll, N.Y.: Orbis; London: SPCK, 1993).

93.   Scholes, *Textual Power*, 75–76.

millions of the world's population, this approach "results in a quietistic acceptance of injustice."[94] In contrast, I argue that "we should take care to salvage those other features of deconstruction"[95] that can further the cause of transformation in the world.[96] By adopting this critical stance, I emphasize that there is so "much destitution, poverty and sheer despair in the world" that people threatened with "debilitating anomie... cannot wait for complete moral certitude before they take action to improve their existence."[97]

7. Ethics, Justice, Mission

In the world of "post" prefixes, this study may thus be located in that stream of postcolonialism aimed toward social transformation and atten-tiveness to the "other". As part of this orientation, it is favorably, if criti-cally, disposed to liberation theology, viewing the Bible as a "safe and unsafe text," a mixture of the "familiar and the distant," rather than a text to be redeemed.[98] On this basis, concepts important in both the biblical text and the contemporary world[99] are able to be explored and made

94. Ibid., 79.

95. Ibid., 110; Sugirtharajah, *Bible and the Third World*, 249–50. Of immense significance in underpinning the validity of this approach, see Edward W. Said, *The World, the Text, and the Critic* (London: Faber & Faber, 1984). Related to biblical studies, see further Schüssler Fiorenza, *Rhetoric and Ethic*. As Paul de Man ("Semiology and Rhetoric," in *Textual Strategies: Perspectives in Post-structuralist Criticism* [ed. Josué V. Harari; London: Methuen, 1980], 121–40 [124]) puts it, this is done at the risk of appearing as "a formalist critic in the morning and a communal moralist in the afternoon."

96. See David Jobling, "Writing the Wrongs of the World: The Deconstruction of the Biblical Text in the Context of Liberation Theologies," *Semeia* 51 (1990): 81–118; also the essays in M. Daniel Carroll R, David J. A. Clines, and Philip R. Davies, eds., *The Bible in Human Society* (JSOTSup 200; Sheffield: Sheffield Academic Press, 1995).

97. Ato Quayson, *Postcolonialism: Theory, Practice, or Process?* (Cambridge, Mass.: Polity, 2000), 155.

98. Sugirtharajah, *Bible and the Third World*, passim; R. S. Sugirtharajah, ed., *The Postcolonial Bible* (Bible and Postcolonialism 1; Sheffield: Sheffield Academic, 1998). See also Bill Ashcroft, Gareth Griffiths, and Helen Tiffin, eds., *Post-colonial Studies: The Key Concepts* (London: Routledge, 2000), and *The Post-colonial Studies Reader* (London: Routledge, 1995); Fernando F. Segovia, "In the Wake of Liberation: Postcolonial and Diasporic Criticisms," in *Los caminos inexhauribles de la palabra: Las relecturas creativas en la Biblia y de la Biblia* (ed. Guillermo Hansen; Buenos Aires: Lumen, 2000), 91–111.

99. In this regard, Schüssler Fiorenza (*Rhetoric and Ethic*, 48) argues that "an emancipatory process of biblical interpretation has as its 'doubled' reference point the contemporary present and the biblical past."

problematic, particularly justice, ethics, and the problem of violence, including foundational and therefore divine violence.[100] This book also, consequently, has a missiological dimension:[101] while predominantly focused on the world of the text,[102] it is also interested in textual appropriation and the extension of meaning directed toward change in the world in front of the text.[103] In addition, the insistence of postmodernism

100.   See Jacques Derrida, "Force of Law: The 'Mystical Foundation of Authority,'" *Cardozo Law Review* 11 (1990): 920–1045. Linking justice, violence, and the divine, John D. Caputo (*Demythologizing Heidegger* [Bloomington: Indiana University Press, 1993], 197) maintains that "the name of justice is no more or less venerable than that of God or truth or peace or freedom, in whose name the most unspeakable atrocities are committed with unfailing regularity." See also Marc H. Ellis, *Unholy Alliance: Religion and Atrocity in Our Time* (London: SCM Press, 1997).

101.   See David J. Bosch, *Transforming Mission: Paradigm Shifts in Theology of Mission* (Maryknoll, N.Y.: Orbis, 1991). For a significant article, appreciative but critical of Bosch, see Kirsteen Kim, "Missiology as Global Conversation of (Contextual) Theologies" (research paper, Queen's Foundation, Birmingham, October 2002). See also H. Daniel Beeby, "A Missional Approach to Renewed Interpretation," in *Renewing Biblical Interpretation* (ed. Craig Bartholomew, Colin Greene, and Karl Möller; Carlisle: Paternoster; Grand Rapids: Zondervan, 2000), 268–83 (283); idem, *Canon and Mission* (Harrisburg, Pa.: Trinity, 1999). In the broad historical context, Barr (*The Scope and Authority of the Bible*, 76) argues that "it is no accident that its [fundamentalism's] flourishing coincided with the great period of Western political imperialism"; similarly, Green (*Theology, Hermeneutics, and Imagination*, 46) observes "that the apologetic appeal to universal reason and common human experience has led to some of the most imperialistic modern claims on behalf of Christianity." Confirming the implication of Western culture as a whole in the imperialistic enterprise, see Edward W. Said, *Culture and Imperialism* (New York: Knopf, 1993). See further Chinua Achebe, "An Image of Africa: Racism in Conrad's *Heart of Darkness*," in Joseph Conrad, *Heart of Darkness: An Authoritative Text, Backgrounds, and Source Criticism* (ed. Robert Kimbrough; 3d ed.; New York: Norton, 1988), 251–62. For some of the implications of this in terms of a violent evangelization, see Leonardo Boff, "Christianity with an Authentic Face: Reflections on the Future of the Church in Latin America," in *Hans Küng: New Horizons for Faith and Thought* (ed. Karl-Josef Kuschel and Hermann Häring; trans. John Bowden; London: SCM Press, 1993), 152–67; idem, *New Evangelization: Good News to the Poor* (trans. Robert R. Barr; Maryknoll, N.Y.: Orbis, 1991). See also Gerald O. West, "Kairos 2000: Moving beyond Church Theology," *Journal of Theology for Southern Africa* 108 (2001): 55–78.

102.   Paul Ricoeur, *Hermeneutics and the Human Sciences* (ed. and trans. John B. Thompson; Cambridge: Cambridge University Press, 1998), 140–42.

103.   Ibid., 142–44. Both appropriation and extension are different from application, which implies a mastery of the meaning of a text; see Hans-Georg Gadamer, *Truth and Method* (trans. Garrett Barden and John Cumming; London:

on the plurality of discourse means that in terms of text, theology, social
vision, missiology, ethics, and justice, the Bible does not speak with one
voice but with many. What is true of the Bible as a whole is also true of a
work as rich and complex in all its aspects as the book of Isaiah. Croatto
argues that for a reading to be intelligible, "the order is *from closure to
polysemy*."[104] Closure is attained through attention to factors such as the
location/interests of the reader, methodological criteria, and the aspect(s)
of the text to be explored.[105] These assist in the production of a coherent
reading, which nevertheless lays no claim to be the only possible meaning of the text. I thus reach for the closure of intelligibility through
exploring the theme of social justice in the book of Isaiah, by application
of a literary methodology, in light of significant experience in the Third
World.

At the outset I noted how D. H. Lawrence warns that trust should
never be placed in the artist but in the tale told. Elsewhere, he compares
the books of the Old Testament to great novels by authors of "passionate
inspiration."[106] This book explores facets of the passion of one of those
great works, the book of Isaiah, knowing that in such works "meaning
vibrates as does a crystal, out of whose hidden clarity pulsate fragmenta-
tion and interference."[107]

Sheed & Ward, 1975), 273–74. As Green (*Theology, Hermeneutics, and Imagination*, 177) observes, "A church whose central activity is the interpretation of scripture is not the guardian of a timeless deposit of faith but rather the *ecclesia semper
reformanda*." See also David J. A. Clines, "Possibilities and Priorities of Biblical
Interpretation in an International Perspective," *BibInt* 1, no. 1 (1993): 67–87; David
Jobling, "Globalization in Biblical Studies/Biblical Studies in Globalization," *BibInt*
1, no. 1 (1993): 96–110.

104.   J. Severino Croatto, *Biblical Hermeneutics: Toward a Theory of Reading
as the Production of Meaning* (Maryknoll, N.Y.: Orbis, 1987), 41 (emphasis in
original); or as Barthes (*Image–Music–Text* [ed. and trans. Stephen Heath; London:
Fontana, 1977], 148) puts it, "[A] text's unity lies not in its origin but in its destination."

105.   Croatto, *Biblical Hermeneutics*, 80, argues: "The text indicates the limit
(however broad) of its own meaning. Textual polysemy does not mean simply what-
you-will. *A text says what it permits to be said*. Its polysemy arises from its previous
closure" (emphasis in original). See also Carlos Mesters, "The Use of the Bible
among the Common People," in *Ministry by the People: Theological Education
by Extension* (ed. F. Ross Kinsler; Geneva: WCC; Maryknoll, N.Y.: Orbis, 1983),
78–92, for a helpful explication of the relationship among text, context, and pre-text.

106.   D. H. Lawrence, *Phoenix II: Uncollected, Unpublished, and Other Prose
Work by D. H. Lawrence* (ed. Warren Roberts and Harry T. Moore; London:
Heinemann, 1968), 418.

107.   George Steiner, "Our Homeland, the Text," *Salmagundi* 6 (1985): 4–65 (4).

Chapter 1

FROM FAILED RHETORIC TO THE HOPE OF JUSTICE:
ISAIAH 1:16–17 TO ISAIAH 58—A TRAJECTORY

רחצו הזכו הסירו רע מעלליכם מנגד עיני חדלו הרע:
למדו היטב דרשו משפט אשרו חמוץ שפטו יתום ריבו אלמנה:

Wash yourselves, make yourselves clean; turn away from the evil of your
doings—take them out of my sight;
Stop doing evil, learn to do right: keep straight on after justice—pursue it,
straighten out oppression, defend the fatherless, advocate for the widow.

(Isa 1:16–17)

1. *Talking about Justice*

A consensus exists that "the concern for justice pervades the entire Old
Testament."[1] For Heschel, "Justice is as much a necessity as breathing is,
and a constant occupation."[2] Justice's most regular linguistic partner,
righteousness, is described as "the mold in which God wants history to
be shaped."[3] This statement, however, raises the question of how justice
is to be conceptually framed. At one end of the spectrum of possibilities
lies the danger of collapsing horizons of various kinds into a universal
concept of justice divorced from the particularities of time and place, as
if justice is always and ever the same.[4] At the other end, the literary idea
of distanciation raises the specter that justice as variously conceived in
the ancient world may in reality be so alien as to be ultimately inaccessible and impenetrable. Attention to the text permits finding a course

---

1. Rolf P. Knierim, *The Task of Old Testament Theology: Substance, Method,
and Cases* (Grand Rapids: Eerdmans, 1995), 88; Abraham J. Heschel, *The Prophets*
(2 vols.; New York: Harper & Row, 1962), 1:199, asserts that "there are few
thoughts as deeply ingrained in the mind of biblical man as the thought of God's
justice and righteousness."

2. Heschel, *The Prophets*, 1:199.

3. Ibid., 1:198.

4. Ibid. Heschel talks about how "its validity is not only universal, but also
eternal, independent of will and experience."

between these polarities, in the awareness that there is no unmediated access to the past, understandings of which are always influenced by the present.[5]

In the biblical text, the primary term for justice is מִשְׁפָּט, which in various contexts refers "to a legal case or lawsuit, legal claim, decision by arbitration, legal decision, or case law."[6] Its use with a range of different words[7] begins to define dimensions of the content of justice. However, "[I]t is an open question whether this word field points to an all-inclusive, homogenous worldview in which all aspects are complementary and operate meaningfully, or whether it points to heterogeneous preunderstandings or concepts which conflict in their canonic juxtaposition" (p. 87). Knierim concludes that the latter is the case in the course of identifying a number of concepts of justice (pp. 89–114). Some of these represent variations of similar conceptual groups, some can be correlated, but significantly some conflict (p. 113). He observes that "the Old Testament itself does not cast its statements about justice in the form of the development of an idea" (p. 113). Canonically, the Hebrew Bible includes them all "in synchronic juxtaposition and, with few exceptions, presents them to its reader without deciding between differences in validity" (p. 113). That is the work of the reader.

Of the types of justice categorized by Knierim, several are related to the interests of this study and offer a way of introducing initial discussion. One of the most important consists of a "dynamistic worldview" in which the doing of justice results in a good life while wrongdoing brings its own just deserts (p. 89). In this cause-and-effect scheme, attested to throughout the Bible (p. 94), "justice organically unfolds as the consistent outcome of a person's actions and attitudes" (p. 92). Furthermore, "Just as in the general ethos the outcome of the individual's life depends on his/her actions, so does Israel's outcome depend even more on its

5. For one approach to this, see Christopher Frey, "The Impact of the Biblical Idea of Justice on Present Discussions of Social Justice," in *Justice and Righteousness: Biblical Themes and their Influence* (ed. Henning Graf Reventlow and Yair Hoffman; JSOTSup 137; Sheffield: JSOT Press, 1992), 91–104.

6. Knierim, *The Task of Old Testament Theology*, 86. Note, though, how Moshe Weinfeld ("Justice and Righteousness," in Reventlow and Hoffman, eds., *Justice and Righteousness*, 228–46 [241]) cites I. L. Seeligmann as seeing "that the original meaning of מִשְׁפָּט is to save the oppressed from the hands of the oppressor, or the enslaved from his enslaver."

7. Knierim, *The Task of Old Testament Theology*, 87, identifies these as "righteousness," "steadfastness," "faithfulness," "kindness," "uprightness," "sufficiency," "peace," "statute," "commandment, ordinance," "instruction," "correction, warning," "completeness." Following page citations are from Knierim.

actions" (p. 96). The concept expresses "a principle of reality that is universally just" and "shows that Yahweh, rather than being himself the principle of universal reality, is committed to that substantive and empirically verifiable principle of universal justice" (p. 90).[8]

One problem arises when, as a consequence of punishment on account of mistreating widows and orphans (Isa 1:17), those who should have been the beneficiaries of rescue and justice—the widows and orphans— themselves also suffer, perhaps disproportionately given their vulnerable position, in the communal punishment. Another arises when an exemplar of justice to widows and orphans, such as Job (Job 29:12–14), experiences suffering rather than the manifestation of justice in the good life. Since the effectual guarantor of this order of justice is God, then the divine self is open to the charge of injustice when the "system" does not function as expected. Exploration of this interface between justice and injustice helps shape this book.

The thrust of this concept of justice is universal. It is virtually an order of creation, which through common wisdom can be discerned in all cultures. It stands in tension with an exclusivistic category of justice grounded in the concept of "Israel's election as Yahweh's people," on the basis of which "justice is what serves Israel's election by and covenant with Yahweh, rather than and regardless of a principle of justice that is the same for all nations" (p. 97). According to this concept, action, even exceedingly violent action, against those outside the elect, is a function of justice. It can be seen in the genocide of the Canaanites to keep Israel pure from polytheism, and in the judgment against the nations for their aggression toward Israel. The question is raised "as to whether the elect witness to the same justice for all nations, or whether all nations are subject to—and victims of—a justice exclusively reserved for the elect" (p. 100). In effect, "[D]oes the God of all nations protect every other nation just as he protects Israel against aggression, or does he only protect his people and not the other nations likewise?" (p. 100). Does Yahweh as the God of universal justice adjudicate "among the nations according to the principle of equal justice rather than of preferred nationalities"? (p. 102). Transposed into Isaianic terms, this provides a conceptual framework for a significant strand of this book: exploring the tension between universalistic and nationalistic aspects of the text as these aspects relate to the theme of justice. A dimension of this framework is

---

8. Heschel (*The Prophets*, 1:216) cites M. Lazarus from 1900–1901, similarly contending, "[J]ustice to the Israelite mind was such an indispensable thing in the universe that it sometimes seems to stand out as some irresistible power independent even of God, as something which God Himself needs obey."

probing how the divine promise of the oppressed in their turn becoming oppressors factors into the theme of justice, especially as it is expressed in violent and humiliating imagery.

Implicit in a number of Knierim's categories is the legitimating of violence and warfare in pursuit of certain understandings of justice. He argues that "Yahweh's own warfare is a manifestation of his justice in history" (p. 100) and that in the Old Testament "war is much more documented as justified than criticized" (p. 103). Knierim recognizes, however, that based on the theology of creation in which "the legitimate symbol of ultimate justice is a perfectly balanced and sufficient world" (p. 118; cf. p. 117), all wars, including Yahweh's, represent "at least a degree of subordinate justice. They are never legitimate in themselves either as means or as ends, especially when compared with their opposite, the justice of peace or the peace of justice" (p. 104; cf. p. 105). He also argues that even Yahweh's war is subject to "his practice of justice, the criterion for which is independent of, supersedes, and opposes the praise of might" (p. 104). The image is of a God who is neither disproportionate nor excessive. In the context of examining the nature of the social justice encoded in the text, this sort of claim will be assessed in light of imagery that suggests a completely unrestrained divine figure gone berserk. What should the attitude of humans in search of justice and peace be to such a representation of God?[9] As Knierim asks, "[W]hat does justice contribute to the understanding of, and trust in, God-Yahweh, and what does God-Yahweh contribute to the understanding of justice?" (p. 113). The answer is neither obvious nor necessarily always flattering to God, given that "justice is not Yahweh or divine, nor is Yahweh-God dissolved into a specific concept of justice, let alone an abstract principle of justice" (p. 113).

At a general level, Knierim indicates factors that contribute to a fuller understanding of any exploration of the theme of justice in the Bible. He reminds us of the need to be alert to "conceptual theological deficiency" (p. 117), exemplified in the way much biblically oriented liberation theology has not sufficiently noticed its manifestation in an exodus theology that portrays the universal God as both liberator of the Israelites and oppressor of the Canaanites (p. 117). He also reminds us that "an Old Testament theology of justice will itself have to be a search for the Old Testament's own quest for justice, an understanding of which is itself hidden in the Old Testament's statements about it. It must do justice to the Old Testament's own search for justice" (p. 111). If this is true of the

---

9. Heschel (*The Prophets*, 1:213) reminds us that in addition to God, "justice is a quality to which human beings, too, lay claim."

Old Testament as a whole, it is also true of a book as long, complex, and rich as the book of Isaiah.

Specifically related to the idea of social justice, Knierim reminds us "that Israel was at all times a stratified society in one way or another" (p. 106) and that the fullness of a just society would only be actualized "in an eschatological future" (p. 107). Within history, therefore, all concepts of justice, including those in the Old Testament, are relativized and rendered penultimate (p. 118). As Knierim puts it: "[T]he inevitability of imperfect justice in the polluted world collides with the perfect justice of the pure eschaton" (p. 121). All justice needs to be searched for (p. 118). In a book such as this, which at one level appropriates the biblical text as a resource in the search for justice in a modern context, I now offer a brief explanation of what is understood by social justice at this historical juncture. The relationship between text and context requires it.

This book conceives social justice as a function of a system of governance, ultimately global in scope, which puts people, especially the poor, before profits[10] and ensures them access to enough of the earth's resources to attain and sustain a life of "comprehensive wellbeing."[11] In the wake of the Fascist victory in the Spanish Civil War, George Orwell asked whether ordinary people would be allowed "to live the decent fully human life" that was "technically achievable."[12] It is a question that is still relevant in our own day. From a contemporary Indian perspective, Arundhati Roy observes: "We have been taught that peace is the opposite of war. But is it? In India, peace is a daily battle for food and shelter and dignity."[13] In light of these comments, the goal of social justice may be articulated as "the balanced satisfaction of all valid human needs in all dimensions of life for all humans, present and future, within a healthy natural context."[14] Primary among these is the need for food. It is the touchstone in the search for justice.

10. See Ulrich Duchrow, *Property for People, Not for Profit: Alternatives to the Global Tyranny of Capital* (London: Zed Books, 2004); Noam Chomsky, *Profit over People: Neoliberalism and Global Order* (New York: Seven Stories, 1999).

11. Klaus Nürnberger, *Prosperity, Poverty, and Pollution: Managing the Approaching Crisis* (Pietermaritzburg: Cluster; London: Zed Books, 1999), 277; his vision is of "the comprehensive wellbeing of all human beings, present and future, within the context of the comprehensive wellbeing of their entire social and natural environments."

12. George Orwell, *Homage to Catalonia* (Harmondsworth: Penguin, 1977 [1938]), 245.

13. Arundhati Roy, *The Chequebook and the Cruise-Missile* (London: Harper Perennial, 2004), 110.

14. Nürnberger, *Prosperity, Poverty, and Pollution*, 279.

Social justice and hunger in a world which produces more than enough for everyone on the planet to have a balanced diet are incompatible.[15] As Knierim argues, "Where there is food and soil for all, there is justice. Where there is hunger and lack of soil for food, the justice of creation is compromised."[16] More than this, for Knierim, the justice, presence, and even the existence of God are "at stake with respect to food and the soil which produces that food. In this sense, the theology of food and soil is intrinsic to the theology of justice."[17]

Authentic social justice thus "must start with satisfying basic material needs"[18] but must also address the underlying causes of poverty and injustice. These causes include:

- developing-world debt, which has changed the overall inflow of finance from rich countries to poor into a perverse and increasing flow *from* poor *to* rich;[19]
- the broader financial context in which wealth is being transferred from poorer to richer people in some developed countries;[20]
- a system of global food production in which a small number of democratically unaccountable players have imposed a large-scale agricultural model in the developing world as part of the trade liberalization agenda, even though this is detrimental to local farmers and the viability of their communities;[21]
- a global trade regime that through the World Trade Organization (WTO) favors the rich rather than the poor, its supposed original beneficiaries;[22]
- an unregulated free-market ideology requiring indefinite exponential growth, which, in the view of its proponents, will

15. See Ben Jackson, *Poverty and the Planet: A Question of Survival* (World Development Movement; Harmondsworth: Penguin, 1990); Frances Moore-Lappé et al., *World Hunger—Twelve Myths* (London: Earthscan, 1998); Marie Augusta Neal, *The Just Demands of the Poor: Essays in Socio-theology* (New York: Paulist, 1987).

16. Knierim, *Task of Old Testament Theology*, 241.

17. Ibid., 241.

18. Karl Müller et al., eds., *Dictionary of Mission: Theology, History, Perspectives* (Maryknoll, N.Y.: Orbis, 1999), 103.

19. Jackson, *Poverty and the Planet*, 94 (emphasis in original); see also Susan George, *A Fate Worse than Debt* (Harmondsworth: Penguin, 1988), 5, 261.

20. David Jenkins, *Market Whys and Human Wherefores: Thinking Again about Markets, Politics, and People* (London: Continuum, 2000), 130.

21. Kevan Bundell, *Forgotten Farmers: Small Farmers, Trade, and Sustainable Agriculture* (London: Christian Aid, 2002).

22. See World Trade Organisation (WTO), *Agreement Establishing the World Trade Organization* (Geneva: World Trade Organisation Information and Media Relations Divisions, 1995).

eventually produce enough for all, but takes insufficient account of the finite natural resources to maintain it.[23]

As the fifth assembly of the World Council of Churches (WCC) in Nairobi put it, the central issue in the search for social justice is not what the well-to-do in the West can do for the poor, but whether they are participating in the struggle of the poor for a "just, participatory and sustainable society"[24] in which ordinary, normally excluded people, particularly small-scale farmers, are empowered to be participants in their future rather than spectators in their fate. Participatory democracy is a key element in social justice.[25] The sixth WCC assembly in Vancouver refined this understanding of social justice by integrating it into a call for justice and peace in the context of seeking the integrity of creation.[26] Justice is inclusive and applies to all of creation.[27]

2. Recent Approaches to the Book of Isaiah

In *New Visions of Isaiah*, a collection devoted to the exploration of recent methodological approaches to the Isaianic corpus that seeks to probe the possibility of moving from diachronic to more synchronic readings of the book as a whole,[28] Melugin writes: "In today's world

23. See Richard Douthwaite, *The Growth Illusion: How Economic Growth has Enriched the Few, Impoverished the Many, and Endangered the Planet* (Devon: Resurgence, 1992), esp. 18–32, 172–92; Sean McDonagh, *The Greening of the Church* (Maryknoll, N.Y.: Orbis; London: Chapman, 1990); further, Jenkins, *Market Whys and Human Wherefores*.
24. Müller et al., eds., *Dictionary of Mission*, 105.
25. Ibid., 105; see also George Monbiot, *The Age of Consent: A Manifesto for a New World Order* (London: Flamingo, 2003).
26. Müller et al., eds., *Dictionary of Mission*, 105; see also Donal Dorr, *Integral Spirituality: Resources for Community, Peace, Justice, and the Earth* (Maryknoll, N.Y.: Orbis, 1990); for the link between food sovereignty and participatory democracy, see Bundell, *Forgotten Farmers*, 5.
27. See Marcus Braybrooke, ed., *Stepping Stones to a Global Ethic* (London: SCM Press, 1992), 138–42.
28. Roy F. Melugin and Marvin A. Sweeney, eds., *New Visions of Isaiah* (JSOTSup 214; Sheffield: Sheffield Academic Press, 1996); for a critical appraisal of the *New Visions of Isaiah* approach, see Yehoshua Gitay, "Prophetic Criticism— 'What are they Doing?': The Case of Isaiah—A Methodological Assessment," *JSOT* 96 (2001): 101–27; for a rejoinder, see Conrad, "Yehoshua Gitay: 'What is *He* Doing?' "; see also Marvin A. Sweeney, "The Book of Isaiah in Recent Research," *Currents in Research: Biblical Studies* 1 (1993): 141–62; H. G. M. Williamson, "Synchronic and Diachronic in Isaian Perspective," in *Synchronic or Diachronic? A Debate on Method in Old Testament Exegesis* (ed. J. C. de Moor; Leiden: Brill, 1995), 211–26.

there is a mind-boggling array of fundamentally different interpretations of the book of Isaiah. There are indeed so many different understandings of Isaiah that a person untrained in biblical studies might well wonder whether they are all interpretations of the same book."[29]

In a review of the state of research into Isaiah that is contemporary with Melugin's, Tate arrives at essentially the same conclusions, observing that "the huge output of written work on the book of Isaiah is almost overwhelming."[30] But perceptively he offers an insight that begins to account for the generally perceived confusion in the field. He notes that the shift from historical-critical, diachronically based studies to the one-book approach "constitutes a paradigm shift in Isaiah studies,"[31] thereby implying that a major upheaval has taken place conceptually and methodologically in how Isaiah is viewed and approached. Given this sea change in direction, it is understandable that the demise of a once regnant critical consensus has inaugurated a state of flux as Isaiah is examined through new, often contradictory and unfocused lenses.[32] Moreover, Tate also helpfully indicates areas in current research where further clarification is needed and directions that might profitably be pursued. Of particular relevance to this book, he notes that "there is a need to sort out, categorize, evaluate and extend the various thematic and intertextual bands of unity in the Isaiah collection."[33]

3. *Isaiah 1 as Prologue*

Chaos and unsettlement notwithstanding, modern scholarship has given several insights into the nature of the book of Isaiah that enjoy reasonably wide critical support, on which this book builds. For example, through the work of Liebreich and those who have followed him, it is now generally accepted that there is a close relationship between Isa 1 and 65–66, although the exact nature of this relationship and the way it frames the work as a whole are disputed. More broadly, Isa 1 is seen by certain writers as an introduction to everything that follows.[34] Miscall asserts

29. Melugin and Sweeney, *New Visions of Isaiah*, 11.

30. Marvin E. Tate, "The Book of Isaiah in Recent Study," in *Forming Prophetic Literature* (ed. James W. Watts and Paul R. House; JSOTSup 235; Sheffield: Sheffield Academic, 1996), 22–56 (50).

31. Ibid., 43.

32. See Leo G. Perdue, *The Collapse of History* (OBT; Minneapolis: Fortress, 1994).

33. Tate, "Book of Isaiah in Recent Study," 52.

34. On the importance of the opening to literary works, see Edward W. Said, *Beginnings, Intention, and Method* (New York: Columbia University Press, 1975).

that "chapter 1 is an introduction to the book of Isaiah as a whole and in its various parts."[35] Seitz views the superscription in 1:1 as referring to the book in its entirety and uses this position as the starting point for developing his thesis that the work should be understood holistically.[36] Melugin observes that "Isaiah 1, rich as it is, does not stand alone. It opens the entire book of Isaiah."[37] Melugin goes on to imply that the book of Isaiah as a whole, as well as the opening chapter, should be read "in synchronic fashion."[38] Brueggemann argues that the opening of the book "provides an overture to the entire book of Isaiah" that "enunciates the themes that will be predominant in all that is to follow."[39]

Within this band of critical thought, O'Connell identifies Isa 1:16–17 as "the structural axis of 1:1–2:5," suggesting "that these verses encapsulate the ideals of Isaiah's prologue—indeed, of the whole book."[40] This conclusion concerning the determinative importance of the theme of social justice within the overall scheme of the book accords well with Brueggemann. In both volumes of his commentary, Brueggemann argues that the central thrust of Isaiah's theology concerns justice and righteousness as the foundation of a community of genuine neighborliness in which the well-being of the marginalized is protected and enhanced.[41] He insists that social relations are always "the primal agenda of the prophetic tradition" in its demand for "policies and actions of a neighborly kind." These policies and actions lead to "a neighborly economics."[42]

Brueggemann also observes that the poetry of justice in ch. 1 has in view a number of later chapters, one of which is ch. 58.[43] However, he does not substantially explore how these two chapters (or indeed the others he links to ch. 1) are related, especially in how they conceive of

---

35.   Peter D. Miscall, *Isaiah* (Readings: A New Biblical Commentary; Sheffield: JSOT Press, 1993), 22.

36.   Christopher S. Seitz, "Isaiah 1–66: Making Sense of the Whole," in *Reading and Preaching the Book of Isaiah* (ed. C. R. Seitz; Philadelphia: Fortress, 1988), 105–26.

37.   Roy F. Melugin, "Figurative Speech and the Reading of Isaiah 1 as Scripture," in Melugin and Sweeney, *New Visions of Isaiah*, 282–305 (295).

38.   Ibid.

39.   Walter Brueggemann, *Isaiah 1–39* (WBC; Louisville, Ky.: Westminster John Knox, 1998), 10–11.

40.   Robert H. O'Connell, *Concentricity and Continuity: The Literary Structure of Isaiah* (JSOTSup 188; Sheffield: Sheffield Academic, 1994), 50.

41.   Brueggemann draws on the terminology of Calvin in using "neighbor" language; see John Calvin, *Commentary on the Book of the Prophet Isaiah* (4 vols.; Edinburgh: Calvin Translation Society, 1850–53), 1:64.

42.   Brueggemann, *Isaiah 1–39*, 48, 186.

43.   Ibid., 22.

and present the theme of social justice. From, so to speak, the other end
of whatever trajectories may be traced from Isa 1 to later sections of the
book, Knight suggests that "chapter 58 contains a timeless sermon" on
account of the fact that "God's Word does not change."[44] The clear
impression is that the passage represents something of a free-standing
unit, the meaning of which can be derived without careful consideration
of how it fits in with and relates to both its immediate and wider contexts. Essentially, this mode of interpretation goes a considerable way
toward legitimating what might be called the "universal truths" school of
exegetical research, an approach that pays insufficient attention to how a
text might be modified or amplified, reinforced or challenged in the
unfolding literary drama of a work in its totality.[45] By contrast, following
up the clue offered by Brueggemann into the wider world of social justice (as represented by the possible connection between chs. 1 and 58), I
seek, in an introductory manner, first to investigate the type of social
justice encoded in Isa 1 and then to probe the relationship between this
and the type depicted in Isa 58. The aim is to see what differences or
developments there might be and what theological implications these
could have in the search for a just social order as envisaged in the world
construed by the full-form text of Isaiah.

4. *Isaiah 1:16–17—Rhetorical Overview*

Isaiah 1:16–17 forms the climax of vv. 10–17,[46] effectually providing a
solution to the disordered religious life depicted. It consists of a battery
of nine imperatives, the cumulative force of which, in the opinion of

44.   George A. F. Knight, *Isaiah 56–66: The New Israel* (ITC; Grand Rapids: Eerdmans; Edinburgh: Hansel, 1985), 22. Brevard S. Childs (*Isaiah* [Louisville, Ky.: Westminster John Knox, 2001], 20), specifically in relation to Isa 1:10–17, but with a more general tenor, opposes the idea of "universal ethical teachings."
45.   Luis Alonso Schökel (*A Manual of Hermeneutics* [The Biblical Seminar 54; Sheffield: Sheffield Academic Press, 1998], 41) correctly observes on the type of exegesis being criticized that "biblical texts are not ahistorical entities, inhabitants of a rarefied atmosphere, floating without ballast in a limbo that is always accessible."
46.   The conclusion of a great many commentators; see Hans Werner Hoffmann, *Die Intention der Verkündigung Jesajas* (BZAW 136; Berlin: de Gruyter, 1974), 92–94. Yehoshua Gitay ("Reflections on the Study of the Prophetic Discourse: The Question of Isaiah 1:2–20," *VT* 33 [1983]: 207–21) places the verses in this broader context. For an early attempt to see ch. 1 as a unified composition, see L. G. Rignell, "Isaiah Chapter 1: Some Exegetical Remarks with Special Reference to the Relationship between the Text and the Book of Deuteronomy," *Studia Theologica* 11 (1958): 140–58.

several scholars, ensures that it can be read as a variant articulation of the great social-justice pronouncements in the Hebrew Bible.[47] Rhetorically, the first group of verbs, in 1:16—"wash" (רחץ), "be clean/pure" (זכה), "turn aside" (סור)—indicates the steps that the audience addressed by Isaiah must undertake before it will be able to judge and defend the cause of the fatherless and to strive after or contend on behalf of the interests of the widow.[48]

In the movement from a clearly implied propensity for wrongdoing to one characterized by the pursuit of equitable social relations that this pericope enacts, three verbs form the rhetorical hinge between these contrasting spheres of existence. In the pattern of the verse, these verbs facilitate and demonstrate the journey from "turning aside" (v. 16) from wrongdoing, to advancing or "going straight on" (v. 17) in what may broadly be called the search for the greater good. Thus, at the heart of these verses lie the injunctions "stop/cease," "learn," "seek." The texture of the poetry suggests that a brake can be placed upon the practice of "evil deeds" by washing and cleansing and turning aside, after which schooling in the ways of doing right purportedly generates and directs energy in the quest for justice.[49] At one level, according to this reading, Isaiah both issues a strong call for solidarity with and advocacy[50] on behalf of the weak (represented by the fatherless and the widows),[51] and in his poetic speech begins to delineate how this might be achieved.

However, as Chomsky has acidly observed in respect of the disparity between what has been said and what has been done by successive U.S. governments in the modern era in Central America, there is the need to be able "to extract the real content [of public discourse] from its

47. E.g. John F. A. Sawyer, *Isaiah* (2 vols.; The Daily Study Bible; Edinburgh: St. Andrews Press; Philadelphia: Westminster, 1984), 1:16; Childs, *Isaiah*, 19.

48. Note that "go straight on" is a possible literal translation of the root אשר, and that this, with its directional orientation, contrasts with the earlier injunction to "stop" doing wrong, where סור literally means "turn aside from." Hemchand Gossai (*Justice, Righteousness, and the Social Critique of the Eighth-Century Prophets* [New York: Peter Lang, 1993], 256) describes this process as "a dramatic turning around."

49. Joseph Addison Alexander (*Commentary on Isaiah* [Grand Rapids: Kregel Classics, 1992 (1867)], 89) captures the sense of the verses well when he observes, "Ceasing to do evil was not enough, or rather was not possible, without beginning to do good."

50. Alexander (*Commentary on Isaiah*, 89) insists that justice is "not in the abstract, but in act." Similarly, Childs (*Isaiah*, 20) contends that the call to justice is constituted of "highly concrete imperatives."

51. Alexander (*Commentary on Isaiah*, 89) determines these as representative of "the whole class of helpless innocents."

rhetorical disguise."[52] Similarly, the case can be made that this pronouncement of Isaiah's needs to be closely scrutinized, particularly in
light of his apparent social position as a member of the ruling elite,[53] to
see if he is the champion of social justice that he presents himself as
being and that popular imagination so often takes him to be. In a sense,
turning the hermeneutic of suspicion against the prophets is not new,[54]
but to a considerable degree this "suspicious" approach has tended to use
categories drawn from the field of historical materialism to make its case.
As indicated, I employ a strategy of close rhetorical reading to see if
clues within the text itself assist in discerning the stance of the opening
material of Isaiah vis-à-vis social justice. This book thus examines the
rhetorical function of the call to social justice in the context in which it is
found and the context it introduces. The book also examines the traditions that have been identified as possibly shaping Isaiah's ethical vision,
with a specific focus on the construals of social justice to which the
traditions give rise.

5. *Cultic Worship and Justice*

As noted, the first part of Isa 1:16–17 consists of a call by the prophet for
those he is exhorting to undertake a process of reorientation. The initial
steps necessary in this reformation are indicated by the word pair רחצו
and זכו, which in this instance may be taken as a hendiadys meaning
"wash in order to be clean."[55] The primary reference is to ritual, cultic
washing (cf. Lev 14:8; 15:13; Deut 23:12; Exod 30:18), but in the verses
as a whole, this washing is given a moral content by being linked to the
adoption of ethical behavior: seeking justice.[56]

52. Noam Chomsky, *On Power and Ideology: The Managua Lectures* (Boston:
South End, 1987), 57.

53. See Robert R. Wilson, *Prophecy and Society in Ancient Israel* (Philadelphia:
Fortress, 1980), 271; Robert Gordis, *Poets, Prophets, and Sages: Essays in Biblical
Interpretation* (Bloomington: Indiana University Press, 1971), 255; Robert T.
Anderson, "Was Isaiah a Scribe?," *JBL* 79 (1960): 57–58; Andrew Davies, *Double
Standards in Isaiah: Re-evaluating Prophetic Ethics and Divine Justice* (Leiden:
Brill, 2000), 57–58.

54. E.g., see M. Lurje, *Studien zur Geschichte der wirtschaftlichen und sozialen
Verhältnisse in israelitisch-jüdischen Exil* (BZAW 45; Giessen: Töpelmann, 1927).

55. J. N. Oswalt, *The Book of Isaiah: Chapters 1–39* (NICOT; Grand Rapids:
Eerdmans, 1986), 98.

56. Sawyer, *Isaiah*, 1:15; Alexander, *Commentary on Isaiah*, 88; John Golding-
gay, *Isaiah* (NIBCOT; Peabody, Mass.: Hendrickson; Carlisle: Paternoster, 2001),
36–37; Thomas L. Leclerc, *Yahweh is Exalted in Justice: Solidarity and Conflict in
Isaiah* (Minneapolis: Fortress, 2001), 38–39 (see also p. 161, where the "relationship

Similarly, the idea of seeking or inquiring of God in the Hebrew Bible also has a pronounced cultic orientation in one strand of thought. God is to be sought (דרשׁ) in the place that God chooses as the dwelling place of the divine name (Deut 12:5). This is the center of a cultic-juridical apparatus that ensures the regulation of a certain concept of justice, based on seeking the Lord and subsequently maintaining boundaries (Deut 13:15; 17:4; 19:18—each of which uses דרשׁ).[57] In a strain of prophetic thought, adherence to a revived cult retains an attraction (Ezek 20:40). When the prophetic voice in Isaiah links seeking (דרשׁ) to an ethical and social-justice agenda in 1:17, this rhetorically challenges what is required of those who worship in a cultic-sacrificial way. It contributes to a redefinition and reorientation of cultic worship.

This sense of challenge to a received form of what constitutes acceptable worship is reinforced with reference to בקשׁ, a common parallel term to דרשׁ, which is found in Isa 1:12 in God's question regarding who requires or seeks (מי־בקשׁ) this cultic worship. The surrounding verses (vv. 11–15) indicate the inadequacy of cultic worship from a divine perspective. In a sense, if cultic worship represents what is not required, Mic 6:8 indicates what is.[58] As part of the rhetorically shaped criticism of cult worship, when Isaiah states "Your hands are full of blood" (Isa 1:15), at one level this refers to the blood of sacrificial animals (1:11), but at another level it is the mark—literal or metaphorical—of the evil deeds of those addressed (1:16). Through this play on imagery, the text again underscores that cultic worship needs to be informed by a concept of justice that includes a moral, ethical, social-justice dimension. Whatever criticisms may eventually be made of the understanding of justice encoded in Isa 1:16 and 17, the unit constitutes a substantial rhetorical challenge to those who divorced the atonement provided by the cult from how they lived in wider society.[59] As Micah, also addressing the relationship between cultic faithfulness and societal injustice, asks for God using a term also found in Isa 1:16, "Shall I justify/make clean (זכה) the one with wicked scales?" (Mic 6:11).

Taken singly, the terms רחץ and זכה in their wider usage enrich a close reading of their deployment in Isa 1:16, contributing to a fuller

---

between cult and justice" is described as "symbiotic" rather than "antagonistic"). Childs (*Isaiah*, 19) argues that "the older hypothesis from the nineteenth century that the prophets were opposed to sacrifice in principle has been generally rejected as misconstrued"; similarly, Joseph Blenkinsopp, *Isaiah 1–39* (AB 19; New York: Doubleday, 2000), 185.

57. Knierim, *The Task of Old Testament Theology*, 116.
58. Whereas Isa 1:12 uses בקשׁ, Mic 6:8 uses דרשׁ.
59. Knierim, *The Task of Old Testament Theology*, 115.

understanding through intertextual resonance, but also raising questions. In the Hebrew Bible, רחץ is widely used,[60] although in addition to Isa 1:16 it is only found in 4:4 in the Isaianic corpus. Here it is used as the prophet looks forward to the day when the Lord will wash away (רחץ) the filth of the daughters of Zion and cleanse[61] the bloodstains of Jerusalem by a spirit of judgment (משׁפט) and burning. The reference to blood echoes references in Isa 1:11 and 15. The method of refinement may be linked to that of 1:25, in which the Lord of hosts, the mighty one of Israel, vows to burn away the dross and remove the impurities of the faithful city turned slut (1:21). Significantly, the dross is understood as rulers (1:23) and judges (1:26) who do not defend the cause of the fatherless or permit the case of the widow to come before them, but instead love bribes and run after gifts (1:23). It should be noted, however, that this cleansing is undertaken by God, whereas in Isa 1:16 the prophetic voice calls the people to wash and cleanse themselves. The wider context raises the question of whether the rulers and judges in particular have the capacity to do this.

6. *The Possibility of Cleansing*

In relation to זכה, Ps 119:9 poses the question, "How can a youth keep his way pure (זכה)?" The answer is by guarding it according to the word of the Lord, by seeking (דרשׁ) God with all his heart, and not straying from God's commandments (Ps 119:9, 10). The blessed are those who seek (דרשׁ) the Lord with their whole heart. In effect, the psalmist presupposes the capacity for human purity through adherence to the law of God in the course of all life's vagaries.[62] However, when use of זכה in Isa 1:16 is compared to other occurrences of the term in the Hebrew Bible, questions begin to arise as to whether this is actually possible.

Of the seven other times the word is used in the Hebrew Bible apart from in Isa 1:16 (the only time it is found in the imperative), four occur in texts where the implication is that it is virtually impossible for humans to cleanse themselves. Two of Job's visitors question whether "one born of a woman" could be either "pure" (זכה) or "righteous," Eliphaz in

---

60. More than 75, of which more than 48 occur in the Pentateuch and 26 in Leviticus alone.

61. The term used is דוח rather than זכה as in Isa 1:16.

62. With regard to Ps 119: in v. 45, the psalmist walks about in freedom because he has sought (דרשׁ) God's precepts; in v. 94, the psalmist has confidence in calling out to God for salvation because he has sought (דרשׁ) God's precepts; in v. 155, salvation is deemed far from the wicked because they do not seek (דרשׁ) God's statutes.

15:14 and Bildad in 25:4. Even accepting that in these cases the question comes from characters best described as one-dimensional foils to the richer theological formulations of Job himself, it is clearly a question that was more generally and didactically pondered, as attested when the author of Proverbs muses, "Who can say, 'I have kept my heart pure; I am clean (זכה) and without sin?'" (20:9). Furthermore, while Sawyer has recognized that Ps 51 is a "major parallel"[63] to Isa 1:16, he has failed to note the inherent tension in that the cleansing in Ps 51 is understood as possible only through the agency of God (in Ps 51:6 [ET v. 4] זכה is used with regard to the judgment of God),[64] whereas Isaiah seems to think that his audience can undertake the task themselves. This tension underscores that if what Isaiah demands is to be taken as at all feasible, it ought rightly to be regarded as exceedingly difficult.

Interestingly, Ps 73:13 juxtaposes the זכה–רחץ word pair in a social context of arrogance, oppression, and violence analogous to that postulated by Isaiah, but there the psalmist, as in Ps 119, assuming that purity was an attainable goal, wonders if there has been any point in his having kept his "heart pure" and having "washed" his hands in "innocence." Even if the cleansing sought by Isaiah is within the realm of the possible, in a world gone awry (as presupposed in Ps 73 and Isa 1), its pursuit and maintenance are of questionable value, again a point illustrating that what Isaiah wants to achieve faces severe obstacles.

While several critics have asked whether such washing and cleansing can in fact be legitimately undertaken by Isaiah's addressees, these critics, from as early as Calvin,[65] pay no attention to any literary role this action might have in shaping the introduction to Isaiah. Instead, they immediately transpose the debate into categories imported from the field of dogmatics, categories that then are effectually imposed on the text.[66] Whatever the merits of this approach, it serves an agenda other than discerning how the material functions as a piece of literature (albeit

---

63. Sawyer, *Isaiah*, 1:15.

64. Various other terms are used to indicate the purifying capacity of God in this psalm: מחה (vv. 3 and 11); כבס (vv. 4 and 9); טהר (vv. 4 and 9); חטא (v. 9).

65. Calvin, *Commentary on the Book of the Prophet Isaiah*, 1:63.

66. An early-modern scholar who opposes this distortion of text in the interests of predetermined doctrinal standards is Johann Salomo Semler, *Vorbereitung zur theologischen Hermeneutik* (4 vols.; Halle: Carl Hermann Hemmerde, 1760–69). As Werner Jeanrond (*Theological Hermeneutics: Development and Significance* [London: SCM Press, 1991], 41) notes, Semler saw himself as standing in the tradition of the proto-historical critic Richard Simon (1638–1712), in that both "aimed at fighting all those theologies which tried to silence the biblical texts through imposing their own doctrines on them."

scriptural literature), from which theological deductions may only be drawn as a second-stage operation (i.e. after a study of literary-rhetorical shaping has been undertaken).[67] So, taking aim at "the ancient error of Pelagianism" (so ancient, apparently, that it stretched back to Isaiah), Young argues that "nowhere is it implied or taught in the Bible that fallen man has the ability to do what has been commanded him."[68] In contrast to this methodological strategy, which seeks to bend the text to predetermined theological norms and conclusions,[69] I suggest that the question as to whether Isaiah's audience is capable, in the world construed by the text, of responding positively to the prophet's call is, first and foremost, a literary device intended to illustrate the magnitude of what is required. This issue, as it is raised in v. 16, echoes and underscores what has already been sounded in the opening verses of the book.[70]

67. See Francis Watson, *Text, Church, and World* (Edinburgh: T. & T. Clark, 1994), 134; see also Schökel, *Manual of Hermeneutics*, 10; Green, *Theology, Hermeneutics, and Imagination*, 182. On the way in which dogmatics has been interpretatively elevated above text, see the seminal work of James Barr, *The Semantics of Biblical Language* (Oxford: Oxford University Press, 1961), esp. 147, 259–60, 275; see also Gerd Lüdemann, *The Unholy in Holy Scripture: The Dark Side of the Bible* (London: SCM Press, 1996), 20; idem, *Heretics: The Other Side of Early Christianity* (London: SCM Press, 1996). In a timely fashion, Schökel (*Manual of Hermeneutics*, 36, 40–41), while appreciative of this methodology, points out that it has its limitations. From a systematic, as opposed to biblical, theologian, see Alister E. McGrath, *The Genesis of Doctrine: A Study in the Foundation of Doctrinal Criticism* (Grand Rapids: Eerdmans, 1990).

68. Edward J. Young, *The Book of Isaiah* (3 vols.; NICOT; Grand Rapids: Eerdmans, 1964–72), 1:71; see also Oswalt, *Book of Isaiah: Chapters 1–39*, 98; note how Alexander (*Commentary on Isaiah*, 89) cites Luther as positing the "evil nature of humanity."

69. In a broader sweep it might be suggested that this tendency is apparent, among others, in the work of Brevard Childs, *Introduction to the Old Testament as Scripture* (Minneapolis: Fortress, 1979); see also J. Gary Millar, *Now Choose Life: Theology and Ethics in Deuteronomy* (Leicester: Apollos, 1998).

70. For a helpful survey of different ways to understand the prophets generally, see Gossai, *Justice, Righteousness, and the Social Critique*, 221–41, esp. 229–34. On Isa 1:2–3, see Eryl W. Davies, *Prophecy and Ethics: Isaiah and the Ethical Tradition of Israel* (JSOTSup 16; Sheffield: JSOT Press, 1981), 60, 62, 64, 114, 117, 119, and passim. Childs (*Isaiah*, 19) argues that there has been much scholarly debate about whether the writing "stems from priestly, prophetic, or wisdom circles. The argument has become quite sterile without much exegetical illumination. All three strains are involved in some fashion, but the search for sharp, form-critical distinctions is quite fruitless." See also R. N. Whybray, "Prophecy and Wisdom," 181–99; Robert Murray, "Prophecy and Cult," 200–16; Anthony Phillips, "Prophecy and Law," 217–32; and John F. A. Sawyer, "A Change of Emphasis in the Study of

According to this reading, which values the fluidity and ambiguity of the text as indicative of the ambiguity and fluidity of life, if—having issued a plea and a summons to repentance that is rightly construed as a tall order—the prophet is unable to offer the hope of the repentance being effected, then not only is the credibility of the prophet called into question, but also the credibility of the one who authorized him. As Magonet pertinently observes, "If a prophet can be wrong, then anything can be wrong and no word is guaranteed."[71]

7. *Schooled in Seeking in Justice*[72]

After issuing his demand for the cessation of wrongdoing, Isaiah next begins to direct his audience towards the measures he sees as necessary to rectifying the social disorder of Jerusalem, Israel, and, more widely, the nations. At the heart of Isa 1:16–17, functioning as the pivot of the nine imperatives of which it is composed, lies the verb למד, meaning "to learn" in the Qal form and "to teach" in the Piel. It is a term that resonates across the Isaianic corpus, and an examination of its various uses raises the suspicion of a perceptible ideological bias within the text, devised to justify and vindicate the failure of the prophet in his commission to elicit the changes necessary in establishing a more equitable society attentive to the needs of the marginalized. Isaiah 2:4 (לא־למד), with its vision of a world where, in the words of the African American spiritual, people

the Prophets," 233–49, in *Israel's Prophetic Tradition: Essays in Honour of Peter R. Ackroyd* (ed. R. Coggins, A. Phillips, and M. Knibb; Cambridge: Cambridge University Press, 1982). Isaiah indicates a situation in which both the terms of the legally rooted covenant have been sundered and the natural order of things has been inverted. In terms of covenant-treaty theology, the "heavens" (v. 2) are called to witness that the junior party to the treaty (the "children") "have rebelled against" their suzerain. In terms of wisdom theology, the profundity of Israel's rebellion is highlighted by the assertion that such utterly aberrant behavior is not even to be found in the natural world, where "the ox knows his master, the donkey his owner's manger." This reading underlines the enormity of the dislocation and degeneracy with which the prophet is dealing. Society is reeling out of control (5:11, 12) to such an extent that the consequences of the unjust order are ultimately presented as cosmic (24:5, 20). It can now be seen that the previously examined question as to whether it really is possible for the people addressed by Isaiah to respond positively to his urging to "wash and make yourselves clean" may rightly be read, in light of vv. 2 and 3, as related to the theme of the gravity of the situation encountered by the prophet.

71. Jonathan Magonet, *A Rabbi's Bible* (London: SCM Press, 1991), 105.

72. Alexander (*Commentary on Isaiah*, 89) cites Musculus and Hitzig as understanding this to mean "forming the habit or accustoming one's self."

"ain't gonna study war no more," sounds an idealistic note that is particularly taken up again in Isa 48:17 and 54:13. In the second of these passages, the poet envisions a situation in which the incomparable Lord (whom no one can teach—למד—anything; 40:14) will himself instruct (למד) the children of the Israelites in a context of great peace and well-established righteousness (54:13): the opposite of the reality in Isa 1. In this new order, the "instructed (למד) tongue" (50:4) of the prophet will be made redundant as God undertakes the task of education God's self. Or perhaps, in something of a self-congratulatory manner, the prophet is implicitly holding himself up as a model, for as he has been attentive to God "like one being taught (למד)" (also 50:4), so, it seems, the whole nation will be taught in 54:13. It all could have come to pass much earlier if it had not been for the people's recalcitrance and rebellion. This tone of elegiac wistfulness is found in 48:17–19, in which the teacher (a derivative of למד) God bemoans that if only the people had paid attention to God's commands they would not have suffered destruction.

Clearly, the blame for what happened to Israel, in terms of a "theological plot of divine goodness, human rebellion and subsequent judgment,"[73] is being firmly fixed on Israel. The groundwork for this conclusion is laid in prior uses of למד. For example, 26:10 posits that "though grace is shown to the wicked, they do not learn (למד) righteousness," while 29:13, in a passage reflective of the same type of situation existing in ch. 1, condemns worship of God that "is made up only of rules taught (למד) by humans." Confronted with such willful disobedience, it seems that all Isaiah can do is bind up his testimony and seal up the law among his disciples (an adjectival form of למד), presumably in the conviction that he will be proved correct at a later date. The important thing to remember, though, is that this counterpointing of the righteous, ignored prophet with the wicked, intransigent people may well be taken as an ideological construct designed to cover over his failure.[74] This is indicated by the fact that the prophet is unable to do what he demands of his audience; he, a man of unclean lips, living among a people of unclean lips, is incapable of "turning aside" (סור) his guilt without the intervening agency of a massive theophany during which one of the attendant seraphim touches his lips with the purifying burning coals (6:7). Yet this סור, "turning aside," is precisely what he expects from those he addresses (1:16).[75]

73. Miscall, *Isaiah*, 23.
74. Davies (*Double Standards in Isaiah*, 11) advises that "the book of Isaiah must be read as ideology rather than revelation."
75. Caputo (*Demythologizing Heidegger*, 201) notes that prophets "make impossible, mad demands on everyone, especially themselves"; in this case, the final element in this formulation is called into question.

Within the Isaianic corpus, Isa 30:11 resonates with the thrust of 1:16 and 17 in the way it calls the rebellious people to turn away from/leave (סור) the way they are going. Similarly, in 52:11, the prophet summons the captives to depart (סור) from Babylon. In 27:9, removal (סור) of Jacob's sin is dependent on the destruction of altars and toppling of *asherim*. This note of one thing being dependent on another is also sounded in 58:9, in which the promise of divine presence is contingent on those addressed removing (סור) oppression and socially corrosive ways of behaving from their midst. There are thus three imperatival calls (1:16; 30:11; 52:11) and two "if–then" constructs (27:9; 58:9). The only demonstrable time that someone turns aside (סור) from evil they become a prey (59:15). In Isaiah's world, responding to the call to turn is not easy and the consequence, at least in 59:15, not encouraging.

Much more closely aligned with its use in 6:7, סור is more regularly depicted as a function of divine activity.[76] By way of contrast to the call of 1:16–17, in 1:25 it is the Lord who will remove (סור) all impurities to ensure justice to the widows and orphans (1:23) in a reconfigured judiciary (1:26). Yahweh will remove (סור) the reproach of God's people from all the earth in the course of swallowing up death forever and wiping the tears from all faces (25:8). Given these aspects of the divine agenda, it is perhaps little wonder that woe is pronounced upon those who deprive (סור) the innocent of their rights (5:23).

A brief exploration of how the term חדל ("cease") is used contributes to this discussion. In 1:16 it forms part of the prophetic call for those addressed to reform their behaviors. However, by 24:8 the noise of the jubilant will have stopped (חדל), ultimately as a result of the Lord indiscriminately laying waste to the earth (24:1–3) as a consequence of the people's disobedience of the laws, violation of the statutes, and severance of the everlasting covenant (24:5). Again things will not go well for them—all of them, including widows and orphans. The justice of God is called into question by the all-encompassing devastation of the earth. In addition, the bald command to turn away (חדל) from man (2:22), envisaged as worthless, reinforces the sense that in 1:16 and 17 the prophet may be demanding what is beyond the capacity of his addressees. Trust or pride in anything of human origin is viewed negatively.[77]

---

76. Isa 3:1, 18; 5:5; 10:27; 11:13 (through the root of Jesse); 14:25 (twice); 17:1; 18:5.

77. Inculcated into the biblical ideology, readers may be induced to sympathize with God's desire to punish the king of Assyria for his pride in being able to remove the boundaries of peoples, but this too is part of the broader Isaianic context, in which anything of human origin is frowned upon.

Perhaps at this rhetorical juncture as much as at any other, the conviction of prophetic faith in "at least the theoretical possibility that there
could be obedience"[78] is called into question.[79] If we are not to conclude
that the prophet is using a privileged position to make inordinate and
unjustifiable demands on the people, then what follows the call to "turn
aside from your evil deeds, stop doing wrong, learn to do what is right"
must contain something that engages them and that is achievable. Otherwise the prophetic discourse risks degenerating into a self-justifying
lambasting from on high of a people whose reorientation the prophet is
finally incapable of assisting and sustaining. Again we must turn to the
rhetoric of the passage to see if it contains anything to justify hope of the
fulfillment of its prophetic agenda.

8. *Rhetorical Strategy: Widening Justice*

The strategy Isaiah adopts is to include the seeking (דרשׁ) of justice in a
proper understanding of the relationship between worship and the just
structuring of society. In this reading, the movement through 1:16–17 is
from cultic to court-judicial reference. The implicit assumption of 1:17
is that the justice system—however narrowly or widely this term is
understood—is not functioning as it should for widows and orphans. In
1:21–27 the leadership is blamed for this failure. The day is envisioned
when a set of judges will deliver justice, thus redeeming Zion. This type
of idealized administration of justice finds further expression in looking
to the establishment of a throne upon which will sit a Davidic heir, who
in the process of judging will seek (דרשׁ) justice and thereby speed up the
inauguration of righteousness (16:5). In the biblical account of the period

---

78. Walter Brueggemann, *Old Testament Theology: Essays on Structure, Theme,
and Text* (ed. Patrick D. Miller; Minneapolis: Fortress, 1992), 13.

79. Davies (*Double Standards in Isaiah*, 35–37) accepts the possibility of
change; so, too, Leclerc (*Yahweh is Exalted in Justice*, 42) and Childs (*Isaiah*, 20).
Georg Fohrer ("Jesaja 1 als Zusammenfassung der Verkündigung Jesajas," *ZAW* 74
[1962]: 251–68) concurs, as does Hoffmann (*Intention der Verkündigung Jesajas*,
95). Significantly, however, A. Vanlier Hunter (*Seek the Lord! A Study of the Meaning and Function of the Exhortations in Amos, Hosea, Isaiah, Micah, and Zephaniah*
[Baltimore: St. Mary's Seminary and University, 1982], 189–90) believes that
"Yahweh's decision to bring judgment has been finalized," and thus "Isaiah never
intends to offer a way of escaping," despite which, however, "requirements for just
living remain fully in effect." See also Georg Sauer ("Die Umkehrforderung in der
Verkündigung Jesajas," in *Wort-Gebot-Glaube: Beiträge zur Theologie des Alten
Testaments* [ed. Hans Joachim Stoebe et al.; Zürich: Zwingli Verlag, 1970], 277–95
[292]), who believes that Isaiah does not offer a possibility for avoiding judgment.

before "the reigns of Uzziah, Jotham, Ahaz, and Hezekiah," there is a well-attested pattern of the Lord being sought through the agency of a prophet (2 Kgs 3:11; 8:8; 1 Chr 15:13; 21:30; 28:9). Even in a scenario in which the prophet is hated, he is still consulted, albeit reluctantly, as a reliable route to God (1 Kgs 22:5–7; 2 Chr 18:7; 34:21). In the wider Isaianic tradition recourse is made to this type of formulation, variations of which articulate the need to seek the Lord.[80]

Initially, however, the object of the seeking in Isaiah is identified as "justice" (Isa 1:17) rather than the Lord, presumably because the audience to whom Isaiah speaks assumed that in their form of worship they already had access to God without further seeking being required. But Isaiah accuses the people of having "forsaken the Lord . . . and turned their backs on God" (1:4), in light of which it may be argued that the injunction to "seek justice" includes the implication that in doing so they will be conforming to a pattern of worship and life acceptable to God. Although it would be an exaggeration to argue that seeking justice is coterminous with seeking God, in this instance, "The religious use of the term *dāraš* in Isaiah argues persuasively for understanding the command 'seek justice' as the social and moral equivalent of the religious and cultic act of 'seeking God.' "[81] In 58:2, those who seek (דרש) God day after day through the religious practice of fasting are told that the divine presence will be manifested in the search for social justice (58:6–10).

Support for this interpretation is found in Amos 5, which famously contains the call for justice to roll down like waters and righteousness like a never-failing stream. The context here is also one in which the type of worship associated with cultic sites (Amos 5:5, 21–24)[82] is divorced

---

80. With reference to the root דרש: Isa 8:19 warns that people should not seek advice from mediums and wizards, but instead should seek their God; 19:3 indicates that such seeking from mediums and wizards is for Egyptians; 11:10 envisages the day when the nations will effectually seek the Lord through rallying to the banner of the root of Jesse; 31:1 condemns those who do not seek the Lord, but instead rely on Egyptian military might; 34:16 calls for people to seek the reassurance of the Lord in the scroll of Yahweh; 55:6 issues a summons to seek Yahweh while he may be found; 65:10 offers a pastoral idyll for those who seek the Lord; 65:1 indicates the readiness of God to be sought by people who did not ask and to be found by those who did not seek (בקש).

81. Leclerc, *Yahweh is Exalted in Justice*, 38; see also J. G. Gammie, *Holiness in Israel* (OBT; Minneapolis: Fortress, 1989), 83–84; Blenkinsopp, *Isaiah 1–39*, 184–85.

82. Note how the divine injunction in Amos 5:4 to "seek [דרש] me" is contrasted with the call in Amos 5:5 not to seek (דרש) Bethel. The reference to Bethel introduces negative comment to the other cultic sites of Gilgal and Beersheeba.

from right social practice. The injunction to "seek (דרשׁ) the Lord and live," directed to those "who turn justice into bitterness and cast right-eousness to the ground" (vv. 6–7), again underlines that authentic wor-ship incorporates participation in shaping a just social order. In addition, in Hos 10:11–12 the same word pairing as in Isa 1:17 (למד and דרשׁ) is used in such a way that being "schooled" in the ways of God leads to the "sowing of righteousness," which in turn is understood as constitutive of "seeking the Lord" (למד, Hos 10:11; דרשׁ, Hos 10:12). Although Hosea does not use the term "justice," he does use "righteousness," so often its pairing in the Hebrew Bible and thus an indication of the direction of his thought. Again, the prophet is operating in a context of corrupted cultic worship (Hos 1:11–13; 4:4–19; 5:1–7; 8:4–7; 10:5–6; 11:2; 13:1–2).

By widening the concept of worship to include the practice of and search for justice, Isaiah configures an arresting challenge. A further reference to דרשׁ ("seek") in Isaiah, however, implicitly raises a question concerning the justice of God. In Isa 9:12 (ET v. 13), the people are reprimanded for not seeking (דרשׁ) Yahweh. Laying aside that their recalcitrance might in part derive from an understandable reluctance to turn again to the one who had hit them (9:12 [ET v. 13]), this failure to seek Yahweh creates the pretext for the announcement of a harsh and inclusive divine judgment, starting with those in positions of leadership (9:14 [ET v. 15]). This judgment also incorporates orphans and widows (9:16 [ET v. 17]), the rights of whom 1:17 implies will be protected through the correction (אשׁר) of oppression. As 9:15 (ET v. 16) and 3:12 clarify through the use of אשׁר, this is the responsibility of those in leadership. Why as part of a comprehensive divine punishment widows and orphans should suffer for the failure of the ruling elite raises an element of doubt about God's course of action.

Furthermore, attention needs to be paid to the ensuing content of the justice envisaged to begin to evaluate if it substantively amplifies the social justice agenda and, crucially, if it is in any way adequate as a solu-tion to the massive societal ills already identified by the prophetic rhetoric. The first element to be derived from the governing imperatival construction "seek justice" is that either the oppressed ought to be encouraged or the oppressor reproved. This may be taken as an example of "undecidability," in which, as Derrida explains, there is "a *deter-minate* oscillation between possibilities."[83] That ambiguity exists with regard to the translation of this phrase perhaps reflects the deeper tension

83. Jacques Derrida, *Limited Inc* (ed. Gerald Graff; trans. Samuel Weber and Jeffrey Mehlman; Evanston, Ill.: Northwestern University Press, 1988), 148 (emphasis in original).

in the prophetic discourse with regard to whether Isaiah's primary focus is on the oppressed or the oppressor.[84] Gordis recognizes this ambivalence, observing rather generously "that Isaiah is opposed to the concentration of wealth not merely because of the impoverishment of the poor, but also because of the demoralization of the rich" and that his concern is "with the well-being of the oppressor and of the oppressed."[85] Certainly the injunction to "encourage the oppressed" introduces and corresponds to the subsequent injunctions to "defend the cause of the fatherless" and to "plead the case of the widow." In this reading, the three imperatives, each developing a related line of thought, follow swiftly and forcefully one after the other, adding up to a cogent extrapolation of what it might mean to "seek justice."

An equally coherent interpretation, however, may be discerned in taking the phrase to mean "reprove the oppressor." According to this perspective, a more morally sensitive element within the ruling elite (much like Isaiah himself[86]) is being called upon to remonstrate with their peers in order that they might discharge their duty in judging the cases of the marginalized in society. Although, in the end, there is little essential difference in these readings, in that both are directed toward those generally doing wrong, the second[87] better fits with both the immediate juridical referent of 1:17 and the wider pattern of the opening chapters of Isaiah, in which the central prophetic concern is not the empowerment of the oppressed but the reformation of the oppressors.

So, 1:23 demonstrates that it is the "rulers" who, despite their dereliction of duty, are responsible for defending "the cause of the fatherless" and for dealing with "the widow's case." However, while 1:17 demands the defense (שפט) of orphans, 1:23 acknowledges the failure of the elite to do so (לא־ישׁפט). While 1:17 calls for the widow's case to be pleaded

---

84. Resonant with this ambiguity, Mailloux (*Reception Histories*, xii) concludes his account of the beginnings of rhetoric by noting that "its legendary origin appears as a theoretical practice *either* for instituting radical change *or* for maintaining traditional power relations" (emphasis in original).

85. Gordis, *Poets, Prophets, and Sages*, 260–61; see also Alexander (*Commentary on Isaiah*, 89), who understands that part of the goal is "to reclaim them [the oppressors] from their evil courses."

86. Ibid., 255; Wilson, *Prophecy and Society in Ancient Israel*, 271; Anderson, "Was Isaiah a Scribe?," 57–58; Davies, *Double Standards in Isaiah*, 57–58.

87. Following J. F. Stenning, ed. and trans., *The Targum of Isaiah* (Oxford: Clarendon, 1949), 4; Franz Delitzsch, *Biblical Commentary on the Prophecies of Isaiah* (2 vols.; Edinburgh: T. & T. Clark, 1910), 1:78; George Buchanan Gray, *A Critical and Exegetical Commentary on the Book of Isaiah* (2 vols.; Edinburgh: T. & T. Clark, 1912), 1:24; Israel W. Slotki, *Isaiah* (London: Soncino, 1949), 6.

(ריב), 1:23 admits the failure of such cases (ריב) to come before the powerful. In these circumstances, this prophetic consciousness envisages justice not as the widows and orphans being incorporated into the system with increased influence, but as God restoring the judges (שׁפט) as in the good old days (1:26): nostalgia rather than social justice. Part of this mindset also looks forward to the ideal ruler of Isa 11:3–4, who will judge (שׁפט) not on appearances (11:3) but in the interests (שׁפט) of the needy and the poor of the earth (11:4). In this thinking, when the powerful do not act on the summons to address ruthlessness (חמוֹץ) of Isa 1:17, God becomes the last court of appeal, as in Ps 71:4, in which the psalmist calls on God for deliverance from the grasp of the ruthless (חמוֹץ). As Isa 3:13 pictures it, Yahweh rises in court to contend (ריב) with the people, but the next verse makes clear that divine judgment is directed against the rulers who have exploited the poor. No doubt there is something attractive in this depiction of the divine, but it does tend to leave the poor as passive objects. It is the rulers or God who exercise real power.

Similarly, 10:1–2 underscores Isaiah's preoccupation with "the elders and leaders" of the people and with those, clearly drawn from the higher echelons of society, "who make unjust laws[,] . . . who issue oppressive decrees to deprive the poor of their rights and rob my oppressed people of justice, making widows their prey and robbing the fatherless." Given this situation, it becomes apparent, in categories developed by Paulo Freire,[88] that Isaiah, in this text and more broadly, conceives of the poor, the marginalized, the widows, and the orphans as objects to whom and for whom things are done. They are viewed as objects rather than subjects capable of constructively acting as agents of their own betterment, or at least having a role to play in that process. That the poor could be anything more than passive recipients of the patronage of the powerful—including a powerful deity—does not, and perhaps could not, register on Isaiah's horizon of thought. This consequently helps explain his constant reformist emphasis on the ruling elite as the best (in his view, perhaps only) avenue for social change.

The narrowness inherent in Isaiah's concept of the route to social justice is, though, open to debate. While Weinfeld is probably correct

88. Paulo Freire, *Pedagogy of the Oppressed* (New York: Continuum, 1992); idem, *Education for Critical Consciousness* (New York: Continuum, 1994); Robert Mackie, ed., *Literacy and Revolution: The Pedagogy of Paulo Freire* (New York: Continuum, 1981); Alice Frazer Evans, Robert A. Evans, and William Bean Kennedy, eds., *Pedagogies for the Non-Poor* (Maryknoll, N.Y.: Orbis, 1987), esp. 219–31.

that the ambit of the legal terminology in Isaiah (i.e. שפט) is wider than a purely juridical context,[89] and at its widest extent suggests an underlying social-justice orientation,[90] the root meaning is located in the world of a court system administered by the powerful. Even if it is assumed that the act of judging or defending the fatherless has an extrajudicial semantic field more aligned to the broader concerns of social justice (as may be the case in Isa 1:17), the basic institutions of justice are accepted and worked within; the question of what to do when these are irremediably corrupted is neither raised nor answered. This acceptance in itself reveals a limited conceptual grasp of the deeper issues involved in the pursuit of a just society. Buying into this flawed, inadequate logic of viewing the poor as objects incapable of independent action, Weinfeld argues that when the prophets refer to matters of justice, "[T]hey do not mean merely that the judges should judge accurately. They mean primarily that the officials and landowners should act on behalf of the poor."[91] This is all very well and may at one level accurately reflect a potential thrust of 1:16–17, but considering the monumentally disordered world constructed by the rhetoric of (to go no further) ch. 1 as a whole, one might well wonder at its relevance and efficacy *for these particular circumstances*.

Further evidence of the circumscribed nature of Isaiah's concept of social justice is found in the rationale he offers for why one should listen to him. He dangles the carrot that if the grouping with which he is engaged is willing to rethink their ways, then they "will eat the good of the land" (1:19).[92] This is tantamount to arguing that social reconfiguration should be inaugurated for reasons of enlightened self-interest rather than, strictly speaking, for reasons of authentic justice. Through the type of reform envisioned by Isaiah, benefits hopefully would accrue incidentally to those most oppressed, but their interests would not be central in initiating or implementing the process. Of course, one could counter that the adoption of an enlightened self-interest was a rhetorical ploy forged in light of an awareness of the harsh realities of societal power relationships, but ultimately this kind of *apologia* only serves to stress Isaiah's

89. For a fuller discussion of this topic, see Pietro Bovati, *Re-establishing Justice: Legal Terms, Concepts, and Procedures in the Hebrew Bible* (trans. Michael J. Smith; JSOTSup 105; Sheffield: JSOT Press, 1994); specifically related to Isaiah, see idem, "Le langage juridique du prophète Isaïe," in *Book of Isaiah/Le livre d'Isaïe: Les oracles et leurs relectures unité et complexité de l'ouvrage* (ed. Jacques Vermeylen; BETL 81; Louvain: Louvain University Press, 1989), 177–96 (188–90).

90. Weinfeld, 'Justice and Righteousness', 242.

91. Ibid., 245.

92. Since this group is composed of members of the ruling elite in a non-egalitarian society, this functionally implies the best of the land.

implication in and acceptance of a system in which the poor are kept voiceless and the interests of the poor never top the social agenda.[93]

9. *Charity, Not Justice: Exodus Betrayed*

Evidence supporting the thesis that Isaiah articulates an atrophied version of social justice may be garnered from the terminology used to depict those deemed most in need of justice. If Isaiah had been the advocate of justice so often imagined, he (or a later redactor[94]) might have been expected to include the term "alien" along with his reference to "orphan" and "widow," since this tripartite formula is the classic Hebrew Bible summary of those to whom society had to be particularly attentive.[95] The significance of the omission of "alien" is that allusion to the liberative dimension of God is being excised. Characteristically, the term "alien" functions as a reminder to Israelites that as they were once aliens in Egypt who had experienced oppression, they therefore needed to organize their liberated social life to ensure that such did not happen to aliens (and thus, by extension, to anyone) living in their midst. As Knierim notes, "Liberation is not only to be received, it is also to be granted by the same people."[96]

Interestingly, some scholars link Isa 1:17 to texts that explicitly include the "alien," as if it should be assumed that Isaiah too intended their inclusion.[97] But the truth is that Isaiah does not make mention of the "alien' in this instance, and, when the Isaianic tradition does, it is exclusively with aliens in roles of servitude to a resurgent Israel (14:1–2; 61:5–6). Too much should not be read into this overall point, but taken with other

93. In the modern world, while recognizing the need in particular historical circumstances for people to speak out on behalf of the poor, it must also be acknowledged that ideally this should only be a temporary measure until the poor are empowered to speak for themselves. As one fine example of speaking out for the poor, see Oscar Romero, *Voice of the Voiceless* (trans. Donald Walsh; Maryknoll, N.Y.: Orbis, 1985).

94. Christiana van Houten (*The Alien in Israelite Law* [JSOTSup 107; Sheffield: JSOT Press, 1991], 116) argues that the reference to "alien" in Isa 14:1 is a post-exilic redaction; therefore, a similar insertion could have been made in 1:17.

95. See F. Charles Fensham, "Widow, Orphan, and the Poor in Ancient Near Eastern Legal and Wisdom Literature," *JNES* 21 (1962): 129–39; Leclerc, *Yahweh is Exalted in Justice*, 37. Blenkinsopp (*Isaiah 1–39*, 185) identifies the marginal and oppressed, among whom he locates orphans and widows, as "charter members of the underprivileged class."

96. Knierim, *The Task of Old Testament Theology*, 114 (see also p. 101).

97. R. E. Clements, *Isaiah 1–39* (NCB; Grand Rapids: Eerdmans, 1980), 34; Delitzsch, *Biblical Commentary on the Prophecies of Isaiah*, 1:80.

evidence, it helps strengthen the case that Isaiah's commitment to authentic social justice was at best only partial. In the broad scope, much of Isaiah is heavily invested not in justice for the alien (or, by implication, for anyone else) but in dreams of imperial grandeur and in the alien's domination.[98]

Whatever the merit of regarding the reference to "alien" as a sort of memory aid to the radicality of a God who could effect liberation, over time this tradition hardened into a pattern, the outlook of which was heavily tilted toward institutionalized charity[99] rather than participatory, structure-changing justice (as had been the case in the paradigm shift from bondage to freedom brought about by God's initiation of exodus).[100] Van Houten delineates the social reality of monarchical Israel well when she argues that "humanitarian concern for the marginalized" arose out of the establishment of "a hierarchical social structure," the economic policies of which "drew the wealth from the land, and made the life of the lower class more precarious."[101] The mechanisms that created and perpetuated such a disparity in wealth, however, were not analyzed or criticized. Thus, appeals to show concern for those abused by such a society (among which can be placed 1:16–17) accept the society's basic organization and frame their understanding of justice in terms of maintaining the dependence of the poor upon the goodwill of the rich. As Gowan notes, "Those people who do not have the power to insist on justice for themselves are thus held up as a special concern for the whole community."[102] Gowan, though, later tacitly admits that in reality it is not the "whole community" that needs to be addressed but "those with power,"[103] since they were the group capable of ameliorating the conditions of the poor. Similarly, van Houten argues that injunctions to show charity to the poor were directed "to well-to-do landowners."[104]

---

98. R. N. Whybray (*The Good Life in the Old Testament* [London: T. & T. Clark, 2002], 218) charts how as the book of Isaiah progresses, "[T]he promise of domination and wealth [for Israel] is expressed in more universalistic terms."

99. Donald E. Gowan, "Wealth and Poverty in the Old Testament: The Case of the Widow, the Orphan, and the Sojourner," *Int* 41 (1987): 341–53 (346).

100. On the enduring importance of the exodus paradigm, see J. Severino Croatto, *Exodus: A Hermeneutics of Freedom* (rev. ed.; Maryknoll, N.Y.: Orbis, 1981), esp. 39–47; idem, "The Socio-historical and Hermeneutical Relevance of the Exodus," in *Exodus: A Lasting Paradigm* (ed. Bas Van Iersel and Anton Weiler; Edinburgh: T. & T. Clark, 1987), 125–33.

101. Van Houten, *Alien in Israelite Law*, 93.

102. Gowan, "Wealth and Poverty in the Old Testament," 349.

103. Ibid., 352.

104. Van Houten, *Alien in Israelite Law*, 106.

While there may be something positive to be said for this paternalistic social arrangement so dependent on the tender consciences of the powerful, in that at least the poor are recognized as having serious problems that the rich have an obligation to help solve, it stops a long way short of the type of justice implied in the exodus account. Further, given the gravity of the context Isaiah is addressing, it is dubious whether this arrangement is a suitable vehicle for tackling the injustices of the time. Indeed, as Davies has argued, it could well be that the ruling elite was adhering to the very legal-ethical tradition appealed to by Isaiah, and were actually using it in furthering and deepening the crisis in society. Davies points out that "Isaiah does not suggest that the means employed by the wealthy to acquire the property of others were in any way illegal, and it is possible that the methods adopted were not acts of open violence but devices which were within the limit of the law."[105] Further, he notes that the Israelite administration "may well have persuaded themselves that they were not changing the ancient stipulations, but merely adapting them to the political exigencies of their age."[106] These statements offer more evidence that Isaiah is using a tool that is not sharp enough to get to the roots of the problem of injustice and to bring genuine hope to the poor.

The wisdom tradition also needs to be examined to see if it illuminates Isaiah's concept of social justice, particularly in light of recent research, which increasingly views the legal-ethical codes in the Hebrew Bible as rooted in and derived from older tribal wisdom. Blenkinsopp suggests that "law may be described as a specialization of tribal wisdom" and also that there is a "confluence of the sapiential-didactic and legal traditions" in that "the writing down of the laws, and especially the provision of motivation for their observation, was intended as another form of moral guidance and instruction, comparable to the collection of aphoristic material in the Book of Proverbs."[107] The significance of this advance in scholarship is that it demonstrates that biblical traditions are not completely isolated or hermetically sealed from each other, but fluidly related. So, it is no longer necessary to attempt to identify one tradition as exclusively influencing and shaping a particular text. Specifically related to the study of Isaiah, Williamson is thus able constructively to push past much of the debate that has surrounded Whedbee's approach to the

---

105. Davies, *Prophecy and Ethics*, 69.

106. Ibid., 81; Goldingay, *Isaiah*, 37; Leclerc, *Yahweh is Exalted in Justice*, 52–54; Davies, *Double Standards in Isaiah*, 40.

107. Joseph Blenkinsopp, *Wisdom and Law in the Old Testament: The Ordering of Life in Israel and Early Judaism* (Oxford: Oxford University Press, 1995), 92, 97.

influence of wisdom teaching on the prophet.[108] In a conclusion commensurate with Blenkinsopp's, Williamson observes that "as with his [Isaiah's] pronouncement of judgement against social sin and injustice, there was what may loosely be called a prophetic element which was combined with other data in wider currency among his contemporaries."[109] The broader context of the article makes it clear that "other data" primarily means wisdom teaching.[110] As regards Isa 1:16 and 17, Sawyer contends that Isaiah's "moral imperatives belong more to the universal ethical teaching of the Wisdom literature than to the more distinctively Israelite laws."[111] Sawyer goes on to suggest parallels to Job 29:12–17 and Prov 17:5 and 2:21, although in its underlying thrust Prov 31:8 and 9 better capture the shape and spirit of Isa 1:16 and 17. Similarly, Knierim roots Isa 1:16b, 17 "in the worldview of the dynamic connection of cause and effect," especially as found in the book of Proverbs.[112] He concludes: "All aspects expressed in Isa 1:16b and 17 are found in the wisdom literature."[113]

As with the legal-ethical tradition, though, the overarching vision of the world held out by Proverbs does not support the struggle for authentic social justice. Although several proverbs praise the moral qualities of the poor (Prov 13:8; 19:1, 22; 28:6), speaking against their exploitation (13:23; 14:31; 17:5; 18:23; 22:16, 22; 28:3, 11; 29:7, 14; 30:14; 31:9, 20) and in favor of the adoption of a charitable attitude toward them (19:17; 21:13; 22:9; 28:8, 27), others suggest that the poor are responsible for their own plight (10:4; 20:13; 21:17; 23:21). Generally, wealth and poverty are seen as inevitable parts of human life.[114] Overall, the world

108. J. W. Whedbee, *Isaiah and Wisdom* (Nashville: Abingdon, 1971); see also J. Fichtner, "Jesaja unter den Weisen," *TLZ* 74 (1949): cols. 75–80.

109. H. G. M. Williamson, "Isaiah and the Wise," in *Wisdom in Ancient Israel: Essays in Honour of J. A. Emerton* (ed. John Day, Robert P. Gordon, and H. G. M. Williamson; Cambridge: Cambridge University Press, 1995), 133–41 (140); see also, for a similar conclusion, J. Barton, *Isaiah 1–39* (OTG; Sheffield: Sheffield Academic Press, 1995), 60–61.

110. Childs (*Isaiah*, 18) endorses the view of several shaping traditions, including wisdom.

111. Sawyer, *Isaiah*, 1:16–17.

112. Knierim, *The Task of Old Testament Theology*, 94.

113. Ibid., 95.

114. As Whybray (*Good Life in the Old Testament*, 185) notes, "[I]nequality is taken for granted." Klaus Koch ("Origin and Effect of Social Critique of the Pre-exilic Prophets," *Bangalore Theological Forum* 11 [1979]: 91–108 [97]) argues that "the attitude of the sages of Israel towards the poor is ambiguous. The poor demand charity but otherwise he is the cause of his own poverty and therefore deserves his destiny"; see also R. C. van Leeuwen, "Wealth and Poverty: System

created by the wisdom perspective is a hierarchical world in which there is a place for everyone so long as everyone accepts their lot (22:2, 7; 29:13).[115] Clearly this is a vision of reality favorable to the rich, and so it may be appropriate to endorse the thesis that wisdom literature as a whole construes an ethic for the elite.[116] Thus there is little in Proverbs to sustain a rigorous analysis of the structural dimensions of injustice as a product of how the world works. Even the proverbial underpinning for the purported "middle way" of Prov 30:8b–9 (cf. Eccl 7:16–18) may at some level be seen as an ideological ploy to keep people in their appointed place, limit their expectations, and inhibit them from actively engaging in a campaign for social change to uplift the poor.

Some have argued that Isaiah was originally a member of the "wise"[117] in elite Jerusalem circles. According to this view, Isaiah subscribed to and propagated this conservative worldview, but somehow—perhaps due to the direct revelation from God in the temple (Isa 6)[118]—broke completely with them and subsequently turned his energies to attacking their social policies. In this reading, he moves from complicit insider to lone prophetic voice with remarkable ease. While there may be something in this idea, it is more credible to understand Isaiah as someone who perceives the social world of regulated wisdom disintegrating due to the rapacious violation of the wisdom ethic itself by the rich. Isaiah is one who, on the basis of that ethic that has served them so well in the past, attempts to call them back to its reimplementation.[119] To a great extent,

and Contradiction in Proverbs," *Hebrew Studies* 33 (1992): 25–36; J. David Pleins, "Poverty in the Social World of the Wise," *JSOT* 37 (1987): 61–78.

115.   In the hymn "All Things Bright and Beautiful," the now quietly dropped verse that speaks of "the rich man in his castle, the poor man at his gate" captures the ethos of this social world.

116.   Though see also Claus Westermann (*Roots of Wisdom: The Oldest Proverbs of Israel and Other Peoples* Louisville, Ky.: Westminster John Knox, 1995]) for a thesis grounding the oldest strata of proverbial wisdom within the wider community.

117.   See Barton, *Isaiah 1–39*, 60–62.

118.   Note, however, Francis Landy ("Strategies of Concentration and Diffusion in Isaiah 6," *BibInt* 7, no. 1 [1999]: 58–86), who demonstrates that the meaning and implications of this key Isaianic passage are neither clear nor stable.

119.   Isaiah's attitude to alcohol in light of that of Proverbs perhaps reinforces this: whereas Proverbs warns how alcohol leads astray (Prov 20:1; 21:17; 23:20, 30, 31) and how rulers should not overindulge (31:4, 5), lest they "forget what the law decrees, and deprive all the oppressed of their rights," Isaiah depicts a society in which the leadership has broken with this wisdom (e.g. Isa 5:22; 22:13; 28:1, 7; 56:12) and therefore needs to be called back to it. Significantly, however, note how proverbial wisdom encourages a "drink to forget"-type attitude on the part of the

through their inordinate, grasping actions, the ruling elite in their blindness are undermining their own position, and this is the heart of the situation Isaiah is struggling to rectify.[120] This interpretation is consistent with the point that in 1:16 and 17 Isaiah is primarily speaking to the rulers and highlights the validity of questioning whether the various traditions on which he draws provide an adequate solution to the social malaise he diagnoses.

In light of the above analysis, it is exaggerated to claim that "the establishment of justice became Isaiah's mission to the world."[121] It may even be gilding the lily to find "in this admonitory instruction [1:16–17] an appeal of permanent relevance to Israel."[122] Both evaluations, much as one may wish to endorse them, are too naively idealistic and fail to pay sufficient attention to the nuances of the text. Certainly, there can be little doubt that at a surface level Isaiah wants to be regarded as an advocate of justice and, according to his lights, may be so. But those lights are dim. Isaiah was able to discern and denounce what was wrong in society but was finally unable adequately to address the problems due to the underdevelopment of the concept of social justice in the traditions on which he was drawing.[123] In the end, challenged by massive injustice, he can only respond in a formulation of conversion that at best can be described as "classic,"[124] but has become "stock"[125] and routinized[126]—"a general rule of conduct"[127] that is incapable of generating a counterforce for

poor: "Give beer to those who are perishing, wine to those who are in anguish; let them drink and forget their poverty and remember their misery no more" (Prov 31:7, 8). If the poor are to be helped, it is not by themselves, but by others speaking for them (31:8, 9). On the drinking motif, see Willem A. M. Beuken, "Isaiah 28: Is it Only Schismatics that Drink Heavily? Beyond the Synchronic versus Diachronic Controversy," in de Moor, ed., *Synchronic or Diachronic?*, 15–38.

120. Knierim, *The Task of Old Testament Theology*, 95.

121. Gordis, *Poets, Prophets, and Sages*, 259.

122. Clements, *Isaiah 1–39*, 33.

123. As Terry Eagleton (*Marxism and Literary Criticism* [London: Routledge, 2002], 32) puts it in a way relevant to this discussion, "[I]n trying to tell the truth in his own way, for example, the author finds himself forced to reveal the limits of the ideology within which he writes." Barr (*The Scope and Authority of the Bible*, 100) observes specifically related to prophetic discourse that "the social perspectives and perceptions of the prophets were essentially conservative. What they declared was the traditional morality exacted by the God of Israel."

124. Leclerc, *Yahweh is Exalted in Justice*, 34, 162.

125. Ibid., 34.

126. Blenkinsopp, *Isaiah 1–39*, 184.

127. Edward J. Kissane, *The Book of Isaiah* (2 vols.; Dublin: Richview Press, 1941–43), 1:12.

justice.[128] This is not to be excessively harsh on Isaiah or to suggest that
he was necessarily cynical in what he believed his oracles could achieve.
It is to observe that Isaiah was part of a social milieu with an insufficiently acute perceptual field and inadequate resources to confront the
problem of gross injustice.[129] As he himself is forced to admit, he is "a
man of unclean lips, living among a people of unclean lips." Or as Duhm,
supporting the thrust of this analysis, remarks in connection to 1:23,
Isaiah complains but does not propose measures that would have begun
to rectify the terrible situation.[130]

10. *Isaiah 58 as an Integrated Unit*

As the comments of Knight[131] indicate, Isaiah 58 has a strong social
justice orientation. It may, in a general sense, be loosely linked to other
texts of a similar theme. For Knight, there is no intrinsic or immediately
compelling reason, however, for doing this, especially as he apparently
views ch. 58 as an independent entity that is virtually incomparable.[132]
Yet, moving away from this stance, it is, in theory, possible to posit a
connection between Isa 58 and any of the many justice pronouncements
in the book of Isaiah or, more widely, the Hebrew Bible.[133] I argue that
within the canonical shape of the Isaianic corpus, a case can be made for
relating ch. 58 to ch. 1. In substantially the same vein as Knight, Hanson
asserts with reference to Isa 58, "Few passages in Third Isaiah reach
across the centuries with as much power as this chapter. It requires no
fancy interpretive ploys."[134] Perhaps so, but the result of arbitrarily

128.   James G. Williams ("The Social Location of Israelite Prophecy," *JAAR* 37
[1969]: 153–65 [162]) contends that Isa 1:16b–17 "simply presents in hortatory
form, the wisdom known not only in Israelite culture, but among all peoples: 'wash!
clean up!'"

129.   John Barton ("Ethics in the Book of Isaiah," in *Writing and Reading the
Scroll of Isaiah: Studies of an Interpretive Tradition* [ed. C. C. Broyles and C. A.
Evans; 2 vols.; VTSup 70.1–2; Leiden: Brill, 1997], 1:67–77 [70]) confirms that
Isaiah "was clearly strongly conservative, believing that the political ideal was the
way things had been in the time of David, when everyone knew his (and especially
her) place"; as such, "Isaiah's vision of society is one of a stable, aristocratic state, in
which the poor are protected by an attitude of *noblesse oblige* on the part of the
ruling classes, and property-owning males are given their 'rightful' pre-eminence."

130.   Duhm, *Das Buch Jesaja*, 33.

131.   Knight, *Isaiah 56–66*, 22–30.

132.   Ibid., 22, where it is referred to as "a timeless sermon."

133.   Miscall, *Isaiah*, 12.

134.   Paul D. Hanson, *Isaiah 40–66* (Interpretation; Louisville, Ky.: John Knox,
1995), 207.

abstracting a text from its immediate literary-rhetorical and wider canonical context in this way is to confer upon it the status of something approaching a talismanic icon. After abstraction it can be deployed in support of a particular agenda, in this instance one arising from justice concerns, although the same technique can operate on behalf of other socio-theological outlooks. This approach, by putting texts on a pedestal and thereby making them untouchable, ignores how they contribute to the nuanced literary-rhetorical development within a complete work.

Interestingly, this abstractionist, proof-texting tendency may be said to have a more sophisticated counterpart in historical-critical research. There, until relatively recently, the validity of comparing and contrasting different texts on a similar theme generally believed to have been produced in widely separated historical eras would have been denied and the text thus fragmented into discrete units. However, consolidating the work of prior scholarship[135] and paving the way for scholars noted earlier, Sweeney in particular has demonstrated that Isa 1 was redactionally designed to serve as the prologue to the entire book "in that it summarizes the message of Isaiah."[136] This foundational assertion, examined in greater detail below for its contribution to understanding Isaiah as a unity and the theme of social justice, thus initially legitimates the study of Isa 58 for how it relates to social justice as sounded in a condensed format in ch. 1.

So, whereas Brueggemann acknowledges the likelihood of Isa 1 as the starting point of a social-justice trajectory that arcs through the text to ch. 58 (among other places),[137] I first examine whether such a proposed linkage is sustainable. I then move to compare and contrast the rhetorical presentation of social justice in both passages to see if the theme is significantly extrapolated, extended, altered, or modified from chs. 1 to 58. I also pay attention to the ways in which these matters are connected to the overall shaping of Isaiah. In addition, though, I turn attention to a dimension of Isa 58 that has avoided close scrutiny by commentators. The question is whether, in a sort of prototypical version of kenotic theology,[138] Isa 58 encourages the embrace of pain, resulting from

135. Fohrer, "Jesaja 1 als Zusammenfassung der Verkündigung Jesajas"; Clements, *Isaiah 1–39*, 28; J. Skinner, *The Book of the Prophet Isaiah* (2 vols.; CB; Cambridge: Cambridge University Press, 1900), 1:2; Delitzsch, *Prophecies of Isaiah*, 1:172; O. Procksch, *Jesaja I: Kapitel 1–39 übersetzt und erklärt* (KAT 9; Leipzig: Deichert, 1930), 20.

136. Marvin A. Sweeney, *Isaiah 1–4 and the Post-exilic Understanding of the Isaianic Tradition* (Berlin: de Gruyter, 1988), 31 and passim.

137. Brueggemann, *Isaiah 1–39*, 22.

138. On this see P. Fiddes, *The Creative Suffering of God* (Oxford: Oxford University Press, 1988); A. Neely, "Mission as Kenosis: Implications for Our Times,"

standing in solidarity with the oppressed, as a means of seeking a reconstituted, just social order. I examine the rhetorical and theological implications of this issue, particularly as they relate to the interface of social justice and wisdom in Isaiah.

11. *Links between Isaiah 1 and 58*

Several scholars have noted in broad terms commonalities between Isa 1 and 58. Operating within a historical field of reference, Watts contests that "Jerusalem in 456 B.C. [his assumed date for ch. 58] was not unlike Jerusalem in 740 B.C. (1:11–17)."[139] Hanson, still adhering to a historical methodology, but dropping specific dating, argues that in ch. 58 "the fidelity of the Third Isaiah circle to the central themes of justice and proper worship developed by Amos, Hosea, Isaiah [presumably 'First'], and Jeremiah comes to clear expression."[140] Similarly, Blenkinsopp argues that 58:5–9a responds to the people "in a manner reminiscent of what earlier prophets had to say about sacrifice," and in his list of supporting texts he includes 1:12–17.[141] More generally, Pleins notes that "Isaiah 58 echoes the very strongest social criticism voiced in First Isaiah."[142]

Moving away from historicity toward a relationship between the texts premised by theological and literary coherence, Motyer notes that "theologically and practically, ch. 58 belongs with 1:10–20. The two passages are the same in content, emphasis and movement."[143] More generally, focusing on the block of material commonly known as Third Isaiah, Schramm observes "that many of the concerns of 56–66 are reflected in the very first chapter of the book of Isaiah."[144] Further, Schramm writes "that Third Isaiah would be a witness that the type of religion that was so often condemned by the pre-exilic prophets persisted into the restoration

---

Princeton Seminary Bulletin 10, no. 3 (1989): 202–22; from a Christological perspective, see L. Richard, *Christ: The Self-Emptying of God* (New York: Paulist, 1997).

139.   John D. W. Watts, *Isaiah 34–66* (WBC; Waco, Tex.: Word, 1987), 273.

140.   Hanson, *Isaiah 40–66*, 204.

141.   Joseph Blenkinsopp, *Isaiah 56–66* (AB 19B; New York: Doubleday, 2003), 179.

142.   J. David Pleins, *Social Visions of the Hebrew Bible: A Theological Introduction* (Louisville, Ky.: Westminster John Knox, 2001), 224.

143.   Alec Motyer, *The Prophecy of Isaiah* (Leicester: InterVarsity, 1993), 478.

144.   Brooks Schramm, *The Opponents of Third Isaiah: Reconstructing the Cultic History of the Restoration* (JSOTSup 193; Sheffield: Sheffield Academic Press, 1995), 109.

period and continued to be practised by leading members of the restoration community."[145]

More specifically related to Isa 58, Schramm contests that vv. 5–7, "by juxtaposing acts of social justice with the common rituals of fasting," represent "typical prophetic" hyperbole,[146] of which "another example . . . can be seen in Isa 1:10–20."[147] However, rather than viewing 1:10–20 as an example of decontextualized rhetorical exaggeration, as Schramm appears to do, I have demonstrated that, integrated into its literary context, the text may equally well be regarded as a failed, though largely genuine, attempt to address a situation of serious injustice in rhetorical terms commensurate to that situation. Therefore, even accepting Schramm's comparison of the rhetoric in 1:16–17 and 58:7–9, a more appropriate response—instead of dismissing both pieces as hyperbolic—would be to explore whether the rhetoric in Isa 58 holds out greater hope of being implemented as a solution to the identified problem than did comparable rhetoric in a similar context in ch. 1. I pursue this question below, as it provides a means of examining the extent to which Isa 58 develops and deepens the concept of social justice, both enunciated and implied, in ch. 1. The question also provides a means of evaluating the extent to which the rhetoric of Isa 58 contains within itself the hope of persuading the people it addresses of adopting its proposals toward social justice. For now, though, the further ties that critics observe between Isa 1 and 58 need to be noted and examined. This will further substantiate closer study of the rhetorical relationship between the two chapters, with special reference to their conceptualizations of social justice and how these might be related in the canonical shaping of Isaiah as a literary-theological work.

12. *The Issue of Religious Observance*

One of the most commonly observed comparisons between Isa 1 and 58 is that both passages deal with the theme of appropriate, acceptable religious observance. Calvin, referring back to 1:11 for a fuller discussion of the point (thereby acknowledging the link), notes "that God approves of no duties which are not accompanied by sincere uprightness

145. Ibid., 111.

146. Ibid., 135. Oswalt (*Book of Isaiah: Chapters 40–66* [NICOT; Grand Rapids: Eerdmans, 1998], 502), linking Isa 58:5 to 1:10–20, also attributes both to "the Semitic love of hyperbole." His aim in doing this is to curtail the radicality of the implications of Isa 58 and to downplay the idea that it could represent a new departure in biblical thought, a viewpoint that I question later.

147. Ibid., 135 n. 3.

of heart."[148] As can be ascertained from the surrounding commentary, the statement ought to be translated into what might be termed uprightness of social behavior.[149] This connection is brought out more immediately and directly in Oswalt and Whybray. Both note that Isa 1 and 58 are "reminiscent" of each other, and both make the link between right worship and right action. Oswalt argues: "The section 58:1–14 is reminiscent of 1:10–20 as it speaks of the folly of formal religion that does not make a difference in human relationships."[150] More circumspectly, Whybray observes that whereas Isa 1 deals with "sacrifice," the focus of ch. 58 is "fasting,"[151] thus underlining that the texts are not identical. Further, even accepting some commonality between the chapters, Whybray locates this resonance more widely, suggesting that Isa 58 stands in relationship not only to Isa 1:12–17, but also to Amos 5:21–25 and Mic 6:6–8.[152] He adds that the relationship extends to other comparable texts in the Hebrew Bible. Whybray does, though, lend his assent to the idea that "traditional [religious] practices" are related to "compassion and kindness towards the poor and unfortunate, which are much closer to Yahweh's heart."[153] Methodologically, the importance of Whybray's careful, judicious approach is that it reminds us that a relationship between Isa 1 and 58 needs to be established on firmer grounds than somewhat vague echoes between loosely connected texts.

Toward the other end of the methodological spectrum from Whybray, with all his judiciousness, lies Watts. Along with his historical-critical orientation, Watts also deploys techniques from the world of drama and theater that, if they could be shown to be reliable and credible as tools of exegesis, would help establish a close structural and thematic tie between the texts in question.[154] Watts conceives of Isa 58 as a play, envisioning it

148. Calvin, *Commentary on the Prophet Isaiah*, 4:229.

149. Ibid., 233, where Calvin outlines "the duties of love of our neighbour" in the following way: "[W]e ought to exercise kindness towards the wretched, and those who need our assistance. . . . [W]e should bestow our wealth and abundance on the poor and needy." While this is heavily influenced by an underlying philosophy of paternalism and charity rather than one of authentic social justice, it recognizes that true religion is more than a matter of an interiorized experience of the divine and that it carries social responsibilities.

150. Oswalt, *Book of Isaiah: Chapters 40–66*, 493–94.

151. R. N. Whybray, *Isaiah 40–66* (NCBC; Grand Rapids: Eerdmans; London: Marshall, Morgan & Scott, 1975), 214.

152. Ibid.

153. Ibid.

154. In this approach, Watts is giving greater latitude to what Schökel (*Manual of Hermeneutics*, 87–90) explores as the role of "imagination" in exegesis. Schökel observes that "among the majority of exegetes, a deep-rooted distrust prevails with

as a scene "set on heaven's balcony,"[155] with Yahweh, Heavens, Earth, and a herald as the principal *dramatis personae*. If it could be demonstrated that the personification of Heavens and Earth as dramatic characters had grounding in the text, then a close connection could be postulated to Isa 1, where, at the very start of the prophetic discourse, heavens and earth are invoked as witnesses to the grievous waywardness of the people. In this way, not only would the texts be linked by a common metaphorical world, but one could say that in both cases a very grave situation was being addressed that warranted the calling of extraordinary witnesses or speakers. However, there is nothing intrinsic to the text of Isa 58 that suggests that heavens and earth could be construed as speech makers, and Watts never justifies his appropriation and inclusion of them in this way. This line of thought, therefore, while interesting, imaginative, and certainly innovative, must be dismissed as speculative and unsubstantiated.[156]

13. *The Theme of Healing Wounds*

In trying to sustain genuine and intrinsic resonances between Isa 1 and 58, which validate the comparison and contrast of the two texts' presentation of social justice, Sawyer is more helpful. He suggests that the healing talked about in Isa 58:8, literally referring "to the new skin that grows over a wound,"[157] recalls 1:5–6. It might be interpreted that the advice offered in Isa 58 is proposed at one level as part of the

---

respect to the interpreters' imagination" (p. 87). Acknowledging "that imagination sometimes goes mad or wanders from the point" (p. 88), Schökel still insists that imagination is an integral part of scholarship and interpretation. As he concludes, "What has been written with imagination must be read with imagination. The imagination is an extraordinary necessary organ of comprehension and interpretation" (p. 90). On the importance of imagination in interpretation, see also Green, *Theology, Hermeneutics, and Imagination*, esp. 187–206; Schüssler Fiorenza, *Rhetoric and Ethic*, 52–55.

    155. Watts, *Isaiah 34–66*, 271.
    156. H. G. M. Williamson (*The Book Called Isaiah: Deutero-Isaiah's Role in Composition and Redaction* [Oxford: Clarendon, 1994], 17) reaches a similar general conclusion on Watts's work, noting that "it is something of a disappointment, however, that Watts rarely pauses to justify his reading, which, as reviewers have remarked, contains many idiosyncratic features."
    157. Sawyer, *Isaiah*, 2:173. Claus Westermann (*Isaiah 40–66: A Commentary* [trans. David M. G. Stalker; OTL; London: SCM Press, 1969], 338) and Whybray (*Isaiah 40–66*, 216) both agree with the meaning of the term, but neither makes a move to connect it to ch. 1.

solution to an ingrained and recurring problem graphically introduced at the very beginning of the book.

Relevant to the thesis of this research, that Isa 58 articulates a form of proto-kenotic theology in which the healing of 58:8 comes through standing in solidarity with and sharing the pain of the disadvantaged,[158] another clear reference to the relationship between suffering and healing occurs in 53:5. This text proposes that through the "wounds" of the mysterious figure that a large section of scholarship has come to call the "Servant"[159] we are healed. According to this line of interpretation, it could either be that the behavior of the figure described in 53:2–6 is being held up as a model for more communitywide emulation in Isa 58,[160] or that in the servant-type of ch. 53 we have a crystallization of a pattern of living already undertaken among people as a result of preaching like that contained in Isa 58.[161] Moving through the text as "sequential readers,"[162] therefore with no particular interest in questions of historicity, the first of these options is dictated by the internal dynamic of the adopted reading strategy. If it is accepted that one of the distinctive movements within the Isaianic corpus is the "democratization" of the Davidic promise from monarch to community,[163] one of the components of this reconfigured community may be its ability to embrace the pain of others as a way of avoiding the open social wounds of Isa 1. Certainly, even if Seitz

---

158.   See Matthew L. Lamb, *Solidarity with Victims: Toward a Theology of Social Transformation* (New York: Crossroad, 1982), ix–xv, 1–27.

159.   See Leclerc, *Yahweh is Exalted in Justice*, 92–94.

160.   This position may be represented by Paul D. Hanson, *The Dawn of Apocalyptic: The Historical and Sociological Roots of Jewish Apocalyptic Eschatology* (Philadelphia: Fortress, 1975), 66–68.

161.   The possibility of adopting this position may be represented by Richard J. Coggins ("Do We Still Need Deutero-Isaiah?," *JSOT* 81 [1998]: 72–92 [80]), who notes that "we may well detect links between two passages, but the direction of influence is by no means always clear."

162.   Katheryn Pfisterer Darr, *Isaiah's Vision and the Family of God* (LCBI; Louisville, Ky.: Westminster John Knox, 1994), 22; see also pp. 23–35 for further ramifications and refinements of this methodology.

163.   As argued by Edgar W. Conrad, "The Royal Narratives and the Structure of the Book of Isaiah," *JSOT* 41 (1988): 67–81 (67); idem, *Fear Not Warrior: A Study of 'al tira' Pericopes in the Hebrew Scriptures* (Brown Judaic Studies 75; Chicago: Scholars Press, 1985), 52–62; idem, "The Community as King in Second Isaiah," in *Understanding the Word: Essays in Honor of Bernhard W. Anderson* (ed. James T. Butler, Edgar W. Conrad, and Ben C. Ollenburger; JSOTSup 37; Sheffield: JSOT Press, 1985), 99–111. Christopher R. Seitz (*Word without End: The Old Testament as Abiding Theological Witness* [Grand Rapids: Eerdmans, 1998], 154–56) is unconvinced.

remains doubtful that the book of Isaiah traces the process by which Davidic promises are embodied by a later community, he is able to assert that Isaiah, read along with Lamentations, generates "a difficult if not powerful theology of suffering."[164]

To a significant degree, much of this argument accords with, illuminates, and supports another connection between Isa 1 and 58. Sawyer makes the connection when he intimates that the reconstituting of Jerusalem in 58:12 should be taken as one of the horizons of hope spoken of in 1:26–27, where "restoration" of "The City of Righteousness, The Faithful City" was promised. Finally, Sawyer offers one other way in which the texts are linked. Modifying Whybray's position that Isa 1 and 58 each deals with a different manifestation of the religious life (the former concerned with sacrifice, the latter with fasting), Sawyer observes that both also deal with Sabbath observance (1:13; 58:13–14) and that both contest that the practice of justice is constitutive of proper Sabbath worship. Although scholarship is divided as to whether vv. 13 and 14 of ch. 58 were originally part of the passage as a whole,[165] Muilenberg[166] and Polan[167] convincingly show on literary grounds that the texts "share in the language and thought of the previous verses."[168]

It may thus be concluded that there are sufficient parallels between Isa 1 and 58 to justify further probing of their rhetorical-theological relationship. Adding to the reasons already mentioned, both passages open by admitting they are addressing a context of rebellion.[169] In rhetorical composition, the passages suggest that what follows should

164. Seitz, *Word without End*, 145.

165. Westermann (*Isaiah 40–66*, 340–42) treats them as a separate unit; D. Michel ("Zur Eigenart Tritojesajas," *Theologica Viatorum* 10 [1965–66]: 213–30) agrees. K. Pauritsch (*Die neue Gemeinde: Gott sammelt Ausgestossene und Arme [Jesaia 56–66]* [AnBib 47; Rome: Biblical Institute Press, 1971], 73) also regards vv. 13–14 as an addition to two other units (vv. 1–9a and 9b–12). H. Kosmala ("Form and Structure of Isaiah 58," *ASTI* 5 [1967]: 69–81) concurs.

166. James Muilenberg, "Isaiah 40–66," *IB* 5:381–773 (684–86).

167. Gregory J. Polan, *In the Ways of Justice toward Salvation: A Rhetorical Analysis of Isaiah 56–59* (American University Studies 7, vol. 13; New York: Lang; Frankfurt am Main: Berne, 1986), 25–26, 275.

168. Oswalt, *Book of Isaiah, Chapters 40–66*, 494; see also Childs, *Isaiah*, 475–76; Leclerc, *Yahweh is Exalted in Justice*, 139. However, Yvonne Sherwood ("'Darke Texts Needs Notes': On Prophetic Prophecy, John Donne, and the Baroque," *JSOT* 27 [2002]: 47–74 [55 n. 27]) observes: "In Isa 58:1–12 a radical reinterpretation of what fasting means squats in considerable conceptual discomfort alongside a thoroughly traditional attitude towards the sabbath in vv. 13–14."

169. See Leclerc, *Yahweh is Exalted in Justice*, 134–40.

ultimately be read as a proposed prophetic antidote.[170] Although פשע has widespread usage throughout Isaiah,[171] Pfisterer Darr substantiates the connection between chs. 1 and 58 since, according to her, "Isaiah 58–59 are pivotal texts for our reader's construal of Isaiah's rhetoric of rebellion." Effectively, the use of פשע in these chapters forms the climax of the theme of rebellion in the book as a whole. As Pfisterer Darr contends, "Intimately linked and reminiscent of Isaiah 1, these two chapters constitute a precise, if proleptic and as yet incomplete, dramatic enactment of events and outcomes first presaged in the initial chapter of Isaiah's vision."[172] Further, after noting the use of פשע in 58:1, Pfisterer Darr explicates the similar "sequence of thought" introduced by the term in ch. 1:

> Readers recall Yahweh's inaugural claim that "my people" (1:3) have "rebelled against me" (1:2), and their leaders' insincere cultic practices, oppression, and acts of violence (1:10–23). Moreover, just as accusation was followed by invitation and the possibility of reconciliation in Isaiah 1, so here condemnation is not the final word. Instead, rhetorical questions (58:6–7) coupled with conditional clauses (vss. 9b–10, 13) spell out God's moral mandate, while interspersed verses (vss. 8–9a, 11–12, 14) disclose, in language reminiscent of Isaiah 40–55, the rich rewards awaiting those who obey Yahweh's demands.[173]

14. *Wider Patterns of Connection*

The correlation between Isa 1 and 58 in subject matter and theme is further strengthened when connections are considered between Isa 1 and the wider block of material in which ch. 58 is located and closely integrated. Sweeney correctly recognizes that "the first sub-unit of Isa 56–66 is chapters 56–59, which focus on the behaviour expected of those who will be members of the new covenant community."[174] But Sweeney does

---

170. Note that Isa 1:2 and 58:1 both use פשע, the former in a verbal, the latter in a noun form, thus creating a link between the passages in the way that they open and in helping determine the similar "sequence of thought" (Kissane, *Book of Isaiah*, 2:238) that they follow; P. A. Smith (*Rhetoric and Redaction in Trito-Isaiah: The Structure, Growth, and Authorship of Isaiah 56–66* [Leiden: Brill, 1995], 99–101) argues for viewing 58:1 to 59:20 as a unit demarcated by the terms "rebellion" and "Jacob"; Blenkinsopp (*Isaiah 56–66*, 176) agrees in a more guarded way.

171. In addition to 1:2 and 58:1, the root is used in 1:28; 24:20; 43:25, 27; 44:22; 46:8; 48:8; 50:1; 53:5, 8, 12 (twice); 57:4; 59:12, 13, 20; 66:24.

172. Pfisterer Darr, *Isaiah's Vision*, 71.

173. Ibid., 72.

174. Sweeney, *Isaiah 1–4*, 89.

not substantiate what the interrelationships among these chapters might be. Polan, arguing "that each of the poems in Isa 56–59 has a unique message but also that the collection of poems forms a structured literary division possessing unity of motifs and themes,"[175] takes up this task in greater detail.[176]

For example, Isa 58 clearly explores the topic of social justice and may thus be regarded as part of the extrapolation of that theme, not only in the book as a whole, but also as it is introduced in 56:1. Rendtorff argues that 56:1 represents a new departure in what he terms "Greater Isaiah," as it, in a canonical framework, presents its textured, nuanced, and unfolding reflection on the subject of justice.[177] According to Rendtorff, the innovative introduction of the term ישעה in 56:1, along with both צדקה and משפט in a combination that occurs "at no earlier point in the book of Isaiah,"[178] can be demonstrated to indicate

> that in the book of Isaiah we find two different concepts of צדקה. The one, dominant in chaps. 1–39, relates צדקה to משפט, thereby emphasizing the righteousness which has to be kept and done. The other, specific to chaps. 40–55, speaks of God's own צדקה, whose coming is announced and whose character will be ישעה, salvation. . . . Both these aspects now appear side by side in 56:1.[179]

These insights are helpful, especially the statement that "Isa 56:1 is the deliberate beginning of something new."[180] However, Rendtorff does not substantially characterize what that "something" is. Therefore, I suggest the following scheme, which concludes with a proposal for the third concept of צדקה.

First there is justice and righteousness that should be practiced by humanity. As Leclerc observes, "Social justice, by definition, is something that only people can enact."[181] However, as has been shown implicit in the rhetoric of 1:16–17, it is doubtful whether humanity of its own devices (including Isaiah himself!) is capable of achieving this aim.

---

175. Polan, *In the Ways of Justice*, vii.
176. Ibid., 27–34.
177. Rolf Rendtorff, *Canon and Theology* (OBT; Minneapolis: Fortress, 1993), 183.
178. Ibid., 183; see also John N. Oswalt, "Righteousness in Isaiah: A Study of the Function of Chapters 56–66 in the Present Structure of the Book," in Broyles and Evans, *Writing and Reading the Scroll of Isaiah*, 1:177–91; Leclerc, *Yahweh is Exalted in Justice*, 131–38, 160–78.
179. Rendtorff, *Canon and Theology*, 183.
180. Ibid., 184.
181. Leclerc, *Yahweh is Exalted in Justice*, 149.

Second is the righteousness that will be inaugurated through the agency of God alone, represented by the dawning of the day of God's salvation and envisaged in the terminology of a second exodus in the great promissory passages in chs. 40–55.[182] Finally, though, is the conception of justice and righteousness that combines these dimensions, resulting in a vision in which the presence and the power of God to bring about a salvific situation will be encountered in the struggle for justice and in the embrace of the pain of the marginalized and the oppressed. In this interpretation, concurring with Rendtorff, 56:1 indeed represents a new avenue of thought concerning justice, which is subsequently more fully developed in 58:6–10. Note in this passage how salvation language drawn most evidently from Deutero-Isaiah[183]—of light breaking forth like the dawn, of healing quickly appearing, of righteousness going before the people, of the glory of the Lord providing a rear guard (all v. 8), of the people's light rising in the darkness (v. 9), and of restoration becoming a reality (v. 12)—is inextricably linked to the practice of justice.[184] Moreover, it is not overstating the case to say that the soteriological promises of God are in some way and to some degree contingent and even dependent on human agency,[185] a topic explored in greater detail later. Additionally, in connection with the theme of righteousness, Rendtorff connects 56:1 and ch. 1 in that both exemplify "one of the key concepts in the 'Greater Isaiah.'"[186] To the extent that the case for linking 56:1 and ch. 58 is persuasive, further justification has thus been

182.   Ibid., 90–130.

183.   Miscall, *Isaiah*, 133–34.

184.   Blenkinsopp (*Isaiah 56–66*, 180) observes: "In later Isaianic passages, and in Jewish end-time imagery in general, 'light' stands for the consummation, the fulfillment of the people's aspirations. The promise that 'I will turn their darkness into light' (42:16) has obviously not been fulfilled, and now they are being told why not." In context, this implies an active human role in the process.

185.   It is hard to avoid the conclusion that Isa 56:1 is premised on the possibility of humanity "observing justice and doing righteousness." For a comparable theological example, see Walter Brueggemann's observation that "something very strange happens in the text of Exodus 3," in that, after uttering "a lot of first-person pronouns in which God takes initiative for what must come next . . . there is an odd, surprising turn in the rhetoric" as "the same God who has been uttering all these 'I' statements" suddenly commissions Moses to accomplish them (*The Threat of Life: Sermons on Pain, Power, and Weakness* [ed. Charles L. Campbell; Minneapolis: Fortress, 1996], 21–22). As Brueggemann notes, "[A]ll of these glorious things God has resolved to do are now abruptly assigned to Moses *as human work*" (emphasis added).

186.   Rendtorff, *Canon and Theology*, 188; also, Leclerc, *Yahweh is Exalted in Justice*, 178.

established for examining the conceptions of social justice articulated in the rhetoric of chs. 1 and 58.

The question of where God may be found is broached in Isa 57 and 58 in similar thematic terms. This reference echoes the subject as it is raised initially in ch. 1, where the group addressed by the prophet assumed they had access to the presence of God through cultic worship. Isaiah 57:15 claims that God dwells both "in a high and holy place [the temple? heaven?] but also with the one who is contrite and lowly in spirit." By way of contrast, refinement, or perhaps a mixture of contextual immediacy and rhetorical necessity, in Isa 58 the ability of God to bi-locate is not expressly mentioned (though perhaps it should still be assumed). Emphasis is on the idea that God—the God who threatens hiding in 1:15 and acknowledges having hidden in 57:17 (עלם in the former case, סתר in the latter)[187]—will reveal God's self and draw attention to God's self. God will do this by saying "Here am I" (58:9) in the midst of a painful movement toward a better society, to people who, in light of 57:15, may be taken to be the "contrite and lowly in spirit." In this scheme, the "lowly" would be represented by those in Isa 58 experiencing oppression, while the "contrite" would be those who came to stand in solidarity with them (their contrition being expressed in their conversion to and alignment with the cause of the poor).

15. *Hints of the Unreliability of God?*

The verb עלם, through which God threatens to hide from the people in 1:15, also occurs in 58:7 in the context of people being asked not to hide themselves (Hithpael imperfect second masculine singular) from their own "flesh and blood." It seems that in 58:7, individuals are being urged to adhere to an ethic of compassion that God's self, whatever the supposed provocation and justification, was unable to sustain: a case of "do as I say, not as I do."[188] Presumably when God withdrew God's presence from Israel in the collapse of the nation and the terrible hiding of the

---

187.   For an introduction to this type of theology, see Samuel Terrien, *The Elusive Presence: Toward a New Biblical Theology* (New York: Harper & Row, 1978); Samuel E. Balentine, *The Hidden God: The Hiding of the Face of God in the Old Testament* (Oxford: Oxford University Press, 1983); specifically related to Isaiah, Davies, *Double Standards in Isaiah*, 164–66.

188.   Note how Alexander (*Commentary on Isaiah*, 355), commenting on 58:3, observes how "Luther understands the last clause as accusing them [i.e. those who complain to God] of wishing to contend with God, and venturing to charge him [God] with injustice."

exile (54:7), the disaster affected both the "oppressed, the widows and orphans" (1:16–17), and those deemed more obviously deserving of punishment.

The question continues to be whether it is credible to suggest that, faced with a God who at one level could be experienced and regarded as fickle and capricious, a source of the search for social justice in Isaiah might be postulated as arising out of human reflection. This reflection would have come within a section of the community of faith, regarding situations perceived to have been abandoned by God: literally God-forsaken areas of life. In this interpretation, the "Here am I" of God in 58:9 would not be the voice of divine assurance guaranteeing God's presence while pursuing a painful course of action urged by God through prophetic announcement. Rather, it would be the embarrassed voice of a God shamed by human initiative in the search for justice to reassert God's presence and solidarity with humanity.[189] This hypothesis, related versions of which are appearing with increasing regularity in recent scholarship,[190] needs to be explored further. For now, suffice it to say that the theme of where God may be found—first sounded in, as it were, its negative form in Isa 1—is taken up and developed more explicitly in chs. 58 and 59. The theme is, in all three instances, related to solidarity with the poor.

Concerning the relationship among Isa 1, 58, and 59, several points can be made. As noted already, both chs. 1 and 58 are at one level religious-worship discourses characterized as occasions of rebellion (פֶּשַׁע). Significantly, variant forms of this root occur three times in 59:12–13, thereby creating the distinct impression of a situation of even more intensified sin, upheaval, and social dislocation. This impression is further underscored by the observation that in the transition from Isa 58 to 59, the idea that "the house of Jacob" (58:1) is "a nation that does what is right"—asking God "for just decisions" and appearing eager "for God to come near them" (58:2)—is shattered. The idea shatters through awareness that "no one calls for justice, no one pleads his case with integrity" (59:4) and that, consequently, justice and righteousness (and, by implication, God) are far away and out of reach (59:9, 14). Moreover, the rising light promised in 58:10 (admittedly on condition of the adoption of

189.   On this theme, see Kathleen M. O'Connor, "The Tears of God and Divine Character in Jeremiah 2–9," in *God in the Fray: A Tribute to Walter Brueggemann* (ed. Tod Linafelt and Timothy K. Beal; Minneapolis: Fortress, 1998), 172–85 (179–85).

190.   Several of the articles in Linafelt and Beal, eds., *God in the Fray*, touch on or tackle the matter in one way or another.

justice-oriented behavior) has been turned to "darkness and deep shadows" by 59:9, resulting in an image of the community groping helplessly about in a pathetic, directionless fashion. It may well be that the people's iniquities have separated them from God and caused God to have hidden God's face from them (59:2; a similar divine ploy to the one threatened in 1:15). Furthermore, as Schramm has noted, "The statement כפיכם נגאלו בדם ('your palms are defiled with blood'; 59:3a) is strongly reminiscent of Isa 1:15, ידיכם דמים מלאו ('your hands are full of blood')."[191] The similarity highlights the close tie between chs. 58–59 and ch. 1 in that both depict a grievously disordered world. However, without conclusive rhetorical proof to the contrary, it may also be construed that at least some of those who doubted that the arm of the Lord was too short to save (59:1) might in fact have implemented, to the best of their ability, the recommendations of Isa 58. They may subsequently still have found no improvement in their painful circumstances (thus the basis for their doubt). On such occasions, though, there is great pressure to conform to received theological wisdom. The deep-seated underlying assumption that God must always be right[192] and that humanity must always be the source of the problem[193] overcomes the temerity to doubt, thereby reasserting the pattern of humanity blaming itself for the delayed manifestation of justice, righteousness, and salvation.[194] Whatever the merit of reading ch. 59 in this way in light of ch. 58, it has been demonstrated that the passages are linked rhetorically to each other and to ch. 1 in terms of the type of religious and social world they portray.

191. Schramm, *Opponents of Third Isaiah*, 138; see also Leclerc, *Yahweh is Exalted in Justice*, 145.

192. As Davies (*Double Standards in Isaiah*, 186) puts it, "[T]here is a strong tendency among commentators to assume that God is always right."

193. In a way that may be allowed to function paradigmatically, Otto Kaiser (*Isaiah 1–12: A Commentary* [trans. John Bowden; 2d ed.; OTL; London: SCM Press, 1996], 119), in relation to Isaiah's call in ch. 6 to harden people's hearts, poses the question: "[D]o we have here the voice of a man who has left his own time and gone wholly over to the side of his God, because he has arrived at the profoundest recognition that his people has fallen victim incurably to the vanity and nothingness of human existence?"

194. A widely recognized concern of Isa 56–66; see Leclerc, *Yahweh is Exalted in Justice*, 152–53. More generally on how human societies blame themselves in order ultimately to retain trust in their Gods, see Daniel L. Smith-Christopher, *A Biblical Theology of Exile* (OBT; Minneapolis: Fortress, 2002). But as Barbara Kingsolver (*The Poisonwood Bible—A Novel* [New York: Harper Perennial, 1999], 327) has a character say, "[Y]ou'll go crazy if you think it's all punishment for your sins."

16. *The Gains of Redactional Criticism*

The acceptability of comparing and contrasting Isa 1 with later passages has arisen from redactional explorations of the final composition of Isaiah in its entirety. In particular, Sweeney is important for having shown that the introductory chapters to Isaiah were intentionally appropriated by a later group and adapted to their agenda. This agenda was, in Sweeney's mind, driven primarily by the necessity to answer theological questions,[195] thereby illustrating that the final redactor has the final say in the literary construction and central focus of a work. Sweeney suggests that "the presentation of the material in First Isaiah reflects the concerns of post-exilic Jerusalem, particularly its concern to understand the destruction of Jerusalem, the Babylonian exile, and the post-exilic restoration."[196] He reiterates this conclusion by arguing that "insofar as Isa 40–66 stem from the late-exilic and post-exilic periods, this means that the material in Isa 1–39 has been interpreted and pre-sented by its redactors in a manner which addresses the concerns of the late- or post-exilic Jewish community."[197] Along the same line, Schramm says that "one is led to the conclusion that [Isa.] 56–66 and the final redaction of the book of Isaiah are somehow related."[198] That he does not in detail say how is less important than the establishment of the likely process of final composition. Establishment of this process permits the examination of links between passages once assumed to be divided by the gulf of history.

While this advance is important, the type of scholarship that produces it is perhaps not best equipped (or, indeed, intended) to identify and accentuate the more strictly literary resonances, tensions, and patterns that come with "traveling through the chronological world of the book."[199] The redactional approach deployed by the likes of Sweeney paves the way for moving through the text from beginning to end in order to see how the text functions rhetorically and dramatically, but does not itself undertake that enterprise (and perhaps questions the validity and worth of embarking upon it).[200] Put another way, Sweeney would be content to

---

195. Sweeney, *Isaiah 1–4*, 98–99.
196. Ibid., 24.
197. Ibid., 24–25.
198. Schramm, *Opponents of Third Isaiah*, 109.
199. Conrad, "Royal Narratives," 72.
200. Williamson (*Book Called Isaiah*, 16–17) recognizes and acknowledges this methodological division when he notes that literary studies "may be bracketed together by virtue of the fact that they do not believe that an approach to the book of

identify the theological questions that shaped the text, and largely to accept at face value the text's own answers to these questions. A literary study, however, would also be interested in examining the rhetorical framing of the questions and answers to see how their presentation contributes to their meaning. Using close-reading techniques, such an approach would be interested in probing whether, for example, conclusions were reached with ease or difficulty, and whether these conclusions were in any way rendered ambiguous or unstable by the rhetoric used to express them.

Applied to the relationship between Isa 1 and 58, this idea of reading chronologically may be useful in both resolving a point of interpretation over which there has been critical disagreement and, at the same time, in accounting satisfactorily for a perceived difference between the texts. The disputed point of interpretation is that one school of thought—the basic delineations of which may be represented by Calvin, who lays them out with incisive clarity[201]—sees the prophet in Isa 58 operating in a typically declamatory and confrontational prophetic mode. Meanwhile, another school, which may be represented by Whybray,[202] conceives of the prophet, behind the initial fiery rhetoric, as much more understanding of and sympathetic toward the people's plight and therefore needing to deploy his subsequent rhetoric accordingly.

Calvin, regarding those addressed by the prophet as "hypocrites . . . who are delighted with their vices,"[203] contends that such people can only be spoken to by means of "a severe and harsh reproof."[204] He insists that "unless they were sharply attacked, and the thunderbolt of words were launched against them,"[205] they would never be jolted from their errant state. Drawing on additional emotive imagery, this process is also portrayed as applying linguistic spurs to a less than compliant beast. In this metaphor, if the horse is the common mass of misguided people and the word of God is the spurs, then the rider wearing the spurs must presumably be the prophet. This is true unless, ultimately, God is taken to be the rider. In the latter case it might be argued that the prophet slips in one

Isaiah by way of tracing the history of its composition will ever lead to a satisfactory understanding of the present form of the work," and that "their work goes beyond my present [historical] interest." He also concedes, however, that he has "no wish to deny the validity" of literary approaches.

201. Calvin, *Commentary on the Prophet Isaiah*, 4:223–25.
202. Whybray, *Isaiah 40–66*, 212–13; see also Blenkinsopp, *Isaiah 56–66*, 179.
203. Calvin, *Commentary on the Prophet Isaiah*, 4:223.
204. Ibid.
205. Ibid., 4:224.

fell swoop from exercising a dangerous amount of power—to the extent that the word of God is subservient to him in the form of an accoutrement attached to his heel—to a position where he logically has no role to play; thrown from the saddle, as it were. The more serious point underlying this discussion is that issues of power—its use and abuse (i.e. who gets to throw the thunderbolts?)—are never far from the surface in any discussion of how the word of God (however that phrase is interpreted) is used.[206] I argue that 58:6–10 articulates an alternative understanding of the exercise of power to that evidently informing Calvin's conceptualization, an understanding grounded in self-emptying (58:10) rather than self-assertion. This strain of thought undercuts, modifies, and stands in tension with the "will to power" as it is expressed in dreams of restoration glory in other parts of the Isaianic text.

Significantly, as far as chronology is concerned, Calvin concludes his comments on the nature and purpose of the prophetic voice in Isa 58:1–2 by asserting that "the state of the people was such, as we have formerly seen *(Is i. 21)*, that scarcely any pure or sound morality remained."[207] Calvin thereby creates the impression that, in this regard at least, Isa 1 and 58 are completely analogous situations. It is as if, narratively, nothing happens between chs. 1 and 58 to impinge on the people as they are inscribed in the text; in each case, the people are in such a permanent and profound state of recalcitrance that one gets the impression that nothing could ever affect them. Perhaps this similarity, derived from a particular interpretation of prophetic discourse, may be construed as an intentional comment on the bleakness of the human condition. It is more likely that the interpretation will turn out to have more to do with dogmatic theology (echoes in Calvin, perhaps, of the intrinsic depravity of humanity and the doctrine of election) than a sensitive approach to how events subsequent to Isa 1 may have contributed to the shaping of ch. 58, influencing its world of thought and its rhetorical function within the work as a whole.

206. See Walter Brueggemann, *The Message of the Psalms: A Theological Commentary* (Minneapolis: Augsburg, 1989), 67, for discussion of the relationship between "triangulation" and the biblical text in the context of Ps 35. As background to the idea of triangulation, see Murray Bowen, *Family Therapy in Clinical Practice* (New York: Aronson, 1978). More broadly on the theme of the relationship between text and power, see Robert B. Coote and Mary P. Coote, *Power, Politics, and the Making of the Bible* (Minneapolis: Fortress, 1990); see further Carlos Mesters, *Defenseless Flower: A New Reading of the Bible* (trans. Francis McDonagh; Maryknoll, N.Y.: Orbis; London: Catholic Institute for International Relations, 1989).

207. Calvin, *Commentary on the Prophet Isaiah*, 4:225 (emphasis added).

In contrast to this analysis, which is an extreme version of the general critical consensus on Isa 58, Whybray contests that after an initial "call from God [in v. 1] to a prophet to denounce the people for their sins in the manner of pre-exilic prophecy," there is an "abrupt change of tone, [in v. 2] which leaves the command of verse 1 unfulfilled."[208] He speculates that this "is probably to be explained by regarding the verse as a quotation or 'text' from earlier prophecy designed to shock the hearers out of their complacency,"[209] but that there is no need for the prophet to persist in this way:

> The picture is that of a people which sincerely seeks to know and to do God's will. They are entirely unaware that their conduct is displeasing to God. . . . they are scrupulous in their efforts to learn God's will through the oracles of priests and prophets. There is nothing to indicate that they limit their concerns to matters of outward ceremonial.[210]

In other words, in the trajectory from Isa 1 to 58, this group has experienced something that warrants their being treated differently from the people of ch. 1, who were so arrogantly complacent that they took for granted their access to the voice and presence of God. Very differently, Schramm writes that "the addressees of this oracle [Isa 58] are the same as in Isaiah 40–55."[211] That is, in the narrative world construed by the full-form Isaianic text, they are the group who have passed through the traumatic abandonment of exile, where they received and were revived by shimmering promises of homecoming and restoration. On the strength of these promises they returned to the land and, by the time of Isa 58 (in combination, perhaps, with their children and grandchildren), are profoundly perplexed by the failure of the promises to materialize. Unless we are to assume that these people precipitously reverted to pre-exilic type (an option that distorts narrative credibility), then clearly their situation is different from that of the people in ch. 1. Narratalogically[212] they have a memory of what their people underwent in the earlier drama, whereas those in ch. 1 are not so positioned. As Schramm, effectually reinforcing Whybray, notes, "[T]here is absolutely no reason to challenge the sincerity of this question ['Why, when we fast, do you take no notice, why, when we afflict ourselves, do you not regard it?'] or of the people who raised it. On the contrary, the prophet accepts the question as

208.   Whybray, *Isaiah 40–66*, 212.
209.   Ibid.
210.   Ibid.
211.   Schramm, *Opponents of Third Isaiah*, 133–34.
212.   See further Mieke Bal, *On Story-Telling* (Sonoma, Calif.: Polebridge, 1991); idem, *On Meaning-Making* (Sonoma, Calif.: Polebridge, 1994).

legitimate and seeks to give an answer to it."[213] Essentially this group is in a very altered pastoral situation to that implied in ch. 1, and, therefore, the rhetorical strategy employed in tackling the situation, even though still on the theme of social justice, may be expected to be nuanced differently. Illustrating this idea, Cheyne perceptively observes that "at *v.* 2 [of ch. 58] the writer passes at once" into what Cheyne describes as a "quiet, expostulating style,"[214] which contrasts markedly with the style of Isa 1. Thus, in this instance, reading chronologically allows us to maintain the canonical link between Isa 1 and 58, while at the same time remaining sensitive to the differences between them. The reading strategy in this case has also assisted in resolving the outstanding problem of how best to interpret the tone of the prophetic speech in Isa 58.

17. *Cycles of Injustice?*

The cumulative effect of the parallels in Isa 1 and 58 is the creation, in the sweep of Isaiah, of a recurring association of defective religious observance with the practice of social injustice. As the French saying goes, "the more things change, the more they remain the same," a proverbial truth reflected in McKenzie's comment on Isa 58 that "the community seemed to have learned nothing from the preaching of the pre-exilic prophets."[215] There does appear to be something intentionally cyclical, considering the final shaping of Isaiah, in the presentation and rhetorical exploration of the theme of social justice in chs. 1 and 58; therefore, this topic merits further attention.

A recent study by Eslinger provides a helpful framework for pursuing this approach.[216] Taking conceptions of history as his starting point,

---

213.   Schramm, *Opponents of Third Isaiah*, 134.

214.   T. K. Cheyne, *Introduction to the Book of Isaiah* (London: Adam & Charles Black, 1895), 325. See also George Adam Smith, *The Book of Isaiah* (2 vols.; rev. ed.; London: Hodder & Stoughton, 1927), 2:417, where he, in relation to Isa 58, touches on the need for what is said to be appropriately related to the way it is said, in light of the context it is said in.

215.   John L. McKenzie, *Second Isaiah: Introduction, Translation, and Notes* (AB 20; Garden City, N.Y.; Doubleday, 1968), 166.

216.   Lyle Eslinger, "Ezekiel 20 and the Metaphor of Historical Teleology: Concepts of Biblical History," *JSOT* 81 (1998): 93–125. Also on the subject of the cyclical pattern in the biblical text, Claus Westermann (*Genesis 12–36: A Commentary* [Minneapolis: Augsburg, 1985], 241) proposes that "A feels disadvantaged by B; A is liberated from the disadvantage; A disadvantages B. This happens in every area of human life, most notably in the political area; the oppressed when liberated becomes the oppressor." Against this viewpoint, Pamela Tamarkin Reis ("Hagar

Eslinger, seriously questioning a thesis proposed by Frye[217] concerning the Judeo-Christian contribution to an understanding of time, ponders whether a linear view of history, ending in an eschatological full stop of consummation, culmination, and closure, predominates over "grand cyclical mythologies"[218] in the Bible as overwhelmingly as has been assumed. After establishing a tension between "Western religion as teleological/historical versus an Eastern consciousness in which history is cyclical and time marches on but goes nowhere,"[219] he pointedly and subversively notes that "the supposed teleological flow of biblical history carries along countless cyclical reversals."[220] From an examination of Ezek 20, he further argues that "the key mythological construction is that history moves on only to repeat itself."[221] Extrapolating more generally, he concludes that "Yahweh and Israel seem doomed forever to be spinning round the same wheel of failing covenantalism"[222]—surely an accurate summation of a strand of thought in the book of Isaiah, especially in the trajectory from Isa 1 to 58.[223] Significantly, he writes that "neither god nor people is willing or able to make a move to break the cycle."[224] Accentuating this point, he insists that "all this mounting failure is a double indictment, obviously of Israel for its incredible unlawfulness but

Requited," *JSOT* 87 [2000]: 75–109 [109]) suggests that "instead of cycling in an endless succession of reciprocal oppression and inequity, humanity progresses in righteousness and compassion." While one would wish to endorse this sentiment, the evidence for it, from the biblical account itself, is far from compelling. As Davies (*Double Standards in Isaiah*, 43) notes with reference to Isa 26:6: "The message is clear, however—those who are presently being oppressed need not worry too much, because one day they too will have the opportunity to oppress"; significantly, he continues, "This seems a strange claim for a prophet—and a God, for that matter—who claims to hate and want to do away with oppression. If oppression is wrong, it is wrong no matter who is doing it. It does not suddenly become acceptable because the oppressor changes."

217. Northrop Frye, *The Double Vision: Language and Meaning in Religion* (Toronto: United Church Publishing, 1991), 45–50.

218. Eslinger, "Ezekiel 20," 93.

219. Ibid., 94.

220. Ibid., 97.

221. Ibid., 100.

222. Ibid., 101.

223. Davies (*Double Standards in Isaiah*, 9) notes that Isa 58 results in "frustration for both God and Israel—the people cannot understand why God refuses to respond (v. 3), so spend more time fasting and observing the rituals without making any effort to change, increasing Yahweh's anger and strengthening his determination not to hear them, and *the cycle continues apace*" (emphasis added).

224. Eslinger, "Ezekiel 20," 106.

also, implicitly, of the god who cannot induce his people to respond as they should, as anyone with any sense of gratitude would."[225] The importance of God's serious implication in a continually failing situation is that it allows for the possibility, at some point, of human initiative, imagination, and innovation in response to that ongoing situation. In the divine–human interface, no matter how much the biblical account has been finally ordered to conform to the picture of a powerful, sovereign God,[226] it perhaps still contains traces of thought that hint that this depiction, while massively predominant, is not quite as monolithic as it at first sight appears.

Eslinger's thinking illuminates the nature of the relationship between Isa 1 and 58 in a canonical reading and may therefore be usefully appropriated as a key component in understanding that relationship.[227] A modification, however, to Eslinger's ideas may increase its effectiveness as a tool for explicating the rhetorical-literary dynamic generated between chs. 1 and 58. Again deploying the methodology of chronological reading and taking into consideration previous discussion, for all the points of similarity between Isa 1 and 58, the latter actually represents an intensification of the former. The reality of ch. 1, like a background whisper or an after-image, is implicitly though unavoidably still operative in ch. 58, helping to shape and determine the reader's reaction to the comparable situation described there. An analogy may be helpful in reinforcing this point: if an initial tragedy occurs, then only that tragedy has to be faced and dealt with, but if a similar tragedy subsequently happens, then the memory of the first tragedy in all likelihood is reactivated to deepen the sense of tragedy in the second. In light of this analogy, the relationship between Isa 1 and 58 is not, strictly speaking, cyclical. Rather, ch. 58 marks a point on what might better be understood as a downward and intensifying spiral. Rhetorically, the effect of interpreting the relationship between the texts in this way is that the search for a way out of the spiral becomes even more pressing and acute. Thus, as the rhetoric of 1:16–17 was closely examined to see if it was adequate to the context it was confronting, so the rhetoric of 58:6–10 needs to be scrutinized to see what it offers in response to its situation. In addition, this

---

225. Ibid., 108.
226. For example, the *tigunne sopherim*, where things considered so theologically outrageous and offensive in the received, accepted, and unadulterated Masoretic text were changed to fit in with the dominant and accepted ideology.
227. Related to the theme of social justice, both Leclerc (*Yahweh is Exalted in Justice*, 161) and Davies (*Double Standards in Isaiah*, 47) reinforce the connection between 1:17 and 58:5–12.

response needs to be evaluated both in terms of its immediate location and also in terms of how it might develop, modify, challenge, or more generally relate to the concept of social justice enunciated in ch. 1. In short, a central question is whether Isa 58 contains anything in its rhetorical-theological configuration that could be taken as the key to breaking out of the spiral or cyclical pattern foregrounded by the application of Eslinger's astute schematization to the text. A related question is the extent to which this answer contributes to an understanding of both the relationship between the spiral/cyclical and the apocalyptic/eschatological, and of the nature of the apocalyptic/eschatological in Isaiah. Eslinger claims that in Ezek 20 we are in "the presence of an unconventional thinker . . . in a period of Israel's history that is usually seen as the seed bed of eschatological historiography."[228] Similarly, an examination of whether anything of the "unconventional" exists in Isa 58 may be undertaken in relation to the overall theme of social justice and eschatology in the book of Isaiah. This is tackled in a close reading and analysis of 58:6–10.

228. Eslinger, "Ezekiel 20," 117.

Chapter 2

THE DEPTH AND DIMENSIONS OF SOCIAL JUSTICE
IN ISAIAH 58:6–10: SOLIDARITY, SELF-GIVING,
AND THE EMBRACE OF PAIN

הלוא זה צום אבחרהו פתח חרצבות רשע התר אגדות מוטה ושלח רצוצים
חפשים וכל־מוטה תנתקו: הלוא פרס לרעב לחמך ועניים מרודים תביא
בית כי־תראה ערם וכסיתו ומבשרך לא תתעלם: אז יבקע כשחר אורך
וארכתך מהרה תצמח והלך לפניך צדקך כבוד יהוה יאספך:
אז תקרא ויהוה יענה תשוע ויאמר הנני אם־תסיר מתוכך מוטה
שלח אצבע ודבר־און: ותפק לרעב נפשך ונפש נענה תשביע
וזרח בחשך אורך ואפלתך כצהרים:

Is not this the fast I choose: burst open the bonds of wickedness, snap the
straps of the yoke, really liberate the oppressed by shattering every yoke?
Is it not breaking your bread with the hungry, opening your home to the
homeless poor, when you see the naked clothing them, and not hiding
yourself from your own flesh? Then your light will break forth like the
dawn and your healing will grow quickly; your righteousness will go
before you, the glory of Yahweh will be your rearguard. Then you will call
and Yahweh will answer, you will cry out and God will say "Here am I."
   If you abandon the yoke from the midst of your life together, pointing
the finger, bent talk, if you empty yourself for the hungry and fill the
hungers of the afflicted, then your light will rise in the darkness and your
gloom will be as noon. (Isa 58:6–10)

1. *Isaiah 58:9: The Rhetorical Pivot*

As a whole, Isa 58 may be taken as a rhetorical unit[1] addressed to a section of society composed of people who are sincerely seeking God and
genuinely trying to follow ways pleasing to God (58:2).[2] The result, however, is a fractured community scarred by discord and discrimination.

---

   1. See the discussion in Childs, *Isaiah*, 475–76.
   2. Goldingay, *Isaiah*, 325. Childs (*Isaiah*, 477) argues that "verse 2a describes
traditional Israelite piety in a way that appears completely positive . . . v. 2a is not a
description of false piety, but a proper response to God."

This situation arises as a consequence of the divorce in society of religious practice from the practice of justice.[3] From the wider rhetorical pattern of the chapter,[4] I place close attention on vv. 6–10 for how they articulate the challenge of seeking justice.[5]

The structural center of the chapter appears in the closing words of 58:5,[6] when the prophet, after underlining the discrepancy between religious observance and social injustice, asks, "Is that what you call fasting, a day acceptable to Yahweh?" Then in the rest of the chapter (vv. 6–14), the prophetic voice rhetorically indicates the type of fasting that God chooses (58:6). The thematic center of the chapter is located in this section, in 58:9a, in the promise of God's presence with God's people.

Watts[7] and O'Connell[8] also locate the rhetorical center of Isa 58 in v. 9a, specifically in the divine announcement הנני. This is the point in the passage, they argue, that unifies the themes of social justice and God's presence in answer to the question raised in vv. 2 and 3a as to the reason for God's absence and ignoring of the people. Watts, structuring the chapter according to a symmetrical pattern, identifies v. 9 as the keystone that holds together the "arch structure."[9] More precisely still (and in agreement with me here), O'Connell regards the phrase "Here am I" in v. 9a as the "axis . . . pivot" of the piece.[10] Other scholars lend their assent to this assessment. Brueggemann notes that "Yahweh's presence, attentiveness, and availability [in v. 9] are exactly what is hoped for in verse 3," but that they are not manifest until "the ethical conditionality of vv. 6–7"[11] (which is the counterpoint to the false religiosity of vv. 3–5) is enacted. The importance Brueggemann invests in v. 9 is reflected in the

---

3. Leclerc, *Yahweh is Exalted in Justice*, 141–42.

4. For the rhetorical structure of the whole chapter, see J. Severino Croatto, *Imaginar El Futuro: Estructura retórica y querigma del Tercer Isaís—Isaías 56–66* (Buenos Aires: Lumen, 2001), 140–41.

5. As an introduction to this subject in Isa 58, see Walter Brueggemann, *Using God's Resources Wisely: Isaiah and Urban Possibility* (Louisville, Ky.: Westminster John Knox, 1993), 61–75.

6. Croatto, *Imaginar El Futuro*, 140. Kosmala ("Form and Structure of Isaiah 58," 69), however, argues that the first part of the chapter, "verses 1–12, consists of two distinct poems, verses 1–2 and 3–11a."

7. Watts, *Isaiah 34–66*, 272.

8. O'Connell, *Concentricity and Continuity*, 223.

9. Watts, *Isaiah 34–66*, 272.

10. O'Connell, *Concentricity and Continuity*, 223. Kosmala ("Form and Structure of Isaiah 58," 76) on textual grounds identifies v. 9a as significant in the redactional process.

11. Walter Brueggemann, *Isaiah 40–66* (WBC; Louisville, Ky.: Westminster John Knox, 1998), 190.

language he chooses to articulate its meaning. He says that it represents the possibility of "full communion with Yahweh,"[12] a comment which, given his insistence on "ethical conditionality," strongly suggests that the fullness of God's presence is inextricably linked to and cannot be divorced from the practice of justice. Similarly focusing on the ultimately integrative importance of v. 9 for the material in Isa 58, Hanson observes that

> persons who have thus experienced the restoration of human community
> [through the practice of justice urged in vv. 6–7] find that they have
> simultaneously become reconciled with God. Healing encompasses all
> aspects of their existence. . . In contrast to those who complained bitterly
> amidst their fasting that God did not hear them, those who have directed
> their attention to the needs of their neighbours in need find that God is
> present with them (v. 9).[13]

Before, however, examining v. 9, particularly for how it implicitly fuses the presence of God in the search for justice to persecution and the embrace of pain, the nature of the social justice envisaged in vv. 6–7 needs to be explored, both for its relationship to social justice presented in ch. 1 and for how its pursuit could lead to crying out for help (v. 9a).

2. *Isaiah 58:6–7: The Content of Social Justice*

After the description of the type of fasting that leads to violence, oppression, and disorder (v. 4), Oswalt notes that this negative and destructive manifestation of a supposedly religious event is linked to its positively presented corrective by means of two similar rhetorical questions. He observes that "verse 5 ended with a rhetorical question that made plain that the people's vision of fasting was not God's vision" and argues that "God's vision" is introduced "through another rhetorical question."[14] So the concluding and condemnatory הלזה תקרא־צום formulation in v. 5 is hooked to its introductory and emphatically positive הלוא זה צום אבחרהו counterpart in v. 6, after which the content of the type of fasting chosen by God is substantiated. This is done rhetorically in a series of verbs (פתח, נתר, and שלח), culminating in the use of נתק in such a way that it "functions like an imperative"[15] (although, interestingly, Oswalt does not translate it as an imperative). As Polan puts it, "[T]he infinitives describe the loosening, unfastening, and freeing" while the concluding verb "orders

---

12. Ibid.
13. Hanson, *Isaiah 40–66*, 206.
14. Oswalt, *The Book of Isaiah: Chapters 40–66*, 502.
15. Ibid., 499 n. 26.

the shattering of every yoke."[16] In keeping with Oswalt, Polan agrees that "one can see a parenetic character in this literary device where, by means of questioning, the new way of fasting is presented."[17]

Regarding the thrust of v. 6 as embodied in its verbal forms, Westermann contends: "The remarkable accumulation of different ways of expressing one single act of proper fasting . . . shows that, in the eyes of the speaker here, of all the conceivable acts of help, one, loosing from bonds and setting men free, was of supreme importance."[18] Whybray closely echoes this statement when he argues that "the four actions required by Yahweh are basically one: the rescue of the oppressed members of the community from harsh treatment by the powerful and unscrupulous."[19] Even from an initial survey of the rhetorical pattern of v. 6, we can thus see that through closely marshaling the verb forms it deploys in the interests of illustrating its overriding aim, v. 6 presents a tightly focused and carefully developed explication of "a day acceptable to the Lord" (v. 5). It concludes "on a very forceful note"[20] in a call for assertive action to be taken in the course of liberation.

"The forcefulness of the language"[21] is further underscored by the cumulative effect of the four verbal constructions in v. 6 and when, additionally, one considers that in this passage the focus of these verbs is liberative action.[22] Light is thus perhaps shed on the conditions endured by those in Isa 58:6 thought to be in need of freedom when, in the case of פתח, one notes that the word appears several times in contexts of extreme peril. Psalm 102:20 uses it to describe the setting free "of those who were doomed to die." Psalm 105:20 uses it in depicting how Joseph is reputedly "released" from the dire straights of a form of slavery characterized by bruising ankle shackles and neck irons (vv. 17–18); the situation resembled that from which the psalmist was "released" (Ps 116:16), just as "the cords of death entangled" him and "the anguish of the grave came upon" him, threatening to overwhelm him with "trouble and sorrow" (v. 3). Indeed, the energy available for release is so forceful that it

16. Polan, *In the Ways of Justice toward Salvation*, 207.

17. Ibid., 206.

18. Westermann, *Isaiah 40–66*, 337; see also Blenkinsopp (*Isaiah 56–66*, 179) on the importance of securing freedom.

19. Whybray, *Isaiah 40–66*, 215.

20. Oswalt, *Book of Isaiah: Chapters 40–66*, 499 n. 26.

21. Ibid., 504.

22. Childs (*Isaiah*, 478) argues that "phrases such as 'loosen the cords of evil,' 'untie the straps of the yoke,' 'letting the oppressed go free,' occur frequently in the earlier prophets," but not together as in Isa 58 and therefore not with the same intensity.

can open the figurative grave for those beyond hope (Ezek 37:12–13, where the פתח root is used in each verse). The range of the power of release is such that it has a cosmic dimension (Job 38:31) and has the restorative ability to be part of the process that turns death and mourning into hope and gladness (Ps 30:11).

Significantly, of the four verb roots used in Isa 58:6, three (נתר ,פתח, and שלח) are found in Ps 105:20 (שלח ,נתר ,פתח). Thus an even closer correspondence may be posited between the world construed by Ps 105 and that of Isa 58. Furthermore, to the extent that Isa 58 may be said to be about the quest for "justice for the oppressed," as Ps 146:7 puts it, these texts (Isa 58:6 and Ps 146) both suggest that the process of "setting free" (נתר) must have as a constituent dimension the feeding of the "hungry" (רעב).[23]

The extent of the power implied in the word נתר is perhaps hinted at in Job 6:9 where the eponymous central character, in the depths of despair and close to suicide, intimates that if God "would let loose" (נתר) God's hand, then that would be sufficient "to crush" him, "cut [him] off," and consequently put him out of his misery. A central aspect of the nature of this power is demonstrated in Hab 3:6, where the prophet envisions the earth being shaken by the Lord and the nations being made to "tremble" (נתר) at just one glance from God. This sense of shaking also occurs in Job 37:1, where Job's "heart trembles, and leaps out (נתר) of its place." This vivid image calls us back to the core idea that the meaning of נתר is associated with and derived from the concept of shaking and that, therefore, the image of the undoing of the thongs of the yoke in Isa 58:6 may at one level be rooted in the literal shaking apart of an instrument of enslavement. This dimension of meaning enriches the imagery chosen to convey how freedom is to achieved by imbuing it with more than a hint of considerable physical force.

This sense of a determined impetus toward the enactment of liberation in Isa 58:6 reaches a fitting climax in נתק, the very forceful form of which, meaning to "tear apart," concludes the verse. That the object of this verb, as was the case with נתר earlier in the verse, is מוטה reinforces the earlier reading that the "undoing of the thongs of the yoke" in that instance involved the likely use of physical force. Further, the relentless insistence on the need for freedom built up by the rhetorical deployment of פתח, נתר, and שלח in relation to various dimensions of freedom's

23. Resonant with this, Blenkinsopp (*Isaiah 56–66*, 179–80) observes that "true fasting is therefore to work to undo the conditions, morally corrupt and corrupting as they are, underlying such conditions. . . . [F]reedom without the means to sustain a decent existence is a hollow promise, then as now."

embodiment fittingly culminates in the summary statement that the ultimate purpose of all this liberative activity is the shattering of every yoke (וכל־מוטה).[24] The type of power implied in use of the term is reflected in that it was chosen to depict Samson's breaking of the cords that bound him in Judg 16:9 and 12.

The image of the yoke being shattered, however, does not always bring beneficial consequences and is not always viewed positively in the biblical account. Quite the reverse is the case in Jer 2:20, in which God, after breaking (שבר) the yoke (על) of the people and bursting (נתק) their bonds (מוסר), is met by the recalcitrant response "I will not serve you!" Further, in Jer 5:5 Israel is portrayed as shattering (שבר) the yoke (על) and bursting (נתק) the bonds (מוסר) of God's commandments in order to break away from God. This state of affairs eventually resulted in the disgrace of captivity. However, in Jer 30:8, using the same terminology, God promised to break (שבר) the yoke (על) off the neck of the people and to burst (נתק) their bonds (מוסר), so that strangers would "no more make a servant of" the people. A similar rhetorical pattern is found in Ps 107, in which, in terminology much like that of Isa 42:7 and 61:1 (which, in its liberation/jubilee orientation, Brueggemann links to Isa 58:6b–7),[25] the psalmist records that "some sat in darkness and the deepest gloom, prisoners suffering in iron chains, for they had rebelled against the words of God" (vv. 10–11a). This course of action led to God subjecting "them to bitter labour" (v. 12; coded language for exile), before God "brought them out of darkness and gloom and broke (נתק) their bonds (מוסר) completely and utterly" (v. 14).

3. *Extending Freedom*

In the rhetorical world of the book of Isaiah, the community encoded in Isa 58 should be seen as standing on the far side of exile. In context, this fittingly accentuates the credibility of the impassioned and sustained appeal for freedom. As people who had an experience and a memory of "the yoke" of exile themselves and who, further, had felt that yoke broken by God in their release from captivity, they should have been the people committed to maintaining and extending the freedom of others, especially the freedom of their neighbors. Moreover, if we accept that those addressed by the prophet were sincere in their religious obser-vance, Isaiah had a genuine opportunity of correcting their behavior in

---

24. As Alexander notes about v. 6, "[T]he terms were so selected as to be descriptive of oppression universally" (*Commentary on Isaiah*, 357).

25. Brueggemann, *Isaiah 40–66*, 189.

that they had a freshly forged paradigm (rebellion–exile–freedom) through which to process the merits of his admonishment and to adjust their behavior accordingly—insofar as they found it compelling and consistent with their experience and understanding of the past. In addition, if one of the prominent concerns of the community in Isa 58 was the delay in the materialization of the promises of Deutero-Isaiah, then the horizon of hope in Isaiah's address (vv. 8–9) at this stage could be viewed as a powerful inducement to the implementation of the terms of the call to justice. In short, a significantly greater degree of rhetorical engagement in terms of potentially persuasive arguments exists in Isa 58:6–10 when compared to the primarily adversarial context of 1:16–17. As Polan has perceptively observed:

> [T]he verbal system describing the fast God chooses is built on a series of infinitives in vv. 6–7 [of ch. 58]; the infinitives stress a mode of action, a way of living, to be put into practice, not something done on a single or specific day. Thus one can see a movement in the text away from understanding fasting as a practice done during a designated time to perceiving fasting as a mode of acting, as a way of life.[26]

It is this way of life, as people freed by God and therefore, in theory, devoted to the practice of freedom, with which the prophet challenges his audience and to which there is reason to hope they could be open.

Much of this analysis, particularly in respect of how the experience of exile essentially forms the foundation of the prophetic delineation of and appeal for just behavior, accords well with Westermann's interpretation of 58:6. He argues: "There can be no doubt that this [the supreme importance attributed to freedom] is to be understood as a direct repercussion of what the entire nation had had experience of, bondage in the exile."[27] So "the nation remembers [or, perhaps more accurately, ought to remember] the bondage which it endured itself, and the release that followed."[28] Thus, "Seen against this background, this exceptionally penetrating and emphatic admonition [58:6] to help to set people free reveals something of the way in which Deutero-Isaiah's proclamation of the release worked out in history."[29] While there is depth and truth here in illuminating the concepts essential to Isa 58, that the admonition was necessary at all shows that a certain portion of the population did not have the propensity to be able fully to grasp the fundamental importance of the idea of freedom for shaping and influencing every aspect of life (a new and

26. Polan, *In the Ways of Justice*, 180.
27. Westermann, *Isaiah 40–66*, 337.
28. Ibid.
29. Ibid.

radical idea for some perhaps). This therefore helps explain the depth and force of the prophet's rhetoric. For Isaiah, elemental issues are at stake, but the freshness of the experience of the exile at least ensures that they should be given a hearing, even in the radical nature of their claim that areas of traditional religious practice are now subject to the imperatives of liberation and justice.[30] In a sense, points of contact are made with the audience in a broadly shared field of reference. Whether these points of contact are sufficient to sustain the deepest level of challenge discerned in the passage will need to be explored and evaluated. For now, suffice to say that Isa 58:6 appears to be a carefully crafted verse, dense with allusions to a concept of social justice that has at its heart the ongoing need for the extension of freedom through the dismantling of "every yoke." To a significant degree, this line of thought may be taken as a riposte to those who perhaps grew complacent after the initial liberation of homecoming was effected; some may have come to see the return from exile or the diasporas as an end in itself, whereas 58:6 in particular regards it as the generative source of a pressing and continuing liberative process.

Rhetorically, 58:7 is linked to 58:6, in that both start with the negative interrogative הלוא, but whereas 58:6 focuses on the actions that precede and eventuate in liberation (loosening, undoing, letting go, breaking), 58:7 concentrates on what it is necessary to do in order to sustain life for those who have been released (sharing, housing, clothing). Liberating the oppressed without also providing resources for life (Exod 3:21–22) is an incomplete exercise likely to lead to little long-term substantive change in the conditions of the poor.[31] The four other times, in addition to Isa 58:6, where חפשי is found in exactly this adjectival form in the Hebrew Bible are all in Jer 34.[32] This passage describes how, threatened by impending exile, the rich agree to let the oppressed go free (חפשים) in order to preserve the existence of the state. In the end, though, having endorsed this policy of jubilee and liberation, they cannot summon the conviction to carry it through thoroughly, so after a temporary release of

30. See Leslie J. Hoppe ("Isaiah 58:1–12," *BTB* 13 [1983]: 44–47), who concludes: "Those who persist in seeking a direct relationship with God apart from their neighbor, those who consider religion to be a private affair of the heart, who ignore the call to justice and confine faith to the interior life are not only guilty of idolatry but of a terrible isolation of the self. By choosing to ignore one's neighbor and the call for justice, one chooses to ignore God as well. The God who is known and loved outside the call for justice is not really the God of Israel but some idol" (p. 47).

31. Blenkinsopp, *Isaiah 56–66*, 179–80.

32. Delitzsch (*Biblical Commentary on the Prophecies of Isaiah*, 2:387–88) notices this connection and regards it as of significance for the understanding of Isa 58.

servants, the rich quickly enslave them again. Contrary to this mentality, Isa 58 not only insists on the implementation of freedom, but also on materially assisting the oppressed (רצץ) thereafter, perhaps to attempt to eliminate the possibility of such an incident being repeated. It may be, at one level of interpretation, that the servant or serving community envisioned by Isa 58 is to be conceived as the agency in society devoted to standing in solidarity with the "bruised reeds" (קנה רצוץ; Isa 42:3). In the narrative progression of the book of Isaiah, this community is to press on with that mission. It needs to trust that, in the face of severe opposition that, as shall be seen, will cause it to "call out" (קרא; 58:9) and "cry" for help (שוע; 58:9), it will not "grow faint" or be "crushed" (a form of רצץ; 42:4). The community will embody a justice-oriented, kenotic lifestyle, as it pursues the aim of "establishing justice in the earth" (42:4).[33] The pressing need for inaugurating and maintaining this focused, disciplined conception of social justice could be that, as indicated by Job 20:19, without it conditions are permitted to develop and eventually flourish in which the poor can be "crushed (רצץ) and abandoned." Exploiters might seize houses "that they did not build" (a comparable situation to that in Isa 5:8, the reverse of which is envisioned in 65:21) and social degeneracy reminiscent of that recounted by Isaiah (5:22; 28:7–8) might lead to the "crushing" (רצץ) of the needy (Amos 4:1).

The connection between Isaiah and Jeremiah discerned above may be continued in how פרס is used in each book, significantly in the only two instances in the Hebrew Bible where it is connected to the breaking of bread. In Jer 16:7, a context of social disintegration is envisaged in which "no one will break (פרס) bread" with those in distress. In what may be taken as a reversal of that text, Isa 58:7 strongly suggests that, in such conditions, it is precisely in acts of solidarity such as the breaking (פרס) of bread with the oppressed—performed as a sign of hope on the journey toward their freedom from hunger (one of the yokes from 58:6 that needs to be broken)—that social cohesion will begin to be established. Rhetorically, פרס in Isa 58:7 stands in continuity with the terms associated with breaking in the previous verse, but it also, in the way it has been used, functions as a bridge to explicating the content of freedom and social justice as filled out in v. 7.[34] In the development of thought in 58:6–7, the inference is that all the different manifestations of breaking in v. 6 should properly lead to the breaking of bread and all that

33. As Childs (*Isaiah*, 478) observes, the action to initiate freedom in Isa 58 "resonates with the commission first given to the servant in 42:6ff."

34. Blenkinsopp, *Isaiah 56–66*, 180.

subsequently follows in v. 7.[35] This progression is facilitated by the location and use of פרם. So the struggle toward freedom properly entails feeding the hungry, sheltering the homeless, clothing the naked, and being available for those in need. As Calvin appropriately notes, "[I]t is not enough to abstain from acts of injustice, if thou refuse thy assistance to the needy."[36] This is echoed by Whybray when he observes that "the rescue of the oppressed is to be followed by positive actions."[37]

4. Isaiah 58:7: A Standard Ethical Injunction?

In seeking to downplay the concept of justice portrayed here and to present it as nothing more than a standard, routine comment on the topic, Whybray observes that obligations such as those of Isa 58:7 "were widely recognized among other peoples of the ancient Near East as well as Israel."[38] On the same tack, Westermann says that "verse 7 goes on to list the traditional acts of help to those in trouble."[39] While there is no doubt some truth in what they say, to a significant degree neither Whybray nor Westermann pays close attention to how these verses function in themselves or as integral parts of a longer poem. Instead, they make them conform to the conventional thought-world not only of the Bible but, more widely, of the ancient Near East. By adopting this strategy, however, exploration of ways in which the conventional might be being reworked in an innovative fashion for rhetorical-theological purposes is automatically precluded. There are, in addition, factors not properly accounted for in such a flat reading,[40] the most important of which is how

---

35. Linking the breaking of bread and social justice in a Christian perspective, see seminally, Tissa Balasuriya, *The Eucharist and Human Liberation* (Maryknoll, N.Y.: Orbis, 1979).

36. Calvin, *Commentary on the Book of the Prophet Isaiah*, 4:233.

37. Whybray, *Isaiah 40–66*, 215.

38. Ibid.

39. Westermann, *Isaiah 40–66*, 337.

40. Along these lines, but specifically related to studies of Jeremiah, Walter Brueggemann ("Jeremiah: Intense Criticism/Thin Interpretation," *Int* 42 [1988]: 268–80) argues (269–70) that a "preoccupation" with a "historical approach . . . holds the imagination of the text-creators hostage to historical experience, as though the writer-speaker could not imagine beyond concrete, identifiable experience. The logic of such a view is to require imagination to live within the limits of known historical experience, obviously an inadequate way of receiving such evocative literature" (ditto Isaiah). Brueggemann further argues that there is a great need to pay close attention "to the strategic and decisive function" of language within a passage rather than simply dismissing it as "rhetoric," "metaphor," or "hyperbole" (p. 271). He adds, consonant with this book, that "the text is more radical than the

the discharging of traditional obligations could have led to the severe crying of v. 9. Furthermore, neither of these readings puts sufficient weight
on the potentially universal ambit of the closing cola of both 58:6 and 7.

Against this tendency to conform the content of 58:7 to general
categories, Brueggemann attempts to read from within the world of the
particular text, and therefore to reflect the richness, density, and emphasis of the text itself. With his sensitivity to the importance of the issues
raised, he is thus able, on the basis of the internal textual categories (the
hungry, the naked, the poor)—and, presumably, because the prophet primarily addresses his audience in the second person singular—to ask if
the thrust of the verse "intends face-to-face charity or refers to public
policy."[41] Brueggemann also asserts:

> To raise that question, however, is to miss the urgency of the mandate.
> The triad of requirements speaks against a selfish preoccupation with
> one's own needs and passions; that is, the imperatives speak against
> individualism in order to assert that we are "members one of another." . . .
> If this mandate be taken seriously, then it concerns all kinds of acts of
> solidarity, both charity and public policy.[42]

Continuing in this way of reading attentively from within a text, one
level of construal in 58:7 might be that the establishment of justice is
connected to the process of reconciliation. The legitimation of this line of
interpretation arises from the impact built up by resonances associated
with various common terms in 58:7.[43] If, for example, only one of these

commentator is [characteristically] prepared to have it be" (p. 274). Further supporting this view, Roy F. Melugin ("Isaiah in the Worshipping Community," in *Worship
and the Hebrew Bible: Essays in Honour of John T. Willis* [ed. M. Patrick Graham,
Rick R. Mars, and Steven L. McKenzie; JSOTSup 284; Sheffield: Sheffield Academic, 1999], 244–64) notes that in traditional biblical studies the "predilection for
original meaning is inconsistent with what redactors of books like Isaiah actually
did" (p. 246) and that "the picture the text presents is so thoroughly figurative that
we cannot penetrate it to reconstruct a literal reality that may have occasioned it"
(p. 256). He concludes that "the case that a supposition that historical scholarship
can reproduce past meanings with full objectivity is quite misguided" (p. 258).

41. Brueggemann, *Isaiah 40–66*, 189.

42. Ibid., 189–90.

43. Jacques Derrida ("Différance," 12–14, 23–25) provides a linguistic-philoso-
phical methodology for reading texts in terms of echoes and resonance. This leads to
the broader field of intertextuality, on which see Julia Kristeva, *Desire in Language:
A Semiotic Approach to Literature and Art* (ed. Leon S. Roudiez; New York:
Columbia University Press, 1980), esp. 36–91. M. H. Abrams ("The Deconstructive
Angel," *Critical Inquiry* 3 [1977]: 425–32) raises questions about and offers
criticisms of this approach. Related specifically to the book of Isaiah, see Peter D.
Miscall (*Isaiah 34–35: A Nightmare/A Dream* [JSOTSup 281; Sheffield: Sheffield

terms had connection to the theme of reconciliation, then the theme could not be considered to have any great implied importance in the passage's rendering of the concept of social justice. But if a web of such associations can be shown, then the theme of reconciliation's presence in the verse gains credibility. So, initially I examine the terms מרוד, רעב (in the compound phrase עניים מרודים),[44] and ערום to test the thesis.

In a terrifying vision of a deranged world where even cannibalism is practiced and where, significantly, in light of 58:6–7, "no one will spare his brother" (9:18 [ET v. 19]), 9:19 (ET v. 20) pictures a situation in which people will "devour but still be hungry" (רעב). The idea of hunger in the midst of vast social dislocation is also sounded in 8:21–22. In this unit, the "distressed and hungry" (רעב) will, in an echo of the condition of the homeless poor in 58:7, "roam through the land." They will be so overwhelmed that, following the logic favored by Job's wife, they "will curse their king and their God." Significantly, in terms of the "light" imagery of 58:8, these are people who have "no light" (8:20) and can only expect that "they will be thrust into utter darkness" (8:22). They are, presumably, the opponents of the prophet, who is so alienated from them and the type of society over which they preside that he is prepared to "bind up the testimony and seal up the law" (8:16) among his disciples. He is prepared to wait for the day when he will be vindicated. That vindication comes, from the prophetic perspective, in the exile, regarded as punishment for the type of social disorder rooted in exploitation of the poor. During the exile, though, in a promissory passage that sounds like an answer to the problem of eating but never being satisfied (9:19 [ET v. 20]), the people are invited to "eat what is good" (55:1–2). Therefore, 58:7 carries the force of a warning that conditions in the community should not be allowed to deteriorate to the previously dreadful level. Those different elements that constitute the community beyond the exile should do all in their power to be reconciled to each other. This process, the text insists, must be grounded in an acceptance of the idea of justice and freedom for all. Memory of what obtained in society when this principle was neglected and of the consequences that ensued ought to have reinforced the need for justice and reconciliation. These dimensions are expressed in breaking bread with the hungry (רעב). As substantiation for these textual associations and echoes, the depth of depravity depicted

---

Academic Press, 1999], 24, 55, 62), who talks of finding "traces and hints of meanings and connotations from parallels," where he develops the idea of "'elusive allusions'" (p. 72). See also p. 122.

44. Alexander (*Commentary on Isaiah*, 358) cites Lowth as the source of the now common translation of this phrase as "the wandering poor."

in 8:20, where some "will feed on the flesh (בְּשַׂר)" of their own offspring, is counterpointed in 58:7 by a call for people not to hide from their own flesh (בְּשַׂר), but rather to be attentive to them in the practice of justice.

With regard to the term מָרוּד, the same sort of dynamic for encouraging the post-exilic community to be a reconciled entity appears. Although there is some debate about the difference in its form between Isa 58:7 and its occurrence in Lamentations (1:7 and 3:19),[45] that these are the only times it is used in the Hebrew Bible calls for analysis of usage. In both texts in Lamentations, homelessness is viewed in the context of and arising as a result of exile. Lamentations 1:5 explicitly mentions "exile" and goes on in 1:7 to bemoan that "in the days of her [Jerusalem's] affliction and wandering (מָרוּד) . . . when her people fell into enemy hands, there was no one to help her for her enemies looked at her and laughed at her destruction." Against this statement, the thrust of 58:7 is that those rendered homeless by the trauma of exile should now not tolerate homelessness in their midst, even if this means opening their doors to the homeless poor.

The ties between Lam 3 and Isa 58 are even closer. In Lam 3, the voice in pain complains that God has driven him away and made him "walk in darkness rather than light" (3:1). Even when the voice calls or cries (שׁוע) for help, the Lord shuts out his prayer (3:8). Yet in the midst of remembering affliction and homelessness (מָרוּד; 3:19), this figure is still able to generate hope (3:21) and to affirm, "Because of the Lord's great love we are not consumed" (3:22). Laying aside for the moment the problematic notion of loving and harsh aspects of the divine character being found in such close proximity without apparent dissonance in the mouth of the person offering the lament, out of this anguished experience of exile, a constituent part of which was homelessness, the firm conviction grew as to the unacceptability of homelessness in any shape or form. This text in Lamentations thus helps illuminate the depth of feeling against homelessness expressed in Isa 58:7: it was to have no place in the restored community that had been reconciled to each other. No doubt, for some (perhaps the vast majority) being reconciled to each other was an outworking and function of being reconciled to God. But for others, given God's role as an agent causing homelessness, there is the possibility that opposition to the condition could have come from more human sources. The wider issue of how the character of God, rendered in the text through the speech and actions of God, may be related to the origination of and commitment to ideas of social justice will be explored in more detail later.

---

45. Oswalt, *Book of Isaiah: Chapters 40–66*, 500; Whybray, *Isaiah 40–66*, 215; Delitzsch, *Biblical Commentary on the Prophecies of Isaiah*, 2:388.

The use of ערום in the Isaianic corpus perhaps gives a clue as to the potential breadth of the reconciliation implicit in the full force of Isa 58:6–7. In an act of prophetic street theater,[46] Isaiah is to walk about naked (20:2–3, where ערום is used once in each verse) as a sign that Israel's erstwhile ally but more usual enemy, Egypt, will be led away by the king of Assyria. Egypt will be shamed and degraded, with buttocks uncovered, naked (ערום) and barefoot. The real focus of the text, however, is not Egypt. As 20:6 makes clear, the sight of columns of naked Egyptians is supposed to force the Israelites to ask themselves "How then can we escape?" This is to say, that in the plight of the Egyptians, the Israelites are to see their own future condition as they are led into captivity. Again, a common term in 58:7 (ערם) is associated with exile. Again the implication of the verse is that as a community that had been refined in the crucible of captivity, into which, presumably, many people had been introduced naked, it is to no longer countenance the degradation of that condition.[47] Indeed, while the primary focus in 58:7 is surely on the need to clothe fellow Israelites, it also carries the sense that even if others (such as Egyptians or even Assyrians) are seen naked, compassion is to be shown to them also, thereby opening the possibility of being reconciled with them (Isa 19:25).[48] The term ערום, along with רעב, is

46. See Bernhard Lang, "Street Theatre, Raising the Dead, and the Zoroastrian Connection in Ezekiel's Prophecy," in *Ezekiel and His Book* (ed. Johan Lust; BETL 74; Louvain: Peeters, 1986), 297–316; idem, "Prophetie, prophetische Zeichen-handlung und Politik in Israel," *TQ* 161 (1981): 273–80.

47. As Pleins (*The Social Visions of the Hebrew Bible*, 297–316 [233]) notes, "Compassion to war refugees is the concrete form of Israel's role in the international arena."

48. W. Vogels ("Egypte mon Peuple: L'Universalisme d'Isa 19:16–25," *Bib* 57 [1976]: 494–515) commences with the assertion of agreement among commentators that this text represents a religious high point in the Old Testament in its universalism. He concludes that despite "divergences," God will say "My People" to others. See also John F. A. Sawyer, "'Blessed Be My People Egypt' (Isaiah 19.25): The Context and Meaning of a Remarkable Passage," in *A Word in Season: Essays in Honour of William McKane* (ed. J. D. Martin and P. R. Davies; JSOTSup 42; Sheffield: JSOT Press, 1986), 57–71; B. Renaud, "La critique prophetique de l'attitude d'Israel face aux nations: Quelques jalons," *Concilium* 220 (1988): 43–53. Giovanni Garbini (*History and Ideology in Ancient Israel* [London: SCM Press, 1988], 148) notes that "it is with some amazement that we read a passage like Isaiah 19.18–25; the explanation of its presence in the Old Testament is perhaps the great authority of the text of Isaiah . . . from which people did not dare to delete an inconvenient passage." For a very different interpretation, see J. Severino Croatto, "The 'Nations' in the Salvific Oracles of Isaiah" (paper presented at the annual meeting of the SBL, San Francisco, 1997).

found in Ezek 18:7 and 16, in the broader context of a chapter widely regarded as introducing the concept of individual responsibility and accountability for wrongdoing (and right doing) into Hebrew thought.[49] Linguistically, in that the second person singular form predominates, Isa 58:6–7 tends to support this position. But as the use of עָרוֹם and רָעֵב, integrated into the overall meaning of the verses, makes clear, these terms and, more generally, the concept of individual responsibility, have a pronounced communal dimension.

Taken together, then, the cumulative effect of the common Hebrew words examined above suggests that Isa 58:7 contains a subliminal reconciliatory aspect underlying but ineluctably linked to its primary social-justice agenda. This point is further strengthened by commentators, who largely agree that Isa 56–66 presupposes a deeply conflicted situation,[50] precisely one in need of intracommunal healing. Isaiah 58 provides an insight into how that might be achieved, always rooting its inferences in the non-negotiable context of justice.[51]

Playing beneath the surface of the important, although somewhat conventional, categories through which the nature of the vision of social justice conceived by 58:7 is articulated, a cluster of allusions adds new depth to that conception of justice. In many ways, this fits in well with 58:6, in that an immensely forceful insistence on the practice of liberation is immediately followed by a commensurately resonant explication of what is then needed to sustain and to make concrete the hope initially engendered in the act of freeing.[52] The rhetorical balance between the verses is further maintained by the way the general call "to shatter and tear apart every yoke" at the end of 58:6 is paralleled at the close of 58:7 by an injunction the force of which is equally generalized. So, when the prophet urges those he is addressing "not to conceal themselves from their own flesh and blood," the clear implication of the rhetorical development of 58:6–7 is that anyone who is hungry or poor or naked or in

49. See Walther Eichrodt, *Ezekiel: A Commentary* (OTL; London: SCM Press, 1970), 237–49; see also Henry McKeating, *Ezekiel* (OTG; Sheffield: Sheffield Academic Press, 1993), 83–85.
50. Hanson, *The Dawn of Apocalyptic*; Schramm, *The Opponents of Third Isaiah*.
51. Although the verb בוא, the meaning of which is given by context, is very common, an exploration of its usage in the specific form found in Isa 58:7 raises intriguing possibilities for how that verse might be interpreted. This is especially true regarding how it is related to the discussion of the theme of reconciliation above.
52. On the importance of concrete actions on behalf of the poor, see Leclerc, *Yahweh is Exalted in Justice*, 143; Blenkinsopp, *Isaiah 56–66*, 179; John D. Caputo, *More Radical Hermeneutics: On Not Knowing Who We Are* (Bloomington: Indiana University Press, 2000), 181.

need is to be considered as kin, even if they belong to a broader grouping that normally would be regarded as the enemy. In contrast to the way
the monarchy was "established" (1 Kgs 2:12, 46; 2 Sam 7:16; 1 Chr
17:14; Isa 2:2) through the adoption of imported exploitative ways
(1 Kgs 5:13–18; 12:4) and alliances with neighboring heads of state
forged through royal marriage (1 Kgs 3:1), here a reconciling vision is
proposed. Reconciliation emerges as the poor, and those prepared to
stand in solidarity with them, reach across traditional lines of enmity,
exclusion, and suspicion in a common search for justice.[53]

5. *The Range and Nature of Justice in Isaiah 58*

Much of this is consonant with, but seeks to build on the conclusions of
other critics, who also recognize, contra Whybray,[54] the universalizing
impetus in the conclusion of 58:7. Calvin, playing on the idea of humanity being made in the image of God, asserts that in 58:7 we ought to pay
attention to "the term flesh, by which he [Isaiah] means all men universally, not one of whom we can behold, without seeing, as in a mirror, 'our
own flesh.' It is therefore a proof of the greatest inhumanity, to despise
those in whom we are constrained to recognise our own likeness."[55]
Likewise, Westermann avers that "the reference is to fellow-men and not
to fellow-country-men."[56] Similarly, after balancing the evidence of the
Septuagint and the Targums, as well as of the wider biblical witness,
Oswalt concludes that "it seems that the more general reference might be
more appropriate here. All humans are of the same stuff; why should I
conceal myself from one whose condition is different from mine, but
whose essence is the same?"[57] Linking the urging of Isa 58 "with the
commission first given to the servant" in ch. 42, Childs observes:

> To share bread with the hungry, to provide shelter for the homeless, and
> to clothe the naked goes far beyond the servant's commission and
> addresses common human compassion in a general imperative. It lies at
> the heart of God's rule to demand mercy and justice for all.[58]

53. From a contemporary perspective, see Miroslav Volf, *Exclusion and
Embrace: A Theological Exploration of Identity, Otherness, and Reconciliation*
(Nashville: Abingdon, 1996).
54. Whybray (*Isaiah 40–66*, 215) holds to the view that, based on similar expressions in Deut 22:1, 3, and 4, "your own flesh" refers only to "your own kinsfolk."
55. Calvin, *Commentary on the Prophet Isaiah*, 4:234.
56. Westermann, *Isaiah 40–66*, 338.
57. Oswalt, *Book of Isaiah: Chapters 40–66*, 504.
58. Childs, *Isaiah*, 478.

In addition, though, I seek to show how this interpretation arises from and is integrated with the thought of the passage in which it is located and, crucially, how it is related to the material-sociological justice in the text.

In beginning to draw together and summarize the conceptualization of social justice as embedded in the rhetoric of Isa 58:6–7, I also make a contrast and comparison to the conceptualization in 1:16–17. First, it should be stressed that the call to justice in 58:6 is forcefully rendered in terms descriptive of concrete actions. The focus is firmly on the steps that need to be taken in the ongoing struggle for freedom. In addition, the verse's final colon gives sufficient authorization to encourage and legitimate independent liberative activity commensurate with the overriding theme of enacting freedom. Whybray encapsulates the balance of the verse, if not the potential range of its application, in observing that "the expressions are metaphorical and the references general, but the action required positive and particular."[59] Thus the prime contrast between 1:16–17 and 58:6 is that the former promotes advocacy, perhaps mainly in a corrupt judicial setting, whereas the latter champions the immediacy of direct action. Furthermore, half of the material in 1:16–17 is preoccupied with what those addressed need to do before engaging in any advocacy at all, whereas in 58:6 the emphasis is relentlessly and consistently on the freedom of the "other." There is no attention paid to the "self."[60]

While both passages deploy stock terminology to indicate the victims of injustice—the oppressed, the fatherless, the widow in 1:17; the oppressed, the hungry, the homeless, the naked in 58:6–7—the categories in ch. 58 are more specific. The level of solidarity in this piece is more intense, involved, engaged, and wide-ranging than in 1:16–17. This is especially true if one accepts that the implication of the climax of 58:7 is that anybody in need is to be regarded as a flesh-and-blood relative deserving of liberative action for no other reason than they are in need. In several respects Isa 58 marks a deepening and a development of the conception of social justice initially extrapolated from 1:16–17.[61]

At this stage, as with 1:16–17, observations concerning the nature of the social justice encoded in the rhetoric of 58:6–7 need to be scrutinized and subjected to the hermeneutic of suspicion to challenge them, to gauge their possible ideological orientation, and finally to ascertain whether

---

59. Whybray, _Isaiah 40–66_, 215.

60. See Leclerc, _Yahweh is Exalted in Justice_, 142–43.

61. As Cyril S. Rodd (_Glimpses of a Strange Land: Studies in Old Testament Ethics_ [Edinburgh: T. & T. Clark, 2001], 171) argues, "[O]ne of the most powerful appeals to care for the poor is expressed in [Isa] 58:6–7."

they are credible. First, the underlying perception of the poor as objects to whom things are done persists in 58:6–7, although perhaps to a lesser extent than in 1:16–17, in that the requirement for close solidarity in ch. 58 potentially dissolves the demarcation between "subject" and "object." The requirement thus undercuts or at least modifies the more glaring detrimental implications for any authentic understanding of justice in the objectification process; genuine solidarity challenges paternalism. So, while the appeal in 58:6–7 is still presumably directed primarily to the more wealthy and powerful members of the community,[62] who have the resources to tackle perceived needs, the identification and mixing together of rich and poor implied in fulfilling the prophetic agenda hold out the opportunity for people from different socioeconomic strata to interact. They can genuinely be led thereby to question commonly held assumptions about how the world operates.[63] This focus on the latent search for justice in 58:6–7 is further supported if one accepts the dynamic toward reconciliation woven into the verses. Essentially, the logic of 58:6–7 opposes the approach to social justice that writes a check and then gets on with "normal" life. This approach accepts apparently unalterable societal structures and divisions (e.g. into rich and poor) without ever really seeing or coming to know intimately some of the human faces composing the general categories of the poor, the oppressed, the hungry, the naked, the homeless, the widow, the orphan.

In the background lies the question of whether Isa 58:6–7 sponsors a charity or justice approach to social problems. Watts, in an attempt at historical reconstruction, appears largely to favor the former. Adopting a very generous attitude to the Persian authorities, he locates the source of social injustice exclusively "in the greed of fellow Jews" (a case of blaming the victim?). Watts suggests, perhaps with some limited merit, that "it was easy to blame the system or the faraway government"[64] for

---

62. Goldingay (*Isaiah*, 326) confirms that the prophetic word is directed toward the powerful, strongly condemning employers both ancient and modern who think they have the right to treat their workers "like animals." Similarly, Slotki (*Isaiah*, 285) infers that the prophet is addressing the powerful and wealthy.

63. In our own day, note how Chinua Achebe (*Home and Exile* [Oxford: Oxford University Press, 2000], 83) implicitly reinforces the need for listening to the "other" by writing: "After a short period of dormancy and a little self-doubt about its erstwhile imperial mission, the West may be ready to resume its old domineering monologue in the world." Also, in the context of the creation of spaces where different stories can be told, he highlights the need for "the process of 're-storying' peoples who had been knocked silent by the trauma of all kinds of dispossession" (p. 79).

64. Watts, *Isaiah 34–66*, 274.

the problems, in response to which he holds up the reforms of Nehemiah (Neh 5:7–17) as an adequate model.[65] Explicitly narrowing the ambit of Isa 58:6–7, Watts insists, to an extent rightly, that "God demanded that people clean up their own affairs, their own neighbourhood."[66] But his conclusion that "that was true liberation" (p. 274)—as if a few measures imposed by a colonial stooge, one of which was opening "his official table to 150 Jews and officials every day" (p. 275), exhausts the passage's concept of social justice—verges on the bizarre and perhaps reveals more about his own ideological investments than the text's. It is as if the implications for justice must be limited to the borders of the colonial province and reduced to a smattering of top-down policies, the purpose of which is the creation of a stable satrapy for the colonial overlord. This interpretation does not begin to account for, among other features, the powerful universalizing tendency of Isa 58:6–7.

Even though Watts acknowledges that as "a Persian colony" Israel would have been subject to forces that would have "led to oppression" (p. 274), he strangely seems to insist that any analysis and strategy for overcoming those forces in a more than parochial vision of justice is illegitimate. Thus, in a way that goes against the expansive and inclusive pronouncements of the book of Isaiah as a whole (e.g. 2:2–5; 60:5–17), the search for justice shrinks to a minimalist intra-Israelite enterprise without taking into consideration wider geopolitical and structural factors. Such factors likely could easily have been identified as contributing to the conditions of poverty and injustice extant in the country. In the modern world, this would be the equivalent of saying that an impoverished Third World country had to solve its own problems and injustices without reference to international institutions, patterns of trade, and power arrangements that helped to foster the problems in the first place.[67]

While such short-sightedness and, in some instances, cynicism are as likely to have existed in the days of Isa 58 as our own, there is no reason why such should be installed as the governing principles of interpretation in respect to 58:6–7. Such interpretation comes at the expense of its more

65. For a much more radical interpretation of Nehemiah's reform, an interpretation that resonates with my approach to Isa 58, see J. Severino Croatto, "The Debt in Nehemiah's Social Reform," in *Subversive Scriptures: Revolutionary Readings of the Christian Bible in Latin America* (ed. Leif E. Vaage; Valley Forge, Pa.: Trinity, 1997), 39–59. Croatto stresses that brothers are the same flesh (p. 47) and the importance of crying out (p. 51).

66. Watts, *Isaiah 34–66*, 274. The next several page citations are to Watts.

67. For a classic introduction and exposition of this field, see Walter Rodney, *How Europe Underdeveloped Africa* (Washington, D.C.: Howard University Press, 1982).

radical thrust, which Watts seems determined to blunt and reduce to a call for charity. In an *apologia* for limited action in the interests of real-politik, Watts worriedly notes that "calls for opening bonds of wickedness, breaking the yoke, and setting free the oppressed . . . might have been heard as a call to rebellion."[68] In response, Watts develops a hermeneutic of reduction and distortion to show that the true agenda of the text is much more modest and that when it talks about smashing every yoke, it does not really mean it. What Watts is apparently incapable of entertaining is the idea that Isa 58:6–7 maintains a resolutely radical stance without advocating rebellion. Yet this reading coheres well with the rhetoric of the passage in the way and to the extent that it presents radical solidarity rather than revolutionary violence as the method through which its aims will be accomplished. Whether this modality for living transformatively in highly conflictual and oppressive contexts is credible has been long debated. That it is consistent with the rhetorical shaping of the verses in a way that Watts's reading is not is the point I have established. This may be an example of using the presuppositions of historical reconstruction to cramp unnecessarily and unconvincingly the rhetorical plenitude of a text.

6. *Justice in Persia's Shadow*

In a way that corresponds closely to the political orientation of Watts's analysis, Berquist has suggested that the oracles that together make up Isa 56–66 were originally produced by the pro-Persian ruling elite in Jerusalem as reports to the colonial center intended to reflect how well things were going in the outlying province of Yehud.[69] In effect they were, according to this view, politico-ideological progress reports. Again, however, this proposal, whatever its merits, fails fully and adequately to account for the content, resonance, and tenor of several passages in Isa 56–66, among which 58:6–7 may justifiably be included. Berquist also develops the idea that sections of the Hebrew Bible, written under the shadow of Persian domination, were designed to show the tensions and ambiguities of living in such a context. These sections intended the creation of "an alternative social world" (p. 221) that presented "a range of different ways in which one can act socially to solve problems with theological correctness" (p. 222). Berquist asserts that these sections "reflect the multiform adaptations of faith to such a pluralistic world," to

68. Watts, *Isaiah 34–66*, 274.
69. Berquist, *Judaism in Persia's Shadow*, 79. The next several citations are to Berquist.

such an extent that they may, at times, even be "mutually contradictory" (p. 223).

The underlying idea in this approach, that certain biblical texts reveal considerable sophistication, subtlety, and plurality in engaging with their realities, may usefully be appropriated and applied to 58:6–7. This hermeneutical key thus forms the basis for suggesting that while seeming not to violate Persian diplomatic sensibilities or to overstep the boundary of what was acceptable, in apparent deference to the might of the imperial machine, 58:6–7 delivers a substantive challenge not only to historically reconstructed Persian exploitation (which may or may not constitute the background to the text), but to every system of injustice. Thus, while 58:7 in particular is couched in terms redolent of a charity-oriented philosophy, when read within its rhetorical context, which is to say v. 6 especially, these two verses taken together raise serious questions about the adequacy of charity as a response to social injustice. As Motyer has correctly perceived, their import leads in the direction of concluding that "it is not enough to work for amelioration."[70]

Perhaps the most telling challenge to the sufficiency of the understanding of social justice in 58:6–7 is that, in a fashion similar to 1:19a, the primary focus ultimately appears not to be on the oppressed but, in this instance, on how the well-to-do can attain the carrot of blessing promised in 58:8. From one perspective, acts of service are conditionally undertaken in order to secure light breaking forth like the dawn, quick healing, and the presence of God covering one's back like a mafia bodyguard. Several scholars have noted this blessing dimension in the text, although none considers how, in the rhetorical shape of the piece, blessing might be interpreted as diminishing the concept of social justice.[71] Further, no one has noticed how undertaking liberative activities on behalf of or in solidarity with the poor in order to receive blessing is undercut in the rhetoric of the passage by the linkage of this blessing to the endurance of pain. In effect, the bestowing of blessing is inextricably bound up with the embrace of pain, as I demonstrate through a close examination of the שׁוע–קרא word pair (v. 9a). As argued at the beginning of this chapter, v. 9a forms the heart of Isa 58. As the rhetorical pivot of the passage, around which its meaning revolves, it calls for close examination.

---

70. Motyer, *The Prophecy of Isaiah*, 481.

71. Ibid., 481. See also Westermann, *Isaiah 40–66*, 338; Whybray, *Isaiah 40–66*, 215; Oswalt, *Book of Isaiah: Chapters 40–66*, 505; Brueggemann, *Isaiah 40–66*, 190.

7. Isaiah 58:9a: The fly of Pain in the Ointment of Blessing

Having urged his audience in vv. 6–7 to adopt a pattern of life representing an acceptable form of fasting, the prophet at the start of v. 8 begins to offer inducements for doing so. These inducements are introduced by the adverb אָז, after which follow the specified terms of blessing, which begin to build up an attractive picture of what is possible in a life with God if the required standards are kept and conditions met. Verse 9 also starts with אָז, and thus, through the use of this repetition, one expects the litany of available blessings to continue, swelling perhaps to an overwhelmingly persuasive crescendo. But instead, the intriguing and somewhat incongruous statement is made: "Then you will call (קרא) and the Lord will answer; you will cry (שׁוע) for help and God will say: Here am I" (58:9a). Rhetorically, the audience has been led to expect that v. 9 will further amplify the state of blessing begun to be envisioned by the introductory אָז of 58:8. But this expectation is challenged, called into question, and confused by the promise of blessing somehow being connected to crying for help. This juxtaposition raises the issue of why such crying would be necessary in a dispensation of bursting light, immediate healing and abundant righteousness, all protected in the rearguard from surprise attack by the glory of the Lord. Certainly, the calling and the crying out eventuate in the blessing of God's intimate presence ("Here am I"), which Westermann equates with "salvation."[72] But this return to the theme of blessing does not erase, explain, or resolve the immediately preceding strong reference to pain. The incongruity is accentuated if one reads straight from the end of v. 7 to the start of v. 9. Then the force of the rhetoric is that if you engage in the type of ethical behavior appealed for in vv. 6–7, "you will call . . . and cry out" prior to God's voice of presence and subsequent promise of blessing in v. 10b. While there is no textual reason to omit v. 8 in a final reading, this exercise illustrates the rhetorical reality of the fly of pain in the ointment of blessing. This issue is made all the more interesting and pressing when one considers that the term used for crying out, שׁוע, is very strong, characteristically deployed in situations of extreme distress. A mapping of the wider rhetorical pattern of 58:6–10 confirms that v. 9a is the nerve center of the passage, governing, moderating, and crucially shaping its meaning as it responds to the expectations expressed in vv. 2b–3a. As the pivot of the piece it should be examined for its relationship to social justice.

---

72. Westermann, *Isaiah 40–66*, 339. Classically on the salvation oracle, see Joachim Begrich, "Das priesterliche Heilsorakel," *ZAW* 52 (1934): 81–92.

8. *The Rhetorical Pattern of Isaiah 58:6–10*

A brief survey of the rhetorical structure of Isa 58:6–10 reveals a pattern in which words and ideas contained in the form of a persuasive speech in 58:6–7 are reflected in a similar order and with a similar intent in 58:9b–10.[73] In both cases, the terms contribute to virtually identical lines of argument. The exception is when 58:6 and 7 utilize the introductory question formulations הלוא זה and הלוא before making the turn to conditionality in אז (58:8). Verse 58:9b starts with the more direct אם of conditionality in the section prior to the one of promises, which starts at v. 10b and is introduced by a *waw*-consecutive carrying the meaning "then." In effect, a rhetorical technique (the use of invitational questions), the purpose of which is to draw the audience into the prophetic discourse and the appeal it is making in 58:6–7, is dispensed with in 58:9b–10 as essentially the same appeal is made through the more direct "if . . . then" formula.[74] Between these two parallel prophetic appeals, the latter of which, by means of comparable form and significant word repetition, reinforces the rhetoric of the former, lies the intrigue of v. 9a.

In this configuration, the double use of מוטה in 58:6 is taken up in 58:9b, when, used singly, it underscores the closing emphasis of 58:6, that is, "break every yoke." This is expressed in 58:9b as "take away from the midst of you the yoke," which should be understood as "oppression of all sorts."[75] Similarly, the injunction to break bread with the hungry (רעב) in 58:7 is paralleled in 58:10 by the implied need to take important measures on behalf of the hungry (רעב again). Although both of the other words used with רעב in the phrase ותפק לרעב נפשך (58:10) are contested by scholars,[76] however they are translated, the strong sense of

73. Childs (*Isaiah*, 480) notes that vv. 9b–12 "are very closely connected with the subject that preceded."

74. Whybray (*Isaiah 40–66*, 216–17) includes v. 9a with the preceding verses and notes that "the tone [of v. 9b] is harsher than in verses 5–9a"; rhetorically, the difference in tone may be accounted for by the idea that vv. 9b–10 is pressing home an argument introduced earlier (vv. 6–7). More important, Whybray does not notice and therefore account for the disjunction in v. 9a with what goes before it; thus, in the present discussion, I suggest that 58:6–7 and 9b–10 articulate comparable messages, between which lies v. 9a, the rhetorical key to the unit.

75. Oswalt, *Book of Isaiah: Chapters 40–66*, 505.

76. See the discussion in Whybray (*Isaiah 40–66*, 217) and Oswalt (*Book of Isaiah: Chapters 40–66*, 505–6). Whybray questions the validity of translating פוק as "pour yourself out," terming it "a rather dubious translation," and amending (with others) from נפשך to לחמך, which would rhetorically increase the connection between 58:7 and 58:10. Oswalt argues against both these interpretative moves.

the need for close identification with the hungry, to the point of self-sacrifice, is retained.[77] In addition, the reference to the poor or afflicted (נענה) in 58:10 corresponds to that in the compound phrase עניים מרודים (58:7). But whereas the focus of the term there is modified and thus narrowed by the word with which it stands in relationship (מרודים), in 58:10 its provenance is widened and generalized to include all categories of the poor and afflicted. Finally, the promise of blessing, conditional upon undertaking serious acts of solidarity with the poor, is in both instances (58:8 and 58:10b) initially represented in terms of light (אור), either "breaking forth" (בקע) or "rising in the darkness" (זרח). Thus, while there are differences between 58:6–8 and 58:9b–12[78]—such as the introduction of doing away with "the pointing finger and malicious talk" of 58:9b[79]—rhetorically speaking they are comparable in the way they outline conditions to be met and consequent blessings. One passage, however, leads up to the threshold of 58:9a; the other leads away from its "Here I am" summation.

9. *Crying Out: The Depth of Pain*

Lodged between the two "conditions-blessings" sections (58:6–8 and 58:9b–12) is v. 9a, which perpetuates the blessings theme in the promise of God's presence, but allies it to calling and crying out for help. The term used for to cry (שׁוע) is very strong and characteristically used of situations in extremis. In one of its grammatical forms, it is used as a forceful introduction to the book of Habakkuk, such that, when confronted by violence all around, the prophet wonders how long he will cry (שׁוע) to the Lord without being heard (Hab 1:2). It is the term used to describe how Jonah cried (שׁוע) to the Lord out of his distress from the belly of the whale, a situation likened to Sheol (Jonah 2:3 [ET v. 2]). In contrast to Habakkuk though, Jonah attests that God hears his cry, raising the interesting and theologically problematic question of which cries God listens to and which God ignores. שׁוע[80] is also the term used of Hezekiah

---

77. Alexander (*Commentary on Isaiah*, 360) captures the underlying sense of the phrase, citing Hendewerk as interpreting it, "if thou wilt turn thy heart to the hungry," and Luther poetically translating it, "if thou wilt let the hungry find thy heart."

78. Duhm (*Das Buch Jesaja*, 438–39) considers vv. 9b–12 as more of the same as what preceded v. 9a.

79. Goldingay (*Isaiah*, 327) argues that these actions have social and political implications, and are not simply routine gossip.

80. Some correct to שׁוה ("to smooth"), but in context שׁוע fits better with the sense of the verse.

when he cries out on the point of death (Isa 38:13 [ET v. 14]). In context, God is envisaged as a breaker of bones (38:13 [ET v. 14]), as opposed to the one who strengthens them in 58:11. Further, the word in Lam 3:8 records the cry (שׁוע) of one whose world has been destroyed and who has had his prayer "shut out" (3:8) by a God experienced, again, as a bone breaker (3:4) and agent of torture who behaves like a beast (3:10), a bandit (3:11), an assassin (3:12–13a), and a boot boy (3:16).

In keeping with what one would expect, שׁוע appears regularly in the Psalter. Psalm 18:7, consonant with the idea emerging that שׁוע appears in contexts of extreme peril, portrays a supplicant on the point of death who cries (שׁוע) to God for help (18:7 [ET v. 6]). In this instance, as in Isa 58:9, שׁוע intensifies an immediately preceding קרא, at which moment, somewhat in the manner of a superhero, God takes decisive action to effect a rescue (vv. 7–19). Thereafter, the rejuvenated supplicant is empowered with superhuman strength and the arrogant confidence to be able to assert that his enemies "cried (שׁוע) for help, but there was no one to save them—to the Lord, but God did not answer" (18:42 [ET v. 41]). The supplicant beats his enemies "as fine as dust" (18:43 [ET v. 42], presumably through taking upon himself the bone-crushing duties previously attributed to God, and perhaps even extending them to bone grinding! The enemies' remains were tossed into the mud (v. 43 [ET v. 42]). The most serious point to be drawn is that whereas Ps 18 trades in a theology of might, arrogance, and self-assertion, leading to domination of foreign nations (vv. 45–46 [ET vv. 44–45]), Isa 58 offers a counter-theology of strength made apparent in weakness, humility, and self-emptying in the struggle for justice everywhere. The route to the heights (על במותי) in Ps 18:34 (ET v. 33) is very different from that in Isa 58:14, where the same phrase, על במותי, appears (see also Hab 3:19).[81] Throughout the psalms in which שׁוע is found, perhaps not unexpectedly the governing paradigm is of the psalmist crying out prior to God hearing and restoring. In the grand claim of Ps 72, which at one level may be interpreted as a piece of royal propaganda,[82] this psalmic pattern as related to the word שׁוע reaches its apogee when the court poet proclaims that the king "will deliver the needy who cry out (שׁוע), the afflicted who have no one to help. He will take pity on the weak and the needy and

81. Alexander (*Commentary on Isaiah*, 363), against the rhetoric earlier in Isa 58, relates this phrase to "conquest and triumphant possession."

82. E.g. Lawrence E. Toombs ("The Psalms," in *The Interpreter's One-Volume Commentary on the Bible* [ed. Charles M. Laymon; Nashville: Abingdon, 1971], 253–303 [282]) describes it as "composed in the inflated style of the court poets for the accession to the throne of a crown prince."

save the needy from death. He will rescue them from oppression and violence, for precious is their blood in his sight. Long may he live!" (72:12–15a). In the psalms that use שׁוע, the one discordant note in this confidence in God is struck in Ps 88:14 (ET v. 13), when, in profound darkness and despair, the psalmist cries (שׁוע) to the Lord for help. For reasons unknown, the psalmist is rejected. The psalm ends on the haunting note—"the darkness is my closest friend" (v. 18)—with no sign of the light promised in Isa 58:8 or 10.

In making the move from the theology predominant in the Psalms of crying to God and being heard and delivered by God, to the troubled theology of crying out and nothing happening, we have well-represented the shift from orientation to disorientation.[83] It is a shift into a much more theologically ambiguous and perplexing world in which the problem of crying out finds no ready or assured answer. This is the world in which Isa 58:9a should be located. In conjunction with its immediate rhetorical context, 58:9a begins to articulate that it is in standing in such close solidarity with the oppressed, so that one shares their pain and joins their unanswered crying, that the energy (human and divine) is generated to work for just change. In the midst of this consciously undertaken struggle, part of which includes the embrace of pain, God is intimately encountered in God's announcement הנני.[84] Underlying this assessment of ch. 58 is the idea that, in the search for justice and reconciliation, pain may have some meaning. This provisional analysis thus brings 58:9a into dialogue and tension with other texts of disorientation that are similarly rooted in the term שׁוע but that depict a different theological understanding of the nature of this term.

To a great extent, as Job is the biblical book containing the largest number of usages of שׁוע (eleven times in Job to nine in the Psalms), Isa 58:9a is consequently connected to that great meditation on the nature of suffering. In Job, the world of Ps 88 is more the order of the day than that of the psalms of confidence and assurance. There is, though, primarily through the aegis of Job's visitors, an attempt, in the dramatic interplay of ideas, to uphold and retain confidence in a theology of orientation and moral coherence. In the extended series of speeches made by Elihu, he argues that people who cry out (שׁוע) under oppression (35:9) go unanswered "because of the arrogance of the wicked" (35:12). That is, if you cry and receive no answer, it is because you were wicked in the first place; you compound your wickedness by being arrogant enough to think

---

83. Brueggemann, *The Message of the Psalms*, 25–28, 51–58.
84. As Fiddes (*The Creative Suffering of God*, 192) argues, "If God suffers with us, he cannot be closer to us."

you deserve an answer. By developing this variety of propositional theology, Elihu establishes a failsafe mechanism that simultaneously defends the integrity of God and delegitimizes the claims of people who receive no satisfactory answer to or resolution of their pain. If pain turns out to be a person's experience, it goes to show that they are, de facto, a wicked person and therefore not deserving of God's attention.[85] Thus Elihu implicitly locates Job's suffering in Job's own defective attitudes and absolves God from any responsibility in the situation.[86] Interestingly, at a later stage of his philosophizing, Elihu suggests that if the arrogant "listen to correction and . . . repent of their evil" (36:10), then they not only will receive the blessing of spending "the rest of their days in prosperity and their years in contentment" (36:11). During (or perhaps on account of) their process of repentance and rehabilitation, their suffering—which he contradictorily depicts them as being too pig-headed to cry out (שׁוע) about (36:13)—will take on meaning. God will speak "to them in their affliction" (36:15)—who knows, perhaps even saying "Here am I." After expostulating his system of moral reform, Elihu concludes with an extended hymn to the utter otherness of God and God's ways from humanity, during which, in unctuous doxology, he exclaims, "How great is God—beyond our understanding!" (36:26a).[87]

Against this hermetically sealed, inherently circular system of thought that functions to justify God no matter what happens, Job insistently maintains that God has responsibility in his painful situation. Yet even though he cries out (שׁוע) about how he has been wronged by God, he gets no response, thereby leading him to conclude that "there is no justice." This sense of moral incoherence fueling moral outrage and anomie is broadened from personal to societal experience: "The groans of the dying rise from the city and the souls of the wounded cry out (שׁוע) for help. But God charges no one with wrongdoing" (24:12). Afterward, the text draws a graphic picture of a society given over to rampant injustice.

However, Job is never able positively and constructively to move beyond the courage of his convictions that the theological formulations of his visitors do not adequately account for suffering and injustice in the

---

85.   This is to say that Elihu has established a "Structure Legitimation" mechanism; see Brueggemann, *Old Testament Theology*, 1–21.

86.   On the essential theology of Job's visitors, see Tryggve N. D. Mettinger, "The God of Job: Avenger, Tyrant, or Victor?," in *The Voice from the Whirlwind: Interpreting the Book of Job* (ed. Leo G. Perdue and W. Clark Gilpin; Nashville: Abingdon, 1992), 39–49 (41–42).

87.   For wider discussion of this topic, see C. B. Labuschange, *The Incomparability of Yahweh in the Old Testament* (Leiden: Brill, 1966).

world. He is unable to begin to propose how, humanly speaking, situations of injustice might be confronted. Instead, looking backward, he emphasizes how he was a model of ethical behavior, rescuing the poor "who cried (שׁוע) for help and the fatherless who had none to assist him." Yet for his efforts he encountered only pain and suffering in both its personal and social dimensions. His experience is of a fractured world bereft of rhyme, reason, and meaning in which, crying out (שׁוע) to God and receiving no answer (30:20), hoping for good but experiencing only evil (30:26), he is reduced to a state of exasperated, disillusioned despair, in which all meaning is drained from life. All he can do is "stand up in the assembly and cry (שׁוע) for help" (30:28), a man unconvinced by reductionist theological schemes. He sees the social order collapsing through a combination of divine and human injustice but cannot generate a vision of or the energy to produce societal hope and reconstruction.[88]

10. *Isaiah 58:9a in Context*

Read in conjunction with the literary-semantic density of שׁוע and the way it potentially illuminates Isa 58:9a, I comment on how this verse functions rhetorically in the wider passage in which it is located. First and most obvious, this analysis supports the view that, in its different grammatical forms, שׁוע is almost exclusively used in contexts of what Ricoeur has termed "limit experience,"[89] that is, situations marked by their powerful, painful extremity and intensity. Therefore, the problem still remains as to how to explain the association of such crying out in extreme pain in 58:9a with the bestowal of blessing. In answer to this overlooked exegetical problem, at the heart of the rhetorical-theological complex constituted by 58:6–10 lies the implicit assertion that to follow the ethical requirements of justice and solidarity enunciated by the prophetic discourse will inexorably lead to crying out in severe pain. This state of affairs arises from an awareness that the degree of solidarity called for in Isa 58 is so intense and its horizon of hope so grounded in the quest for authentic justice that it poses an inherent challenge to those in power. The challenge is such that the powerful will mobilize their forces of oppression against anyone adopting a lifestyle geared to reconciliation and justice, thereby, in the ensuing conflict, causing them to cry out.

According to this reading, in response to the people's complaint that God has ignored them, the prophet, initially through asking questions,

---

88. See, in addition, Clines, *Interested Parties*, 122–44.

89. See Paul Ricoeur, "Biblical Hermeneutics," *Semeia* 4 (1975): 23–148 (108–45).

invites them to consider a more equitable and generous form of living in relation to the poor as the way to regain God's attention. He enhances the attraction of his proposal by linking it to the promise of abundant blessing. But then, having rhetorically drawn his audience in, he reveals the cost of commitment: all this grace will not come cheaply, for it will entail crying out to God in deep distress. Yet, so the rhetoric claims, it is precisely in the midst of this struggle for justice alongside the poor that God will reveal God's self and indicate God's presence. By more emphatically reiterating the conditional pattern of "if . . . then" from vv. 9b–12, the prophet reinforces the idea that the vision of the restored community of vv. 11 and 12 is premised by and rooted in the reality, expressed in the pivotal v. 9a, that this can only be achieved through radical solidarity and being prepared to suffer in the search for justice.[90]

What might be called the self-sacrificing aspect of 58:6–10 has in some way been noticed by several scholars. Brueggemann observes the need for "self-transcending generosity."[91] Oswalt, explicating what he considers to be the "profound" thought of the passage, insists that "a sacrifice of oneself for the sake of those who have been oppressed" is one of its key components.[92] Highlighting these aspects of identification and solidarity, Calvin notes that, regarding the poor, "To 'pour out the soul,' therefore, is nothing else than to bewail their distresses, and to be as much affected by their own poverty as if we ourselves endured it."[93] Perhaps, though, closest to what I have argued, Webb posits that "the great paradox of the life of faith to which we are called is that blessing comes through self-denial, that we receive through giving, and that we gain our lives through laying them down."[94] However, none of these commentators adequately captures the depth of pain that will be involved in enacting the prophetic message, the sense that embarking on a course of behavior characterized by generosity toward the poor (58:7, 9b–10a) will not result in the warm glow of self-satisfaction or the commendation of wider society for performing good deeds, but the deep cry of anguish. This perplexing reality at the rhetorical-theological center of the text may best be explained as an indication of the radical nature of the prophet's challenge. He is not interested in charity but in an order of life that involves a deep embrace of pain and a profound willingness to endure

---

90. See Brueggemann, *Old Testament Theology*, 22–44.

91. Brueggemann, *Isaiah 40–66*, 188.

92. Oswalt, *Book of Isaiah: Chapters 40–66*, 506.

93. Calvin, *Commentary on the Prophet Isaiah*, 4:237.

94. Barry Webb, *The Message of Isaiah* (BST; Leicester: InterVarsity, 1996), 226.

hardship in pursuit of justice. While Webb, with his reference to laying down lives, operates in this field of thought, his terminology is stock and platitudinous, failing to stress sufficiently that the purpose of kenotic behavior and the embrace of pain is not primarily in regaining our lives but in responding to the needs of the neighbor. The ultimate horizon of kenosis and crying out is not personal salvation, but social justice. As Leclerc insists, "Discipleship is undertaken not so much for individual salvation as for the building of God's Kingdom on earth."[95] Similarly, Blenkinsopp argues that the "high level of specificity" regarding action for justice becomes "the *exclusive* criterion for salvation or reprobation."[96]

Isaiah 58:6–10 challenges the precepts of conventional wisdom theology, both in the Isaianic corpus and more widely in the canonical context. The challenge extends to, unlike in wisdom theology, refusing to accept the existence of wealth and poverty as givens embedded in the natural order, and rejecting the characteristic wisdom notion of prudence as the best guide to behavior. Within the book of Isaiah, the theological proposal woven into the rhetoric of 58:6–10, that solidarity and the embrace of pain are the avenue to justice and restoration, represents a counterpoint to and route of escape from the re-emergence of something comparable to the pre-exilic context. In the earlier time, "lack of understanding" (5:3) prevailed in a world of moral equivocation in which those "wise in their own eyes" (5:21) called "evil good and good evil . . . put darkness for light and light for darkness" (5:20), as they presided over a degenerate world of corruption and injustice (5:22–23). Isaiah 58:6–10, as interpreted here, implicitly claims to be a method by which "the wisdom of the wise will perish, the intelligence of the intelligent will vanish" (29:14).[97] It is a modality for living by which the shelter and safe places of 32:2 may be created, during which blindness and deafness will be alleviated and, in general, clarity of vision concerning the reality of the world will be attained:

> No longer will the fool be called noble, nor the scoundrel be highly respected. For the fool speaks folly, his mind is busy with evil: He practices ungodliness and spreads error concerning the Lord; the hungry he

95. Leclerc, *Yahweh is Exalted in Justice*, 144.

96. Blenkinsopp, *Isaiah 56–66*, 179, 180 (emphasis in original). Blenkinsopp suggests that Isa 58 may lie behind and influence "the final judgment scene in Matt 25:31–46." Focusing on the importance of neighbor, see Walter Brueggemann, "The Need for Neighbor," *The Other Side* (July–August 2003): 32–36.

97. Sweeney (*Isaiah 1–4*, 57) notes the importance of this theme, but leaves it open as to how and when in the world of the Isaianic text it might be construed as being fulfilled.

leaves empty and from the thirsty he withholds water. The scoundrel's methods are wicked, he makes up evil schemes to destroy the poor with lies, even when the plea of the needy is just. But the noble man makes noble plans, and by noble deeds he stands. (32:5–8).

The community envisaged by Isa 58, resonant with the terminology and the implied agenda of ch. 32, may be construed as just such a community of "the noble." Pursuit of the program of ch. 58, through standing in solidarity with the poor, may be taken as the necessary prerequisite to eyes and consciousness being turned to comprehending the world aright and to stammering tongues being cut loose in fluent defense of justice (32:4). In effect, 58:6–10 offers a new way to live beyond the wisdom of old, bankrupt stratifications and epistemological paradigms; but there is a cost to inaugurating the new order of justice and reconciliation.[98]

Caution is due when schemes are proposed involving the embrace of pain. Such schemes can fail to differentiate between categories of pain (some of which should be embraced while others should not) and can easily degenerate into mechanisms by which people are blackmailed into a quiescent acceptance of pain and suffering by what could be called theo-babble—that is, theological constructs designed to justify a status quo that as part of its inevitable function produces injustice. Elihu, as noted earlier, is just such a practitioner. He says to Job, "Beware of turning to evil, which you seem to prefer to affliction" (Job 36:21). Effectually, Job is advised to put up, shut up, and simply accept his lot rather than turn to evil, which the context suggests is conceived of as a protest against perceived injustice. After this attempted imposition of a coercive system of thought to quell any theology of protest, Elihu launches into the recitation of how God is majestically beyond human reason (Job 32:22–33). I cite the passage again now in order to illustrate that, in substance, it is not unlike some sections of Deutero-Isaiah (e.g. Isa 40:12–14, 25–26) and is similar to Isa 55:8–9, in which God declares, "My thoughts are not your thoughts, neither are your ways my ways. . . . As the heavens

---

98. Isaiah 32, with its affirmation of the role of human structures in creating justice, occupies what might be called a mediating position on the road to exclusively eschatological texts (e.g. 9:2–7; 11:1–16), where it is the future eschatological king alone who will be the source of justice. Whybray (*The Good Life in the Old Testament*, 217) argues: "In 32:1–2 the coming of a righteous king is prophesied, one who *together with other leaders of the community* will restore the security of the city" (emphasis added). Gossai (*Justice, Righteousness, and the Social Critique*, 154) corroborates this, noting that "32:1 points to the future rule of the princes and kings of Israel. . . . [T]his new age of justice is meant to be understood as one which will be in the life of Israel in the foreseeable future. It is not explicitly a messianic oracle." See also Pleins, *Social Visions of the Hebrew Bible*, 252.

are higher than the earth, so are my ways higher than your ways, and my thoughts than your thoughts." While this formulation in Isaiah is used as an attempt to engender confidence in God on the part of a justifiably doubtful people, that is, as a way of illustrating that this God is worth believing in and worshiping,[99] in changed circumstances it could be used, as in the Elihu–Job dialogue, in the interests of another agenda.[100] However, bearing this warning in mind, and aware of the dangerous distortions possible in advocating embracing pain, the rhetorical-theological thrust of Isa 58:6–10 is positive and its intention generative. Thus, in the theologies of "crying out" discerned through examination of שׁוע in its various contexts, 58:6–10 offers a theological formulation in contrast to both the theology of assurance exemplified in the Psalter (with the exception of Ps 88), and to the protest exemplified by Job. As Clines, in a provocative discussion of Job 24 and the absence of God, argues, "The suffering of the poor is a human problem, created by humans and soluble, if it is soluble at all, by humans. To collapse the social problem into a theological one, to make it God's problem, is . . . an abdication of responsibility."[101] Isaiah 58:6–10 affirms human responsibility in the solution of problems of poverty and injustice. In the claim of הנני placed in the mouth of God, it also retains a theological dimension,[102] perhaps suggesting that through the humanly initiated search for justice, God will be called back to a sphere of life for which God had abdicated responsibility.[103] However this is interpreted—as God revealing God's self in the midst of pain or as God, through human agency, being drawn into situations of pain—the shared affirmation is that God is encountered in pain experienced in the search for justice for all.

99. Sweeney, *Isaiah 1–4 and the Post-exilic Understanding*, 94, 98, 99. In line with what I suggest, Sweeney notes that people "would have believed that YHWH was powerless since He was unable to stop the disasters which befell them. The book of Isaiah is designed to counter such a belief." Within that structure Isa 55:8–9 has the same goal.

100. See further Labuschange, *Incomparability of Yahweh*.

101. David J. A. Clines, "Quarter Days Gone: Job 24 and the Absence of God," in Linafelt and Beal, eds., *God in the Fray*, 242–58.

102. Dorothee Sölle (*Thinking about God: An Introduction to Theology* [London: SCM Press; Philadelphia: Trinity, 1990], 192–93) talks of the need for a transcendent referent, noting that "those who lack transcendence also fall short on immanence. Moreover they lack clarity and compassion."

103. Kingsolver (*The Poisonwood Bible*, 499) writes poignantly of a mother, cradling an "innocent wreck of a baby" who is dangerously ill, confessing, "[H]ere I was, banging on heaven's door again. A desolate banging, from a girl who could count the years since she felt any real presence on the other side of that door."

11. *Isaiah 58:6–10:*
A Theologically Challenging Minority Voice

There is some justification in scholarship for attributing such importance to Isa 58. For example, Westermann identifies 58:6 as "the beginning of that great change which declared, in God's name, that men and women are of greater importance than cultic rite directed towards himself" (cf. Hos 6:6).[104] It is thus pivotal in the developing conception of the relationship between religious practice and justice. In addition, Westermann also claims that 58:9 "is of particular importance for the understanding of what the Old Testament means by salvation."[105]

One of the predominant theological strains in the book of Isaiah, rooted in the vision of Isa 2:2–4 and emphasized in the closing chapters, concerns what might be called world relationships: Israel's place in the world; the relationship of the nations to Israel; Jerusalem or Zion's role in the ultimate scheme of things.[106] Sweeney contends that one of the Isaianic foci concerns "developing the picture of the restored kingdom into a world empire," which might legitimately be seen as forming part of "YHWH's plan for world domination."[107] The imagery is overtly imperialistic and expresses an explicit will to power.[108] Operating within the same type of worldview, Hanson presents chs. 60–62 as a "glorious picture of shalom,"[109] although how being subjugated by and subordinated to a reconfigured and resurgent Israel could be construed as "shalom" for the nations involved is never explained.[110] Also with regard to this

104. Westermann, *Isaiah 40–66*, 337.
105. Ibid., 338.
106. Christopher Seitz, *Zion's final Destiny: The Development of the Book of Isaiah—A Reassessment of Isaiah 36–39* (Minneapolis: Fortress, 1991), 119–48; Barry Webb, "Zion in Transformation: A Literary Approach to Isaiah," in *The Bible in Three Dimensions* (ed. D. J. A. Clines, S. E. Fowl, and S. E. Porter; JSOTSup 87; Sheffield: Sheffield Academic Press, 1990), 64–84.
107. Sweeney, *Isaiah 1–4 and the Post-exilic Understanding*, 42, 97.
108. In its religious grounding it may perhaps be categorized as an example of what Achebe (*Home and Exile*, 12) terms "the psychology of religious imperialism."
109. Hanson, *Dawn of Apocalyptic*, 62.
110. Similarly, Klaus Baltzer (*Deutero-Isaiah* [Hermeneia; Minneapolis: Fortress, 2001], 330), describing how victory parades "ending with the people [i.e. the vanquished non-Israelites] falling on their faces in the prokynesis . . . must have been good fun," does not identify how or for whom exactly. Although this may not be a major issue in Isaiah, it is important for the resonance it has in the modern world. Naim Ateek (*Justice, and Only Justice: A Palestinian Theology of Liberation* [Maryknoll, N.Y.: Orbis, 1989], 78) poses the question, "How can the Old Testament be the Word of God in light of the Palestinian Christians' experience with its

section of the book, specifically 60:1–22, Brueggemann determines it to be "a foundational theological-evangelical announcement" in that "the great reversal in geopolitics is good news for Jerusalem."[111] Again, though, from the perspective of the nations, which are somewhat disparagingly referred to as "insects" (p. 205), how domination by Israel is to be understood as a function and expression of the evangel remains something of a mystery.

Brueggemann reveals his conscious investment in the world of power when he argues that "theological submission to Yahweh entails political submission to Jerusalem," an overall process that he says the poet envisions as "a wondrous capitulation of the nations who have for very long been superior to Israel in exploitative ways."[112] As far as can be determined, Brueggemann's thinking, on a revolving freedom–oppression/exploitation axis, accepts as legitimate the dreams of domination of the oppressed once the old order is overturned, the boot is on the other foot, and they are in the saddle. This comes dangerously close to justifying the cycle of the oppressed themselves becoming oppressors on attainment of power. Brueggemann himself acknowledges the possible risks inherent in his position when he notes that 60:1–22 "is shot through with latent imperialism that imagines not only theological and evangelical guarantees but also political, economic, and material advantage" (p. 211). Confronted with this dangerous mixture, he suggests

> that the church's best hope also lives at the seductive edge of such claims that invite arrogance beyond joy. There is no sure protection against such a posture. It is kept in check, surely, only by the continuing awareness that it is the God of mercy who gives the newness and appoints *shalom* as taskmaster. (p. 211)

If this has been understood correctly, Brueggemann argues that the desire on the part of the oppressed to exercise power in a way not much different from that of the oppressors is to be checked by the thought that God

use to support Zionism?" Graham Usher and Brian Whitaker ("Israeli Troops Seize West Bank Town in Terror Hunt," *Guardian Weekly* [21–30 January 2002]) talk of how Israeli actions were aimed at "the public humiliation" of Yasser Arafat. Suzanne Goldenberg ("Israeli Army Pays Gaza Refugees a Visit," *Guardian Weekly* [19–25 April 2001]) recounts a Palestinian observing, "[T]he Israelis want to treat us like master and servant."

111.   Brueggemann, *Isaiah 40–66*, 203, 204. The next several references are to Brueggemann.

112.   Ibid., 206. Similarly, Smith-Christopher (*A Biblical Theology of Exile*, 134) argues that "acts of obeisance . . . do not imply defeat or humiliation, but rather that humbling acceptance of transformation," but ultimately this seems strained.

is merciful and that therefore they too should display mercy when the tables are turned and they are elevated to positions of authority. While there is some merit in this, it is finally not convincing, particularly the way in which it accepts and participates in the ideological mind-set of domination. Isaiah 58:6–10, as interpreted here, represents a much more substantive challenge to the imperial consciousness in all its forms, and to the dreams (delusions?) of power and glory it invariably fosters and harbors.[113] Isaiah 58:6–10 insists that the actual practice of and struggle for justice goes on no matter who is in control. The dawning of an imagined golden age is unlikely to be inaugurated simply by replacing a foreign ruling elite with an indigenous one, which is every bit as likely to pursue exploitative policies, especially if it is invested in an imperial theology of power and glory. Indeed, read against a background of injustice within Israel (consonant with conditions as portrayed in the closing chapters of the book of Isaiah), passages such as Isa 60–62 may be interpreted as nationalistic propaganda produced by the ruling elite in order to divert the attention of the oppressed away from the true causes of their problems. In this way the oppressed are to be seduced and co-

113. Dwight W. Van Winkle ("An Inclusive Authoritative Text in Exclusive Communities," in *Writing and Reading the Scroll of Isaiah: Studies of an Interpretive Tradition* [ed. C. C. Broyles and C. A. Evans; 2 vols.; VTSup 70.1–2; Leiden: Brill, 1997], 1:423–40) demonstrates how "the Qumran community invoked the nationalistic portions of Second and Third Isaiah" to essentially avoid the radical implications of Isa 56:6 (p. 426). Smith-Christopher (*Biblical Theology of Exile*, 16) poses the key question to which I propose Isa 58 as part of the answer when he asks, "[I]f 'nationalism' is only a transitory tactic of liberation, which can lead uncritically to the same politics of dominance and privilege characteristic of the old colonizing states, what is the potential for avoiding this?" Assessing the present context in Palestine as it has been influenced by the idea that the establishment of the state of Israel represents the fulfillment of biblical prophecy and Jewish prayer, Yossi Klein Halevi ("Adrift in Israel's Dreamless Present," *Guardian Weekly* [7–13 December 2000]) contends, "There is neither a biblical past to escape to nor a peaceful future to anticipate. We are caught in a dreamless present. . . . Perhaps for the first time since the birth of Zionism a century ago, we are a people without a vision. . . . We are in mourning for the passing of our messianic delusions." Catherine Dupeyron ("Israeli Patriots Who Refuse to Join a 'Racist' Army," *Guardian Weekly* [3–9 January 2002]) writes of one conscientious objector to serving in the Israeli defense forces. The objector says, "When political reality is replaced by messianic hopes, it's a disaster. . . . Every people has its myths, but when they are realised at the expense of others it's a tragedy." Miscall ("Isaiah: Dreams and Nightmares," 164) relates this type of thinking to Isa 60–62 in his comment "that Jerusalem's dream is a nightmare for others." On how murderously destructive the mixture of theology and nationalism can be, see Michael Karpin and Ina Friedman, *Murder in the Name of God: The Plot to Kill Yitzhak Rabin* (London: Granta, 1999).

opted into accepting the predominant ideology, and to transpose their hopes for a better life into a distant future when external enemies will be overturned. Isaiah 58:6–10 resists this maneuver. Furthermore, 58:6–10 also contains the dimension of reconciliation, which at least holds out the possibility of the oppressed-turning-into-oppressors cycle, as winter follows autumn, being broken.[114]

12. *A Common Humanity: Exodus Modified*

Isaiah 58, perhaps intentionally, blurs the lines of demarcation between the categories into which the world is usually divided in order to be understood. Watts essentially agrees with this approach when he argues that "the shift in v 5 to singular address coincides with the use of עדם 'a human being'. What is announced applies to any person seeking Yahweh."[115] So, read through this lens, the exodus language used throughout chs. 40–55,[116] in continuity with which 58:6–10 stands, is given new and added meaning. Effectually, the rigidity of exodus categories is called into question and the meaning of the exodus paradigm in the life of the community reified. Thus, where the story of the exodus conceived the world as divided between the "them" and "us" of oppressed Hebrews against oppressive Egyptians, 58:6–10 implies that this objectification

114. This does not deny the validity of what R. S. Sugirtharajah (*The Bible and the Third World: Precolonial, Colonial, and Postcolonial Encounters* [Cambridge: Cambridge University Press, 2001], 249) terms the second stream of postcolonial thought devoted to resisting the colonizer. Classically see Frantz Fanon, *The Wretched of the Earth* (trans. Constance Farrington; New York: Grove Press, 1963). As Achebe (*Home and Exile*, 72) observes, "The psychology of the dispossessed can be truly frightening." Robert J. Schreiter (*Reconciliation: Mission and Ministry in a Changing Social Order* [Maryknoll, N.Y.: Orbis; Cambridge, Mass.: Boston Theological Institute, 1992) argues that reparations to the dispossessed precede reconciliation. Against using God to buttress dreams of eventual domination, Sölle (*Thinking about God*, 195) argues: "The certainty of God in us does not then grow as a certainty of authoritarian might that it will be right in the end, but as the certainty of the subversive power of justice."

115. Watts, *Isaiah 34–66*, 272.

116. See Bernhard W. Anderson, "Exodus Typology in Second Isaiah," in *Israel's Prophetic Heritage: Essays in Honor of James Muilenburg* (ed. Bernhard W. Anderson and Walter Harrelson; London: SCM Press, 1962), 177–95; idem, "Exodus and Covenant in Second Isaiah and Prophetic Tradition," in *Magnalia Dei: The Mighty Acts of God* (ed. Frank Moore Cross, Werner E. Lemke, and Patrick D. Miller Jr.; New York: Doubleday, 1976), 339–60; Alexander, *Commentary on Isaiah*, 359. More generally, Childs (*Isaiah*, 479) and Goldingay (*Isaiah*, 325) both note how Third Isaiah takes over the language of Second.

and externalization of the agency of oppression as being outside the community of faith cannot be sustained. The line demarcating the oppressed from the oppressor is relocated within, and thus the exploited across the frontier are not necessarily the enemy.[117]

Consequently, the logic of the rhetoric of Isa 58:6–10 strongly suggests that the horizon of exodus hope is opened for anyone suffering oppression anywhere, and is no longer confined to Israel (Amos 9:7).[118] Exodus may be effected in any context of oppression in which people move to stand in solidarity with the oppressed in order to struggle with them for liberation.[119] While this may happen most often within a homogenous religious-ethnic grouping, there is, theoretically, nothing to preclude acts of solidarity in search of exodus taking place across transreligious and ethnic lines.[120] Thus, interpreted in this fashion, Isa 58:6–10 challenges the exclusive application of the exodus paradigm to Israel and undermines how it can be utilized by ruling elites in buttressing a nationalist ideology intended to inculcate a sense of suspicion of and superiority to those outside the elect nation.[121] Whereas ruling elites, using old

117.   John Goldingay ("Isaiah 40–55 in the 1990s: Among Other Things, Deconstructing, Mystifying, Intertextual, Socio-critical, and Hearer-Involving," *BibInt* 5 [1997]: 225–46 [233]) paves the way for this type of interpretation by arguing that Isa 40–55 "makes a point of subverting the division between insiders and outsiders." Miscall ("Isaiah: Dreams and Nightmares," 151–52) argues that "in his book as a whole, I find that Isaiah, the poet and prophet who narrates . . . does not make clear and final distinctions between Israel and the nations, between righteous and wicked, and salvation and judgment."

118.   Walter Brueggemann (*Theology of the Old Testament: Testimony, Dispute, Advocacy* [Minneapolis: Fortress, 1997], 520–22) counts this as among what he terms "Texts of Radical Hope," arguing that "the way in which Israel is treated by Yahweh in the Exodus is the way in which every people may expect to be treated." My comments on Isa 58:6–10, as they relate to exodus, build on and contribute to this theme.

119.   As Caputo (*Demythologizing Heidegger*, 190) puts it, "The whole idea behind justice is not to exclude anyone from the kingdom, which means the kingdom is nowhere in particular." Corroborating this statement, Derrida ("Force of Law," 955) insists that "justice always addresses itself to singularity, to the singularity of the other, despite or even because it pretends to universality."

120.   Caputo (*More Radical Hermeneutics*, 64) understands Derrida as calling for "communities that are rendered porous and open-ended, without homogeneity and self-identity" on account of practicing "an unconditional hospitality" and issuing "an open-ended invitation to every wayfarer."

121.   Jon D. Levenson (*The Hebrew Bible, the Old Testament, and Historical Criticism: Jews and Christians in Biblical Studies* [Louisville, Ky.: Westminster John Knox, 1993], 127–59) vehemently opposes any application of the exodus paradigm to peoples other than Jews. Magonet (*A Rabbi's Bible*, 136–48), also from

nationalist myths, exacerbate division between peoples, while simultaneously perpetuating injustice against their own people, 58:6–10, allusively
reclaiming one of those old, core myths of Israel, offers a different,
radically subversive way to live, committed to exodus and liberation for
the oppressed everywhere. The universalism in the book of Isaiah[122] is
given a further dimension by 58:6–10, in that this text puts the idea of the
embrace of pain on the horizon of universalism.[123] Moreover, the kenotic
dimension noted in Isa 58, if taken seriously, significantly ameliorates
the dangerous potential for the exodus paradigm becoming the occasion
for the domination, if not obliteration, of the "other."[124]

13. *The Theory of the Rise of Apocalyptic*

Hanson's theory of how apocalyptic thought originated in Israel can be
analyzed to see if Isa 58:6–10 modifies it or calls into question its
credibility. Hanson believes that the prophetic community that produced
the closing chapters of the book of Isaiah increasingly found itself
"hopelessly remote . . . from the brilliant promises of Second Isaiah."[125]
At this point, as "an oppressed minority" (p. 151), it became "detached
from participation in the political order" and thus relinquished "the task
of interpreting the prophetic message and corresponding vocation of the
chosen people within the historical context." The result of this process
"heralds the death of prophecy and the birth of apocalyptic eschatology"
(p. 161). In essence, through upsetting "the delicate balance between myth
and history" (p. 130) and thereby uncoupling itself "from the weighty
vocation of serving within the political order" (p. 131), the community

a Jewish perspective, takes the opposite view. Further, see Alice Ogden Bellis and
Joel S. Kaminsky, eds., *Jews, Christians, and the Theology of the Hebrew Scriptures*
(Atlanta: Society of Biblical Literature, 2000), 173–275.

122.   Joseph Blenkinsopp, "Second Isaiah—Prophet of Universalism," *JSOT* 41
(1988): 83–103.

123.   In this analysis, Isa 58:6–10 may be taken as an "example of the universalism that saves cultures from nationalist viruses" (Carlos Fuentes, *The Years with
Laura Díaz* [London: Bloomsbury, 2001], 307).

124.   Caputo (*Demythologizing Heidegger*, 201), resonant with the kenotic
dimension I perceive in Isa 58, defines prophetic justice in Levinas and Derrida as
"the expenditure of self without demanding a return. It is even violent—toward
oneself: one is held hostage, one allows oneself to suffer deprivations and outrages
that one would protest if it befell the Other." See also Caputo, *More Radical
Hermeneutics*, 56–57, 64–65; Jacques Derrida, *Politics of Friendship* (trans. George
Collins; London: Verso, 1997).

125.   Hanson, *Dawn of Apocalyptic*, 123. Subsequent bracketed references in the
main text are to this source.

from which, in Hanson's estimation, the oracles at the end of the Isaianic corpus came, resorts to a new form of literature in which a future era of salvation for the elect—distinct from and with no connection to the present—is envisaged:

> The redeemed in the visionary group of the post-exilic period feel responsible only to their own eschatological circle, which makes it possible for them to remain aloof from the political sphere. Prophetism has here begun to move out of the national cult toward exclusive sectarianism, ceasing to address the world of political realities and narrowing its vision to the sanctified community of the new era, giving up interpreting divine activity within the context of plain history and choosing instead to announce deliverance to the faithful in terms highly influenced by mythology and disinterested in conditions of human instrumentality and historical contingency. (p. 132)

Much of this argument, especially as it conceives the community inscribed in Isa 58 as a depoliticized entity devoted to "exclusive sectarianism" and "disinterested in considerations of human instrumentality and historical contingency," stands in marked contrast to my interpretation of the chapter. My interpretation is grounded in a vision of potential and theoretical inclusivity as people in any context of oppression are encouraged to engage in concrete acts of human liberation within history. Certainly any grouping following the instruction of Isa 58 may be considered to have been small on account of the demanding commitment required to fulfill the prophetic ethic. But the logic of the passage is outward-looking rather than inward-looking, and rooted in the realities of society rather than some projected future.

Two misconceptions dominate Hanson's thinking and lead him to a less-than-satisfactory reading. First, taking the experience of certain disaffected middle-class North American groups in the 1970s as normative, not to mention predictive of how collections of people will behave when alienated from the prevailing structures of power, he assumes that the only reaction to social exclusion is a flight into a socially disengaged never-never land. Second, his conception of what constitutes history is, as he himself admits, concerned with "the destiny of nations and kings" (p. 151). Thus, when these terms of reference are not immediately apparent in shaping the discourse, he too quickly concludes that what is being talked about is necessarily apolitical and ahistorical. When these critical factors are taken into account, Isa 58:6–10 can, consistent with its rhetoric, be read, not as a piece of early apocalyptic detached from the conditions of the world, but as a call to profound engagement in the midst of present history, which has as its aim manifesting signs of social transformation. In this interpretation, faced with harsh circumstances, solidarity and struggle are options at least as valid as flight. Furthermore, history is not only the story of kings and countries and the high officials of government, but also, more importantly, is the often overlooked and untold story of the world's little people. These persons, in conjunction with those who will stand with them, take responsibility for their own destiny through undertaking acts of historical liberation in the creation of a better world. The vision is of history "from below"[126] in which poetic renderings of a world transformed to justice are not the selfishly hoarded escapist dreams of a disaffected few, but the horizon toward which the modalities of freedom and solidarity articulated in Isa 58 are moving, as those modalities are enacted and realized. Thus, Hanson's conceptualization of apocalyptic, whatever its surface attractions, is undermined, certainly as it is applied to Isa 58, by an interpretation that more appropriately accounts for the "plain" data.

Isaiah 58 and the Pattern of Biblical Prayer

Another way in which Isa 58 may be considered to contribute something new to the different theological formulations in the Hebrew Bible is brought to light in considering Miller's extensive discussion of the form and theology of biblical prayer in *They Cried to the Lord*.[127] Taking as a focus the worship life of Israel as it, in its particularity, is located in the broader context of prayer in the ancient Near East, he derives an Old Testament theology from this examination of the nature of prayer. On the strength of his research, he is able to categorize the wide range of different types of petition that are scattered throughout the Bible and to identify characteristic divine responses to these petitions. This is a massive undertaking that, in the end, understands the pattern of prayer, stripped of variations, to be encapsulated in the movement from crying out to divine response:

> Time and again . . . the people cried out to God and God responded. It is one of the primary threads binding the whole together. When the people, in one voice or in many, cry out for help, the ears of God are open, and God responds in ways to deal with their situation, to provide the help that is needed. (p. 140)

126.   This is a common idea in liberation theology; for example, see a section in Gustavo Gutiérrez, *The Power of the Poor in History* (London: SCM Press, 1983), 169–221, entitled "Theology from the Underside of History."

127.   Patrick D. Miller, *They Cried to the Lord: The Form and Theology of Biblical Prayer* (Minneapolis: Fortress, 1994). Subsequent bracketed references in the main text are to this source. See also idem, "Prayer and Divine Action," in Linafelt and Beal, eds., *God in the Fray*, 211–32, which summarizes the longer work.

This is described as "the structure of human pain and divine compassion, a framework of existence that takes shape in prayer and God's response." In this scheme, it seems, the act of crying out is always presented as arising from something that happens to befall the supplicant (pp. 105–6). The something may be illness, or the effects of war, or the result of sin, or any of a great number of other possibilities. But in all cases, events beyond the supplicant's control break out in some form of chaos to reduce him to crying out for help, in response to which he wants and perhaps expects to hear an oracle of assurance (pp. 98–99). In a sense, Isa 58:9a conforms to and mirrors this pattern in the way that it projects a condition of life when crying out will immediately be followed by God's presence. However, the act of crying out in 58:9a is ultimately understood as deriving, not from something happening beyond the expectation of the supplicant, but as the result of a conscious and deliberate course of action, initially outlined in vv. 6 and 7. The heart of this action is conceived as the embrace of pain involved in the pursuit of activities to secure social justice. There may be an element of warning in 58:9a, in that it suggests that acts of justice and liberation such as those called for by the prophet, if followed rigorously and profoundly, will lead to crying out in distress. Here the crying out is preceded and predicated by the adoption of a type of ethical behavior that the supplicant knows beforehand will lead to suffering. This is different from crying out as a consequence of the misfortunes that occur in the normal and regular pattern of life's affairs. Yet it is in this conscious embrace of pain that God promises to say "Here am I," perhaps, given the context, the most poignant and intimate expression of God's attention, but one that Miller does not mention in his enumeration of comparable formulations (p. 99). Isaiah 58:6–10 introduces a small, easily overlooked, yet significant variation into Miller's otherwise extensive and compelling theology of prayer.

Miller observes concerning the issue of social regulation that "when the human systems of justice and its administration fail to deliver the oppressed, they cry out for help and vindication, for a right judgment by God that will sustain them before the plots and deceits of others" (p. 109). Further, he notes:

> In the face of human oppression, the innocent victim appeals to a righteous judge in heaven (Ps 7:11) to confirm that innocence, to render a fair verdict, and to preserve the life and well-being of the one who has been done in by the forces and agents of injustice, malicious witnesses, the ruthless (Ps 54:3), and the bloodthirsty (Ps 26:9), people whose hands are "full of bribes" to manipulate the human machinery of justice. (pp. 109–10)

Generally and ideally this might be so. Generally and ideally that crying out elicits a word of divine assurance "rooted in the reality of God's presence and power" might illustrate that, for the most part, "With these divine words of assurance, we are not only at the center of what is going on in prayer in the Bible. We are at the center of the whole structure of faith to which it bears witness" (p. 174). But what happens when the structure fails to operate as postulated and believed in?

In Miller's broad understanding of the pattern of biblical prayer, it may justifiably be assumed that the early stages of Isaiah involve the calling out to God for justice over the heads of a corrupt judiciary, but that this failed to engender the expected oracles of assurance. This failure perhaps begins to explain, within the world constructed by the full form of the book, the development, in the face of persistent and entrenched injustice that God did not alleviate, of a trajectory from insistence on the need for advocacy on behalf of the poor (1:16–17) to insistence on the need for direct action on behalf of the poor. Thus Isa 58:6–10, in this thinking, marks the emergence of an underlying line of prophetic reflection more openly invested in a commitment to human action to tackle problems of social justice. Rather than call to God and wait, people are being encouraged to participate in a life of justice in order, at some level, to (re-)mobilize God on behalf of the poor and oppressed. Assuredly this is still a very theological proposition that, in its way, stands in line with some recent studies that have explored how human agency might interact, by prompting and motivating, with divine response.

In one such piece, Lee states that her essay has two purposes: "(1) to consider Exodus 1–2 as a hopeful paradigm for *human response to genocide*"[128]—thus the focus on a positive human agency, in the case of Isa 58, in response to injustice—"and (2) to highlight what is rarely suggested: that in the book of Exodus . . . *the divine response to genocide . . .* is highly problematic."[129] This second point, reformulated and applied to the Isaianic corpus, offers a similar possibility of exploring the divine response to injustice in the book, to see whether it might also be deemed "problematic." Characteristic of perhaps the bulk of biblical theology (and Miller fits into this mold), which, as a matter of dogmatic course, assumes the goodness of God, thereby automatically absolving the divine from any whiff of implication in wrongdoing, Calvin simply asserts that righteousness "as meaning just government . . . is the gift of God."[130] Calvin suggests that God's governance is always just and that just

128.   Nancy C. Lee, "Genocide's Lament: Moses, Pharaoh's Daughter, and the Former Yugoslavia," in Linafelt and Beal, eds., *God in the Fray*, 66–82 (67–68 [emphasis in original]).

129.   Ibid., 68 (emphasis in original).

130.   Calvin, *Commentary on the Prophet Isaiah*, 4:235.

government in the world is impossible for humanity without a divine hand of assistance. If, however, in deploying the deconstructionist methodology of reading against the grain it can be shown that the God rendered in the book of Isaiah (and more widely in the Hebrew Bible) is involved in violence and abuse disproportionate to any reputed offense to God, then the source of justice in the world is not necessarily exclusively divine. The way is opened for at least considering that 58:6–10, beneath its invariable and important theological contributions, could be a resource for human motivation in the struggle for social justice. Perhaps Isa 58 is rhetorically supple enough that it allows for different people to embark on the search for justice for different reasons. People can accept and respond to the prophet's message as an act of faith to a word of advice and correction. In addition, people wanting to commit to the imperative of justice who, on the basis of memory and experience, have reason to doubt the justness of God can still fully, if perhaps more suspiciously,[131] devote themselves to the prophetic agenda. To the former, the voice of God saying "Here am I" in the midst of the pain of the struggle comes as fulfillment of promise; to the latter, if heard at all, it comes as the voice of a God virtually shamed by their initiative into trying to move back into right relationship with them. The rhetorical route to the "high places" (על במותי; Isa 58:14) is via the embrace of pain and the questions that raises.

14. *The Challenge to Exclusivism*

At the start of *Now Choose Life: Theology and Ethics in Deuteronomy*, Millar claims "that not only does the message of Deuteronomy take us to the very heart of biblical theology, but that it is unmatched in its relevance for the affluent western church of today."[132] There may be some truth in this, but as short a text as it is, Isa 58:6–10 seriously challenges some of the central tenets of Deuteronomic theology. Whereas, as Millar insists,[133] Deuteronomy is almost exclusively concerned with ethics within the community of Israel alone, 58:6–10, at its deepest level, envisions that wherever the search for justice is joined in the terms enunciated by the prophet, and for whatever motivation, whether among the elect or

---

131.   As Goldingay ("Isaiah 40–55 in the 1990s," 232) observes specifically in regard to chs. 40–55, but with a broader application, "Israel will be well advised not to listen too naively to the prophet's encouraging message about its being God's servant."

132.   Millar, *Now Choose Life*, 11.

133.   Ibid., 99, 145, and passim.

not, then God will say "Here am I." What is important is the actualization of the prophetic charter.[134] Moreover, notwithstanding Millar's ultimately unconvincing attempt to defend theologically the parts of Deuteronomy that call for the extermination of the Canaanites—leading to the suffering of others, in obedience to God[135]—58:6–10 proposes suffering on behalf of others. In this, people are called to choose an ethic grounded in the solidarity of suffering as the way to life, rather than, as in Deuteronomy, an ethic of national identity rooted in exclusion, charity, and a form of ethnic cleansing.[136] Further, whereas in Deuteronomy the presence of God is to be found in the cult, at the place that God will choose as a dwelling for God's name, in 58:6–10 God's presence ("Here am I") is to be encountered, if at all, in the course of a common quest for justice.

At one point, turning toward the New Testament, Millar suggests that "while one would hesitate to ascribe Pauline soteriology and eschatology to Deuteronomy, it is hard to resist the temptation when the correlation between this book and the apostolic teaching is so close!"[137] Be that as it may, even in this sphere of perceived inter-Testament echoes and

134. See Joseph W. Groves (*Actualization and Interpretation in the Old Testament* [Atlanta: Scholars Press, 1987], esp. 209), where in discussing "the religious dimension of actualization" it is argued that "biblical actualization is different from a general theory of literary actualization. The religious motive for the re-use of old traditions gives Biblical actualization an intensity and complexity lacking in most other applications of the general concept." This is certainly true of the implications for social justice, especially as related to the embrace of pain which I discern in Isa 58.

135. Millar, *Now Choose Life*, 160. For a trenchant criticism of apologies for violence in the Bible, see Regina M. Schwartz, *The Curse of Cain: The Violent Legacy of Monotheism* (Chicago: University of Chicago Press, 1997).

136. As Daniel Smith (*Religion of the Landless: The Social Context of the Babylonian Exile* [Philadelphia: Fortress, 1989], 205) notes, "Exodus is the road to nationalism and power." Caputo (*More Radical Hermeneutics*, 81) talks movingly of "the powerful and revolutionary command to recognize the trace of God in the face of the neighbor and the stranger, of the friend and the enemy." Significantly, given my interests in this book, he goes on, "[T]he most deeply ethical, let us say, the most friendly, moment in Christianity is found in the story in which the master says that whenever you befriended the least of mine—whenever you fed them or visited them in prison—you befriended me. . . . [T]he trace of God is inscribed on the face of the neighbor, especially of those laid low by circumstance—the widow, the orphan." For a poignant example of what can happen when the neighbor is not respected, see Jan T. Gross, *Neighbors: The Destruction of the Jewish Community at Jedwabne, Poland* (Princeton: Princeton University Press, 2001).

137. Millar, *Now Choose Life*, 66.

parallels, 58:6–10 has a contribution to make, for it prefigures and perhaps is a taproot of New Testament kenotic theology. This assertion finds support in Knight's observation that the verb used in 58:10 to call for self-giving is the same verb "used of the Suffering Servant at 53:12 and of the eternal Christ at Phil. 2:7."[138] Differences in theological focus not only exist between the Testaments, but also within them. The assumption of a gulf between "Old" and "New" may be a gulf more rooted in the dogmatics of different religious or faith traditions than the text itself. It may be that Isa 58:6–10 has more in common with Phil 2:5–11 in rhetoric and theology than with Deuteronomy. Likewise, Deuteronomy may have more in common with whatever passages Millar would choose to exemplify "Pauline soteriology and eschatology" than with Isa 58. However the term "Bible" is defined, it speaks in many different theological voices,[139] which do not necessarily harmonize.

In conclusion, although Isa 58:6–10 is a short passage that may not articulate a fully developed theological position, it occupies an important position within the book of Isaiah as a whole, and indeed within the broader scope of the Hebrew Bible for the suggestive proposals it makes, especially in relation to the theme of social justice. It may be said to represent a minority voice, but one that challenges, calls into question, and causes us to ponder the claims of more predominant theological positions. Through deepening the concept of social justice to such an extent that it adds new dimensions of meaning to the broader theological traditions of Israel, 58:6–10 presents radical solidarity, protokenosis, and the embrace of pain as the route to a new order of justice, not only in postexilic Israel, but around the world. In this construal, justice for the "other" takes precedence over personal salvation. Sobrino has eloquently and forcefully said:

> Solidarity is another name for the kind of love that moves feet, hands, hearts, material goods, assistance and sacrifice towards the pain, danger, misfortune, disaster, repression or death of other persons or a whole people. The aim is to share with them and help them rise up, become free, claim justice, rebuild.[140]

Although he does not acknowledge any direct dependence on Isa 58, his words faithfully encapsulate the heart of the message uncovered in this

138.   George A. F. Knight, *Isaiah 56–66: The New Israel* (ITC; Grand Rapids: Eerdmans; Edinburgh: Handsel, 1985), 28.

139.   John Goldingay, *Theological Diversity and the Authority of the Old Testament* (Carlisle: Paternoster, 1995).

140.   Jon Sobrino, quoted on a Lenten campaign poster by the Irish non-governmental organization Trócaire, 1988.

rhetorical exegesis and theological exposition. Considerable weight has been placed on and significant freight extrapolated from a brief passage. However, the close reading, through integrating the meaning of the passage into the world of the book, is able to sustain the weight and affirm the freight.

Chapter 3

THE RHETORIC OF PUNISHMENT AS QUESTIONING VOICE

והעם לא־שב עד־המכהו ואת־יהוה צבאות לא דרשו: ויכרת יהוה מישראל
ראש וזנב כפה ואגמון יום אחד: זקן ונשוא־פנים הוא הראש ונביא
מורה־שקר הוא הזנב: ויהיו מאשרי העם־הזה מתעים ומאשריו מבלעים:
על־כן על־בחוריו לא־ישמח אדני ואת־יתמיו ואת־אלמנתיו לא ירחם
כי כלו חנף ומרע וכל־פה דבר נבלה בכל־זאת לא־שב אפו ועוד ידו נטויה:

But the people did not turn to the one who strikes them, nor seek out
Yahweh of hosts. So in one day Yahweh cut off head and tail, palm frond
and reed from Israel—the elder and honored man is the head, the prophet
teaching lies the tail; for those who lead this people lead them awry, and
those who are led are left reeling and engulfed. So the Lord does not take
pleasure in their youths, and has no compassion on their orphans and
widows, for all are godless evildoers and every mouth spouts foolishness:
for all this, God's anger is not deflected and God's hand is still upraised.
(Isa 9:12–16 [ET vv. 13–17])

1. *Questioning Assumptions, Generating Meaning*

The purpose of this chapter is primarily twofold.[1] It is first to assess
whether key passages concerned with punishment, taking the book of
Isaiah as a whole, are as rhetorically secure and convincing as has often
been assumed. Second, the purpose is to probe hints in the text indicating
a capacity—exceeding what the majority of interpreters traditionally
have assumed—on the part of the final redactor or implied author to
doubt the nature of the character of God. As Heschel writes, "Israel's
misery seemed out of all proportion to her guilt, and its justice belied by
other facts of history."[2] Given this experience of the divine, he is justified

---

1. For a discussion of the phrase "questioning voice" used in the present
chapter's title, see Fredrick Holmgren, *With Wings as Eagles: Isaiah 40/55—An
Interpretation* (Chappaqua, N.Y.: Biblical Scholars Press, 1973), 4.

2. Heschel, *The Prophets*, 1:147. Prophetic language in its original form was
more perlocutional/rhetorical than "historical," on which see J. L. Austin, *How to do
Things with Words* (London: Oxford University Press, 1963); John R. Searle, *Speech*

in asking the key question, "Can He Who 'has destroyed without mercy all the habitations of Jacob,' Who 'has become like an enemy' (Lam 2:2, 5), still be trusted as the God who is our Father?"[3]

Heschel makes these comments during discussion of what he takes to be Second Isaiah. The possibility is thus raised of construing the relationship between Isa 1–39 and what follows as more tension-filled and dialectical than has generally been acknowledged. According to Heschel, Second Isaiah, in addition to his proclamation of the good news of release from captivity for the exiles, "does not passively accept Zion's lot" but also "challenges the Lord,"[4] in part at least for what has happened. If true, then one of the more unnoticed aspects of the blocs commonly designated First and Second Isaiah is that the justice of the punishment announced so insistently in the opening section of the book is subtly called into question. This is not to say that it is crudely eroded or obviously undermined, but rather to emphasize the nuanced dramatic qualities inherent and available in a close reading of the text as opposed to one shaped by firm and fixed *a priori* theological commitments.

This chapter also explores ways that careful attention to the text, rather than the text filtered through external dogmatic categories, opens up possibilities for reading the book of Isaiah as a sequential whole. I examine how the predominant characterization of God may have been challenged and partially reified during the course of the book and how the implied author's use of irony may help integrate the work as an entirety. The irony may be traced to the stance the implied author takes to the dramatization of the book's unfolding events. Related to this second point, later I examine whether *some* of those who turn their back on God (e.g. 1:4; 59:13), especially in the latter stages of the book, and who resist the poetic ingratiatory appeals of God (e.g. 49:15–18), may not, in the developing drama of the text, be justified in doing so. The theological and indeed missiological implications underlying this literary reading are examined for relevance to Isaiah's presentation of the concept of social justice.

As a point of departure, I explore texts that deal with "widows and orphans" in connection with the theme of universal condemnation and punishment for how they contribute to an understanding of social justice within the Isaianic corpus. I pay particular notice to who exactly is condemned, the nature of their sin or crime, and the wider implications the punishment has in Isaiah's construal of social justice. Focus on

---

Acts: An Essay in the Philosophy of Language (Cambridge: Cambridge University Press, 1972).

3. Heschel, *The Prophets*, 1:147.
4. Ibid., 1:146.

"widows and orphans" is appropriate as a way into this topic in light of the fact that these are the groups explicitly mentioned in 1:16–17 as deserving of justice activity on their behalf. Further, these verses have been shown to be of prime importance in introducing the theme of social justice in the book of Isaiah.

Following this, I study texts that at some level appear to entertain the idea of God having acted excessively in the divine treatment of Israel. These texts are studied both for how they function in their immediate rhetorical contexts and for how they more broadly affect the concept of justice if God is lexically or semantically implicated in injustice.[5] Due to the number of texts, a full rhetorical analysis of each is not possible. Instead, aspects of relevant passages are placed in the foreground. In essence, my reading stresses the allusive, nuanced nature of the text and explicates how this leads to fresh theological insights. I consequently oppose the closure that comes with readings grounded in prior convictions, such as the immutable nature of God's justice. As has been the pattern in this book so far, text receives primacy over theological dogma.

2. Certitude beyond All Reasonable Doubt?

Clements's scholarship contributes to viewing the prophecy of Isaiah as an integrated piece in which the Assyrian and Babylonian parts are more than "only peripherally related to each other."[6] On the basis of redaction criticism—in order to illuminate what he takes to be assured historical events—he argues that "a more intrinsic connection between the two parts of the book should be recognized" (p. 434). For Clements, "the

---

5. As a point of hermeneutical practice, the goodness and justice of God will not be assumed (e.g. see M. S. Bryan, "The Threat to the Reputation of YHWH: The Portrayal of the Divine Character in the Book of Ezekiel" [Ph.D. diss., Sheffield University, 1992]). Such assumptions characteristically predetermine interpretation. In much the same way, the assumption of the benign intentions of the United States in world affairs has tended in a significant swathe of historical interpretation to ameliorate the worst excesses of U.S. foreign policy. Thus, serious engagement with the global consequences of that policy, which have regularly been more brutally self-interested than they have been presented, is precluded. For a recent example of this hermeneutic at work, see Michael Lind, *Vietnam: The Necessary War* (New York: Free Press, 2000). For a critique of this approach, see Noam Chomsky, *The Culture of Terrorism* (Boston: South End Press, 1988); idem, *Necessary Illusions: Thought Control in Democratic Societies* (Boston: South End Press, 1989); idem, *Year 501: The Conquest Continues* (Boston: South End Press, 1993).

6. R. E. Clements, "The Prophecies of Isaiah and the Fall of Jerusalem in 587 B.C.," *VT* 30 (1980): 421–36 (434). Subsequent bracketed references in the main text are to this source.

events which befell Jerusalem in 587 B.C. provided a pivotal point" (p. 436) around which many of the oracles in the Isaianic corpus revolve and through which those oracles can be integrated. This involves those oracles taken by Clements to be original, in addition to those understood to be secondary glosses or "interpretative comments" (p. 423). In effect, "that ancient Israelite scribes saw some sort of connection between certain prophecies given by Isaiah and the destruction that came upon Jerusalem in 587 B.C." (p. 423) provides the unifying principle in the book of Isaiah. The connection enables us to "discern traces of a connected and relatively systematic process of redaction in passages which have already, for the most part, been seen to be secondary for formal and stylistic reasons" (p. 424).

Clements perceives that the underlying aim of the final form of Isaiah "clearly seems to be to provide some kind of theodicy which would show why such massive destruction [as occurred in 587 B.C.E.] had to be inflicted upon Judah" (p. 438).[7] "Prophecies emanating from the aftermath of the events of 701," in which Israel had been miraculously delivered from impending doom, "appeared to offer further confirmation that some sin on the part of the citizens of Jerusalem had evoked from Yahweh the need for further and fuller judgment in the years that had followed" (p. 430). In this redactional-historical construal, "prophecy has been used to provide a theodicy, explaining the necessity for events which otherwise appeared to contravene the established expectations concerning the purposes of divine providence" (p. 432). In other words, prophecy has been called upon to account for a massive and potentially inexplicable dislocation in Israelite perception of its relationship to the divine.

While Clements's observations help support reading Isaiah as a unity and in emphasizing the centrality in the book of the destruction of Jerusalem prior to "exile,"[8] in certain important regards his methodological

7. More generally on the subject of theodicy, see James L. Crenshaw, ed., *Theodicy in the Old Testament* (Issues in Religion and Theology 4; Philadelphia: Fortress; London: SPCK, 1983). In this frame, the book of Isaiah in one of its aspects becomes an example of "structure legitimation" (see Brueggemann, *Old Testament Theology*, 1–21). See also John Barton, "History and Rhetoric in the Prophets," in *The Bible as Rhetoric: Studies in Biblical Persuasion and Credibility* (ed. Martin Warner; London: Routledge, 1990), 51–64. John Milton ("Paradise Lost," bk. 1, line 26, in *The Portable Milton* [ed. Douglas Bush; Harmondsworth: Penguin, 1977], 233) proposes that his poem is an attempt to justify "the ways of God to men"; one dimension of the final form of Isaiah may be construed to have a similar goal.
8. As Smith-Christopher (*A Biblical Theology of Exile*, 104) observes, "That 'exile' becomes a central myth in biblical literature is clear, but what I believe must

approach precludes him from pursuing significant interpretative questions. He is content to postulate the theodic dimension of Isaiah but does
not examine the rhetoric in which it is couched to assess its persuasiveness. This example of redaction criticism is able to identify the way the
text, viewed as a relationship between primary and secondary material,
highlights the importance of theodicy, but lacks the inclination and the
critical tools to evaluate its presentation. Redaction criticism thus casts
light on how, given key historical assumptions that are increasingly
being questioned in quarters of the scholarly community, a text *may* have
come to assume its final form. But apart from the larger interpretative
claims necessary to support its thesis, redaction criticism is disinclined to
read the fine detail of the work as a unity.

Consequently, Clements accedes too readily to what at first sight
seems to be the surface ideology of the text, without questioning what
other strategies, in the rhetorical context of the work as a whole, the
implied author may have had. It may finally be that the text supports and
unequivocally endorses the idea that God acts justly and proportionately
in punishing Israel's sin, but before the certitude of such a conclusion
can be asserted the text needs to be scrutinized to see if any other dynam-
ics can be discerned that might erode and destabilize this certitude. A
close reading of the most pertinent sections of the book, from which more
general conclusions may be drawn, adequately fulfills this requirement,
which is beyond the purview of redaction criticism. Furthermore, if the
purported events of 587 B.C.E. were as momentous as Clements and
others imply,[9] exploding completely and perhaps exposing Israel's expectations of the divine, then any serious accounting would have to participate in the profound depth of communal loss in order to be given a serious
hearing. To have attempted to explain the unexplainable[10] in a glib,
schematic, or neatly formulaic way would have been to risk immediate

also be clear is that there is not necessarily a fictional, contrived, or exaggerated
event behind the use of such influential motifs." While this book operates with
"exile" as a literary construct, see also Lester L. Grabbe, ed., *Leading Captivity
Captive: The Exile as History and Ideology* (JSOTSup 278; Sheffield: Sheffield
Academic Press, 1998); James Scott, ed., *Exile: Old Testament, Jewish, and Chris-
tian Conceptions* (Leiden: Brill, 1997); Hans Barstad, *The Myth of the Empty Land:
A Study in the History and Archaeology of Judah during the "Exilic" Period* (Oslo:
Scandinavian University Press, 1996).

9. E.g. see Walter Brueggemann, *Hopeful Imagination: Prophetic Voices in Exile*
(Philadelphia: Fortress, 1986).

10. Analogously, D. H. Lawrence (*Selected Literary Criticism* [ed. Anthony
Beal; London: Heinemann, 1956], 107) describes the novelist's task as describing
the "indescribable."

rejection. A deeply perplexing issue demanded a deeply pondered response: immediately, the idea of easy certitude is punctured.

3. *Divine Justice and Divine Wrath: Easy Bedfellows?*

To a considerable extent, the concept of the wrath of God is related to the theme of divine punishment and may therefore be surveyed for how it impinges on the assurance of the proposal that God's punishment is always fair. A tendency in handling this matter, however, is that, parallel to Clements's underlying fiduciary frame of reference, the justice of God is simply assumed, as if any idea to the contrary could not be entertained. Representative of this position, Locke, without seriously substantiating his central point, asserts that

> [a] sharp contrast exists in the Old Testament between the righteous indignation of God and the angry outbursts of man. On the one hand, God's anger is justifiable and develops as a result of the wrongdoing of man. . . . While God's anger is just and deserved, man's anger is often an exhibition of his sinful nature and contradicts the will of God. Man's anger is usually associated with hate and consists of passionate actions intended for the harm of others. These are not righteous actions, and God therefore punishes them.[11]

No doubt there is a generalized grain of truth here. But if, within the internal rhetoric of Isaiah, it can be demonstrated that some of the actions of God are both passionate and intended for the harm of others, then this assertion is undermined. It is undermined especially if the constant though seldom-achieved human task is seeking the well-being of those same "others." Specifically, I examine this issue with respect to the "widows and orphans" category as used in the Isaianic corpus.

Locke also offers the largely unsubstantiated opinion that God's love "is the guiding force in executing judgment. He desires to show mercy, but the nations are often arrogant and proud and do not glorify God."[12] Locke's case is rendered less secure if it can be shown that God also participates in activity motivated and driven by pride (e.g. Isa 48:9–11). According to Locke's conclusion, "Chaos and despair result from his [God's] acts of vengeance; yet he uses these events in order to shape and mold future events. His hope is for a renewed relationship with Judah and for recognition of his justice and righteousness among the nations."[13]

---

11. Jason W. Locke, "The Wrath of God in the Book of Isaiah," *Restoration Quarterly* 35, no. 4 (1993): 221–33 (223–24).

12. Ibid., 233.

13. Ibid., 233.

However, in a literary Isaianic world this proposition is not as convincing as the interpreter would like to think. Textually there is evidence to unsettle it. Thus the perceived experience of excessive punishment by God might not result in the maintenance of an adherence to the idea of justice as intrinsic to the divine character. Instead, justice may be pursued by humanity in the face of divine abandonment. A God who divorces (50:1) and walks out of the covenanted relationship (54:7–8), no matter how justifiably,[14] opens the way for the divorced party to retain a commitment to a value of the former partner. The commitment can be retained without necessarily ever re-embracing the partner with the same degree of trust (if at all). Thus the concept of justice might well emerge from the book of Isaiah more unscathed than the concept of the God of justice.

In his essay "The Meaning and Mystery of Wrath," Heschel initially follows quite closely the contours of Locke's opinions. Arguing that the wrath of God is a contingent and transient matter, he contests that in respect of the divine character, "Anger is an act, a situation, not an essential attribute."[15] It is not, therefore, constituent of and intrinsic to God's being. Moreover, Heschel contends that concern is the central dimension of any manifestation of divine wrath, writing that "the secret of anger is God's care"[16] and concluding that God's "wrath is not regarded as an emotional outburst, as an irrational fit, but rather as part of His continual care" (p. 73). Further, he proposes that:

> The divine pathos, whether mercy or anger, was never thought of as an impulsive act, arising automatically within the divine Being as the reaction to man's behaviour and as something due to peculiarity of temperament or propensity. . . . It comes about in the light of moral judgment rather than in the darkness of passion. (p. 78)

However, in his discussion, Heschel makes a comment that damages the credibility of his argument and raises a serious question concerning the justice of divine ethics. Observing how God's wrath is often concretized and realized within historical processes, he notes that "once the fury

14. At this point, one way to defend the integrity of God is to argue that the divine is leaving a covenant already broken by the other party.
15. Heschel, *The Prophets*, 2:71. Colin Gunton ("Trinity and Trustworthiness," in *The Trustworthiness of God: Perspectives on the Nature of Scripture* [ed. Paul Helm and Carl Trueman; Leicester: Apollos, 2002], 275–84 [282]) observes that "one can conceive of love without wrath, at least in some hypothetical paradisal world, but not without trustworthiness."
16. Heschel, *The Prophets*, 2:72 (subsequent bracketed references in the main text are to this source). One nevertheless is tempted to suggest that with "care" like that inscribed in, say, Isa 24:1–13 the world has no need for the term "abuse."

of the events is unleashed, the innocent suffer as much as the wicked" (p. 75). This is obviously problematic in the way it implicitly acknowledges that God's anger is not always visited exclusively on those who deserve it. The certainty inherent in the rigid polarity of the proposition that divine wrath is always a just and proportionate response to perpetual human sin, which is always deserving of punishment, is thus undercut and invested with a sense of ambiguity rather than absolute assurance.

In light of this observation, some of the "innocent" who are at the receiving end of an acute form of divine anger could be validated in approaching with trepidation divine overtures intended to turn them back toward God. So, Heschel's viewpoint may well not enjoy universal assent when he says:

> The anger of God may bring misery and distress. Nevertheless, there is an agony more excruciating, more loathsome: the state of being forsaken by God. The punishment of being discarded, abandoned, rejected, is worse than the punishment of exile. Anger, too, is a form of His presence in history. Anger, too, is an expression of His concern. (p. 76)

As Laytner, in the words of post-Holocaust poetry, writes:

> O God of mercy
> For the time being
> Choose another people. . . .
> Take back the gift of our separateness.[17]

Or in the tradition of *din Torah*, which re-emerged in the Nazi extermination camps, Laytner quotes the following: "Creator of the worlds, You are mighty and terrible beyond all doubt. But from the circle of true lovers of Israel, we . . . *forever shut You out*."[18] Postbiblical justification of this strain of resistance to God is rooted in the Hasidic milieu, representative of a strand of which the Kotzker rebbe, in something like an echo of the situation implied in Isa 50–54, protests to God, "If You do not keep Your covenant, then neither will I keep the promise, and it is all over: we are through with being Your Chosen People, Your unique treasure."[19]

The nature of divine characterization—inclusive of elements of excess, unreliability, vindictiveness, and violence—that gives rise to this sort of

---

17. Anson Laytner, *Arguing with God: A Jewish Tradition* (Northvale, N.J.: Aronson, 1990), 203. For examples of poetically rendered counter-readings of the biblical text, see Eleanor Wilner, *Sarah's Choice* (Chicago: University of Chicago Press, 1989), esp. 8–9, 21–24.

18. Laytner, *Arguing with God*, 206 (emphasis added).

19. Ibid., 189.

exchange is attested to in the biblical witness. In the Jewish tradition, for example, the Aqedah is problematic for the way God demands the sacrifice of Isaac, the son through whom the promise of family and national growth is supposed to be fulfilled.[20] Focusing on the prophetic material, Brueggemann discerns disconcerting evidence that Jeremiah is abused by God, perhaps even with the undertone that the divine is responsible for rape.[21] The word that gives rise to this possibility, פתה, is also used in 1 Kgs 22:20–22, in which God fully participates in plans to "entice" Ahab to his death. As Brueggemann observes, "Yahweh is at the head of the conspiracy to cause a wrong death in royal Israel. Yahweh here obviously exercises no covenantal self-restraint, but is determined to have Yahweh's own way no matter what the cost, even if it means deceptive violence."[22] The brooding quality of the Bible as a whole in respect of God's character is further accentuated by the way 2 Sam 24:1 attributes David's misguided census of Israel and Judah to incitement by the Lord, while 1 Chr 21:1 charges Satan with responsibility.

Within the Bible there is evidence of suspicion of God and frank acknowledgment of the experience of God as a disturbing agency.[23] There is thus little basis for assuming unquestioningly the probity of God as a fixed point of hermeneutical certitude in the shifting drama of the canonical constellation, since the biblical writers themselves did not do so. On this theme, as noted above, Brueggemann raises the issue of divine commitment to covenant standards. This has implications for the world constructed by the book of Isaiah, for as Holmgren observes, "The conviction that God had bound himself to the Davidic monarchy as well as to the city of Jerusalem was, no doubt, widespread in Judah."[24] The downfall of Jerusalem was consequently a massive challenge to Israelite faith, in reaction to which voices arose questioning whether the "punishment for the nation's sin" was not "excessively cruel."[25] Holmgren identifies the composer of Lamentations as one of the key sources of this

20. See, e.g., Jon D. Levenson, *The Death and Resurrection of the Beloved Son: The Transformation of Child Sacrifice in Judaism and Christianity* (New Haven: Yale University Press, 1993), esp. 82–142.

21. Brueggemann, *Theology of the Old Testament*, 360.

22. Ibid., 361. For a defense of the integrity of God in this passage, which is ultimately not convincing, see P. J. Williams, "Lying Spirits Sent by God? The Case of Micaiah's Prophecy," in Helm and Trueman, eds., *Trustworthiness of God*, 58–66.

23. See, e.g., James L. Crenshaw, *A Whirlpool of Torment: God as Oppressive Presence* (OBT; Philadelphia: Fortress, 1984).

24. Holmgren, *With Wings as Eagles*, 2; see also Otto Eissfeldt, "The Promises of Grace to David in Isaiah 55:1–5," in Anderson and Harrelson, eds., *Israel's Prophetic Heritage*, 196–207.

25. Holmgren, *With Wings as Eagles*, 3, 4.

type of thinking.[26] If, as has been suggested, the book of Lamentations may rightly be construed as occupying a liturgical position between Isa 39 and 40,[27] then one may ask whether Isaiah in its final form participates in this "questioning voice" more than has been recognized.[28]

Brueggemann above also raises the issue of God's overriding determination to get God's own way. Transposed into the world of Isaiah, Brueggemann's point asks about the extent to which the rhetoric of Isa 40–55, representative as it is of a close alignment between prophetic discourse/ideology and the divine voice, is coercive rather than, as has been widely argued, persuasive and inviting.[29] Generally, scholars who have taken seriously the relationship between chs. 1–39 and 40–55/66 have done so in a judgment–promise schema in which the justified punishment announced in the first part of the book gives way to the gracious offer of the second. The implication is that anyone who would resist this graciousness is virtually incomprehensible. However, if the destruction of Jerusalem was, in part at least, experienced as both excessive and covenant-rupturing on the part of God, then those in the text who resist or are wary of God's rapprochement are considerably legitimized. I will be sensitive to these matters to see how they might affect a full-form reading of the text. In essence, the aim is to explore how the decentering of the idea of the justice of God affects viable interpretative options, rendering the text more pondering, questioning, and brooding than has generally been allowed.

4. *Methodological Considerations*

A few methodological points need to be made in order to underpin and clarify what has been said. I scrutinize texts related to the theme of punishment in the spirit of "entering an old text from a new critical

26. See Kathleen M. O'Connor, *Lamentations and the Tears of the World* (Maryknoll, N.Y.: Orbis, 2002), esp. 110–23; see also Tod Linafelt, *Surviving Lamentations: Catastrophe, Lament, and Protest in the Afterlife of a Biblical Book* (Chicago: University of Chicago Press, 2000), esp. 19–79.

27. So Brueggemann, *Isaiah 40–66*, 15–16.

28. Holmgren, *With Wings as Eagles*, 4. However it is understood, the exile is biblically presented as one of those "limit experiences" that challenges simplistic theological articulations. Analogously, Kingsolver (*The Poisonwood Bible*, 368) describes how the fundamentalist missionary in the novel, on the tragic death of his child, for once "had no words to instruct our minds and improve our souls, no parable that would turn Ruth May's death by snakebite into a lesson on the Glory of God." The old simplistic theology was inadequate.

29. For example, as evidenced by the title of Richard Clifford's *Fair Spoken and Persuading: An Interpretation of Second Isaiah* (New York: Paulist, 1984).

direction."[30] Reflexive adherence to the concept of the justice of God is precluded in the interests of generating interpretative possibility and enriching the conceptualization of social justice presented in Isaiah. As Schüssler Fiorenza argues in support of this approach, "[I]t is necessary to uncover the mechanisms and incoherencies of such texts, to see the inconsistencies of our sources, to elaborate the . . . political-theological functions of such texts."[31]

Further underscoring the necessity of a critical, close-reading technique to elucidate how a text functions, Greenblatt writes: "No-one is forced—except perhaps in school—to take aesthetic or political wholes as sacrosanct."[32] One might add that this tendency to force people into accepting certain texts as sacrosanct and therefore beyond question also exists in different forms of religious tradition with regard to what are taken to be sacred texts. However, as Johnson contends concerning texts of clear moral content and import, of which the book of Isaiah in the history of interpretation may be taken as an example:[33]

> If certainty had never produced anything but just and life-affirming results, there would be no need to analyse it. It is because of the self-contradictions and ambiguities already present within the text and the history of even the clearest and most admirable statements that careful reading is essential. Such a reading does not aim to eliminate or dismiss texts or values, but rather to see them in a more complex, more *constructed*, less idealized light.[34]

This represents a helpful programmatic statement of the philosophy of this chapter. It affirms both the seriousness with which the text should be treated and the necessity of paying skeptically close attention to it for how it yields meaning.

In addition, I support Sweeney's assertion that

30. Elisabeth Schüssler Fiorenza (*Bread Not Stone: The Challenge of Feminist Biblical Interpretation* [Boston: Beacon, 1984], 113) cites this as the way "to break the hold of androcentric biblical texts over us," although more generally it may be utilized as a method of ensuring that biblical ideology is not uncritically accepted. It is thus a means of bringing to the surface and observing dimensions of texts that have characteristically been overlooked.

31. Ibid., 113.

32. Stephen Greenblatt, "Resonance and Wonder," in *Literary Theory Today* (ed. Peter Collier and Helga Geyer-Ryan; Cambridge, Mass.: Polity, 1990), 74–90 (76).

33. See John F. A. Sawyer, *The Fifth Gospel: Isaiah in the History of Christianity* (Cambridge: Cambridge University Press, 1996).

34. Barbara Johnson, "The Surprise of Otherness: A Note on the Wartime Writings of Paul de Man," in Collier and Geyer-Ryan, eds., *Literary Theory Today*, 13–22 (21 [emphasis in original]).

scholars can no longer consider the short, self-contained prophetic speech to be the primary basis for the interpretation of prophetic literature. Exegesis can no longer begin with the literary dissection of a prophetic book; this only produces an artificial text. Instead, interpreters must begin with the largest literary unit available, that is, the final form of the prophetic book as a whole, in order to understand the significance of the smaller texts that constitute the text.[35]

Applied to the Isaianic corpus, this means, for example, that a passage like Isa 3:10–11 can no longer be understood simply as a wisdom text.[36] At one level, 3:10–11 is (or more precisely was) a wisdom text, but it ultimately must be placed in the widest possible literary context within the book of Isaiah.[37] Placing it in the larger context enables one to see how that shapes and modifies its meaning, perhaps through the deployment of juxtapositional irony on the part of the implied author or final redactor. In other words, against the atomistic propensity inherent in form and to a degree redaction criticism, this approach takes seriously how the final form of texts in relationship to each other affects meaning in important ways.

Brueggemann, in considered reaction to proposals by Marty,[38] stresses the need to highlight the aniconic[39] as opposed to the iconic aspects of the biblical text. He contests that the Bible

must now be read as the aniconic text of church and synagogue. While the Bible may indeed offer images for the construction of public life, the key task now entrusted to theological education is to see the Bible's aniconic power, its power as a text that breaks images, critiques religion, exposes ideology, identifies hidden interest—out of which comes room for the holiness of God and the newness of humanity.[40]

35. Marvin A. Sweeney, "Formation and Form in Prophetic Literature," in *Old Testament Interpretation: Past, Present, and Future* (ed. James Luther Mays, David L. Petersen, and Kent Harold Richards; Nashville: Abingdon, 1995), 113–26 (115).

36. W. L. Holladay, "Isaiah 3:10–11: An Archaic Wisdom Passage," *VT* 18 (1968): 481–87.

37. As Sweeney notes, "Interpreters must consider not only the *Sitz im Leben* or 'setting in life' of prophetic texts, but the *Sitz im Literatur* or 'literary setting' as well" ("Formation and Form in Prophetic Literature," 115).

38. Martin Marty, "America's Iconic Book," in *Humanizing America's Iconic Book* (ed. Gene M. Tucker and Douglas A. Knight; Chico, Calif.: Scholars Press, 1982), 1–23.

39. See Ronald S. Hendel, "The Social Origins of the Aniconic Tradition," *CBQ* 50 (1988): 365–82.

40. Walter Brueggemann, *Interpretation and Obedience: From Faithful Reading to Faithful Living* (Minneapolis: Fortress, 1991), 104 (emphasis in original). Subsequent bracketed references in the main text are to this source.

Pursuing this contextualized insight regarding the needs of our age, I seek to locate the aniconic within the overall shaping of the book of Isaiah. There is the proviso that, in contrast to Brueggemann's assumption about how the aniconic virtually automatically creates space for human regeneration in tandem with divine holiness, the aniconic might, applied more rigorously, be corrosive of the idea of God's holiness and justice. It might, furthermore, support the analysis that new human possibility emerges in struggle with perceived divine excess.

By being this open to reconceiving the portrayal of the nature and origins of social justice in Isaiah, this reading conforms to Brueggemann's suggestive proposal of the canon as "a *field of authorized possibility* in which we practice new interpretation" rather than "a *field of certitude* for which we already know the right conclusions" (p. 125 [emphasis in original]). For him, the necessity for "a fresh entry into the canon itself for new reading" (p. 125) has been occasioned by "a profound epistemological crisis" rooted in the twin causes of (p. 1) a loss of faith in "Enlightenment objectivity" and (p. 2) "the loss of Western political and economic hegemony, so that traditional claims of power are no more convincing than the old reliable opinions of certitude" (p. 124). Furthermore:

> The loss of *certitude* and the loss of *domination* together open up new interpretive questions. The normative accepted interpretations of canon, either in church or academy, no longer prevail. We are driven back to the literature itself for norming, but that norming no longer honors or conforms to old certitudes or domination. (p. 124 [emphasis in original])

Prospectively aniconic readings are authorized, challenging even such concepts as the justice of God, so long as they can be substantiated by a close reading of the text (p. 134).[41] The text is related, in this instance, to the devastating effect of national humiliation and exile on the Israelite consciousness. As Brueggemann, drawing on an image of interpretation being like "a ship voyaging to an unknown destination, but never arriving and never dropping anchor,"[42] writes: "Literarily, the canon is open literature in which 'every effort of exegesis is justified without argument', as Kermode has observed."[43]

41. Interpretation is governed or, in Brueggemann's terms, rendered "not rudderless" by knowing "the One to whom we must give answer." As Brueggemann says, "This One is the subject of text and interpretation"; however, if the aniconic cuts deep, this relationship to God is eroded, creating more opportunity for the human voice to be heard in its own right, rather than exclusively in relationship to the divine in a perpetual posture of the lesser answering the greater.

42. Mary Douglas and Aaron Wildavsky, *Risk and Culture* (Berkeley: University of California Press, 1982), 192.

43. Brueggemann, *Interpretation and Obedience*, 133–34.

5. *Isaiah 9:16 (ET v. 17): Preliminary Rhetorical Remarks*

Turning toward texts that deal directly with punishment, from the rhetorical perspective in a sequential reading, one is struck with the tension between Isa 9:16 (ET v. 17) and 1:17. Whereas the latter insists on advocacy on behalf of the fatherless and the widow (יתום and אלמנה), the former indicates a withdrawal of divine compassion from them (יתמיו and אלמנתיו). In a sense, the puzzling quality of 9:16 (ET v. 17) is intensified by its proximity to 10:2, where widows and the fatherless are reinstated as the object of divine concern.[44] Before explicating this tension between 1:17 and 9:16 (ET v. 17), I survey the passage in which 9:16 (ET v. 17) is located to determine its basic structure, its thematic interests, and its connections to the wider Isaiah material.

Isaiah 9:7–20 (ET vv. 8–21) is organized around the refrain "Yet for all this, God's anger is not turned away, God's hand is still upraised" (בכל־זאת לא־שב אפו ועוד ידו נטויה; vv. 11, 16, 20 [ET vv. 12, 17, 21]). The recurring image, "which hammers home the point that Yahweh's hand is still stretched out,"[45] is of a more powerful figure threatening a weaker one. Perhaps the image, in light of 1:1 and 1:4–5, is of an already beaten child being further confronted by a father with his hand still upraised in promise of more punishment to come. Young captures the force of the repetition, although without any awareness or acknowledgment of its implied abusive excess, when he graphically and with a disturbing degree of *sangfroid* records how the consequence of the phrase God's "hand is still outstretched" will be

> stroke after stroke and blow after blow. The judgment must run through many stages and courses before its final end is reached. Each day will bring new plagues, new blows, new strokes. What appears to the people to be the end will be followed by still more punishments. Judgment in its completeness will finally come, for the hand of God is still outstretched.[46]

44. David Carr ("Reading Isaiah from Beginning to End," in Melugin and Sweeney, eds., *New Visions of Isaiah*, 188–218 [194–95]) holds the opinion that "very few receivers of Isaiah would have read a text of Isaiah silently and alone" because "reception of ancient texts like the Bible was predominantly oral. . . . Thus most people would have heard the book of Isaiah read aloud," effectively in sections. However, withdrawal of divine support from widows and orphans strikes such a discordant note that even in these circumstances questions might well have been raised in the minds of hearers; furthermore, this reconstruction does not preclude approaching Isaiah as a unity now.

45. Hans Wildberger, *Isaiah 1–12* (trans. Thomas H. Trapp; Continental Commentary; Minneapolis: Fortress, 1991), 224.

46. Young, *The Book of Isaiah*, 1:353.

Laying aside the relish with which Young lingers over this punishment, we can more objectively say that one of the functions of the repetition of this phrase is to underline that we have entered a world in which the rod will certainly not be spared (Isa 10:5).[47] Or perhaps, in terms of the ending of Ps 62, which adroitly summarizes the heart of theodicy, the context is one in which the strength of God is not in doubt (Ps 62:11), although God's love is rather less obvious and pronounced (Ps 62:12).

Rhetorically, the repetition of this phrase divides Isa 9:7–20 (ET vv. 8–21) into three seven-line strophes.[48] The first of these (vv. 7–12 [ET vv. 8–13]) deals with what the prophetic discourse perceives as "pride and arrogance of heart" (9:8 [ET v. 9]), a theme that will be studied more fully later, especially for how it relates to the Isaianic idea of trusting in God alone. The polarity between utterly condemning human pride, arrogance, and haughtiness for relying on human resources and encouraging absolute trust in the Lord is, however, rendered more complex if there is reason to doubt the divine, evidence of which may be discerned in traces of the text. The second strophe (vv. 13–16 [ET vv. 14–17]) presents the whole people of Israel as having gone astray. In this, the reference to "the fatherless and widows" having divine support withdrawn from them ostensibly reinforces the extent and depth of the malaise in national life, although I examine below how rhetorically convincing this ultimately is. The third strophe (vv. 17–20 [ET vv. 18–21]) depicts the destructive and degenerative nature of a society fuelled by "wickedness" (9:17 [ET v. 18]), a society in which "no-one will spare his brother" (9:18 [ET v. 19]) and where there is no satisfaction to be found for hunger (9:19 [ET v. 20]). The image of each feeding "on the flesh of his own seed"[49] (9:19

47. Goldingay (*Isaiah*, 79) recognizes that this is a passage in which the reliability of the character of Yahweh is potentially in doubt, but concludes that "the purpose of the rod is to save the child, not kill it." Goldingay records 10:3 as using "*sho'ah*, the word for total desolation that modern Judaism took as its term for the Nazi attempt to annihilate the Jewish people" (p. 76). In a sense, to frame comments in this way is implicitly to question the proportionality of the justice. In this regard, Suzanne Goldenberg ("Holocaust Outburst Widens Israeli Rift," *Guardian Weekly* [10–16 August 2000]) writes of the furore caused by maverick Rabbi Ovadiah Yosef, who said that "the millions killed in the Nazi Holocaust were sinners," the "reincarnations of earlier souls who sinned time and again and did all sorts of things that shouldn't have been done, and were reincarnated . . . so that things could be set right."

48. Kaiser, *Isaiah 1–12*, 22.

49. Although the Masoretic text literally means "flesh of his own arm," slight emendation of זְרוֹעַ can render "arm" as either "seed/offspring" (זֶרַע) or "neighbor" (רֵעַ) (see Childs, *Isaiah*, 82–83). In my view, the former of these emendations fits in better with the context. Following this option, see the discussion in Oswalt, *The

[ET v. 20]) captures the horror of this world. By way of contrast, the passage counterpoints the world envisioned by 58:6–10, where social solidarity, although costly, generates sharing. A "scorched land" (9:18 [ET v. 19]) is contrasted with "a well-watered garden" (58:11).

That this same phrase also occurs in 5:25 and 10:4 gave rise, in scholarship with the aim of identifying the "original" text and the history of redactional additions, to various theories about how best to reconstitute the different passages in which it is located by a process of "cutting and pasting."[50] In a helpful survey of proposals in this regard, Sweeney observes:

> On the one hand, formal similarities have led many scholars to conclude that 9:7–10:4 constitutes a secondary editorial assemblage and that the original texts were 9:7–20 + 5:25–30, characterized by the refrain "in all this, his anger has not turned and his hand is stretched out still," and 5:8–24 + 10:1–4, characterized by the "woe" form. Although there is some justification for this view, the result of this complication has been a failure to assess adequately the formal and generic characteristics of the *present form of this text.*[51]

Thus, while "10:1–4 clearly corresponds to 5:8–24," for Sweeney it is equally true "that 9:7–20 does not appear to be designed to stand independently from 10:1–4."[52] In other words, 10:1–4, with "its mixture of forms and content from both 9:7–20 and 5:8–24 indicates that it presupposes both passages."[53] Essentially, single categorization of texts precluding a relationship to other texts of a different form or genre is shown to be unnecessary and unsustainable. Consequently the impulse to rearrange texts is supported by no absolute and overriding methodological imperative; they can be read as they are received.

The significance of this is that, viewed rhetorically, Isa 9:6 (ET v. 7)–10:4 is legitimately linked back to 5:8–30 in its present canonical position, which in turn is linked to other passages dealing with "crime and

---

Book of Isaiah: Chapters 1–39, 256; and Blenkinsopp, *Isaiah 1–39,* 216–17. This is the translation favored by the NIV, NLT, and NRSV. For following the latter option and emending "arm" to "neighbor," see Kaiser, *Isaiah 1–12,* 220; John D. W. Watts, *Isaiah 1–33* (WBC 24; Waco, Tex.: Word, 1985), 140–41.

50. See Kaiser, *Isaiah 1–12,* 220–23; also, Marvin A. Sweeney, *Isaiah 1–39* (FOTL 16; Grand Rapids: Eerdmans, 1996), 188–96; Childs, *Isaiah,* 41–44, 83–85; Blenkinsopp, *Isaiah 1–39,* 208–19; W. P. Brown, "The So-Called Refrain in Isaiah 5:25–30 and 9:7–10:4," *CBQ* 52 (1990): 432–43; S. A. Irvine, "The Isaianic *Denkschrift*: Reconsidering an Old Hypothesis," *ZAW* 104 (1992): 216–31.

51. Sweeney, *Isaiah 1–39,* 190 (emphasis added).

52. Ibid., 193.

53. Ibid.

punishment" in related previous chapters of the book. As the call and commissioning of Isaiah (6:1–13) falls between these descriptions of a society given over to bloodshed and cries of distress (5:7), the difficulty (impossibility?) of his mission is heavily underscored, although some sense of future hope is maintained by the eschatological passages 7:13–17 and 9:1–6 (ET vv. 2–7).[54] Furthermore, the idea of Assyria being an instrument of God's punishment, introduced in 7:18b and 8:7, is, as Sweeney has demonstrated, modified and further explicated in 10:5–19 in the way "that Assyria is condemned for the same crimes as northern Israel, including arrogance (10:12–15) and plundering the weak (10:6–11)." As a consequence, "it will suffer the same fate of burning (10:16–19)."[55] For him, "it is clear that the refrain in 9:7–10:4 is intended to lead the reader or hearer not only to the condemnation of the leadership of the northern kingdom of Israel but ultimately to the condemnation of Assyria as well."[56] In this way, the impression is given that God treats Assyria and Israel the same. To a degree, this represents the decommissioning of Israel in the sense that it is divested of its special status before God. Another way of articulating this is to say that God treats all peoples the same, an idea that offers a basis for extrapolating a relationship between 9:7 (ET v. 8)–10:34 and the series of oracles against the nations that starts at ch. 13 and concludes with the judgment in ch. 24. (For example, note how the "head and tail . . . palm branch and reed" formula applied to Israel in 9:13 [ET v. 14] is transposed to Egypt in 19:15.) Whether this treatment is proportionate and just, however, is another matter, especially in light of the violent imagery of 10:26 and 24:1–13.

It may thus be concluded that 9:6 (ET v. 7)–10:4 is a coherent unit (despite reservations by some on the inclusion of 10:1–4) that, in general terms, is integrated and connected to the wider material in which it is found.

6. *Hints of Instability in Meaning*

To those connections already noted, one may be added for its rhetorically curious nature and the issues it raises. In 9:12 (ET v. 13), following the

54. Blenkinsopp (*Isaiah 1–39*, 211) argues that "we thus have three distinct series arranged deliberately so as to provide a framework for the autobiographical and biographical centerpiece." He adds, "It is important to resist the temptation either to impose more order on the book than was ever intended by its redactors or to privilege unduly putative original arrangements" (pp. 211–12). See also Childs, *Isaiah*, 84–85.
55. Sweeney, *Isaiah 1–39*, 191.
56. Ibid.

refrain "Yet for all this, his anger is not turned away, his hand is still upraised" (9:11 [ET v. 12]), the assertion is made that "the people have not (re)turned to him who smites them." The immediate context leads to the conclusion that "to him who smites them" (עד־המכהו) refers directly to God, although the mention of Arameans and Philistines (9:11 [ET v. 12]) means that this (re)turning may, at a remove, carry the implication of arising through the use of these peoples as divine agents. But in 10:20 the referent of "to him that smites them" (על־מכהו) is clearly not God, but Assyria, reliance upon which (שׁען) is presented in opposition to reliance upon Yahweh, the Holy One of Israel. Use of this term is also found in 31:1 (שׁען), again in the context of relying on something that is not God (Egyptian horses), and is immediately contrasted detrimentally with God. Thus, in both cases, God is ostensibly shown as completely different from another option on which one could rely. So, while the broader context of ch. 10 (10:5) and, indeed, the book of Isaiah more generally (8:7), may indicate that Assyria can be understood as God's retributive instrument, in the specifics of 10:20, the rhetoric portrays God and "him that smites them" as distinct and in opposition to each other. Moreover, the language looks toward the day when Israel will refrain from relying on allies who are likely to let down and turn violent, when Israel will "in truth rely on the Lord." The rhetoric of the verse seeks to mask and deny divine sponsorship of violence, as if to, in this verse at least, disassociate the divine from involvement in "striking down." Since, however, this involvement is clearly indicated in 9:12 (ET v. 13), the text is invested with a degree of instability. In a disturbing sense, the projected situation in which Israel finds itself (10:20) is that in abandoning "him that smites them," they will rely on the Holy One of Israel who also smites them, even if only by proxy: a rock-or-a-hard-place scenario. Through close reading of terms that could easily be overlooked as similar, but which, upon closer examination, prove to contain a curious disjunction, the possibility emerges that in its final form the text harbors questions and reservations about the nature of God.

Along the same lines, activities that cause grave offense to God in 10:1–2 are precisely the activities that God sponsors in 10:5–6. So, in a "woe" oracle clearly directed against the ruling elite (10:1, "those who make unjust laws, those who issue oppressive decrees"), this group is castigated for making "widows their spoil" (אלמנות שללם [שׁלל]; 10:2) and "plundering the fatherless" (ואת־יתומים יבזו [בזז]; 10:2). At this point, moreover, God identifies closely with the marginalized in society as indicated by the possessive in the phrase עניי עמי ("the poor of *my* people"). But a few verses later, through God's chosen agency, the

Assyrians, God is implicated in "taking spoil and seizing plunder" (לשלל
שלל ולבז בז; 10:6). In this case the divine purpose is ultimately not
totally destructive (e.g. 10:20–23, with its corrective implication), and,
finally, the king of Assyria will require punishment "for the willful pride
of his heart and the haughty look in his eyes" (10:12). This occurs as if
the king of Assyria has perhaps exceeded divine intentionality, but these
mitigating factors do not erase the fact that lexically God has authorized
and been associated with actions that God previously had condemned.[57]
When not glossed over in the interests of a harmonized reading,[58] this is
another point, perhaps trivial in the eyes of some exegetes, that gives
cause for concern about the character of God.

In additional support of this line of thought, the idea of Assyria being
sent "against a godless nation" (בגוי חנף; 10:6) echoes a similar phrase
(כלו חנף; "everyone is godless") used in 9:16 (ET v. 17). The use of גוי in
relation to Israel, the chosen people, rather than, as is more usual in the
Hebrew Bible, those outside the circle of election, is perhaps another hint
that all nations are being treated alike.[59] In both cases, the designation
"godless" applies to everyone, a conclusion further endorsed by the
wording ועל־עם עברתי ("against the people who anger me"; 10:6). In
this phrase, the term "people" carries the force that it is all the people
who are under divine judgment via the Assyrian rod wielded in God's
(outstretched?) hand. Yet, if the judgment is universal, lacking any
differentiation as to whom within the nation should be punished, it is
peculiar that located between and related to these two passages (9:13–16
[ET vv. 14–17] and 10:5–6), which bespeak condemnation for all (note
how the first explicitly includes "widows and the fatherless"), one
passage forcefully insists that the "woe" will be to those who oppress the
poor, inclusive of "widows and the fatherless." To the extent that God
promotes and initiates such oppressive behavior (i.e. the shadow of the
divine behind the "seizing" and the "plundering" of the Assyrians in

57. Goldingay (*Isaiah*, 79) observes that "Yahweh is quite happy for the Assyrians to loot and pillage, without at first seeming to worry too much about atrocities,
war crimes, or the ethics of just war." He also writes that even if human violence is
divinely encouraged, "This does not resolve the difficulty of the fact that violence
seems invariably to beget violence, even when its vision is to terminate it, and even
when the violence is Yahweh's" (p. 79).

58. A hermeneutical principle advocated by Packer, "Hermeneutics and Biblical
Authority," 153.

59. Sawyer makes a similar point in relation to 3:1–15 when he says that "the
'elders and princes' of Judah take their place in the dock alongside the leaders of all
the other nations of the world. Their greed and inhumanity are no better than that of
their gentile neighbours" (*Isaiah*, 1:37).

10:6), God may legitimately be construed, according to the logic of the text, as authorizing and indulging in "godlessness." Again, the text is less determinate, unambiguous, and stable in meaning than might at first be supposed, affirming that "all texts have some degree of openness."[60]

7. The Fatherless and Widows Not Pitied

Perhaps the most striking example of this type of incongruity between thematically and linguistically related texts in proximity to each other is found in the tension generated between 9:16 (ET v. 17) and 10:1–2. Whereas in the former "the fatherless and widows" are prophetically castigated as being as reprobate as everyone else in a disordered society,[61] in the latter "Yahweh emerges again as the defender of *the weakest of my people*, that is, the poor of Judah."[62] What is more, from this book's perspective, which has established the importance of 1:17 as a programmatic statement indicative of the nature and grounding of a concept of social justice in Isaiah as a whole, the *volte face* in the divine attitude reflected in 9:16 (ET v. 17) is contradictory and problematic. The problematic dimension of the text is illuminated and cast into obvious relief by the way in which 10:2 closely corresponds to the thrust of 1:17, thus making 9:16 (ET v. 17) stand out in a more pronounced way.

It may be that 9:16 (ET v. 17) represents something of an exasperated "curse on everybody concerned"-type attitude on the part of the prophetic voice when confronted with perceived widespread wrongdoing that "has reached every level of society."[63] This kind of generalized pronouncement, though, fails to appreciate how the mechanics of an oppressive state apparatus regularly force the poor to make choices and exhibit patterns of behavior that are less than "honest" and "lawful," however these socially conditioned terms are understood.[64] Besides, this

---

60. John Goldingay, "How Far Do Readers Make Sense? Interpreting Biblical Narrative," in Trueman, Gray, and Blomberg, eds., *Solid Ground*, 172–89 (183).

61. Part of what Crenshaw terms "a *massa damnationis*" ("Introduction: The Shift from Theodicy to Anthropodicy," in his edited volume, *Theodicy in the Old Testament*, 1–16).

62. David Stacey, *Isaiah 1–39* (Epworth Commentaries; London: Epworth, 1993), 77 (emphasis added).

63. Oswalt, *Book of Isaiah: Chapters 1–39*, 255.

64 This, perhaps, should not come as much of a surprise since, as 10:1 concedes, the laws are themselves unjust (see Blenkinsopp, *Isaiah 1–39*, 212–13; Childs, *Isaiah*, 86–87). In this general area, the late Pope John Paul II said that in situations of extreme oppression, it is moral and legitimate for the poor to expropriate what they need from the rich in order to survive and sustain life.

analytically inadequate blanket condemnation,[65] so often the approach of the socially privileged (amongst whom, so far as can be discerned, the literary character Isaiah is located), still does not satisfactorily resolve the rhetorical disjunction between texts that urge the defense of the poor and a text that, against this grain, denounces them as being as guilty of sin as those who have oppressed them. It may be that the poor do participate in wrongdoing, but the precise nature of this wrongdoing would need to be identified in order to show how the poor, in a sweeping universal condemnation, warrant the same punishment as those who oppress them. Attention thus needs to be devoted to the specific terms by which "the fatherless and widows" are condemned alongside the elders, prominent men, and prophets (9:14 [ET v. 15]) to evaluate how rhetorically persuasive this strategy is. The rhetorical strategy also needs to be assessed in light of the broader pattern of prophetic denunciation, particularly in the opening chapters of Isaiah, to see if the idea of "universal Israelite sin," in the main, accords with that broader pattern.[66]

A sense of the perplexing and peculiar quality of 9:16 (ET v. 17) is reflected in the comments of several scholars. Sawyer dubs the passage in which it is located as "a unique attack on the whole of Israelite society ... whatever their status." Sawyer subsequently writes that "even widows and orphans are godless fools (v. 17) and can expect no compassion. This is the only passage in the Old Testament where their suffering is included in a picture of judgment."[67] Stacey acknowledges that "it is a shock to read that Yahweh intended the slaughter of 'the fatherless and widows,' the very groups whose cause he champions in 1:17, 23 and elsewhere."[68] Skinner speaks of "the unwonted severity of the threat against the widows and orphans," even if he adds contradictorily that the threat "is justified by the universal corruptness of the nation."[69] A similar feeling

---

65. This issue still has an afterlife in the Middle East. Jonathan Steele quotes a disaffected Israeli soldier who terms the present policy of the Israeli government toward the Palestinians as a "mechanism of collective punishment" ("Soldier Battling for His People's Soul," *Guardian Weekly* [31 October–6 November 2002]). Similarly, a *Guardian* editorial acknowledges that "that the men and women who created Israel wanted it to be a country based on freedom, justice and peace" (*Guardian Weekly* [24–31 May 2001]). The editorial further argues that "it is difficult to see the treatment of the Palestinian population as a whole as anything other than an indefensible form of collective punishment for the deeds of the few."

66. As Derek Mahon writes, the idea seems to be that "the something rotten in the state / Infects the innocent" ("The Sea in Winter," in *Poems, 1962–1978* [Oxford: Oxford University Press, 1979], 111).

67. Sawyer, *Isaiah*, 1:104–5.

68. Stacey, *Isaiah 1–39*, 76.

69. Skinner, *The Book of the Prophet Isaiah*, 1:80.

concerning the unusual and arresting nature of this verse can be adduced when Delitzsch comments that God "will deny his wonted compassion *even* to widows and orphans,"[70] as if this contains a shocking strand of meaning. Furthermore, Widyapranawa acknowledges that the totality of condemnation meant that "innocent babes and defenceless widows would necessarily suffer along with the leadership that was responsible for setting the nation's policy."[71]

Similarly, Calvin also reveals a level of unease at the intention of God in respect of punishing the fatherless and widows. In comments that derive from and are influenced by his broader ethical thought-world,[72] Calvin nervously observes that "vengeance of God against all ranks" invariably means "that neither boys nor youths, nor widows, will be exempted, who are usually spared even among heathens at the sacking of towns, as we learn from history."[73] Essentially, Calvin is anxious that by inaugurating a campaign in which widows and orphans will be treated as mercilessly as everyone else, God will be leaving God's self open to the accusation of operating by moral standards lower than those of an average heathen.

For Young, who views the society addressed by Isaiah as antediluvian in the depths of its sinfulness, the use of the rhetorical question "What, however, about the widows and orphans, over whom God had expressed concern and to whom he had shown mercy?"[74] indicates that at least he recognizes there potentially is a case to answer that God will be acting out of character if God directs divine anger against widows and orphans. The implication of his conclusion, however, that God is fully justified in pursuing this course of action, is that Isaiah's Israel is actually worse

70. Delitzsch, *Biblical Commentary on the Prophecies of Isaiah*, 1:254 (emphasis added).

71. S. H. Widyapranawa, *The Lord is Saviour: Faith in National Crisis—A Commentary on the Book of Isaiah* (ITC; Grand Rapids: Eerdmans, 1990), 56. He seeks to explain this in a way comparable to Skinner.

72. See D. F. Wright, "Accommodation and Barbarity in John Calvin's Old Testament Commentaries," in *Understanding Poets and Prophets: Essays in Honour of George Wishart Anderson* (ed. A. Graeme Auld; JSOTSup 152; Sheffield: JSOT, 1993), 413–27. See also E. A. Dowey, *The Knowledge of God in Calvin's Theology* (New York: Columbia University Press, 1952); F. L. Battles, "God was Accommodating Himself to Human Capacity," *Int* 31 (1977): 19–38; S. D. Benin, "The 'Cunning of God' and Divine Accommodation," *Journal of the History of Ideas* 45 (1984): 179–91; A. G. Baxter, "What Did Calvin Teach about Accommodation?," *Evangel* 6, no. 1 (1988): 20–22.

73. Calvin, *Commentary on the Book of the Prophet Isaiah*, 1:325.

74. Young, *Book of Isaiah*, 1:352.

than "the time before the flood,"[75] for no Noah-figure can be found who merits exemption from the divine ire. The further logical implication of this line of thought is that (e.g. contra 3:10) there is not one "righteous" person in Israel for whom "it will be well." Thus, since there is no righteous figure to be spared the coming doom and to make a fresh start when it has passed, the Isaianic concept of the remnant (e.g. 1:25–26; 10:20–23) must be understood as being composed of well-punished "sinners." These "sinners," through experience of divine wrath, return to a God who initially, in the world constructed by the book of Isaiah, advocates the defense of "widows and orphans" (1:17 etc.). But this God later deems them worthy of inclusion in a general damnation (9:16 [ET v. 17]).

Related to this point, Seitz, in connection with 9:13–17, observes that

> just as in chapter 1, where the survivors should have taken care to incul-cate righteousness and justice in Jerusalem, so too Israel's *leaders* fail to learn from the preceding episodes of judgment visited upon the Northern Kingdom: "the people did not turn to him who struck them, or seek the Lord of Hosts" (9:13). So extensive is Israel's refusal to turn that God has no compassion even on those normally deserving of mercy: the orphans and widows (9:17). Everyone—even the orphan and the widow—is god-less.[76]

There is, however, something here that is forced, logically questionable, and overstretched without sufficient substantiation. If it is "Israel's leaders" who are principally responsible for the state of the nation and who "fail to learn from the preceding episodes of judgment," it is not obviously or immediately apparent why ultimately punishment is also extended to widows and orphans.[77] Again there is an equivocal quality inherent in the text, which, as represented by Seitz, some commentators attempt to resolve by recourse to a chain of reasoning bereft of key links.[78] In conjunction with the comments above in relation to the implications of Young's analysis, within the text itself the concept of (re)turning to God is from the outset signaled as fraught with grounds for reservations, questions, and problems. On this evidence, the God encoded in Isaiah deserves to be approached with a high degree of trepidation; the decision to turn toward this deity with the hope and intention of inclusion

---

75. Ibid.

76. Christopher R. Seitz, *Isaiah 1–39* (Interpretation; Louisville, Ky.: John Knox, 1993), 90 (emphasis added).

77. As Davies (*Double Standards in Isaiah*, 133) observes, "The suggestion that all Israel is culpable perhaps makes for a surprising conclusion, since just about all the evils Isaiah lists . . . seem to be far more applicable to the governing classes."

78. See also Childs, *Isaiah*, 86, for an example of this.

in the remnant community is not one that can be made with transparent ease.[79]

For all of the unease and reservation cataloged above, several scholars hastily move on to justify the divine will in its punitive intent toward the fatherless and widows. One scholar, displaying an attitude verging on the callously dismissive, notes that people "are all utterly corrupt on all sides."[80] Another, having registered "shock" at what God is about to do, then immediately casually concludes, "Nevertheless, so wicked is the nation that the punishment must be as harsh as this."[81] Yet another, with only a slight, but never seriously entertained, acknowledgment that anything might be amiss, writes that "it is a righteous judgment, for all of the people . . . are profane."[82] In a like fashion, Calvin, so that people "may not accuse God of cruelty," argues that the divine "shows that there are good reasons why he [God] is so severe, because they are all wicked, and therefore that they deserve to be cast headlong to ruin without any distinction."[83] Along the same lines, Motyer asserts that since "God's truth had been openly preached to them," both "leaders and led" are consequently "culpable," although interestingly he is quick to explain that "the lord is not a God of capricious fury."[84]

This approach is grounded in the circular reasoning that if God is understood to have said something, then it must be simply accepted as true. Consequent interpretation of the specific terms by which the universal punishment is justified is significantly determined by this prior hermeneutical presupposition.[85] These terms will be closely examined below to see if they contain seeds of an alternative reading that acquiesces less immediately with the surface rhetoric and theology of the text. The purpose is to explore if the text, read as part of the work as a whole, is more nuanced, tensive, ponderingly reflective, and subversive than has been proposed.

79. Especially, perhaps, on the part of the poor. As Davies argues, "God rarely punishes only the right people. . . . [A]s ever, it is the underprivileged groups of society which suffer most" (*Double Standards in Isaiah*, 131).

80. Delitzsch, *Biblical Commentary on the Prophecies of Isaiah*, 1:254.

81. Stacey, *Isaiah 1–39*, 76.

82. Young, *Book of Isaiah*, 1:352.

83. Calvin, *Commentary on the Book of the Prophet Isaiah*, 1:325.

84. Motyer, *The Prophecy of Isaiah*, 109.

85. In Calvin, Delitzsch, Young, Motyer, and Oswalt, for example, usage of these terms from the wider biblical literature is only quoted if it is perceived to support the case being made. Usage that might call into question this homogenization and possibly open different, perhaps more tensive, lines of interpretation, is not cited.

From a slightly different perspective and introducing a new element into the discussion, Wright, wary of and resistant to the concept of "the preferential option for the poor,"[86] highlights Isa 9:14–17 precisely because in it God does not turn "a blind eye to the sins of the poor, as if poverty and oppression in themselves rendered their victims spotless and innocent."[87] According to Wright, "Rather, this group in society receives God's special attention because they are on the 'wronged' side of a situation of chronic injustice which God abhors and wishes to have redressed. For God's righteous will to be done requires the execution of justice on their behalf."[88] While there is an element of truth in this, it is also problematic, first in the way it precludes the poor from being subjects of their own liberation from injustice. The second problem is the extent to which Wright never clarifies how the "chronic injustice" experienced by the poor, symbolized by widows and orphans, is going to be rectified while at the same time they are severely punished (looted and plundered, 10:6) for their reputed contribution to "the total corruption of the nation."[89]

To be fair, Wright does not pretend to treat this Isaianic passage extensively or in depth, either in itself or for how it is related to the rest of the book of Isaiah. It is rather marshaled as a proof text for a particular argument. But his comments, rooted in the assumption that God is beyond reproach in punishing everyone, even the socially sinned-against widows and orphans,[90] illustrate the need for identifying as accurately as

---

86. There is a sizeable literature on this subject, but see, *inter alia*, Gustavo Gutiérrez, *A Theology of Liberation: History, Politics, and Salvation* (trans. and ed. Sister Caridad Inda and John Eagleson; London: SCM Press, 1974), esp. 287–306; idem, *We Drink from Our Own Wells: The Spiritual Journey of a People* (London: SCM Press, 1984), esp. 122–27; idem, *The Power of the Poor in History*, esp. 111–24; idem, "Option for the Poor," in *Systematic Theology: Perspectives from Liberation Theology* (ed. Jon Sobrino and Ignacio Ellacuria; London: SCM, 1996), 22–37; idem, "A Preferential Option for the Poor," in *Classic Texts in Mission and World Christianity* (ed. Norman E. Thomas; Maryknoll, N.Y.: Orbis, 1995), 193–95; Maria Arlinda Rodriquez and Heloise da Cunha, "Living with the Poor in Brazil," in *Trends in Mission: Toward the Third Millennium* (ed. William Jenkinson and Helene O'Sullivan; Maryknoll, N.Y.: Orbis, 1993), 216–25.

87. Christopher J. H. Wright, *Living as the People of God: The Relevance of Old Testament Ethics* (Leicester: InterVarsity, 1983), 147.

88. Ibid.

89. Ibid.

90. Davies captures the anomaly in the situation in his assessment that "the young, the orphans and widows would suffer as a result of God's judgment on the corrupt leaders who had left them hopeless and helpless, and, once again, they are not principally the ones to blame" (*Double Standards in Isaiah*, 133).

possible who, in Isaiah, is condemned and for what. Finally, what is the sin of the poor? Does their condemnation cohere with the general pattern of the rhetoric of punishment, especially in the opening stages of Isaiah? If there is a degree of dissonance and disjunction in this, how may it be accounted for?

By deploying an interpretative strategy that envisages the widespread and indiscriminate suffering in Israel as a necessary function or by-product of warfare, a few scholars take a step toward moderating and ameliorating the most objectionable aspects of the idea of God directly and flagrantly acting as an agent of retribution, especially against widows and orphans. Illustrative of this stance, Stacey contends that "when villages are overrun by a savage enemy, no one is spared."[91] Explicating the mechanics by which this process occurs, Oswalt infers that upon the withdrawal of divine support from the young men (עַל־בַּחוּרָיו לֹא־יִשְׂמַח אֲדֹנָי; 9:16 [ET v. 17]), who may be understood as warriors, "they are defeated and there is no help for the defenceless at home."[92] Operating in the same conceptual stream, Brueggemann conceives that divine "pun-ishment, instigated by Yahweh and executed by foreigners, has caused a brutal diminishment of the people, especially the leadership (vv. 14–18), so that Israel must now live in a context where there is no pity, compas-sion, or mercy (v. 17a)."[93] In this view, which Calvin considers only to reject,[94] the impression of distance is put between God and the actuality of war-induced mayhem by the attributing of this mayhem to the "natu-ral" processes derivative of and attendant on the reality of war. The focus is more on the human element that creates the horror of war than on the divine root cause, which is consequently downplayed. This construal, however, attractive for the way it sequences and unifies divine will and its expression in felt experience, contains the implicit difficulty that while God can announce the need for punishment, God cannot finally control its enactment with precision. In the mess of war the innocent suffer, for God does not have any "smart" bombs at the divine disposal.[95] On account of this difficulty, to function coherently this understanding must of necessity presuppose the guilt of everyone, even though, as noted earlier, this then opens the possibility of God being accused of war

91. Stacey, *Isaiah 1–39*, 76.
92. Oswalt, *Book of Isaiah: Chapters 1–39*, 255.
93. Brueggemann, *Isaiah 1–39*, 89.
94. Calvin, *Commentary on the Book of the Prophet Isaiah*, 1:325. Concluding his discussion of this issue, he notes that this possibility "does not greatly affect the general meaning" of the verse, which is likely true.
95. The intelligence of which has been belied in our own age by the amount of "collateral" damage they have caused.

crimes and crimes against humanity for what is planned against widows and orphans. The assertion that "the prophet insists that the public process is a moral fabric" may be more partial than absolute, carrying no ringing conviction or unalloyed persuasiveness.[96]

Still operating within this interpretative ambit, perhaps the most generous and appealing understanding of 9:16 (ET v. 17) from a social-justice perspective would be, in light of a text like Exod 22:22–24, to view the reference to the fatherless and widows as part of the outworking of the punishment visited on the exploitative oppressors of Israel.[97] Accordingly, those among the upper echelons of Israelite society who have participated in the abuse of Israel's widows and orphans will themselves be punished by having their families reduced, at their own demise, to the state of widow- and orphanhood. In this reading, those who have taken advantage of widows and orphans (contra Exod 22:22), as reportedly happened in the society addressed by Isaiah, will be killed by the sword (22:24). In this instance it will be the sword of the invader, as a result of which rulers' wives "will become widows" and their children "fatherless" (22:24). There are advantages to this interpretation: it retains some sense of retributive justice in the way that what is done to others ("the least of these") by the ruling elite is eventually done to them. Although themselves being dead, they would not be aware of the poetic symmetry to which their punishment gave rise. Furthermore, the disturbing notion of God attacking even the poorest of the poor in society is considerably reduced: true to the exodus tradition, God can still be conceived as being on the side of the poor.

There are also, however, disadvantages and problems. At one level, it stretches credulity to imagine that the attentions of an invading army could be directed solely to those who most deserved it (as a concept, "smart swords" is no more trustworthy than "smart bombs"). It probably is credible, though, that invaders focused on members of the ruling establishment more intentionally and provided them more "individual" treatment than those further down the hierarchy (Jer 29:2). Nevertheless, the brutality of war adversely affected all levels of society, even widows and orphans. Moreover, this reading, particularly amenable to a liberationist hermeneutic, is not supported by a close reading of the text.

96. Brueggemann, *Isaiah 1–39*, 89. The problem persists that "by far the greater part of Isaiah's ethical system is really only applicable to the upper classes of society, and hardly a mention is made of the sins and temptations to which the lower classes would have been drawn" (Davies, *Double Standards in Isaiah*, 135).

97. Kaiser (*Isaiah 1–12*, 225), by reference to Exod 22:21–24, acknowledges the possibility of this interpretation.

Strictly speaking, it might be argued that in 9:16 (ET v. 17) the fatherless and widows are actually singled out as worse than everyone else since the כלו ("every one") refers immediately back to them. This is likely, though, being too rhetorically fastidious, and the "every one" should be taken in context to condemn the whole of society equally.

Furthermore, this approach by no means resolves the problem of violence related to the characterization of God, for the essential thrust of this depiction of justice and punishment is that God acts very much like those God condemns. If widows and orphans are oppressed, God generates more widows and orphans in response. Heschel, effectually arguing in support of the exercise of divine anger on behalf of the poor, rhetorically asks, "Is it a sign of cruelty that God's anger is aroused when the rights of the poor are violated, when widows and orphans are oppressed?"[98] But how the mobilization of God's anger against the oppressor actually assists the oppressed is not detailed. Thus, if Exod 22:22–24 is posited as governing the meaning of Isa 9:16 (ET v. 17) intertextually, a pattern of punishment effected in terms replicating the original offence is manifest. Analogous to this, in comments on another biblical passage in which God sides with the wronged poor against the rapacious rich (1 Sam 12:11–12), Linafelt acerbically observes that God's punishment of David is for God to propose acting in the same way as the original transgressor: "Yahweh says 'I will take your women in your sight and give them to your neighbor, and he shall sleep with your women in the sight of this sun.'"[99] In both these cases, not only is God implicated in behavior equivalent, if not identical, to the initial wrong, thereby perpetuating a cycle of violence, but the wronged party is not substantially assisted, healed, or offered the possibility of just reconciliation with their oppressor.

However this reference to the divine relationship to widows and orphans is explained, God is to a greater or lesser degree tainted by association with disturbing violence and implicated in its perpetuation.[100] Again the question is raised as to whether a careful full-form reading of Isaiah offers clues about how this particular cycle might be broken. In pursuit of both an answer to this and further elucidation of why God

98. Heschel, *The Prophets*, 2:65.

99. Tod Linafelt, "Taking Women: Readers/Responses/Responsibility in Samuel," in *Reading between Texts: Intertextuality and the Hebrew Bible* (ed. Danna Nolan Fewell; LCBI; Louisville, Ky.: Westminster John Knox, 1992), 99–113.

100. See also Isa 13:14–16 for a graphically presented example of divine sponsorship of prisoners of war summarily executed ("thrust through . . . by the sword," 13:15), infants dashed to pieces before their parents' eyes, houses looted, and wives raped (13:16).

condemns everyone in Israel, I examine the terms by which this condemnation is supported and justified for any illumination they might give
about how this problematic passage functions when read closely.

8. *Ungodliness, Justice, and Divine Reliability*

The unsettling announcement that the nation in its entirety, inclusive of
widows and orphans, is so corrupt that it is utterly deserving of punishment is justified by the threefold accusation that everyone is "godless"
(חנף), "an evildoer" (ומרע), and, further, that they are speaking "folly" or
senselessness (נבלה; 9:16 [ET v. 17]). Rhetorically, the first two categories are introduced by כלו, as is the third (וכל). In this configuration, the
initial reasons given for punishing the whole nation come in the form of
general designations of wrongdoing, while, as Motyer notes, "The only
sin specified by name is the sin of speech."[101]

The pattern adopted by some commentators in dealing with these
categories is to pass over them in silence,[102] as if they are self-explana-
tory. More representatively, others cite a few scattered examples of their
usage in the wider biblical literature (presumably to act as some sort of
control group of texts). In addition, these scholars relate the categories to
other Isaianic passages to which they are not strictly speaking connected
on any intrinsic grounds, as if to suggest that these uses are typical illus-
trations. So, addressing the meaning of חנף, Motyer, in support of his
thesis that the word "is used particularly of apostasy,"[103] links its usage to
Jer 3:1, 9, and Ps 106:38, all of which represent verbal forms of the term.
He does not first explore how the word is used within the world of Isaiah
and in comparable adjectival formulations to see if they more immediately clarify, modify, or add nuance to its meaning. This would be a
more exegetically sound methodology.

With respect to נבלה, Motyer cites 1 Sam 25:25 and Ps 14:1 as
illustrative of the phenomena and Isa 3:8 and 6:5 as manifestations of its
spoken form.[104] Oswalt concurs with the citation of Ps 14:1 as a member
of the control group of texts and Isa 6:5 as an example of its appearance
in the Isaiah text, in addition to which he adds to each category, respectively, Gen 34:7; Josh 7:15; Judg 19:24; and Isa 5:20. It is accepted that
מרע has such a wide biblical usage that it warrants no particular further
attention. However, against general scholarly practice, I propose that חנף

---

101. Motyer, *Prophecy of Isaiah*, 109.
102. So, e.g., Sawyer, *Isaiah*, 1:105.
103. Motyer, *Prophecy of Isaiah*, 109.
104. Ibid.

and נבלה occur a sufficiently restricted number of times in their variant forms to justify a closer and more systematic examination. This is to see if other levels of meaning may plausibly be perceived in 9:16 (ET v. 17) in addition to and perhaps in conflict with those determined by the methodology outlined above.

Young helpfully directs our attention to 32:6 as a characteristic example of the nature of "folly," but does not draw out the implications that this depiction of the term, grounded as it is in the concept of social justice, has for how 9:16 (ET v. 17)[105] might be read, especially in light of the fact that the חנף–נבלה word pair is also found in this verse. In this instance (32:6), both folly and godlessness are constituted by a pattern of behavior that leaves the hungry empty, that withholds water from the thirsty (32:6), and that is devoted to concocting "evil schemes to destroy the poor with lies, even when the plea of the needy is just" (32:7). In essence, "folly" and "godlessness" have a particular social-justice connotation in the thought-world of Isaiah.[106] That this type of godless folly is more the sin of the rich and powerful rather than that of the poor and helpless (widows and orphans?) is underscored by the way in which nobility (נדיב) is associated with foolishness, and apparent social respectability (שוע) with actual knavery in 32:5. The implication is that folly and godlessness, so defined, are much more prevalent among the ruling elite of society, who have the scope to indulge themselves in them on account of their societal position.

Furthermore, this social-justice dimension inherent in Isaiah's use of חנף is maintained in 33:14 (חנפים), the only other time the word is used in an adjectival or noun form in the book. Here, godless sinners, it may be inferred, are those who do not "speak what is right," those who exact "gain from extortion," derive income "from accepting bribes," turn a deaf ear "against plots of murder," and close a blind eye "against contemplating evil" (33:15). To the extent that these crimes are more characteristically perpetrated and/or tolerated by the upper echelons of society, who are entrusted with its just governance, again godlessness is linked more closely and directly with the rich than with the poor.

Thus, if, as has been demonstrated, "godlessness" in Isaiah is more representatively a function of how the rulers treat the ruled, then the reference in 9:16 (ET v. 17) to everyone being godless stands in disjunction. No doubt, in a disordered world, the poor are as capable, in the lesser

---

105. Young, *Book of Isaiah*, 1:352.

106. Gutiérrez quotes a Bolivian peasant, Paz Jiménez, as saying that an atheist, that is, a "godless" person, is one who "fails to practice justice toward the poor" (*Power of the Poor in History*, 140).

ways open to them, of pursuing some of the ways of injustice as the rich.[107] But even this construal still implies that there are some poor who are being mistreated by a combination of people: those presiding over and benefiting from an unjust social order; and folk from their own social strata who, for whatever reason (perhaps in order to survive), have broken solidarity with their own class and participated in activity ultimately detrimental to its best interests. Given these contexts of how חָנֵף is deployed in the Isaianic corpus, the universal condemnation of 9:16 (ET v. 17), reinforced by 10:6 (חָנֵף), is undermined and rendered insecure. This is true particularly, as noted above, for the way God in 10:6 is associated with the type of looting and plundering disavowed in 10:2.

There is also evidence in the wider biblical literature to support the contention that the practice of godlessness is related to a mode of behavior that damages the poor. In Ps 35, the beleaguered poet asserts that the Lord rescues "the poor from those too strong for them, the poor and needy from those who rob them" (Ps 35:10). In this assertion, the poet states his confidence that God will rescue him from the "attackers gathered against" him (Ps 35:15), amongst whom "the ungodly" (חָנֵף) are to be found. This confidence, however, may be less than assured, for the psalmist has continually to try to motivate God to what he considers appropriate divine intervention on behalf of himself as a representative of the poor.[108] The psalmist presents himself as someone who has acted with self-sacrificial righteousness, who should, therefore, be able to rely on the righteousness of God. But instead, he encounters a situation in which his prayers return to him unanswered: in the silence of God, the reliability of God is called into question. This issue of divine reliability is one that, in variant form, has concerned the exploration of Isa 9:16 (ET v. 17).

---

107.   For example, in Mobutu's Zaire, if low-ranking government functionaries and police officers had not taken bribes, they would never have received any income, for central government had ceased to pay them. No doubt taking bribes was corrupt, but it was a different order of corruption (in some ways it was a necessary part of survival) than that of Mobutu and his Western backers, who were the originators and perpetuators of a vast system of exploitation geared to their self-aggrandizement. See George, *A Fate Worse than Debt*, 106–18. To condemn such "corrupt" officials in the same breath as Mobutu in a blanket condemnation is to misunderstand the issues and compound the injustice; Western commentators are prone to this kind of superficial analysis. The parallels to the world of Isa 9:16 (ET v. 17) need not be labored.

108.   "Contend, O Lord, with those who contend with me, fight against those who fight against me" (35:1); "O Lord, how long will you look on?" (35:17); "O Lord, you have seen this; be not silent. Do not be far from me, O Lord. Awake, and rise to my defense! Contend for me. . . . Vindicate me . . ." (35:22–24).

Related to this theme of divine reliability, the only other time חנף is used in Isaiah occurs in 24:5. The same type of announcement of all-inclusive punishment (24:2) as is found in 9:13–14 (ET vv. 14–15) is extended to global (and ultimately cosmic) proportions ("See, the Lord is going to lay waste the earth" [24:1]).[109] Again, God is depicted as an agent of plunder, this time in a particularly intensive form (והבוז תבוז, 24:3). This intensity is accentuated by the way the reference to the plundering God follows immediately after another infinitive-absolute construction (הבוק תבוק הארץ, 24:3), through which God is identified as the ultimate source of the projected wasting of the earth. In an atmosphere redolent with destructive force, in which, in the first verse of the chapter, God is linked to a barrage of verbs of violence (עוה ,בלק ,בקק, פוץ [all in 24:1]), the destructive impulse is acutely maintained in the infinitive-absolute constructions of v. 3. By v. 4, the earth "withers" (נבל; used twice in the verse) and "languishes" (אמל; also used twice).

At this point of exhaustion, after the divine onslaught, it is asserted that "the earth is defiled" (חנף).[110] Webb argues that "this passage shows us a world so abused by those to whom it was entrusted that it can no longer sustain life: it has been 'defiled by its people.' "[111] Significantly though, Webb does not point out that even if this "withering" and "languishing" of the earth in part originates as a result of having been defiled by humanity rather than divine punishment, God's intended judgment for the initial offense will arguably cause more damage to the earth than the offense itself. In a similarly one-eyed view that looks only at human wrongdoing, Motyer writes: "It is intrinsic to the doctrine of creation that human beings in sin are the supreme environmental threat."[112] The potential impact of 24:1 for the earth eludes him in this evaluation, for in punishing humanity for defiling the earth, God will reduce the earth to a wasteland. Could it speak, the earth might well complain about the efficacy of this treatment.[113] This may be taken as another example of the

---

109. Interpreting this text as the start of an apocalyptic (or at least eschatological) piece, the majority of the scholarly community agree that הארץ refers to the whole earth (so Otto Plöger, *Theocracy and Eschatology* [Oxford: Blackwell, 1968], 73). See also, *inter alia*, Kaiser, Webb, Oswalt, Motyer, and Brueggemann in their commentaries. While Watts (*Isaiah 1–33*, 315–17) cautions against this somewhat, the context of 24:1 does suggest a comprehensive ambit.

110. This sense of "pollution" or "defilement" is also found in Jer 3:1, 2, 9; Ps 106:36; Mic 4:11; Num 35:33 (twice).

111. Webb, *The Message of Isaiah*, 106.

112. Motyer, *Prophecy of Isaiah*, 197.

113. One of the dangers of aligning oneself too closely and easily with a God of such wanton destructive power is that, in the modern world, this power has, in

disturbing nature of punishment with respect to 2 Sam 12:11 and Isa 9:16 (ET v. 17), if Exod 22:22–24 is thought in any way to lie behind the meaning of the Isaiah text.

Interestingly, with regard to 24:1–4, commentators tend not to jump immediately to the defense of God for the proposed massive destruction. Rather, it is as if the scale and intensity of the looming apocalyptic horizon gives momentary cause for unease, even if this is swiftly resolved in support of the divine intent. Motyer, a convinced adherent of the school of thought that automatically places God above reproach, correctly notes that "the emphasis is on total devastation" and that "no-one will escape." But he adds, "[Y]et no charge is levelled. The word of the Lord has been spoken . . . but the verses offer no justification for it."[114] In other words, the poetry of the passage does not necessarily portray God's intended activity as reasonable, rational, or proportionate: other interpretative options are viable and available.

Motyer, however, finds a way of maintaining his reading stance by saying that the disturbing "section cannot stand alone but needs the remainder of the poem, and especially . . . verses 18b–20, to complete the picture."[115] Strictly speaking, those verses are themselves largely descriptive, and the inference that the guilt of the earth's rebellion is so heavy that it deserves anything and everything it gets from God is only convincing and plausible if there is a prior commitment to the idea of God being above reproach. Motyer's reading is thus based on a version of circular reasoning and does not expunge the sense that, in the opening verses of Isa 24, God is presented in a disturbing fashion.

Addressing this presentation, Oswalt argues that "it must be asserted that the writer is more concerned with images than with logic. He wants his hearers to picture the teeming, abundant earth as an abandoned heap

---

certain quarters, been translated into a positive understanding of the threat of nuclear holocaust (e.g. Hal Lindsay, *The Late Great Planet Earth* [Grand Rapids: Zondervan, 1970]). Even more dangerously, some (e.g. Ronald Reagan) were comfortable with the idea of conceiving of themselves as the human agency through which the holocaust could come about. It is one thing to posit that the divine has such awesome power, but quite another to imagine that one has the right, in human capacity, to assist in the exercise of it. One should consider Num 35:33, which links pollution or defilement to bloodshed, atonement for which can only be made "by the blood of the one who shed it." Since certain Isaianic texts clearly identify God as having blood on the divine hands—for example, Isa 13:16 graphically depicts infants having their heads battered as part of God's punishment of the "world for its evil" (13:11)—this God needs to be reconceptualized.

114. Motyer, *Prophecy of Isaiah*, 197.
115. Ibid.

when God finishes with it." Oswalt concludes, "Precisely how it becomes that way does not seem to be a major concern of his."[116] Noticeably, that God is heavily involved in this vast destruction, and the implications deriving from this fact, are not a major concern of Oswalt. It does not register that one of the reasons "that the writer is more concerned with images than with logic" could be the artistic intent of presenting God as acting beyond logic and thus rightly to be wondered at, doubted, feared, and questioned. One supposes that such things do not need to be acknowledged, much less pondered, if on grounds extrinsic to but regularly imported into the text the righteousness of God is always assumed.

Also focusing on the imagery of the text, Brueggemann insists that because the poem "is completely lacking in geographical and historical specificity . . . one must stay 'inside the poem' . . . attending to the rhetorical import and emotional intent of the text."[117] Since, however, Brueggemann classifies both 13:9–16 and 24:1–23 as apocalyptic,[118] and the passages are thematically and linguistically linked, it is reasonable to assume that Brueggemann's general comments on the former may apply equally well to the latter. He says, "Yahweh's commitment against pride and insolence[119] is not a reasonable, calculated matter. It is Yahweh's 'gut reaction,' Yahweh's deepest interest completely beyond calculation."[120] According to this reading, although it is not pursued, the text potentially is more open, allowed to speak in its own voice(s) without being controlled by external theological categories. Consequently, the text generates the possibility that, on account of its description, some readers might feel justifiably that God's actions are excessive and disproportionate in their violence.

The legitimacy of understanding the text in this more questioning way is strengthened when one takes account of the way Isa 13:9–16 is linked

116. Oswalt, *Book of Isaiah: Chapters 1–39*, 445.
117. Brueggemann, *Isaiah 1–39*, 190.
118. Ibid., 119 and 190.
119. Oswalt identifies human pride as a central motivating factor for the action of God in Isa 24 (*Book of Isaiah: Chapters 1–39*, 444). He asserts that "human pride and God cannot coexist." Another, more problematic, way of articulating this is to say that divine pride cannot countenance human self-assertion; again God is implicated in the sin God dislikes.
120. Brueggemann, *Isaiah 1–39*, 120. Brueggemann adds: "One might observe that Yahweh's negative energy is paralleled to that of the insolent and the proud, as though Yahweh beats his enemies at their own game by their own weapons," which sounds like yet another example of God exercising punishment in the same terms as the initial sin, thereby becoming associated with it and adding a divine dimension to its perpetuation.

linguistically to 24:18 and, more important, Job 9:6.[121] In the latter, the power (Job 9:4b–14), but neither the trustworthiness nor justice of God is acknowledged (Job 9:19–24).[122] In light of Ps 35, Isa 24, and so on, evidence accumulates that God may be unreliable at one end of the spectrum for the way the divine remains silent in the face of injustice and, at the other end, for the way God's discharge of power may not always be an absolute expression of justice.[123]

The dimensions of meaning teased out above—that חנף is regularly identified with those at the top of the social hierarchy and that it is often used in contexts with a justice orientation—are further supported by Jer 23:9–15, in which the word arises twice. In this passage it is "prophet and priest," that is, the religious sector of the governing class, who are deemed "godless" (חנף [Jer 23:11]). Within this overall religious category, "the prophets of Jerusalem," who may be understood as those closest to political power, are accused of being responsible for the spread of "ungodliness" (חנפה [23:15]). The context of the passage as a whole implies that "ungodliness" consists of religious apostasy ("the prophets of Samaria . . . prophesied by Baal and led . . . Israel astray" [v. 13]); sexual impropriety (vv. 10, 14); a generalized category dubbed "wickedness" (vv. 10, 11, 14); the strengthening of "the hands of evildoers" (v. 14); and, significantly, exercising "power unjustly," in an inappropriate manner (וגבורתם לא־כן [23:10]). As one would expect, חנף carries several connotations of meaning, one of which is the manifestation of injustice in society.

On two occasions, חנף appears in passages in which the idea of a remnant or group that truly knows God is juxtaposed with those who push and peddle in profanity and defilement. In Dan 11:32, a corrupt leader will lead into corruption (חנף) those who have violated the covenant, but the people who know their God will stand firm and take action. As presented here, there is a clear divide between those given over to corruption, pollution, and defilement, and the stalwarts who are on the Lord's side.

---

121.   The root רעש occurs in Isa 13:13 and 24:18, while the word pair רגז and ממקומה, in reference to cosmic upheaval, is found in both Isa 13:13 and Job 9:6.

122.   Job suggests that God is beyond the "matter of justice" (v. 19); "destroys both the blameless and the wicked" (v. 22); "mocks the despair of the innocent" (v. 23); and "when a land falls into the hands of the wicked, blindfolds its judges" (v. 24).

123.   Thus, the wisdom-oriented assertion that "with his mouth the godless (חנף) destroys his neighbor, but through knowledge the righteous escape" (Prov 11:9) cannot naively be accepted as an adequate description of the way the world operates; while there may be truth in it, lived experience also undermines its certitude.

More significantly for a full-form reading of Isaiah, Micah envisages a remnant of exiles, composed of the lame and those God has brought to grief (Mic 4:6–7). This remnant, although promised a new reign of God in Mount Zion and a restoration of its former dominion (Mic 4:7–8), is nevertheless confronted by many nations threatening its "defilement" (חנף [4:11]). These nations, however, "do not know the thoughts of the Lord" or understand God's plan (4:12) to empower Daughter Zion to savage them and to break them to pieces (4:13). In this construal, similar to a strain of thought already observed in the Isaianic corpus, a rampant and revived remnant returns from exile to the homeland ready to put the past behind it and to pick up the threads of its old life, reassuming its old ways of domination, with everything blessed by the Lord.

With regard to the biblical image of the remnant resulting from a harsh process of smelting (e.g. Isa 1:25–27), this understanding proposes the drawing of a neat line under the past, as if the remnant, now apparently safe and secure, can be distanced and divorced from its origins. However, I show that such distinct delineations and segmentations into hermetically sealed eras are textually illusory, certainly in the book of Isaiah, in which the God encoded in the text is continually problematic, even for the remnant, and never easily trusted, even by the remnant. Thus, the remnant of Isa 24:13, who act as cheerleaders to an awesome display of divine destructiveness and "raise their voices" joyously in acclamation of God's brutalization of the earth (24:14), finding such a manifestation of divine might something to glory at (24:15, 16), discover, in a sequential reading of the text, that such a power is unpredictable and that there is no guarantee that it will not one day be directed against them.[124] In Isaiah, the remnant, to a significant degree, is an

---

124. No doubt Brueggemann is right to argue that this remnant community "is so committed to praise of Yahweh that it is willing to see the world system condemned, if that condemnation enhances the splendor of Yahweh," and that "we may allow for a socioeconomic dimension to such praise" (*Isaiah 1–39*, 193). By this, Brueggemann means that the members of the remnant community have no investment in the present world order and, therefore, as "they do not benefit from the system[,] . . . they are glad to see it go, given their deep confidence that Yahweh will have for them a better future." It is also no doubt right that it is a shock "to the key players in the destructive world system to imagine that some will be glad to see it terminated" and that those at the margins of exploitative global arrangements (then or now) are likely to be "the 'they' who join in praise and celebration of the destructive potential of Yahweh; it is 'they' who wait for a new creation that is always at the edge of this sort of radical rhetoric." Nevertheless, this flirtation with the language of destructive power, which can variously manifest itself in sectarianism or, in some strands of liberation theology, in the notion of revolutionary violence as an expression of love, aims at the obliteration of the "other." Even if that "other" is

insecure entity that by the end of the book, in part at least, seems to have exhausted its capacity to keep on believing in the promise of God to inaugurate an era of justice (59:9–11). What is more, some have internalized the logic that insists that their rebellion and sins are the factors that have inhibited the dawning of this new era (59:12–15a) to such a degree that they are immobilized by despondency and despair (59:15b–16a).

Perhaps, though, there is a beneficial aspect. This time, when Yahweh goes on a divine rampage of destruction (59:16b–20), there is no one cheering the warrior God to the rafters. The pain of refinement, having started globally, does not seem as if it is ever going to end, as it moves to encompass those who had once prided themselves on being counted among the elect. Faced with this process within the book of Isaiah, people are confronted in narrative with the choice of (1) continuing to accept the justness of God's apparently unremitting punishment, in hopes that a refined core will eventually emerge; or (2) languishing in resignation at the violent nature of God; or (3) summoning the courage to turn their backs on this God as the divine is reified. I explore the nuances contained in the idea of the remnant more fully below, especially for any ironic intent that might be perceived in a final-form reading of Isaiah.

9. *Godlessness and Senselessness: Job as the Lens*

The highest incidence of חנף in the Hebrew Bible occurs in the book of Job, in which it is used eight times, always in the same form as in Isa 9:16 (ET v. 17).[125] It recurs in the series of conversations between Job and his visitors,[126] which, taken together, probes the nature of divine justice.[127] This usage warrants closer examination for meaning it might uncover in the Isaiah text.

patently an oppressive force, thereby making this approach more understandable, the language stands in tension with the reconciliatory element in the Isaianic text, such as that, for example, expressed in Isa 58:6–10.

125. In the Hebrew Bible as a whole, the root חנף appears a total of 26 times: eight in Job; six in Jeremiah; five in Isaiah; twice each in the Psalms and the book of Numbers; and once each in Micah, Daniel, and Proverbs.

126. For an introduction to this material, see Norman C. Habel, *The Book of Job: A Commentary* (OTL; London: SCM Press, 1985), 25–35.

127. The term is found five times in the mouth of Job's visitors and three times in the mouth of Job himself in the following pattern: 8:13, Bildad; 13:16, Job; 15:34, Eliphaz; 17:18, Job; 20:5, Zophar; 27:8, Job; 34:30 and 36:13, Elihu. Sometimes, after the term has been used by one of the visitors, an interchange of several speeches may take place before it appears in Job's mouth.

Job, in what constitutes a cry for human freedom from divine attention, which is felt as an intrusively oppressive presence,[128] ends by confronting God in such a way that his sin is by no means acknowledged. He conditionally says "*if* I have sinned" (7:20), and from that position of conditionality argues that God's treatment of him is still disproportionate: divine interest would be better served by pardoning Job's offenses and forgiving his sins (7:20–21), if it turns out there are any. Responding to what he hears as the blasphemous implication of Job's line of thought, Bildad asks rhetorically, "Does God pervert justice? Does the Almighty pervert what is right?" (8:3). This is to suggest that the impugning of divine justice is to think the unthinkable. For Bildad, based on the wisdom of former generations (8:8–12), the death of Job's children is evidence of their sin (8:4): "Such is the destiny of all who forget God; so perishes the hope of the 'godless' (חָנֵף)" (8:13). In essence, Job's questioning of the nature of God and of divine justice experienced in the world is met with a defense rooted in circular reasoning: if something appalling happens, this indicates sin on the part of the person to whom it happened. The *a priori* assumption is of God's righteousness. As Bildad says consolingly to Job in the midst of his despair, "[I]f you are pure and upright, even now God will rouse himself on your behalf" (8:6), for "surely God does not reject a blameless person or strengthen the hands of evildoers" (8:20).

As the debate intensifies, Zophar rejects Job's thinking (11:2b–3a) and insists that if God "convenes a court, who can oppose him?" He strongly suggests that if God charges, guilt must be assumed. Putting words into Job's mouth, Zophar is especially scandalized that Job could say to God, "My beliefs are flawless and I am pure in your sight" (11:4). This contravenes Zophar's conception of the relationship between human sin and divine justice. According to him, Job's only hope is to turn toward God (11:13), to "put away the sin that is in" his hand (11:14), and simply to forget his troubles (11:16). Then "life will be brighter than noonday, and darkness will become like morning" (11:17).[129] But first, Job must desist from questioning God.

---

128. In a series of rhetorical questions, Job asks, "Am I the sea, or a monster of the deep, that you put me under guard?" (Job 7:12), and, in an irritated reversal of the awed, reverential attitude of Ps 8, "What is man that you make so much of him, that you give him so much attention, that you examine him every morning and test him every moment?" (Job 7:17–18), concluding, "Will you never look away from me, or let me alone even for an instant?" (7:19). Habel views Job 7:17–18 as a parody of Ps 8 (*Book of Job*, 43).

129. In this construal, none of the protokenotic suffering of Isa 58:6–10, for example, is necessary to reach a comparable position of "enlightenment," which is depicted in terms resonant with 58:8b–9a.

Replying to this construal of reality, of which he is contemptuous (12:2), Job itemizes instances of the power of God (12:13–25), concluding in contrast to Zophar's imagery of darkness becoming like morning that God "deprives the leaders of the earth of their reason. . . . They grope in darkness with no light" (12:24–25).[130] This deity is a much more unfathomable, unpredictable, and unreliable character than the one depicted by Zophar, a fact in which, curiously, Job finds a nugget of hope and comfort. As Job says, "[N]o godless (חנף) man would dare come before" such a God (13:16). Only a man utterly convinced of his righteousness would even consider doing so. In his own mind, Job is the man, so certain is he that he has suffered abuse at the hands of the divine wildly in excess of any offense he could have committed; in truth, though, he will not confess to having committed any.

Appalled at what he takes to be dangerous talk that undermines piety and hinders devotion to God (15:4), Eliphaz, grounding his theological wisdom in the "grey-haired and aged" (15:10), says that Job has condemned himself out of his own mouth and testified against himself with his own lips (15:6). In Eliphaz's perspective, "What is man, that he could be pure, one born of woman, that he could be righteous?" (15:14). Lest anyone should give a positive appraisal of human potential, Eliphaz immediately follows his rhetorical question with a prototypical total-depravity statement in which he insists: "If God places no trust in holy ones, if even the heavens are not pure in God's eyes, how much less man, who is vile and corrupt" (15:16). For him, wickedness, which interestingly he conceives as social injustice,[131] leads to sharing "the company of the godless (חנף)," whose end is finally destruction (15:34). Significantly though, as shall be seen, Job is not part of the socially oppressive class "who love bribes" (15:34). Therefore, Job does not conform to Eliphaz's all-encompassing schema and reveals it to be flawed: there is data, in the person of Job, with whom the schema cannot adequately cope.

Having listened to this analysis of his situation, Job presents himself as akin to the suffering servant of Isa 50:4–11,[132] except that he will not

130. This language is similar to Isa 59:9–10.
131. The wicked are described as overweight folk (Job 15:27), who, in order to generate the wealth (15:29) in which they have misplaced so much trust (15:31), take bribes (15:34), "conceive trouble and give birth to evil" (15:35). The disordered world of the wicked (15:22–25) is reminiscent of what awaits wrongdoers according to Isa 8:21–22. Job's enumeration of God's acts of power (Job 12:17–25), the conclusion of which calls to mind Isa 59:9–10, echoes Isaianic themes more generally.
132. Habel observes: "The general theme of a suffering individual may suggest connections with the suffering servant of Isa 53." He concludes, though, that "no real parallel exists" (*Book of Job*, 41).

keep silent. He does not "suffer submissively," but is, rather, "defiant and vitriolic in his opposition to God."[133] Whereas the Servant does not rebel (Isa 50:5), but offers his cheeks for abuse and accepts being spat upon (50:6), Job rebels loudly when his cheeks are struck in scorn (Job 16:10) as "a man in whose face people spit" (17:6).[134] Further, instead of trusting in God, as does the Servant (Isa 50:7), Job regards God as the force mercilessly attacking him, even though he insists that "my hands have been free from violence and my prayer is pure" (Job 16:17). Yet in the midst of his struggle, Job recognizes that for all his reservations about the divine, God is the only power that can bring him security (17:3). Allied to this, though, Job appears to hope that the sight of him will so disturb upright people that "the innocent" will be "aroused against the ungodly (חָנֵף)" (17:8).[135]

In a recent article, Frolov has gone against the scholarly current and taken the part of Jonah in resisting participation in the divine mission of that book. Significantly for the present discussion, he argues that this makes the author of Jonah

> an opponent of Deutero-Isaiah (admiring the fate of a righteous servant of God—a designation that may be applied to Jonah as well—who gets afflicted and ultimately dies for "the sin of many"; cf. Isaiah 53) and thus, indirectly, of the later Christian doctrine of vicarious suffering. It would be hazardous to claim that the book of Jonah was written as a polemical response to Isaiah 53 (or vice versa); at the same time, there is no doubt that the ideologies underlying these texts are at odds with each other.[136]

Similarly, especially with respect to relationships proposed between disparate texts,[137] an ideological tension exists between Job 16–17 and Isa 50 in their differing attitudes to comparable experiences of abuse.

---

133. Ibid., 42.

134   לֶחִי in Job 16:10 is paralleled by precisely the same form of the word in Isa 50:6. נכה in Job 16:10 is found in Isa 50:6, whereas Job 17:6 uses תֹפֶת, the only time this term is used in the Hebrew Bible. Isaiah 50:6 uses רק, which is also found in this exact form in Job 30:10.

135. May this be taken, in its intention, to be an ancient example of the charity-campaign poster, which aims at pricking the conscience of people and mobilizing them for "godly" action?

136. Serge Frolov, "Returning the Ticket: God and his Prophet in the Book of Jonah," *JSOT* 86 (1999): 85–105 (102–3).

137. Robert Gordis (*The Book of God and Man: A Study of Job* [Chicago: University of Chicago Press, 1965], 216) contends that the Joban author has adapted the idea that suffering need not always result from sin (which Gordis traces to Deutero-Isaiah) to suit individual, as opposed to national, circumstances. Robert H. Pfeiffer ("The Dual Origin of Hebrew Monotheism," *JBL* 46 [1927]: 193–206

As the debate in Job, traced through the term חנף, continues concerning the relationship among innocence, suffering, and God, the independently minded protagonist of the poem, prepared trenchantly to resist conventional theological wisdom, protests that God has wronged him. Even though he calls for help, "there is no justice" (19:6–7). Poignantly detailing his alienation from everyone in society (19:13–19), Job pleads with his "friends" not to pursue him as God has done (19:21–22). Effectually, he is asking them to allow their prefabricated theological ideas to be dismantled and dissolved in an act of human solidarity. But their spokesperson in this instance, Zophar, distancing himself from the profundity of Job's challenge, repeats the mantra (20:4) "that the mirth of the wicked is brief, the joy of the godless (חנף) lasts but a moment" (20:5). Zophar speaks as if, at one level, to suggest dismissively that suffering in this world caused by wicked people is transient and to be endured without the exaggerated antics of a Job. At another level, more darkly, Zophar may be hinting that if, on account of his behavior, Job may be considered among the wicked, then he deserves what he is getting.

Returning to the theme of divine power, Bildad, in response to Job's graphic description of a society given over to injustice (24:2–11) and his questioning stance about lack of divine intervention to redress the situation (24:1, 12), blithely asserts: "Dominion and awe belong to God; God establishes order in the heights of heaven" (25:1). This assertion comes before Bildad renders illegitimate any attempt to question the justice of God on the grounds that nobody can be "righteous before God" because nobody "born of woman" can be pure (25:4). Taking a decidedly low opinion of humanity, he designates people as maggots and worms.[138] Even after he is so dismissed, Job, however, clings to his viewpoint. He will never admit his opponents are in the right and will never deny the integrity and essential righteousness of his position (27:5–6). In what is functionally a curse, Job wishes his enemies (may his visitors be included among them?) to be treated "like the wicked," his adversaries "like the unjust" (27:7). As he observes, "[W]hat hope has the godless (חנף) when he is cut off" (27:8). The conclusion to be drawn is that Job is not among the godless, for although he has suffered, wished for death, and railed against God, he is still alive and therefore still has hope for a restoration

---

[202–6]), however, had argued for the primacy of Job over Second Isaiah. As Habel observes, "[W]hile Job was no doubt familiar with literary and oral traditions of Israel, clear lines of dependency for establishing a particular date for the book are not demonstrable" (*Book of Job*, 41).

138. Picking up on this imagery, see Stuart Lasine, "Bird's-Eye and Worm's-Eye Views of Justice in the Book of Job," *JSOT* 42 (1988): 29–53.

of his previous relationship with God (29:2–6), which was marked by intimacy and blessing (29:4). In his struggle, Job does not reject God, but neither does he accept that his hardship is a consequence of his sin.

The final two occurrences of חָנֵף in Job come from the mouth of Elihu, who, like his associates, rests his "just deserts" theological beliefs on the foundation of God's supposed righteousness. As he says, "Far be it from God to do evil, for the Almighty to do wrong. God repays a man for what he has done; God brings upon him what his conduct deserves. It is unthinkable that God would do wrong, that the Almighty would pervert justice" (34:10b–12). In Elihu's view, God's "eyes are on the ways of men" (34:21) so closely that men only have to come before God to receive instantaneous, non-summary justice (34:23). Interestingly, Elihu also incorporates a social-justice dimension in his worldview in the way he focuses on how the wickedness of those God watches causes "the cry of the poor to come before" God, so that God hears "the cry of the needy" (34:28). The depiction of a deity attentive to the cries of the poor is immediately and crucially undermined, however, by the subsequent question, "But if God remains silent, who can condemn Him?" (34:29a). This is to accept that God is beyond and not to be held to what would be considered normal human standards of consistency in questions of justice. Consequently, if a situation arises in which it seems that God does not respond appropriately to the cry of the poor, this, conveniently for Elihu, but problematically for Job, should not be considered sufficient grounds for casting aspersions against the reliability of the divine character. Notwithstanding the obvious fissure Elihu has introduced in his rhetoric to the concept of the integrity of God, he maintains that the purpose of divine governance over individual and nation alike (34:29b) is "to keep a godless (חָנֵף) man from ruling" (34:30). God's justice is unquestionable; therefore, there are no grounds for human protest against the divine. For not accepting this proposition, Job, according to Elihu, "speaks without knowledge" and "lacks insight" (34:35). Unlike the Servant of Isa 50, who has "not been rebellious" (v. 5), Job "to his sin . . . adds rebellion" (34:37).[139]

Further extrapolating his theological construct, Elihu, claiming to be "one perfect in knowledge" (36:4), has more to say "on God's behalf" (36:2). He holds to the opinion that although "God is mighty," the divine "does not despise men" (36:5), but rather presides over a just jurisdiction of rewards and punishments (36:6–7). The picture is of a God willing to

---

139. A different Hebrew word is used for rebellion in each case: מרה in the former and פֶּשַׁע in the latter. The פֶּשַׁע root, as noted, enjoys wide usage throughout Isaiah.

explain where people have gone wrong (36:8–9), so that they might turn from the error of their ways to once again "obey and serve" God, spending "the rest of their days in prosperity and their years in contentment" (36:11). Faced with such a transparently fair, accessible, generous, emollient God, those recalcitrant enough still to harbor doubts about divine justice are deemed "the godless (חנף) in heart" for the resentment they feel (36:13). Rhetorically, Elihu is attempting to shame and cajole Job into a change of attitude (36:16). His strategy, however, implodes in self-contradiction when, speaking of the "godless," among whom he wants Job to see himself if his present attitude persists, he says that "even when God fetters them, they do not cry for help" (36:13). To the considerable extent that Job has never kept silent about his condition, but has, even in the midst of his accusations against God, paradoxically expressed his reliance on God, he clearly is not to be counted as "godless." His understanding of God and, more importantly, of legitimate human rights before God in situations of pain in which God is perceived to be implicated, is radically different from that of his parade of visitors.

A number of observations can now be made. First, the potentiality for innocence is clung to so doggedly that the universal designation of everyone as "godless" in Isa. 9:16 (ET v. 17) is further called into doubt. This sense of doubt increases when one notes that, according to Isa 9:16 (ET v. 17), everyone is guilty of the sin of improper speech ("every mouth speaks vileness/folly [נבלה]"). In contradistinction, from the outset Job is presented as one who, despite everything, "did not sin in what he said" (Job 2:10; see also 27:4). Furthermore, in the way Job "rescued the poor who cried for help, and the fatherless who had none to assist them" (Job 29:12), it is difficult to avoid the conclusion that at a certain level Job is presented as an exemplar of Isa 1:17[140] and consequently should not be condemned. Indeed, in his own defense, Job, resisting the inference of his visitors that he is being punished on account of his participation in injustice, insists that he has always acted justly toward the poor (Job 31:13, 16, 17, 21). Thus, while none of this is in itself conclusive, it does strengthen the grounds intertextually for calling into question the type of

---

140. In a discussion of the setting and possible dates for the book of Job, Habel surveys links to other texts, concluding that "while the cumulative evidence may tend to suggest a postexilic era, the book's literary integrity, paradoxical themes, heroic setting, and uncomfortable challenge are pertinent for students of wisdom and life in any era and far more important than the precise date of this ancient literary work" (*Book of Job*, 39–42). See also the section on form and focus (pp. 42–46). Nevertheless, without arguing for a formal relationship between the texts, Job as a character resonantly discharges the injunction of Isa 1:17.

all-encompassing pronouncement of guilt delivered in Isa 9:16 (ET v. 17), rendering it less than completely secure in its claim to truth.

Viewed through the lens of Job, those parts of the Isaianic corpus (such as 9:16 [ET v. 17]) that propound a theology of total guilt without consideration of innocence may be identified as examples of the kind of discourse articulated by Job's visitors. In the case of Job's visitors, the experience of pain on Job's part led them to the assumption of his guilt and punishment; in the case of a certain strain of thought in the book of Isaiah, the experience and reality of exile (however that is understood)[141] led to the necessity of attributing guilt to the whole nation. Devastatingly for this order of theology, with its propensity for neat schematization, however, Job 42:8 condemns Job's visitors as purveyors of "folly" (נבלה). This is the same form of the term found in Isa 9:16 (ET v. 17) in the accusation that every mouth speaks "folly" (נבלה). Again, the sweeping claims of Isa 9:16 (ET v. 17) are undermined. As I have argued elsewhere, those "who theologically conceived the world as a neatly ordered place in which there was no dissonance between events in life and the discernment of God's activity and justice" are branded as speaking folly: "The fool may say in his heart that there is no God, but those who understand God too simplistically are also foolish."[142] Instead God vindicates those, like Job, who seek "God in the struggles, setbacks and vagaries of existence. God is thus implicated and encountered in the 'stuff' of life."[143]

Within the Isaianic corpus, "folly," like "godlessness," is also associated with the practice of injustice. Isaiah 32:6 portrays how a "fool" (נבל) speaking "folly" (נבלה) contributes to the hungry being left empty and water being withheld from the thirsty (32:6). This occurs in a distorted context in which the poor are destroyed by lies, "even when the plea of the needy is just" (32:7). Faced with this situation, the prophet looks forward to a time of reversal when the "fool" (נבל) will no longer be thought of as noble (32:5). The genuinely noble will assume leadership positions devising noble plans (32:8), which by implication have the establishment of an equitable social order as part of their agenda. Yet if, as has been shown, "folly" is linked with injustice, then once more the issue is raised of why those at the receiving end of such foolishness

---

141. See further Grabbe, *Leading Captivity Captive*; James Scott, *Exile: Old Testament, Jewish, and Christian Conceptions*; Barstad, *Myth of the Empty Land*; Smith Christopher, *Biblical Theology of Exile*, 27–73.

142. Mark Gray, "Amnon: A Chip Off the Old Block? Rhetorical Strategy in 2 Samuel 13:7–15. The Rape of Tamar and the Humiliation of the Poor," *JSOT* 77 (1998): 39–54 (52).

143. Ibid.

(understood as an expression of exploitation) are to be condemned alongside its chief perpetrators.

In the biblical literature more broadly, the case has been made that injustice is significantly wedded to "folly." Although in context the term "regularly bespeaks sexual transgression (Jer. 29:23), with a particular focus on rape (Gen. 37:4; Judg. 19:23; 20:6)," a usage which accords well with נבלה in 2 Sam 13:12, 13, this text, in conjunction with Isa 32:6, illustrates

> that in the Israelite consciousness there is a shrewd conviction that debased actions such as Amnon's [in 2 Sam 13] (constitutive of sexual perversion), are integrally part of the degenerative process which eventuates in societal injustice. . . . Ancient Israel knew, better than many modern social analysts, that private morality is intimately linked to more general public policies and practices, especially vis-à-vis the disadvantaged.[144]

Thus, while "like all communities, Israel always had its rapists and ne'er-do-wells[,] . . . in Amnon we stand at the start of a trajectory where the values of such are . . . being elevated to the level of and embedded in the modalities of established governance."[145] In other words, since in narrative the society conceived by the book of Isaiah represents a point further along that trajectory, once again, consistent with a perspective embedded in the biblical account, the rulers are identified as more culpable of wrongdoing than the ruled.

10. *Heads, Tails, and Textual Uncertainty*

One of my concerns in this chapter has been to explore the extent to which the condemnation of "everyone" in Isa 9:16 (ET v. 17) is rhetorically convincing. Evidence indicates valid grounds for postulating a lack of stability in the claims of the text. This lack of stability is reinforced by a brief examination of the rhetorical pattern of the preceding verses (vv. 12–15 [ET vv. 13–16]), which indicates a degree of tension as the passage moves toward its conclusion of universal guilt.

Following the refrain "Yet for all this, his anger is not turned away, his hand is still upraised" (9:11b [ET v. 12b]), the unit that concludes in universal condemnation is introduced by the claim that "the people have not returned to him who struck them, nor have they sought the Lord Almighty" (9:12 [ET v. 13]). The reference to העם, which also occurs in v. 15 (ET v. 16), suggests that the whole nation is being spoken of.

144.   Ibid., 51.
145.   Ibid., 49.

Consequently, the immediately succeeding pronouncement, in the form of an allusive metaphor, that "the Lord will cut off from Israel both head and tail, both palm branch and reed" (ראש וזנב כפה ואגמון; 9:13 [ET v. 14]) initially pushes the interpreter in the direction of understanding this phrase as similarly applying to all the people. Reinforcing this reading, Kaiser argues that "as the comparison with Deut. 28:13, 44 shows, the head and tail of the people are its rulers and the subjects who serve them."[146] Motyer concurs with this assessment: "The pairs of opposites, *head and tail, palm branch and reed*, denote totality. Head and tail signify from one end to the other while branch and reed . . . signify from the eminent to the lowly."[147]

In light of this, the explanatory comment that "the elders and prominent men are the head, the prophets who teach lies are the tail" (9:14 [ET v. 15]) creates a sense of restrictive disjunction. From a historical-critical perspective, Kaiser observes: "Remarkably enough, the editor responsible for this verse wants to see the judgment as a blow only against the elders, the men of reputation at court and the false prophets."[148] Contrary to this line of thought, which implicitly acknowledges a fault line in the text, Motyer contends that "the metaphor of verse 13 [ET v. 14] is spelled out in a balanced scheme in the following verses."[149] Operating in the same historical-critical field as Kaiser (if only to attempt to refute it), but with a hermeneutic grounded in the theological-ideological assumption of textual unity and harmony, Motyer further argues that "Isaiah often explains his metaphors." He adds, "To have observed this stylistic feature would have prevented some commentators from finding glosses in this verse."[150]

In opposition to these approaches, which joust at each other in the historical-critical arena and either attribute angularity in the text to the

---

146. Kaiser, *Isaiah 1–12*, 225. Against this, Oswalt takes "head and tail, palm branch and bulrush" to refer to "the totality of leadership," a reading he supports by saying that Isa 19:15 "uses the same language for the foolish leadership of Egypt" (*Book of Isaiah: Chapters 1–39*, 255). While it is accurate that the phrase ראש וזנב כפה ואגמון in 19:15 appears to apply primarily to the Egyptian leaders, in its use in 9:13 (ET v. 14), the most secure conclusion, even without Kaiser's supporting Deuteronomic references, is that the rhetoric at this stage is leading the reader to understand that it is the whole people that is being alluded to. Oswalt eliminates the tension and nuance of the rhetoric by interpreting 9:13 (ET v. 14) according to the after-the-fact clarification of 9:14 (ET v. 15).

147. Motyer, *Prophecy of Isaiah*, 108 (emphasis in original).

148. Kaiser, *Isaiah 1–12*, 225.

149. Motyer, *Prophecy of Isaiah*, 108.

150. Ibid.

hand of a later redactor or devise strategies to deny the existence of such angularity, the tension and indeterminacy inherent in the rhetoric, viewed from a literary standpoint, reflect the difficulty of the subject being addressed. As indicated by the rhetorical pattern of the passage, there is a struggle as to whether guilt should be apportioned mainly to those who determine policy or whether it should be extended throughout the nation's population, from king to widow to orphaned infant. On the one hand is the underlying conception that the ruling elite is more responsible collectively for the nation's situation than those whom it rules. On the other hand is the perceived need to cast the net of blame so that it covers everyone. The text says, "Those who guide this people mislead them, and those who are guided are led astray" (9:15 [ET v. 16]). Characteristically among commentators, this has been used as part of the overall justification of "Yahweh's act of annihilation of his people," the reason being that the "leaders have failed by leading the people on a false path, while the people have incurred guilt by allowing themselves to be led."[151]

However, it is not immediately apparent that those who lead and those who are led should be condemned equally. That power in all of its dimensions to coerce, persuade, and confuse is disproportionately available to the leaders suggests that they are in fact more culpable than those whom they lead.[152] Oswalt contends that on account of a "self-serving attitude on the part of the leaders of the nation the people can receive no truly objective guidance."[153] This being the case, there is at minimum an obvious need for differentiation or gradation in punishment, rather than an ethical postulation that brackets a marginalized widow or orphan with the representatives of the system that has oppressed them. There is an evident degree of tension, indeterminacy, and inadequacy in the way the question of universal guilt and punishment is rhetorically presented in this passage. I now place this evaluation in the context of other texts in the opening chapters of Isaiah that attribute blame for Israel's plight. It is beyond the scope of this study to analyze these texts exhaustively. Instead, I survey them for the illumination they might bring to the discussion of Isa 9:12–16 (ET vv. 13–17).

---

151.   Kaiser, *Isaiah 1–12*, 225.

152.   Analogously, with regard to the issue of racism, it has been argued that, properly understood, racism is constituted by racial prejudice *plus the power to implement this programmatically*; thus, while people of color may be prejudiced, they cannot be racist in white-dominated societies. See Nibs Stroupe and Inez Fleming, *While we Run this Race: Confronting the Power of Racism in a Southern Church* (New York: Orbis, 1995).

153.   Oswalt, *Book of Isaiah: Chapters 1–39*, 255.

11. *The Attribution of Guilt in the Opening Chapters of Isaiah*

As far as the accusation of "rebellion" (פֶּשַׁע; 1:2), lack of understanding (לֹא בִין; 1:3), "sin" (חֵטְא; 1:4), "iniquity" (עָוֹן; 1:4), evildoing (מְרֵעִים; 1:4), and corruption (מַשְׁחִיתִים; 1:4) is concerned, the Isaianic corpus opens by attributing these errant qualities to generalized, socially inclusive groupings. These groups are introduced by the familial term בָּנִים (1:2), which also occurs in this form in 1:4, thus creating an *inclusio* around the other inclusive terms. In this way, it is rhetorically indicated that "Israel" (1:3), עַמִּי (1:3), גּוֹי (1:4), and עַם (1:4) all ultimately refer to constituent individuals who are sons of God.[154] The opening of the introduction to the prophecy of Isaiah consequently lends support to the idea that the nation in its entirety is guilty of wrongdoing.

An element of social differentiation is introduced in v. 10 when the rulers (קְצִינֵי) are addressed, although, immediately afterward, the people (עַם) are again included in the equation. Indeed, in the way the rulers are linked with Sodom and the people with Gomorrah, rhetorically the point is made that together they have created a society of absolute debasement. From the social-justice perspective, however, 1:16–17 implicitly recognizes that not all people can be equally condemned: there is a specific sector of society responsible for the oppression of the poor, and it is to this sector that the injunction to "seek justice . . . [d]efend the cause of the fatherless, plead the cause of the widow" (1:17) is chiefly directed. In this instance, those represented by the widow and orphan categories are presumably absolved from oppressing themselves.

This implicit recognition is made explicit in 1:23, in which it is expressly the rulers (שָׂרַיִךְ [literally, "your princes"]) who, in a litany of corruption contributing to an overall context of social injustice,[155] are charged with failing to defend (שָׁפְטוּ) the cause of the fatherless (1:23).[156] Furthermore, whereas in 1:17 pleading the case of the widow (אַלְמָנָה) is mandated, in 1:23 the widow's (אַלְמָנָה) case does not even come before the authorities: there is thus a gulf between what is enjoined and what the rulers do.

At this juncture, therefore, condemnation, according to Clements, is "of the political leaders and officials in Jerusalem." "[T]he clear implication"

---

154. The sense of inclusivity in the condemnation is increased if, as happens in several translations (e.g. the NIV), the term בָּנִים is taken as "children."

155. These rulers are designated as "rebels, companions of thieves," lovers of bribes, and chasers after gifts.

156. The same root for "to defend" is used in 1:17, also in conjunction with the fatherless (יָתוֹם).

is "that it is they who are responsible for the unhealthy state of the moral, social and political life of the city. . . . It is the leaders of Jerusalem themselves who have become Yahweh's enemies."[157] With specific respect to v. 23, Clements identifies the rulers as "men of authority who held high civil and military administrative posts."[158] Watts agrees that this prophecy is against "Zion's corrupt leaders,"[159] as does Seitz. In arguing that "the chapter does not single out the king for special condemnation," Seitz asserts that "the leadership in general is indicted."[160] Kaiser contends that the purpose underlying this oracle "does not mean the final annihilation of the city but its liberation from the ruling circles which are sapping its strength and corrupting it."[161]

Oswalt substantially echoes this line of interpretation: "The ruling class . . . has become so perverted that they who are to promote order and obedience are themselves rebels, while they who are entrusted with responsibility for justice are through their own greed actively promoting injustice."[162] He also contends that "social injustice is ultimately the result of refusal to entrust oneself to a fair and loving God."[163] But the way in which the divine self condemns (9:16 [ET v. 17]) those (widows and orphans) previously identified as objects of special divine and human concern (1:17, 23) casts a shadow over the sustainability of this statement. The core reason for plausible doubt about Oswalt's positivistic claim with regard to the character of God is that it is not derived from the full rhetorical presentation of God in the text.

A number of comments are in order: in the opening chapter of Isaiah one observes the tendency towards both a socially encompassing condemnation and one more sharply focused on the rulers as primarily responsible for the state of the nation. From a social-justice viewpoint, however, the relationship between these two aspects of the text is unclear in terms of understanding how the oppressed may also be construed as participating in oppression in order to incur guilt. If vv. 29–31 are

157. Clements, *Isaiah 1–39*, 35.
158. Ibid., 36.
159. Watts, *Isaiah 1–33*, 26.
160. Seitz, *Isaiah 1–39*, 35–36.
161. Kaiser, *Isaiah 1–12*, 44.
162. Oswalt, *Book of Isaiah: Chapters 1–39*, 105–6. This understanding of the "proper" function of a ruling elite follows the thinking of Calvin (*Commentary on the Book of the Prophet Isaiah*, 1:75). A more materialist and less idealistic reading might wonder if such a leadership has ever existed; moreover, a materialist reading might well view social exploitation as inextricably linked to the rise, establishment, and perpetuation of a ruling elite.
163. Oswalt, *Book of Isaiah: Chapters 1–39*, 106.

accepted as rhetorically integrated into ch. 1, then the sin of the poor may not be social injustice but idolatry. This suggestion, though, is not without a problem. It conflates idolatry and social injustice in a general attribution of guilt in which, contradictorily, the socially marginalized, while deemed worthy of assistance on account of their exploitation, are also deemed deserving of obliteration for their idolatry. Moreover, Oswalt has noted "the connection between idolatry and social justice":[164] the implication is that idolatrous behavior fuels injustice. This understanding of the social justice–idolatry nexus logically suggests that the socially advantaged are more responsible for both these dimensions of sin in the life of the people than the socially disadvantaged.

This conclusion is supported by 2:6–8, in which the land being filled with idols (וַתִּמָּלֵא אַרְצוֹ אֱלִילִים; v. 8) is linked rhetorically to the land also being filled with silver, gold, endless treasures, horses, and chariots. The importance of this list is that, by allusion to Deut 17:16–17, the inference is that the king is ultimately the source of a combination of acquisitive greed and idol worship in the land. In a noteworthy discussion of these verses in their broader context of 2:6–21, O'Connell perceives "the prophet's strategy of reticence openly to criticize the Judean monarchy."[165] While acknowledging "the culpability of the monarchy for the aberrations listed in the accusation" of 2:6–8, O'Connell proposes that "the condemnation of Judah's royalty" in these verses "remains obscured . . . for perhaps two reasons."[166] These are:

> First, such indirectness might afford the prophet some measure of insulation against reprisal at the hands of the king(s) he was thus incriminating. Second, by refraining from specifying the social class that was the object of these denunciations, as well as the threats that follow, they could be seen to apply equally well to those who followed misdirection as to those who misled. Thus, it is the lack of specific addressee that extends culpability both to those who followed apostate policies and to the king and judicial heads who instituted them.[167]

While this subtle interpretation is illuminating in some regards, it can only be accepted with qualification. Fear of the power of the monarchy determines the prophetic policy of not confronting this central institution openly. Therefore, it is the king who, as first among equals in the ruling elite and the one invested with supreme authority, is primarily responsible for the ethical-religious condition of the nation. Failure to maintain a

---

164. Ibid.
165. O'Connell, *Concentricity and Continuity*, 59.
166. Ibid., 65–66.
167. Ibid., 66.

distinction between the monarchy and whoever else is secondarily associated with corrupt and proscribed royal practices potentially introduces
a lack of precision and consistency into O'Connell's analysis. The intention of identifying the root of the problem as the king could be seriously
diminished through the move to extend a shared "culpability" too easily,
especially since it is by the literary device of allusion that the monarchy
is condemned as the source of national malaise. The reference "to those
who followed misdirection/apostate policies" should not be understood
in a generalized way as applying to society as a whole, but to those
among the lower echelons of the ruling class who had the capacity to
play their part in the process of accumulation.

In the following chapter, 3:14, directed against "the elders and leaders," in which they are accused of ruining the vineyard and hoarding "the
plunder from the poor" in their houses, fits in well with this reading and
is well-attested in the secondary literature.[168] Clements asserts that "the
theme of misgovernment is here taken up afresh in a further piece of
invective addressed to the elders and officials of Judah. It is their mis-
deeds which have made necessary the punishment which will shortly
come."[169] In other words, as far as punishment for social injustice is concerned, the leadership deserves punishment more than those whom they
oppress, an assessment that Clements underscores:

> The ruling classes are assumed by Isaiah to bear responsibility for the
> behaviour of the people as a whole. More particularly, however, they are
> guilty because they have oppressed those for whom they should have
> been concerned, and to whom they should have shown charity.[170]

In keeping with this insistent focus on the guilt of the ruling elite, Sawyer
discerns in this wider passage a word of comfort for "the *innocent* victims of injustice and oppression." God, in Sawyer's estimation, has considerable affection for the victims; they should be told "that they at any
rate are not responsible for the topsy-turvy world in which they live."[171]

Brueggemann also pursues this line: "The poet is discerning enough to
see that the distortion of social relationships is not in the first instance a
work of all citizens, but characteristically the work of 'opinion makers'
who are on the make at the expense of their fellow citizens."[172] On the

---

168. Ibid., 69, where it is correctly observed that the broader context in which
this verse is located (3:1–4:1, according to O'Connell) "focuses upon the form that
YHWH's judgment would take against the nonregal upper classes in Zion's society."
169. Clements, *Isaiah 1–39*, 49.
170. Ibid., 50.
171. Sawyer, *Isaiah*, 1:36 (emphasis added).
172. Brueggemann, *Isaiah 1–39*, 36.

basis of this differentiation between rulers and ruled, and the subsequent designation of the poor as God's people, Brueggemann asserts that "this is a strong example of God's preferential option for the poor, for the God of Hosts is particularly allied with the poor as their legal advocate against the leadership class."[173] Commensurate with this analysis, Oswalt observes:

> When government becomes corrupt it is usually those who are helpless who are hurt first and most often, especially if the leaders think of the people as their own preserve which they can use to their own advantage. But God says that the people, especially the helpless, are his and asks . . . how the rulers dare to treat his heritage as they do.[174]

In a particularly graphic way, the disparity between leaders and led, reflective of the extent to which the former warrant judgment and the latter do not, is encapsulated in the image of the poor being crushed and having their faces ground (3:15).[175] The identification, however, in v. 15 of the poor as God's people[176] in no way helps explain why God eventually also turns on them in punishment. Rather, a further question mark is placed against the character of God.

The reference to vineyard (כֶּרֶם) in 3:14 acts as a bridge to and is more fully explicated in the famous Song of the Vineyard of 5:1–7, in which variations of the כרם root recur six times.[177] Here, in keeping with the meaning of 3:14, the ruination of the vineyard is attributed to social injustice, concluding in v. 7 with the forcefully poetic assertion that God "looked for justice (מִשְׁפָּט) but beheld bloodshed (מִשְׂפָּח), for righteousness

---

173.　Ibid., 37.

174.　Oswalt, *Book of Isaiah: Chapters 1–39*, 138–39.

175.　Alexander understands this as depicting how the poor, already bent over, are walked on until their faces are ground into the road (*Commentary on Isaiah*, 116).

176.　In addition to the examples already noted, Watts contends that the poor "are seen as virtually identical with God's people" (*Isaiah 1–33*, 42–43). Thus, essentially, "The Lord identifies himself with the poor"; consequently, "The elders are judged for crime against God." Against the general critical consensus and the rhetoric of the text, Young (*Book of Isaiah*, 1:158) is more circumspect about identifying the poor as the object of God's special concern ("my people"). He says, "*Probably* we are not at this point to identify the 'my people' with the entire nation, but rather with those who were in poor condition and helpless" (p. 158 [emphasis added]). Perhaps this reserve reflects an awareness at some level that if God is identified too closely with the interests of the poor, then a problem is created if the divine subsequently includes that category in a universal judgment.

177.　Twice in v. 1 and once each in vv. 3, 4 (as in v. 3), 5 (as in vv. 3 and 4), and 7.

(צדקה) but heard a cry (צעקה)."[178] Clearly this context presupposes that those so crying out on account of being deprived of justice warrant action on their behalf, not inclusion in a sweeping category of guilt. Furthermore, consonant with the denunciation of the unjust accumulation of wealth in 3:14, the succeeding woe oracle of 5:8 also contains this opposition to unjust acquisitive activity, reflected in the formulation "woe to you who add house to house and join field to field."

As the passage progresses, however, a note of dissonance and incongruity is sounded. Blurring the previous distinction between the leadership class, who are worthy of rebuke, and the exploited, who merit divine support, is a movement in the direction of envisioning a punishment that will include all social classes. Rhetorically, the two woe oracles of vv. 8–10 and 11–12 lead to the pivotal "therefore" (לכן) of v. 13, which introduces a poetic vision of what will happen to people on account of their injustice (v. 8) and their recourse to excess alcohol (vv. 11–12). If the designation of the poor as God's particular people in 3:15 carries that same connotation through to 5:15,[179] then the announcement that "my people will go into exile" is rhetorically perplexing and arresting.

The sense of a universal judgment is indicated even more explicitly by the way the initial pronouncement of punishment is explicated as the men of rank prospectively dying of hunger and the masses (המונו) being parched with thirst. This inclusive punishment is reiterated and underscored in v. 14 when, parallel to v. 13, after the repetition of לכן as the first word of the verse, we are informed that Sheol has opened its mouth to accommodate the "nobles and masses" (המונה) who will descend to it without limit. That the coming judgment will encompass both ends of the social spectrum is further indicated by the formula "both high and low will be humbled" (v. 15).

The basic rhetorical pattern of this section is for two series of woe oracles (vv. 8–10, 11–12, and vv. 18–19, 20, 21, 22, respectively), each introduced by the interjection הוי, to culminate in the rhetorical point לכן (v. 13, reinforced by being repeated at the start of v. 14 and v. 24). Afterward, the punishment arising from the preceding woe oracles is announced. As observed in vv. 13 and 14, this punishment is articulated as a universal judgment. This pattern, though, loses clarity in the conclusion to the woe oracle of v. 22, when the condemnation of those "who acquit the guilty for a bribe" and "deny justice to the innocent," in a

---

178. This wordplay is widely noted; see, among others, Klaus Koch, *The Prophets: The Assyrian Period* (2 vols.; London: SCM Press, 1982), 1:114.

179. עמי is found in the same form in both verses; this, though, is a common form of a common word.

return to the language of social justice, implies that there are those who do not merit inclusion in a general attribution of guilt.

A hint of this type of slippage appears in v. 17. The image of lambs grazing in their pasture while fatlings and kids feed among the ruins gives the impression that not everyone will be included in the coming judgment and, what is more, not everyone should be. It might thus be argued that the all-encompassing articulation of punishment only applies to those sections of the "masses" who have emulated the degenerate and dissolute practices of the ruling elite.[180] While this is an attractive solution to the problem to a certain degree, it is never, however, clearly delineated as a viable interpretative option. Moreover, the portrayal of punishment as an all-consuming fire in v. 24 resonates with the similar imagery of 9:17–18 (ET vv. 18–19), which appears in a context of universal condemnation. In addition, 5:25 introduces the formula "yet for all this, his anger is not turned away, his hand is still upraised," which punctuates 9:7 (ET v. 8)–10:4, with its already-noted thrust of universal guilt. Again it may be safer to conclude that instability, tension, and indeterminacy in this passage seem to advocate an inclusive punishment, but that the passage also contains elements that effectually undermine the justice of this approach.

In summary, while there are precursors in the opening chapters of the Isaianic corpus to the full-blown universal condemnation in 9:12–16 (ET vv. 13–17), the focus, in the initial stages of Isaiah's prophecy, is primarily on the rulers as responsible for the disordered state of the nation. They therefore are more deserving of reprimand than those within their governance. How precisely these divergent strains of thought are related is left unresolved.

O'Connell has validly observed that different passages at the beginning of the book of Isaiah "play the complementary roles of setting into the foreground the two main covenant offences against which YHWH contends throughout the remainder of the book: the offences of religious apostasy and social injustice."[181] This analysis opens the possibility of postulating the innocence of the poor as far as crimes against the ideal of social justice are concerned. There is also the possibility of permitting their inclusion in a general attributing of guilt on the grounds of religious deviancy. A combination of the strained logic of this thinking and the existence of a proposed link between idolatry and social injustice results

180. Along these lines, Kaiser, speaking of 3:12, notes that "as a rule such rapacity is not limited to the ruling class but also extends to the people who look up to them and imitate them" (*Isaiah 1–12*, 76).

181. O'Connell, *Concentricity and Continuity*, 79.

in the approach being less than convincing. There is thus an insurmountable angularity and incongruity in the poor being firmly identified as God's special people, warranting divine and human support, while on the other hand being designated as worthy of inclusion in fierce divine punishment. When examined closely, the rhetoric of punishment casts doubt on the efficacy of divine justice.

The comments of Kaiser concerning 3:13–15 reverberate in significance beyond their immediate context.[182] The inference is that even action undertaken by God to punish those who deserve it will have repercussions detrimental to those who do not. Moral ambiguity is never far from the behavior or character of the divine. This must be borne in mind when the text, read without a governing theological agenda, suggests that God sometimes exceeds what is justifiable.[183] As Davies asserts, "An impartial observer might ask if the punishment announced by Yahweh upon his people is really in proportion to their crimes. In certain instances it plainly is not."[184]

In comments that echo one of my interests in exploring the importance of human solidarity as the basis for a just human society, Kaiser writes:

> The violation of human solidarity is in any form and in any circumstances a sign of forgetfulness of a humanity whose existence is meant to be co-existence; of one who receives himself not only physically, but also spiritually, from others; and is reminded of the fact that others accept him, work with him and for him, and support him. Anyone who refuses to accept others as human beings devalues them so that they become mere objects and thus violates their very persons. This rebounds on those who act in this way in solitude and as hatred. Thus movements are set in train the violence of which ultimately destroys the whole of society.[185]

182.   "God's judgment is a struggle for and against man: the advocate for his people must call the rulers to account as those who bear the utmost responsibility, but if he inflicts punishment, all will be affected by it" (Kaiser, *Isaiah 1–12*, 77).

183.   For example, Brueggemann concedes that the invective directed against the "women of Zion" in 3:16–4:1 may be "sharply sexist and inordinately abusive of women" (*Isaiah 1–39*, 37). It is indicative of God acting inappropriately on two accounts: in deploying unacceptable violence and in attacking the leaders' wives rather than the leaders themselves. For a more recent example of this type of dynamic, see Fabrice Virgili, *La France "Virile": Des femmes tondues à la libération* (Paris: Éditions Payot, 2000). Laurent Douzou quotes the French poet Paul Eluard writing from 1944, "In those days, so as not to punish the guilty, they ill-treated girls. They even went so far as to shave off their hair" ("Close Shave that Still Troubles France," *Guardian Weekly* [2–8 November 2000]).

184.   Davies, *Double Standards in Isaiah*, 136.

185.   Kaiser, *Isaiah 1–12*, 77.

There is much to affirm in this statement, especially the connection it makes between human solidarity and the creation of an equitable social order. However, where Kaiser views human solidarity as a function of "taking God seriously,"[186] in circumstances in which the divine is experienced, in part at least, as unjust and violent, then the source of solidarity in the search for justice is not located solely in the divine but also in humanity's reaction against the perception of God's excess. In other words, if, as has been demonstrated, the text supports the thesis that God is implicated in "movements . . . the violence of which ultimately destroys the whole of society," then the search for social justice may be found in human solidarity in opposition to God's sometimes unreliable character. This more nuanced interpretation more faithfully accounts for and reflects the nuances of Isaiah read in its full form.

12. *Indeterminacy as a Hermeneutical Principle*

The indeterminacy and ambivalence noted at several points above may be variously accounted for depending on the methodological approach. The different branches of historical criticism have attempted to identify within a text the periods in which its constituent parts were produced. In this method, there is no imperative to explain jarring incongruity or inconsistency in the flow of a passage, for this can be attributed to texts from different eras simply having been juxtaposed in the final compilation of disparate materials. Thus, in this tradition of scholarship, the theology of a passage like Isa 3:10–11 can be presented in isolation from its broader literary setting. Similarly, statements about God such as Isa 5:16 can be exegeted without considering how such a statement might function in the wider literary context. Laato helpfully assigns this methodology to "the Modern (M-reader)" who "reads the book [Isaiah] diachronically and historical-critically and tries to give an account of its historical development."[187]

In addition, however, in "the Ideological reader (I-reader)" Laato identifies a distinct but equally valid methodological practitioner who, attentive to "the resultant texture of resonance and meanings" in the final form of a text, "attempts to produce a coherent ideological interpretation."[188] According to this method, therefore, whatever the meaning of a

186. Ibid., 77–78.
187. Antti Laato, *About Zion I Will Not Be Silent: The Book of Isaiah as an Ideological Unity* (CB 44; Stockholm: Almqvist & Wiksell, 1998), 7; see also pp. 10–11.
188. Ibid., 7, 10–11.

text viewed as a discrete unit, this meaning might be altered when read as part of the complete literary work in which it is located. Thus, on the basis of the evidence, the apparent meanings of both Isa 3:10–11 and 5:16, taken in isolation, are significantly subverted when read as part of the unfolding drama of Isaiah as a whole by having their core assertions undermined. In a similar vein, rather than acceding to the surface meaning of Isa 9:16 (ET v. 17), or taking it as an ideologically inept attempt to introduce universal condemnation in order to account for the crushing and inclusive punishment of exile, it too should be interpreted as being undermined by a close reading of the full form of the Isaianic text, with particular reference to its immediate literary context.

In this perspective, the negative reference to widows and orphans in 9:16 (ET v. 17), followed closely by the positive reference in 10:2, functions in a literary framework to destabilize the character of God, especially when also read in light of the key introductory reference to widows and orphans in 1:17. This sense of doubt about the character of God is deepened in the way, outlined above, the divine is further called into question by association with activities that God otherwise condemns. These inconsistencies and incongruities perhaps derive from accidental arrangement in the process of transmission or, less dependent on the vagaries of fortune, are the result of an ideologically naive or ham-fisted final redactor.[189] But it might be countered that the inconsistencies are too obvious and glaring to be completely accounted for in either of these ways, particularly when issues of literary sophistication are taken seriously. Thus, whatever pronouncements of judgment, punishment, or the nature of divine justice may have meant as isolated oracles identified by a specific methodology, operating by its own internal standards, a reading of the Isaianic text in its entirety offers grounds for perceiving such pronouncements as imbued with indeterminacy. They can be seen as functioning to undermine the stability and assurance of the presentation of the character of God.

If, as seems correct, it is accurate that the canonical form of the biblical text largely comes from the hands of an educated scribal class serving the interests of political power in the Yehud period,[190] the historical distance scribes had from the events of exile enabled them, for both artistic and theological reasons, to indicate that those events had not been as determinate and clear-cut as had once been thought in certain quarters, even as far as the role of Yahweh was concerned. Effectively,

189. See Barton, *Reading the Old Testament*, 45–60.
190. Philip R. Davies, *Scribes and Schools: The Canonization of the Hebrew Scriptures* (Louisville, Ky.: Westminster John Knox, 1998), 10–12, 15–17, 74–78.

they were able to indicate that the distinction between good and evil, between a just God and a people so corrupt that every one of them deserves severe punishment, is a questionable proposition.[191] A pondering, questioning element is consequently introduced to the text.

This rhetorical approach is rooted in and governed by a sense of the ironic located in the final redactor's stance toward the poetic voice in the material.[192] In one way, consequently, the text may be read in adherence to its immediately accessible surface ideology (and has been by most commentators). But by pursuing a close-reading strategy and being attentive to clues, this surface ideology is ironically destabilized. At its subtle and elusive best, irony can legitimately entertain both readings virtually simultaneously, as, in moving between the two to decide which is more authentic and convincing, a reader is consequently decentered and wrong-footed.[193] This may be taken as an example of one of "the

191.   Analogously, the further we get from the events of the Second World War, the more the presentation of that historical period as manifesting a clear-cut division between good and evil is eroded. It emerges that, before the war, the right wing in France were whispering "Better Hitler than Blum" (the leader of the French socialists); similarly, elements in the British ruling class were quite receptive to the ideas of fascism, a perspective brilliantly rendered in Kazuo Ishiguro's *Remains of the Day* (London: Faber & Faber, 1989). Some Western businesses operated amicably with the Nazi regime throughout the war (see Edwin Black, *IBM and the Holocaust: The Strategic Alliance between Nazi Germany and America's Most Powerful Corporation* [New York: Crown, 2001]); similarly, the reputation of the Swiss as a neutral nation friendly to the allies has suffered considerable damage by revelations concerning Swiss collusion with the Nazis. The collusion occurred especially in the banking sector and especially in deriving benefit from Jewish money, which survivors of the Holocaust and relatives of Holocaust victims have had immense difficulty reclaiming. The list proliferates, including now the Dutch, the Belgians, and the Ford Motor Company.

192.   Following the urging of David M. Gunn ("New Directions in the Study of Biblical Hebrew Narrative," *JSOT* 39 [1987]: 67–75 [71–72]), the movement is from innocent or credulous readings to readings more ironic or suspicious. Transposing Gunn's comments from the narrative genre to the prophetic-poetic, this may be viewed as an example of irony being located "in the treatment of the narrator"/poetic voice "by the (implied) author"/final redactor. See also Good (*Irony in the Old Testament*, 115–67) for a more conventional treatment of the subject of irony in Isaiah. As Mahon poses the issue, "who would trade self-knowledge for / A prelapsarian metaphor, / Love-play of the ironic conscience / For a prescriptive innocence?" ("Beyond Howth Head," in *Poems, 1962–1978*, 52).

193.   As Goldingay suggests, texts are "capable of being allusive and ambiguous, designed to provoke thought rather than to render thought unnecessary" ("Isaiah 40–55 in the 1990s: Among Other Things, Deconstructing, Mystifying, Intertextual, Socio-critical, and Hearer-Involving," *BibInt* 5, no. 3 [1997]: 225–46 [231]). This is

means by which a text establishes and manages its relationship to its audience in order to achieve a particular effect."[194]

The description of Israelite society in the opening stages of the book of Isaiah as being the equivalent in degeneracy to the debauchery of Sodom and Gomorrah (Isa 1:9, 10; 13:19; with a reference to Sodom alone in 3:9) implicitly calls for an Abraham figure to argue against the justice of a socially all-encompassing condemnation in which the righteous will be swept away with the wicked (Gen 18:23–33). It calls for a mode of discourse that argues with God, reasons with God (18:24), and rhetorically proposes, "Will not the judge of all the earth do right?" (18:25). Significantly, however, such a figure and such a discourse are conspicuous by their absence. Among later references to Abraham (Isa 29:22; 41:8; 51:2; 63:16), 41:8 indicates a state of friendship between the patriarch and the divine. Ironically, though, we are being led to conclude that such a friend, who would contest with God on behalf of the people, was lacking in Israel's hour of need.

Through this type of interpretation, the suggestion is raised intertextually that in one perspective the Isaianic discourse aligns itself too readily with and acquiesces too easily in God's universal condemnation of the people. By so acquiescing, the inadequacy of the discourse is subtly indicated and God's justice rendered dubious. Among other commentators, O'Connell rightly observes that "YHWH accused Zion's leaders of practicing Sodom's excesses," from which he extrapolates: "Thus, by implication, YHWH may be portrayed here as threatening Zion with becoming a heap of destruction like that which resulted from Sodom's judgment."[195] This being the case, the gravity of such a situation cries out for someone with the brass neck and sly theological acumen of an Abraham, especially since it is "Zion's *leaders*" who are charged with "practicing Sodom's excesses."[196]

At one level, modern literary theory has demonstrated that ambiguity rather than certitude is inherent in both texts and, therefore, their interpretation(s). Even a progressive evangelical like Goldingay concedes that "ambiguity is then a fact to be acknowledged and made the most of," positively noting that "it can be creatively provocative."[197] Goldingay also suggestively proposes "that allusiveness and ambiguity in portraying

true especially if, on account of "nagging doubts, questions, and suspicions," the audience dares "to sit in judgment on God" (p. 227).

194. Patrick and Scult, *Rhetoric and Biblical Interpretation*, 12.
195. O'Connell, *Concentricity and Continuity*, 78.
196. Ibid. (emphasis added).
197. Goldingay, "Interpreting Biblical Narrative," 175.

biblical characters do not stop short of the character of God."[198] Derrida speaks of "the pure discursivity of meaning" and "the essential incompleteness of translation."[199] Along the same lines, Jabès, with pointed wit, writes: "Sense would be a simple convention of reading or listening, if the frustrated letters did not have to add their grain of salt."[200]

Derrida, effectually refining the general category of indeterminacy, also develops the concept of "undecidability," by which he does not simply mean confusion or ambiguity in a text, but "a determinate oscillation between possibilities."[201] This, given the prior comments about the nature of irony, is a form of what occurs in the movement and negotiation between a "flat" or accepting reading of Isaiah and a more ironically oriented reading. Along comparable lines, Hartman postulates the "frictionality" of the biblical text,[202] while Reed argues that "the conflict of interpretations that the critic of the Bible faces may be understood as a symptom of struggles acted out within the text."[203] In the same field of thought, Boyarin, elucidating his idea of "double-voicedness" in the biblical text, says that "built into its very structure is contradiction and opposition."[204]

All of these studies, representative of a broader trend in literary criticism, point to and affirm the tension-filled, ambivalent quality of texts. These interpretations are rooted in the reality of indeterminacy,[205] even if this term is challenged and modified. What is more, the interpretative possibilities opened by this arena have moved beyond theoretical-methodological considerations to generating new readings of texts.[206]

198. Ibid., 177.

199. Jacques Derrida, *Aporias* (Stanford, Calif.: Stanford University Press, 1993), 10.

200. Edmond Jablès, *The Book of Margins* (trans. R. Waldrop; Chicago: University of Chicago Press, 1993), 19.

201. Derrida, *Limited Inc*, 148.

202. G. H. Hartman, "The Struggle for the Text," in *Midrash and Literature* (ed. G. H. Hartman and S. Budick; New Haven: Yale University Press, 1986), 3–18 (13).

203. W. L. Reed, *Dialogues of the Word: The Bible as Literature according to Bakhtin* (New York: Oxford University Press, 1993), 15.

204. Daniel Boyarin, *Intertextuality and the Reading of Midrash* (Bloomington: Indiana University Press, 1990), 77.

205. Helpfully, see Neil Douglas-Klotz, "Midrash and Postmodern Inquiry: Suggestions toward a Hermeneutics of Indeterminacy," *Currents in Research: Biblical Studies* 7 (1999): 181–93.

206. For example, see Walter Brueggemann ("The Uninflected *Therefore* of Hosea 4:13," in *Reading from This Place*. Vol. 1, *Social Location and Biblical Interpretation in the United States*, 231–49 [241]), where, in speaking of two possible meanings of the word for "land," he notes: "We cannot *determine* which is intended"

Further, to the extent to which the concept of polyvalency may be related to that of indeterminacy in that both presuppose a plurality of interpretative options, Miscall stresses the polyvalent, allusive nature of the Isaiah text.[207] Miscall also highlights the difficulties of affirming allegiance to "the God encoded in the Isaiah text,"[208] substantially as a result of divine participation in unexplained and disturbing violence.

In an important article concerned with the meaning of ברך in the book of Job, Linafelt has persuasively argued that the whole work "is an adventure of theological subversion and theological dialogue, a crack in biblical discourse . . . a faultline in religious language that runs to the very character of God."[209] This is true especially for the way it evinces "a fundamental ambivalence about the character of YHWH."[210] On the strength of the above research, there are cracks in the biblical discourse in addition to those identified by Linafelt. A similar process to what Linafelt traces in Job is also evident in a close and nuanced reading of the opening chapters of Isaiah in its presentation of the theme of divine judgment and punishment. Furthermore, using "the classic Kantian formulation of the beautiful and the sublime"[211] as an analytical category, Linafelt concludes that "if there is a divine presence in this text, it is neither beautiful nor just, but perhaps sublime."[212] Indications in the rhetoric of the book of Isaiah suggest the same conclusion.

(emphasis added). Related to this general subject, see also Shalom M. Paul, "Polysensuous Polyvalency in Poetic Parallelism," in *Sha'arei Talmon: Studies in the Bible, Qumran, and the Ancient Near East—Presented to Shemaryahu Talmon* (ed. Michael Fishbane and Emanuel Tov, with the assistance of Weston W. Fields; Winona Lake, Ind.: Eisenbrauns, 1992), 147–63.

207.   Mark Gray, review of Peter Miscall, *Isaiah 34–35: A Nightmare/A Dream, Themelios* 25, no. 2 (2000): 71–72 (71). Supportive of Miscall's insistence "that the text should not be conformed to prior theological categories in a reductionist way," Dale Patrick notes that "biblical theologians should be free from the dogmatic constraints of interpretive communities. The text is too multivalent to be captured by any one interpretive tradition" (*The Rhetoric of Revelation in the Hebrew Bible* [OBT; Minneapolis: Fortress, 1999], xix).

208.   Gray, review of Miscall, 71.

209.   Tod Linafelt, "The Undecidability of ברך in the Prologue to Job and Beyond," *BibInt* 4, no. 2 (1996): 154–72 (154).

210.   Ibid., 156.

211.   Ibid., 170.

212.   Ibid., 171. Or as Linda Grant acidly quips, "The God of the Old Testament who visited 10 plagues on the Egyptians, including the slaying of the first-born, is beyond the jurisdiction of Amnesty International" ("Winners and Losers in a Hard Land," *Guardian Weekly* [2–8 November 2000]).

Chapter 4

THE MATTER OF TRUST:
"ON WHAT ARE YOU BASING THIS TRUST OF YOURS?"

The issue of trust is related to the foregoing discussion about ambiguity
in the divine character and is also a prominent theme in its own right
within the Isaianic corpus. I now explore the issue of trust to gain further
illumination concerning the nature of the character of God in the book of
Isaiah as a whole. I then assess the impact of my conclusions on the
subject of social justice. Finally, I place the results of this research in
critical dialogue with a range of theological and missiological scholars
who take the biblical text as their point of departure.

1. *The Untrustworthy Nature of Man*

Intrinsic to the book of Isaiah, this topic of trust first occurs in the
formula חדלו לכם מן־האדם (2:22),[1] which may literally be translated as
"cease from man," or more idiomatically "stop trusting in man."[2] This

1.　This verse is omitted altogether in the Septuagint. In the modern era, B. Duhm
discounts its originality (*Das Buch Jesaia*, 43–44). R. B. Y. Scott, after arguing that
v. 17, to which v. 22 is closely linked linguistically, should govern its lexical confusion and consequently provide the concluding refrain of the chapter, dismisses the
latter as a "meaningless (or at least unsuitable) sentence which the copyist extracted
from a partly illegible text" ("The Book of Isaiah, Chapters 1–39," *IB* 5:151–381
[183]). Summarizing this trend, Otto Kaiser notes, "We may take it as certain that
this verse is the addition of a later reader" (*Isaiah 1–12*, 63). However, as J. N.
Oswalt observes, "Thus v. 22, in a very effective way, sums up the general statement
of 2:6–21 and moves into the specific and concrete statement of 3:1–4:1" (*The Book
of Isaiah: Chapters 1–39*, 129). Moreover, from a rhetorical as opposed to a historical perspective, it is appropriate to deal with the text (in this case the Masoretic text)
in its received form. As Childs argues, "The real issue . . . turns on how this difficult,
but far from incoherent, text now functions in its present form" (*Isaiah*, 31).
2.　So the NIV. See also Motyer, *The Prophecy of Isaiah*, 58; Brueggemann,
Isaiah 1–39, 31–32; Oswalt, *Book of Isaiah: Chapters 1–39*, 128–29; Watts, *Isaiah
1–33*, 36; Webb, *The Message of Isaiah*, 48. Even taking into consideration the

injunction effectually concludes a passage (2:6–22) that envisions the severe reduction of human hubris (2:9, 11, 17[3]) as God alone is exalted.[4] Thus pride or trusting in humanity is negatively counterpointed to reliance on God. As Barton observes, the book of Isaiah encapsulates an "insistence on trust in God and the avoidance of all human expedients."[5]

This configuration may be justified in the context of divine exaltation occurring as the section of humanity that has displayed excessive arrogance and pride is cut down to size.[6] But if this group is taken to be socially inclusive and therefore representative of all humanity,[7] then once again, in parallel fashion to the above discussion concerning the probity of universal punishment, the justice of God is called into question. In this instance, the specter is raised of a God of overweening pride,[8] who, in pursuit of divine exaltation, is prepared to humble both those who are arrogant and those who are not.

further survey of interpretative options in Kaiser (*Isaiah 1–12*, 63), the balance of probability, both taking v. 22 by itself and in its literary context, suggests a sense of turning away from or not trusting in humanity. In a different form of words, ארור הגבר אשר יבטח באדם, Jer 17:5 arrives at the same idea ("cursed is the man who trusts in man").

3. These three verses all contain the word pair שחח ("to humble") and שפל ("to bring low").

4. Verses 11 and 17 both end ונשגב יהוה לבדו ביום ההוא ("In that day Yahweh alone will be exalted"). Of the 20 times the שגב root is found in the Hebrew Bible, these verses are the only places it is found in this Niphal form. Barton argues that "the theme of pride and humility seems almost to be the uniting theme of the whole work" ("Ethics in the Book of Isaiah," 73). He adds, "Humility is seen as the appropriate response to the majesty of God" (p. 75), and that "the whole book might be seen as a treatise on human folly and divine wisdom" in which "humans sin against God's supremacy . . . by self-aggrandizement, arrogance, and refusal to trust in God" (p. 76).

5. Barton, "Ethics in the Book of Isaiah," 72.

6. The phrases גבהות אדם and רום אנשים are found in 2:11 and 17.

7. As seems to be indicated by 5:15, in which man (אדם) will be "bowed down" (שחח), man (איש) will be "humbled/brought low" (שפל), and the eyes of the haughty "humbled/brought low" (שפל).

8. Walter Houston points out that "in the courts of the Lord none but the Lord will be allowed honour" ("Tragedy in the Courts of the Lord: A Socio-literary Reading of the Death of Nadab and Abihu," *JSOT* 90 [2000]: 31–39 [34]). Supportive of this thinking, Barton argues that "the distinctively Isaianic approach to ethics involves tracing ethical obligation to its highest source, which lies in the supremacy of God, from whom all good and all power derives, and doing, saying, and thinking nothing which might derogate from that supremacy" ("Ethics in the Book of Isaiah," 77). This approach, though, simply accepts without question the beneficent, trustworthy nature of God.

Based on previous rhetorical analysis, other interesting and potentially problematic issues are also raised concerning the character of the divine by the "stop trusting in man" formulation. In 2:22, the command to "turn away" from humanity is found in precisely the same form as in 1:16 (חדל), where it is an integral part of a significant exhortation to turn toward humanity, particularly those most marginalized and oppressed. Thus a note of uncertainty is introduced to the text. What is it that the Lord requires? An abandonment of wickedness as part of the process of embracing the cause of the poor, or a turning of one's back on all of humanity in the interests of holiness and abetting the exaltation of God?[9]

Oswalt offers a partial solution to this conundrum when he argues that the thrust of 2:22 is against "the tendency of human beings to make our-selves the centre of all things"[10] and consequently to establish a culture of "dependency upon man."[11] Likewise, Webb insists that the import of the verse is to reinforce that "as objects of ultimate trust" human beings "are of no account at all."[12] This *interpretation*, however, while plausible from a certain theological perspective, is a considerable step away from the immediate rhetorical impact of the injunction with which the verse starts. Moreover, if the character of the divine as inscribed in the text (which, as demonstrated, is marked by a degree of unreliability and excess) is not conflated with the concept of God as an extratextual postulation of cer-tainty and reliability, then the exclusivist polarity of a choice between humanity or God is significantly dissolved. Humanity may yet be legiti-mately understood as a source of ethical values in relation to the search for social justice.

This note of uncertainty and dissonance is further accentuated when it is observed that whereas 2:22 urges a turning away from humanity (האדם),[13] 58:5–10, which Watts identifies as being addressed "to אדם 'a human being' rather than to Israel and Jerusalem" and therefore constitu-tive of "Yahweh's requirements for worship . . . to anyone who seeks him,"[14] encourages a turning toward humanity in a profound way. Not-withstanding the extensive number of times אדם occurs in the Hebrew Bible, its deployment as part of a sustained denigration of any reliance

9. Walter Brueggemann explores this dialectic ("Vision for a New Church and a New Century Part II: Holiness Become Generosity," *Union Seminary Quarterly Review* 54 [2000]: 1–2, 45–64).

10. Oswalt, *Book of Isaiah: Chapters 1–39*, 128.

11. Ibid., 129.

12. Webb, *Message of Isaiah*, 48.

13. This reading is particularly underscored by the NEB translation of v. 22a as "Have no more to do with man."

14. Watts, *Isaiah 34–66*, 271.

upon humanity[15] may be contrasted legitimately with a passage in the same book that exhorts an embrace of humanity in the quest for reconciliation and social justice.

In addition, however the confused syntax of v. 22b is handled, it is difficult to avoid the conclusion that the reference to "breath" (נשמה) is part of a devaluation of the worth of human life, the essence of which is this elusive, insubstantial material. This thrust stands in tension with the first biblical occurrence of נשמה (Gen 2:7), in which "the breath of life," as a gift of God, is that which transforms an inanimate creature of dust into a "living being," and thus carries a positive connotation.[16]

Commentators attempt to ameliorate the negative dimension of 2:22b in a number of ways. Following the likes of Duhm,[17] Kaiser holds out the possibility that it constitutes a "reference to man's transitoriness" and consequently should be interpreted as a cause for "God to be merciful."[18] However, while attractive in a sense, this reading is undercut and rendered less than secure by the wider context of Isa 2, which is significantly opposed to any positive or sympathetic evaluation of humanity. Interpreted as a call not to trust in man on account of the inconsequential nature of the breath in his nostrils, v. 22 fittingly concludes the development of thought that arrives at this juncture.

Approaching the verse from a different perspective, Webb argues that it "does not deny the truth, taught elsewhere, that human beings are made in God's image and therefore have a certain dignity. It does assert, however, that as objects of ultimate trust they are of no account at all."[19] This interpretation does not place much importance on the immediate

---

15. As Brueggemann observes, "Leave off trust in 'mortals.' The Hebrew is bald: *'adam* = humankind. The same term has been used in verses 9, 11, 17 and 20, there rendered 'people.' Leave off human self-securing" (*Isaiah 1–39*, 32).

16. This positive connotation, perhaps not unsurprisingly for historicist reasons rooted in the study of traditions, is also found in Isa 42:5. But in Job 4:9, in a context in which Eliphaz is postulating a closely correlated relationship between evil and punishment, so that the innocent do not perish and the upright are not destroyed, Eliphaz insists that "at the breath (נשמה) of God . . . those who plough evil and those who sow trouble . . . are destroyed" (4:8–9). In this instance, the reference to "breath" carries a negative connotation as the breath of God ends life in punishment. Eliphaz argues that "if God places no trust (אמן)" in human beings (4:18), then neither should human beings themselves (vv. 19–21). This statement occurs to support the thesis that no mortal can be more righteous than God and no person more pure than their maker (4:17). In other words, the position of God to do whatever God pleases, without question or critical comment, is defended.

17. Duhm, *Das Buch Jesaja*, 43–44.

18. Kaiser, *Isaiah 1–12*, 63.

19. Webb, *Message of Isaiah*, 48.

context in which the verse is found, and is governed by the theological necessity of protecting the integrity of the divine from any accusation of inconsistency or wrongdoing. In effect, Webb's analysis functions in a way comparable to that of one of Job's visitors.[20]

2. *A Voice of Protest in Favor of Humanity*

Responding to the concluding argument of Bildad, in which he, in an echo of earlier comments by Eliphaz (4:17), posits the unrighteousness of humanity before God and humanity's intrinsic impurity (25:4), Job scathingly commends his "comforter" for how he has helped the power-less (26:1) and questions whose נשמה ("spirit") has spoken from his mouth (26:4). He then, interestingly, acknowledges the power of God (26:7–14), before going on to assert that this God who surely lives has denied him justice (27:2). Next, in a trenchant defense of the integrity of his humanity, Job insists that as long as he has breath (נשמה) within him, the wind (or spirit) of God in his nostrils (27:3), he will never accede to his opponent's theological formulation. Instead he asserts his righteous-ness and the clear nature of his conscience (27:6). Functionally, this is someone who is prepared to trust in humanity even against received theological wisdom.[21]

Against this perceived blasphemy, Elihu is angry that those who have previously contended with Job have condemned him but found no way to refute him (32:3).[22] So he sets out to do so. With a self-deprecating display of modesty, which finally smacks of being feigned, he avers that it is "the breath (נשמה) of the Almighty" that gives a person understand-ing (32:8). Consequently, "It is not only the old (or many) who are wise, nor only the aged who understand what is right" (32:9). Therefore, young as he is (32:6, 7), he feels himself sufficiently wise as a result of divine inspiration to offer a conclusive rebuttal to Job. Indeed, in a colorful metaphorical flourish, he claims to be "like bottled-up wine, like new

---

20. See Mettinger, "The God of Job," 41–42.
21. Job's apparent renunciation of this position in 42:1–6 is dealt with below.
22. This verse is one of the *tiqqune sopherim*, the eighteen emendations of the scribes in the Jewish tradition made to eliminate a reading that may have been theo-logically offensive to God. So the Masoretic reads "they declared Job to be in the wrong/guilty" instead of the original "condemned God/made God guilty." The uncor-rupted text, prior to the theologically motivated changes instituted by the Masoretes, reflecting a "conversion" of Job's first three visitors, indicates that in the tradition that produced the book of Job, in a certain quarter and at a certain time, Job's position was not considered completely outlandish.

wineskins ready to burst" (32:19): he must speak and find relief (32:20) as the "spirit within"[23] compels him (32:18).

Elihu continues with the orthodox formulation that the "spirit of God" (note the use of רוח again) has made him and that "the breath (נשמה) of the Almighty" gives him life (33:4), from which he concludes that he and Job are alike before God in that both are children of clay (33:6). For him, however, there is such a disjunction between God and humanity that the nature of the relationship between the two is marked, guarded, and encapsulated in the conviction "God is greater than man," and that, there-fore, self-evidently, what Job has been saying is "not right." According to Elihu, it is thus impossible for any human to claim to be "pure and without sin . . . clean and free from guilt" (33:9). Then, in a self-impor-tant and self-righteous way, he implies that if God "has found fault" with him (even him!) and considers him "God's enemy" (32:10), the same must hold true universally.[24]

On the basis of this insecure theological foundation, Elihu proceeds to address Job's complaint that God "answers none of man's words"[25] by arguing that "God does speak" in various ways "though man may not perceive it" (33:14). Confronted with situations of pain, Elihu maintains the hope of restoration through divine intervention (33:25, 26), so long as afterward the restored person publicly comes clean by confessing, "I sinned and perverted what was right, but I did not get what I deserved. God redeemed my soul from going down to the pit" (33:27, 28a).[26] In effect, with substantially no more theological originality than his prede-cessors who have engaged in dialogue with Job, Elihu builds a theology designed to defend the divine from accusations of complicity in wrong-doing. Everything—especially with regard to contexts of pain in life—

---

23. Rhetorically, note the repetition of רוח in vv. 8 and 18.

24. In this case the functional claim to universal application is undermined by the ironic way it is presented. This perhaps further warns us to be wary of universalist claims, such as the one examined above with respect to universal punishment.

25. This may literally be translated "that all of his words God will not answer," perhaps with the connotation that God does not answer for what God brings about. In any case, the idea seems to be that God does not feel obliged to give an account of divine activity.

26. In a sense Elihu affirms the Psalmic pattern of restoration as exemplified, for example, by Ps 30:11–12, but in the process eliminates and renders illegitimate the haunting voice of Ps 88. Moreover, Elihu links all calamity, pain, and misfortune ultimately to sin. In making this move, he is theologically much narrower than many of the Psalms (and elsewhere in the Hebrew Bible), where no such linkage is pre-supposed. See Fredrik Lindström, *Suffering and Sin: Interpretations of Illness in the Individual Complaint Psalms* (Stockholm: Almqvist & Wiksell, 1994).

must be amenable to a neat explanation that contains no ambiguity and that, more importantly, casts no shadow of doubt over God's character.

Concluding his contribution at considerable length, Elihu continues his rebuttal of Job's assertion that Job is innocent and that God has denied him justice (34:5) by insisting that God does neither evil nor wrong (34:10), but rather "repays a person for what they have done, bringing upon them what their conduct deserves" (34:11). According to Elihu's theological lights, "It is unthinkable that God would do wrong, that the Almighty would pervert justice" (34:12). He then reasons that if God withdrew God's "spirit and breath" (34:14; note the רוח and נשמה combination again), "all humankind would perish altogether," resulting in humanity's return to dust.[27] It does not necessarily follow that because God sustains life, God is also just: the character of God as a God of justice cannot be derived directly from this premise. In further explicating his restricted theological agenda, Elihu asks rhetorically, "Can one [One?] who hates justice govern?" (34:17),[28] before resoundingly asserting, "The Almighty is beyond our reach and exalted in power; in God's justice and great righteousness, God does not oppress" (37:23).

This reference to the strength of God, reflected in the use of כביר (34:17; 36:5) and כח (found in the similar expressions ישׂגיב בכחו in 36:22 and שׂגיא־כח in 37:23), forms a *leitmotif* through Elihu's closing argument. Again, however, a non sequitur is evident, this time in the linkage of God's might and God's justice,[29] in that the latter is not necessarily

27. A similar idea is expressed in Ps 104:29, though using different terms. The flood also achieves this end (and more!) in Gen 7:22 in that it deprives "everything on dry land that had the breath (נשמה) of life in its nostrils" of existence. Disturbingly, in light of my interest in humanity carrying out divinely sanctioned violence, Israel is endowed with the same authority to take life. Regarding its conquest of the land of promise, Israel is told "in the cities of the nations the Lord your God is giving you . . . do not leave alive anything that breathes (נשמה)" (Deut 20:16). Joshua fully follows through on this injunction, destroying all who breathed (נשמה; Josh 10:40), not sparing anything that breathed (נשמה; Josh 11:11), putting to the sword anyone who breathed (נשמה; Josh 11:14). Within Israel, the same sort of thing happens when "anyone who breathed (נשמה)" (1 Kgs 15:29) in Jeroboam's whole family is destroyed "according to the word of the Lord."

28. This question can be related to a similar question in Ps 94:20, which asks of the divine, "Can a corrupt throne be allied with you?" In this instance the implication is that a God of justice cannot sanction a corrupt earthly regime (throne), one "that brings on misery by its decrees" (Ps 94:20). In Elihu's question, the claim that God is the God of justice is made more explicitly.

29. In 34:17, צדיק and כביר are portrayed as divine attributes, while in 37:23, שדי is described as being: שׂגיא־כח ומשפט ורב־צדקה ("great in power and justice and abundant righteousness").

a function or expression of the former, as Elihu presupposes. In terms of the theodic formulation of Ps 62:11b–12, the rumor or witness that God is strong and loving leads the psalmist to hope for divine justice, but this hope is articulated without the absolute conviction and certitude of Elihu's fundamentalist assertion. This issue, of the relationship between divine power and justice, is explored further below.

In light of the preceding discussion, the call of Isa 2:22 to "stop trust-ing in man" is rendered unstable. This is done by the Joban account of one person who is prepared to trust in his convictions of innocence and of having been unjustly treated by God, even against God and God's self-appointed theological apologists. Furthermore, in situations of extreme suffering, either in the putatively individual example of Job, or in the communal example of Israel with regard to the biblical representa-tion of exile, to defend the integrity of the divine too insistently and in too fundamentalist a way places one in theological company of dubious value.[30]

3. *Isaiah 36 and the Theme of Trust*

The choice between "trusting" in God or "trusting in man" (or something associated with or deriving from humanity) is characteristic of both the book of Isaiah and, more generally, an aspect of the sweep of biblical rhetoric.[31] With respect to Isaiah, this theme may be further explored for the light it casts on the character of God through tracing the use of the various terms for trust deployed within the book, primary among which is בטח.

Watts, after wondering why "a narrative about 8th-century Jerusalem" should "appear where one would expect a description of the last days of the Kingdom of Judah in the 6th century B.C.,"[32] suggests that Isa 36–39

---

30. Anson Laytner makes the connection between the theology of Deutero-Isaiah and Elihu. He states, "Deutero-Isaiah, in particular, has God answering all the charges that Israel (or Job) raise against Him. As opposed to the protest and argu-ment of Job and company, these works [Ezekiel, Zechariah, Malachi, Deutero-Isaiah, and Elihu] advocate trust in the Lord" (*Arguing with God*, 37). He further maintains that these theological articulations "state that it was Israel's sins that led God to withdraw, and that it is for the people to repent and for God to pardon."

31. See R. Laird Harris, Gleason L. Archer Jr., and Bruce K. Waltke, eds., *Theological Wordbook of the Old Testament* (2 vols.; Chicago: Moody Press), 1:233, where in explaining the key term בטח the editors write, "In general, the Old Testa-ment contrasts the validity of that sense of confidence which comes from reliance upon God with the folly of any other kind of security."

32. Watts, *Isaiah 34–66*, 23.

was generative for the composition of the book of Isaiah as a whole.[33] He terms these chapters as "the seedbed of ideas, vocabulary, and plot that echoes in the chapters preceding and following."[34] First among these, he then identifies "confidence and trust, which are one Hebrew word, בטח."[35]

Reinforcing the idea of the importance of the theme of trust, specifically in relation to Isa 36, Brueggemann writes that "the governing term *bth* dominates this speech and occurs six times (vv. 4, 5, 6, 6, 7, 9)."[36] As noted above with respect to the example of this theme in 2:22, again the choice presented to Israel is one between trust in Yahweh or trust in a range of constructs originating in humanity.[37]

Interestingly, though, the primary speech (36:4–10) in which the term בטח recurs is found not in the mouth of an Israelite, but of an Assyrian field commander. Through the speech, issues of faith are indeed raised for Israel. Issues pertaining to the reliability of God are also raised. So, during an Assyrian military campaign against "the fortified cities of Judah" (36:1), the Rabshakeh, an envoy of the king of Assyria, approaches Jerusalem to outline for the city's leadership the futility of their position confronted with Assyrian power. The envoy comes also to offer peace terms that promise security (36:16) until captives are resettled in "a land of grain and new wine, a land of bread and vineyards" (35:17). In an opening gambit designed to begin the erosion of Israelite confidence, the

---

33. Ibid. Watts asks the question, "Can it be that the reading of this narrative was the inspiration that led to the composition of the Vision?" Context leads one to assume that Watts implies an affirmative answer. See also Childs, *Isaiah*, 259–66, for a helpful survey of discussion.

34. Watts, *Isaiah 34–66*, 23.

35. Ibid. See also Goldingay, *Isaiah*, 204–7.

36. Brueggemann, *Isaiah 1–39*, 285. More broadly, Brueggemann intimates that "this entire unit of chapters 36–39 functions to *summon Israel to faith* in a circumstance that bespeaks doubt, timidity, and fear" (p. 282 [emphasis in original]). Underscoring the importance of the theme of trust in Isaiah as a whole, he asserts that "the key religious obligation of the Isaiah tradition is 'faith,' a capacity to trust in Yahweh in situations of risk" (p. 284). The term further occurs in connection to the narrative impulse of this passage as it is carried into 37:10, on which see below.

37. Ibid. As Brueggemann observes, "The speech . . . is Isaianic theology summoning Judah to the risk and danger of bold faith in Yahweh as the only alternative to life on the harsh, demanding terms of the empire." Laato, also making the thematic link between Isa 2:22 and ch. 36, observes, "Isa 2:22 takes up another important message which IR [implied readers] can relate to the texts of Isaiah 1–39. The people cannot expect help from human beings. The people must turn to Yahweh to seek help from him and him alone" (*About Zion I Will Not Be Silent*, 177). He adds, "Hezekiah is described in Isaiah 36–39 as he who acted aright by turning to Yhwh and asking his help against the Assyrian army."

Rabshakeh, on behalf of his sovereign, poses the question מה הבטחון הזה
אשר בטחת ("On what are you basing this trust [בטח] in which you are
trusting [בטח]?") before going on specifically to undermine the two main-
stays of Israelite confidence: their ally, Egypt, and their God, Yahweh.

With regard to the former, he contemptuously acknowledges that Israel
speaks of "strategy and power" (36:5). But in answer to the demand for
more detailed and substantive information contained in the question, "On
whom are you relying (בטח) now that you have rebelled?" (36:5), when
he reveals that he already knows that the object of trust (בבט; 36:4a) is
Egypt, he attempts to undermine Israelite confidence by asserting that
Egypt is a "broken reed of a staff" that lacerates the hand of anyone who
leans on it (36:6). Underlining the unreliability of the Egyptian Pharaoh,
the mouthpiece of the Assyrian king intimates that this untrustworthiness
is characteristic for "all who rely (בטח) on him" (36:6).

The Rabshakeh then sows seeds of doubt in the minds of some Israelites by suggesting that if Israel says, "On Yahweh our God we rely (בבטח)"
(36:7), then their object of trust is one who may not be best pleased with
Hezekiah, the Israelite king, on account of his having removed Yahweh's
high places and altars in a centralizing religious reform. The suggestion,
which may have found a sympathetic ear in certain quarters of Israelite
society,[38] is perhaps being made that Hezekiah's reforms were motivated
by the desire for self-aggrandizement (self-exaltation?) and the consoli-
dation of power, rather than having been solely divinely inspired.[39] In
light of this point, there might well be understandable grounds for
supposing that God's intent was to punish Hezekiah rather than to come
to Israel's defense.

Having thus attempted to demoralize the representatives of the Israelite leadership that he is addressing directly, the Assyrian envoy suggests
making terms (36:8). But before clarifying what the terms might be, he
returns to the worth of the Egyptian alliance, arguing that Israel will
derive no benefit from relying (בבטח) on it, such is Assyrian superiority.[40]

---

38. As Oswalt observes with regard to Hezekiah's reform, "Thus the Assyrian
officer's confident assertion that God did not want to bless Judah probably touched a
raw nerve of doubt which was very near the surface of many a Judean consciousness" (*Book of Isaiah: Chapters 1–39*, 636). Similarly, Motyer notes that the Rabshakeh "may have been playing also on the frayed nerves of any who were less than
convinced of the rightness of what the king was doing" (*Prophecy of Isaiah*, 277).

39. For an illuminating exposition of this theme with respect to the centralizing
reforms of Josiah, see Shigeyuki Nakanose, *Josiah's Passover: Sociology and the
Liberating Bible* (Maryknoll, N.Y.: Orbis, 1993).

40. Condemnation of reliance on Egypt forms a pattern in Isaiah that is linked to
the theme of trust: in 30:2, those "who go down to Egypt without consulting" God

Returning to the subject of Yahweh, Israel's other basis of hope, he makes the decisive claim that the Lord has requested the Assyrian king "to march against this country and destroy it" (36:10). In effect, Israel's God is in league with Assyria against God's chosen people (or so at least the Assyrian field commander claims). Understandably, the Israelite leadership wants this potentially devastating information kept from the populace of Jerusalem as a whole—indicating, perhaps, that even if it cannot be demonstrated that they believe it, they at least treat the claim with some level of seriousness and plausibility. But in an attempt to spread doubt in the ranks of the enemy, the Rabshakeh proclaims in the common Hebrew tongue, "Do not let Hezekiah persuade you to trust (בטח) in the Lord" (36:15). As Kaiser puts it, "Thus with the first speech of the Rabshakeh the narrative asks whom man should trust in extremity, himself, the help of other people or God?"[41] Or as Watts observes, perhaps with a touch of understatement given the potentially detrimental implication for the character of God if the divine is indeed in cahoots with the Assyrians, this speech "raises the issue of true and false confidence (בטח) and its foundation."[42] The trustworthiness of God cannot be left out of this adjudication.

Commentators approach the matter of God reportedly encouraging (and thereby validating?) the Assyrian assault on Judah in a variety of ways. Brueggemann allows that the assertion "that the armies of Sennacherib have come against Judah *at the behest of Yahweh*" is a "daring claim."[43] He then, however, diminishes the incongruity of the claim by suggesting that it "could be part of rather routine propaganda" and that, besides, "the prophetic tradition of Israel is not averse to identifying invaders of Judah as tools of Yahweh's judgement."[44] Three points can

---

and who trust/take refuge (חסה) in Egypt's shade are condemned. Use of this term in the broader Isaianic corpus highlights the prophetic claim that refuge taken in and thus trust placed in anything not ordained by God is futile. Isaiah 14:32 effectually asserts that it is only in Zion that God's afflicted people will find refuge (חסה), while 57:13 maintains that the person who makes God their refuge (חסה) "will inherit the land and possess God's holy mountain." This pattern is also seen in the use of two other terms for trust within the Isaianic corpus, בטח and יחל.

41. Otto Kaiser, *Isaiah 13–39* (trans. R. A. Wilson; OTL; London: SCM Press, 1974), 387.

42. Watts, *Isaiah 34–66*, 25.

43. Brueggemann, *Isaiah 1–39*, 286 (emphasis in original). Childs terms the two arguments of the Rabshakeh "especially startling" (*Isaiah*, 273).

44. Brueggemann, *Isaiah 1–39*, 286. Oswalt also follows this line: "Other evidence from the Ancient Near East shows that it was not unusual for a conqueror to claim that his conquest was made possible because the god of the vanquished had joined the side of the conqueror" (*Book of Isaiah: Chapters 1–39*, 636–37). See also,

be made: first, while this might be an example of propaganda, equally it might not. The nature of the text leaves the matter open, undecided, and ambiguous, a function of the narrative that does little to bring assurance concerning the reliability of the character of God. For all the reader knows, God could be testing Judah in some sort of Joban fashion. Second, citing further examples of an unreliable action, while helping to establish a pattern of behavior, hardly makes it ethically more acceptable. Third, in this instance, the claim is that Yahweh goes beyond merely using a foreign nation as a tool (which could be achieved without the nation knowing the divine purpose it had served),[45] to communicating God's intention to that nation and thereby involving it in God's will against God's people. Also able to entertain the thought of God initiating an alliance with an enemy of Israel, Watts observes that the Rabshakeh "closes with an insinuation that Yahweh had instigated the invasion in the first place."[46] For reasons that may be surmised, the use of the term "insinuation" considerably modifies the way in which the claim itself is made in the text.

As might be expected, a certain school of scholarship reflexively marshals arguments to defend the integrity of the character of God. Motyer, on the basis of no supporting evidence, attributes the knowledge of the Rabshakeh to the work of espionage, noting that "spies are not a modern invention."[47] Webb argues that "this speech is a classic study in the Satanic art of sowing doubt and unbelief through subtly twisting the truth."[48] Developing his case in a way that is worth quoting at length, he goes on:

> The speech is so persuasive precisely because it contains so much that is true. But its basic premise is false: namely, that the LORD has forsaken Judah, and that therefore trust in him is futile. It is always Satan's way to make us think that God has abandoned us, and to use logic woven from

following Oswalt, J. B. Pritchard, ed., *Ancient Near Eastern Texts* (3d ed.; Princeton: Princeton University Press, 1969), 277–78, 283, 286, 289–91, 293, 301, 312–15, 462.

45.   Oswalt argues, "We do not know whether the Assyrians were aware of Isaiah's claim that God would use the Assyrians to punish his people (8:7–8; 10:5–6)" (*Book of Isaiah: Chapters 1–39*, 637). If they were, this claim could be dismissed as propaganda derivative of that knowledge, but since we do not the text is consequently imbued with a degree of indeterminacy/undecidability which adds to the narrative strength of the passage. It also draws the issue of the character of God into that web of indeterminacy/undecidability.

46.   Watts, *Isaiah 34–66*, 25.

47.   Motyer, *Prophecy of Isaiah*, 278.

48.   Webb, *Message of Isaiah*, 148.

half-truths to convince us of it. This speech is so subtly devilish in character that it might have been written by Satan himself. The truth is that the LORD had brought Judah to the end of her own resources so that she might learn again what it meant to trust him utterly. But he had not abandoned and would not abandon her.[49]

These arguments, however, are governed and determined by theological presuppositions about the nature of God rather than the evidence of the text itself. Webb is so intent on defending a pre-established theological formulation (in a fashion reminiscent of the strategy of Job's visitors) that claims are made that not only go beyond what the text in its wider ramifications supports, but that actually contradict it. There is thus a disjunction between the assertion that God "had not abandoned and would not abandon" Israel and Isa 54:7, in which God confesses to having abandoned Israel.[50]

The nature of the text, on account of the rhetorical strategy adopted, will not sustain this degree of closure based on *a priori* theological assumptions. If anything, the narrative, even if one accepts that it is finally intended to illustrate trust in God on the part of Hezekiah, tends more to support a reading that at least continues to host reservations about the reliability of Yahweh. This is reinforced when one considers that the final appeal by messengers of Sennacherib to Hezekiah not to depend (בטח) on God (37:10) has been undercut by the prior disclosure (37:7) that God is going to put a spirit (רוח) in the Assyrian king that will lead him to be assassinated.[51] The impression is thus created that God is, as it were, working both sides of the street. Further, that God is in communication with Assyria via this spirit adds credence to the claim of the Rabshakeh in 36:10: the Assyrian army could well have been at the gates of Jerusalem on the instruction of Yahweh.

If this narrative is important with regard to the theme of trust and of significance in the composition of the book of Isaiah as a whole,[52] the

---

49. Ibid., 149.

50. See Brueggemann for a much more text-based exploration of the theme of abandonment (*Deep Memory, Exuberant Hope* [Minneapolis: Fortress, 2000], 77–90).

51. Although the term רוח has wide usage in the Hebrew Bible, the idea of sending a spirit to achieve a divine purpose legitimately calls to mind 1 Kgs 22:22, in which a spirit is sent from the heavenly court as part of a ruse to deceive Ahab, king of Israel. The spirit is described as רוח שקר ("a lying spirit," the expression also occurs in 1 Kgs 22:23). The term שקר is also found in the commandment "you shall not bear false witness (שקר) against your neighbor" (Exod 20:16). God in 1 Kgs 22 effectively is party to breaking one of God's own commandments; thus, the character of God is further called into question.

52. See Seitz, *Zion's Final Destiny*; and Laato, *About Zion I Will Not Be Silent*.

manner of its telling, while doubtless skilful and entertaining, militates against easy or unreserved accession to the God encoded in the text. The narratological suggestion of divine participation in the modalities of unreliability invariably leaves a residual effect. Even if it is understood that the intended or implied reader of the final form of the book is to take some degree of delight that their God took part in subterfuge against a more powerful enemy, the doubt remains that at some point God could act similarly against them.

As far as this text is concerned, the God presented retains traces of the character of "Yahweh the impish God who refuses to conform" rather than "the great אני הוא of the Isaiah scroll."[53] In other words, a degree of tension exists between whatever trust might be engendered and affirmed in the ambiguously rendered God of Isa 36–37 and the nature of trust expressed in the assured conviction of 12:2, in which it is confidently proclaimed, "Surely God is my salvation: I will trust (בטח) and not be afraid."[54] Trust in the God of Isa 36–37, while possible (as displayed by Hezekiah), is something of a leap of faith.[55]

---

53. K. L. Noll, "Is there a Text in this Tradition? Readers' Response and the Taming of Samuel's God," *JSOT* 83 (1999): 31–51 (50). Noll contrasts the unstable character of God in the book of Samuel (p. 48) with the unitary characterization of the divine in Isaiah, Deuteronomy, Exodus, and elsewhere (p. 50). This interpretation of the character of God in Isa 36–37 suggests that the division Noll argues for is not that decisive, to the extent that God continues to display elements that destabilize the concept of a coherent God of absolute moral rectitude, reliability, and integrity.

54. Along the same lines, 14:30 looks to the day when "the needy will lie down in trust (בטח)," but the concept of universal punishment as explored above, even against the most marginalized and needy in society, undercuts confidence in this statement.

55. This sort of idea is also found in 50:10–11. The sense of trust in God being a leap of faith in the dark becomes more pronounced when one considers that syntactically it is possible to read 50:10 as indicating that even the servant of Yahweh walks in darkness and has no light, yet even in this condition the servant still trusts in the name of Yahweh and relies on his God. Interestingly, Ellen van Wolde argues that "Job's faith will be only truly disinterested when he continues to believe without a direct reason and without a special purpose" (*Mr and Mrs Job* [London: SCM Press, 1991], 138). It is only after he has accepted that functionally he is in the dark about certain matters, that he is once again, in parallel to 1:8 and 2:3, designated "my servant" (עבד; 42:7 and three times in 42:8). Indicating the significance of this switch, van Wolde stresses, "Neither in the dialogues nor in God's speech is Job called God's servant, but only in the prologue," then, "Four times in two verses God calls Job 'my servant'" (p. 143). The idea of faith being a leap in the dark reminds one of Søren Kierkegaard, *Fear and Trembling* (trans. Walter Lowrie; New York: Anchor, 1954).

4. *The Challenge of Trust*

The challenge of maintaining trust in God is also reflected in the rhetorical development of Isa 26.[56] It opens with a confident declaration of faith, similar to those in 12:2 and 14:30,[57] in which the text proclaims that Yahweh will keep in profound peace the one who has a steadfast mind, because that person trusts (בטח) in God (26:3). This is immediately followed by an injunction, "[T]rust (בטח) in Yahweh forever" (26:4). As Brueggemann notes, "To trust means to continue to rely [on Yahweh] with dogged determination, without respect to circumstance."[58] This definition aptly encapsulates the nature of trust in God endorsed by the wider Isaianic corpus and substantiated by the above analysis. However, as Brueggemann goes on to suggest, the imperative of v. 4 may be necessary to summon a community "wavering to reaffirm its confidence in Yahweh."[59] Thus, again the issue is mooted that trust or confidence in God is not always easily conceded.

By the latter stages of ch. 26, the incipient crisis of confidence in God has intensified. From v. 11 onward, "the wicked," who are alleged to have failed to learn righteousness from the graciousness of God (v. 10), are referred to as "they." In v. 16, the text asserts that "they came to you in their distress; when you disciplined them, they could barely whisper." Applied to the wicked, this statement, in the view of a certain type of retribution-oriented theology, might not only appear understandable, but expected, acceptable, and entirely justifiable—indeed the function of a certain concept of justice.[60] But the switch in the succeeding verse from the third person plural to the first person plural jarringly indicates that this abused condition is being experienced not by those who arguably might deserve it according to a certain theological outlook, but by

56. For a survey of historical-critical analyses of this passage in respect of dating its various strata, see Kaiser, *Isaiah 13–39*, 205–6 n. f. See also Oswalt, who notes that "there has been an almost incredible variety of opinions concerning the literary integrity of ch. 26" (*Book of Isaiah: Chapters 1–39*, 469–70; Childs, *Isaiah*, 188–90).

57. When the root אמן, which sometimes carries the connotation "to have faith" in or "to trust," is considered, this list may be extended: see 28:16; 49:7; 55:3. However, that trust in the actions of God is not easily acknowledged may also be indicated by 53:1–12, which is introduced by the question, "Who has believed (אמן) what we have heard?" It is as if that which follows stretches credulity and is therefore difficult to acknowledge.

58. Brueggemann, *Isaiah 1–39*, 202.

59. Ibid., 203.

60. Blenkinsopp correctly observes that "we may readily admit the danger lurking in this claim to be God's righteous people when it is linked with the demand that punishment be visited on 'the others'" (*Isaiah 1–39*, 369–70).

members of the grouping who have retained trust in God.[61] What is more, their abased position has been caused by God. The nature of their extreme anxiety appears in the image of the group likened to a woman writhing and crying in the toils of childbirth (26:17), but ultimately being unable to produce a child.[62]

By this point in the chapter, as Watts perceives, the mood has "turned away from the pious thoughts with which it began." Watts notes further "that despair lies not far beneath the surface"[63] of the group that has been steadfastly loyal to Yahweh. Explicating the same idea, Brueggemann argues that

> now the "they" are not the wicked of verse 11, but they are the desperately needy, the forlorn righteous. They have turned incessantly and trustingly to Yahweh. They have sought and poured out. They have given themselves passionately over to Yahweh. They have done that even while under the severe pressure of Yahweh. They have not, for any reason, ceased to turn to, rely upon, and trust in Yahweh. But all for naught![64]

Effectually casting doubt on the character of God, Brueggemann labels these verses (26:16–18) as "daring utterance" in which "Yahweh has not given the victory due such zealous faith."[65] Brueggemann concludes, "The picture is of this little passionate community of faith, surrounded by adversaries, having cast its lot with the only alternative power it knows or trusts."[66] On the strength of Brueggemann's own comments, however, this trust is considerably strained and not given without protest due to the perception that God is in some degree unreliable. This sense of unreliability legitimately opens the way for humanity to initiate attempts to establish structures, systems, and practices of justice.[67]

The potential depth of the crisis in the nature of God inherent in these verses is reflected in the way the issue registers seriously in the commentaries of conservative scholars, even if, as might be expected, ultimately

---

61. See Childs, *Isaiah*, 191.

62. On this imagery, see Darr, *Isaiah's Vision and the Family of God*, 205–24.

63. Watts, *Isaiah 1–33*, 342; see also Goldingay, *Isaiah*, 147–48.

64. Brueggemann, *Isaiah 1–39*, 207.

65. Ibid.

66. Ibid., 208.

67. Against this, Oswalt argues that 26:16–19 "illustrates what the entire first thirty-nine chapters of the book are about: trust in human potential must bring disaster . . . but an awareness of human weakness which results in trust in God will bring life forevermore" (*Book of Isaiah: Chapters 1–39*, 483). The neat mathematical quality of this formula, however, is unsettled by the way the text is able to host the idea that God is not always trustworthy, thereby reactivating the proposition that humanity has a proper place in the search for justice.

they reach conclusions that keep the integrity of the divine intact. Oswalt acknowledges that "however strong the conviction of God's ultimate triumph, there come those moments when the believer is brought face to face with the contradictions which the present sets over against that conviction."[68] In other words, there are times when theological dogma is challenged by felt experience.

Webb terms the implications of 26:16–17 "perplexing" for "the *apparent* harshness with which the LORD treats the ones who are looking to him to save them. . . . Their commitment to the LORD brings them nothing but frustration and a sense of complete failure."[69] Owning up to the reality that "there is surely an acute crisis of faith here," he adds, as a prelude to what is for him a satisfactory resolution to the problem, that such a situation "must issue in either despair or a breakthrough to a new understanding of God's ways." Then, with an assurance that verges on the platitudinous, he continues, "It is a testimony to the resilience of Old Testament faith that such crises *always do*, in fact, turn out to be occasions for fresh light to break through, and that is certainly the case here."[70] For him, the answer to the crisis is that "the LORD has come to rescue his people time and again in the past . . . and he will certainly do so again."[71] How this standard and quite banal articulation of a version of Old Testament faith conforms to the claims made for it as constituting fresh light breaking through is unclear.

Even with this proposal to safeguard the character of God, however, there is a further problem. Oswalt identifies it by posing the question, "It is fine to believe that God will one day be crowned on Mount Zion and invite all his saints to feast with him in the presence of their enemies, but what about all those saints who have lived and struggled and died in the meantime with no apparent result?"[72] Similarly, dubbing the matter a "further perplexity to be faced before the breakthrough can come," Webb also asks, "What about those who die in the time of waiting, who have put their trust in the LORD but experienced no fulfilment? Will they suffer the same fate as the wicked . . . and miss out on the triumph to come?"[73]

Both turn to 26:19 to answer their question. Webb asserts that this group of faithful departed "will be raised from death to share in the final

---

68. Ibid., 482.
69. Webb, *Message of Isaiah*, 111 (emphasis added).
70. Ibid., 111 (emphasis added).
71. Ibid., 111 (emphasis added).
72. Oswalt, *Book of Isaiah: Chapters 1–39*, 485.
73. Webb, *Message of Isaiah*, 111.

victory,"[74] and Oswalt that they "will be revived with shouts of joy to partake in the festivities of God's final triumph."[75] Brueggemann also follows this line of thought:

> In the conventional, liturgical practice of Israel, complaint characteristically evokes a response from Yahweh, promising presence and intervention. . . . But now in an unprecedented circumstance, Israel receives from Yahweh an unprecedented response. The dead, the ones done in by the "lofty city" (v.5), will be raised to life. . . . Those who have died will be raised.[76]

In addition to his assessment that the context of Isa 26 represents "an unprecedented circumstance" that elicits "an unprecedented response" from God, Brueggemann reinforces the extraordinary nature of the content of 26:19 by suggesting that it "is surely beyond anything the righteous could have anticipated, an answer that breaks the categories of all of Yahweh's traditional responses."[77] On the basis of this statement, the profound nature of the crisis depicted in Isa 26 generates an equally profound reaction from God. This proposal, however, is not without problem, for it is tantamount to saying that the initial crisis, implicit in and central to which was doubt about the character of God, has been satisfactorily resolved on the strength of a promise by God. Effectively, reliance is to be placed in the word of one about whose reliability and probity grounds for reservation exist.[78]

---

74. Ibid.

75. Oswalt, *Book of Isaiah: Chapters 1–39*, 485. Oswalt also states that this verse, "along with 25:8, represents the highest conception of resurrection in the Old Testament" (p. 485). For a survey of approaches to this verse, see p. 485 n. 46. Brueggemann notes that 26:19 "is of uncommon interest because it is one of only two places in the Old Testament where resurrection of the dead is clearly attested" (*Isaiah 1–39*, 208). See Childs, *Isaiah*, 191–92; see also T. Desmond Alexander, "The Old Testament View of Life after Death," in *Solid Ground: Twenty-five Years of Evangelical Theology* (ed. Carl R. Trueman, Tony J. Gray, and Craig L. Blomberg; Leicester: Apollos, 2000), 120–33. For more in-depth study, see Elizabeth Bloch-Smith, *Judahite Burial Practices and Beliefs about the Dead* (JSOTSup 123; Sheffield: JSOT Press, 1992); further, H. Birkeland, "The Beliefs in Resurrection of the Dead in the Old Testament," *VT* 3 (1950–51): 60–78; John F. A. Sawyer, "Hebrew Words for the Resurrection of the Dead," *VT* 13 (1973): 218–34.

76. Brueggemann, *Isaiah 1–39*, 208.

77. Ibid.

78. In this instance, Brueggemann, against his own reading strategy, too easily resolves a troublesome text by not taking "the direct statement of the text with full seriousness" (*Deep Memory, Exuberant Hope*, 81). Effectually, he has reached for a "closure" which "eliminates the candour of the text itself" (p. 89).

Interestingly, Kaiser, in connection with 26:19, which he regards as a later addition to the text, proposes that it opens up "a vista which makes it *easier to believe in the righteousness of God.*"[79] The implication is that without this verse of absolute conviction about the righteousness of God, the belief would be difficult to sustain. However, even with it, the use of the comparative "easier" indicates that worries about the character of God may yet justifiably linger. Consequently, notwithstanding the charged character of 26:19, however it is interpreted, residual questions remain about the behavior of God in this case. The rhetoric of the passage does not lay them conclusively to rest.

Without belaboring the matter, Brueggemann, for all his endorsement of 26:19, recognizes one aspect of its potential inadequacy in his comment that it concedes "perhaps, that there is no remedy for the troubles of Israel's circumstance 'in this life.'"[80] If God has the power to raise the dead to life, it might be asked why, instead of pushing the horizon of hope into the eschatological end-time ("the sweet bye and bye"), the divine does not channel at least part of that power toward transforming the present, particularly a present filled with torment for those who cling faithfully to God. Thus the issue is raised in a pointed and poignant way of the relationship between rhetoric, especially promissory rhetoric originating in the divine,[81] and praxis for justice. This praxis for justice originates at least in part in human analysis and impulse, in the face of a

79. Kaiser, *Isaiah 13–39*, 215 (emphasis added).
80. Brueggemann, *Isaiah 1–39*, 208.
81. On possible approaches to the apparent failure of such promissory rhetoric, see Robert P. Carroll, "Second Isaiah and the Failure of Prophecy," *Studia Theologica* 32 (1978): 119–31. In a contemporary context not utterly dissimilar from that under discussion, the political commentator Simon Hoggart describes one of Tony Blair's speeches in the 2001 general-election campaign. Blair was surrounded by Labour Party posters, of which Hoggart writes, "It was unclear whether these represented claims of actual results, or further pledges for next time. But it doesn't matter. In New Labour there is no difference. The aspiration is already accomplished fact, the promise is the only reality" (*Guardian Weekly* [17–23 May 2001]). Similarly, on Blair's House of Commons speech about the threat of weapons of mass destruction, which convinced many British members of Parliament of the necessity to go to war with Iraq, Polly Toynbee writes, "As for Tony Blair's veracity, with him there is a wavy line between deception and self-deception. He is so easily carried away by the persuasiveness of his own words and the force of his own arguments that you can hear him mesmerise himself: the truth with him is bound up with extraordinary optimism. There is an almost childish blurring between the wish and the fact: if he says something strongly enough, his words can magic it into truth" ("Did Blair Lie about WMD?" *Guardian Weekly* [5–11 June 2003]).

God of occasional character lapses,[82] who through the prophetic Isaianic voice insists that no trust can be placed in anything of human origin.

5. *Trust and the Shaping of Isaiah*

The theme of trust also relates to the relationship among what have, in certain quarters, been taken to be the three component parts of the book of Isaiah. Laato writes that "Isaiah 40–55 is so full of great expectations that if Isaiah 55 were the Book's closing chapter I R [implied readers] would have difficulty in understanding the dissonance between these expectations and their realisation in the postexilic period."[83] He goes on to explain that "the *apparent* divergence between the reality and the expectations of Isaiah 40–55 needed hermeneutics which can be found in Isaiah 56–66." For Laato, consequently, "I R's view of Isaiah 40–55 is restrained" by being followed "by Isaiah 56–66[,] which explain why the great expectations of Isaiah have not been fulfilled." Although Laato maintains that "Isaiah 40–55 is of great importance to I R,"[84] the idea that the unconditional promises of those chapters are restrained by what follows means that functionally the content of the promises is undercut. From one perspective, these could be interpreted as understandable grounds for a diminished confidence in the glowing promises of 40–55 and, by extension, in the God who made them. As Barton observes, "Deutero-Isaiah and his predecessor are alike confronted with an audience that cannot believe the message they are being offered, and not wholly without reason in either case."[85]

Against this tendency to doubt, however, Laato insists that "the last discourse of the Book (Isaiah 56–66) explains to I R why the marvellous programme of salvation did not come to pass." According to him:

> The heart of the discourse of Isaiah 56–66 deals with the dissonance inherent in the fact that the people have returned from exile to Jerusalem, but the plan of salvation promised in Isaiah 40–55 and predicted in Isaiah 1–39 has not come to fulfilment. It is clear that Isaiah 56–66 is the crux of the argument of the I A [implied author] which he addressed to I R [implied readers].[86]

82. See Brueggemann, *Deep Memory, Exuberant Hope*, 88.

83. Laato, *About Zion I Will Not Be Silent*, 185; idem, "The Composition of Isaiah 40–55," *JBL* 109 (1990): 207–28; also, Antje Labahn, "The Delay of Salvation within Deutero-Isaiah," *JSOT* 85 (1999): 71–84.

84. Laato, *About Zion I Will Not Be Silent*, 185 (emphasis added).

85. Barton, "Ethics in the Book of Isaiah," 73.

86. Laato, *About Zion I Will Not Be Silent*, 200 (subsequent bracketed references in the main text are to this source). On this theme, Laato presents Isa 40–55 as "a

He argues that "Isaiah 56–66 contains salvation-historical themes similar to those presented in Isaiah 40–55," although, as he notes, "these themes are no longer unconditional" (p. 173) in the former. This admission of a shift from unconditionality to conditionality reflects a considerable change in underlying meaning. Similarly, while the exiled grouping is "exhorted to put its trust in Yahweh's plan of salvation which will be realised in the near future (= 'now', עתה)" (p. 190) in Isa 40–55, by 56–66 those who continue to trust in God are forced "to present arguments why the promised salvation has not taken place . . . why salvation has not yet ensued" (p. 202). The movement from immediacy to futurity again constitutes a significant underlying alteration in meaning. The way that "only in Isaiah 56–66 does it become clear to I R that salvation pertains to the future" (p. 173) accentuates a sense of disjunction and fosters a feeling of letdown. Furthermore:

> Whereas I R understand Isaiah 40–55 as presupposing that the returned exiles would be loyal and will therefore inherit the promised salvation in Zion, Isaiah 56–66 raises the problem that the people who came back still continue to live without regard for the will of Yahweh. (p. 194)[87]

This problem, and the other problems indicated here, are effectually and rather conveniently resolved by attributing the delay in the materialization of the promises of Isa 40–55 completely to the sin of the people:

> A strong argument is made in the Book of Isaiah that Yahweh has always distinguished between obedient and disobedient members of his people and saved the former while destroying the latter. . . . The obedient are those who seek the best for Zion and eagerly await its coming glory. Isaiah 40–55 proclaims that this salvation is at hand but Isaiah 56–66 reiterates that its fulfilment was postponed because of the people's disobedience. (p. 209)[88]

It is difficult, however, not to conclude that at one level this assertion derives from latching on to a ready-made solution in which one

---

turning-point in the history of Judah (and Jerusalem)" while "Isaiah 56–66 explain[s] to I R why this marvellous time of salvation has not yet come to pass" (p. 171). When Laato here argues that the last section of Isaiah "explains" and "deals with" why earlier promises have not come to pass in the way they were given, he presumably means satisfactorily and convincingly. This, though, is not conclusively proven, even in terms of the evidence he presents.

87. This point is underscored when Laato writes, "[N]ot all of those who have returned to Judah are willing to follow the commandments of Yahweh even though the texts in Isaiah 40–55 presuppose such fidelity" (p. 200).

88. The neatness of this balance between "obedient" and "disobedient" is challenged by the analysis above of Isa 9:16 (ET v. 17), in which everyone is presented as sinful and therefore disobedient.

ideological strain in the Isaianic text is elevated to the position of governing hermeneutical principle by the ideological predisposition of the reader. Besides which, this proposal, in the way it diverts attention away from the reliability of the divine character by attributing the failure of the promises of Isa 40–55 solely to humanity, does not fully account for the way unconditional divine promises become conditional, for the way the divine word bespeaking immediate salvation becomes pushed into the future, and for the way divine expectation of human obedience becomes a reality marked by human disobedience. In all of these issues, the matter of God's trustworthiness is implicitly impugned. As Michael Taylor, speaking more generally of the nature of God in the context of theodicy, writes:

> [I]f God's redemptive enterprise is frustrated because of our continuing sinful opposition, that only underlines how ineffective it is in dealing with the very reality it sets out to redeem. What are we to make of a gospel which claims to rescue sinners but has little impact on their sinful and destructive behaviour? It looks like impotence.[89]

In the context of the book of Isaiah,[90] putting all the blame for God's promises not coming to pass when and how God said they would on humanity is an unduly protective maneuver, part of which may be designed to defend God from the charge of impotence (50:2; 59:1). What is more, humanity is presented as little short of obdurately perverse if it is unable to follow the ways of God sufficiently to ensure the realization of the glittering promises of which it has been the recipient. That some of those who considered themselves loyal servants of Yahweh could accuse the Lord of making them wander from God's ways through hardening their hearts (63:17) indicates that, even for those who viewed themselves as insiders, the character of God was not unproblematic. Significantly, this lament also indicates that this section of humanity at least was not prepared to accept total responsibility for its behavior.[91]

---

89. Michael Taylor, *Poverty and Christianity* (London: SCM Press, 2000), 48.

90. In which, according to Brueggemann (*Deep, Memory Exuberant Hope*, 13, 37), the gospel is represented by the word בשׂר in Isa 52:7.

91. With regard to Isa 59:1–21, Laato argues that "the rhetorical 'we' in 59:9–15 are apparently the group of the righteous servants who attempt to explain to the group of 'you' (= disloyal members of the people) why salvation has not yet ensued. That the 'we' group present themselves in relation to the 'you'-group demonstrates the former's attempt to persuade the latter to share in the programme of salvation which belongs to the whole people" (*About Zion I Will Not Be Silent*, 202). However, 63:17 appears to demonstrate that in due narratological course, doubts began to arise even among the righteous servants; see further below.

Laato intimates that one of the core purposes of the book of Isaiah is to clarify for the implied readers "that they are asked to put their trust unreservedly in great promises about Zion when the city will become the centre of the whole world" (p. 194).[92] Ultimately therefore, "The Israelites may worship Yahweh and Yahweh only and trust in him in order to bear witness among the nations" (p. 208). Yet Laato also tacitly acknowledges that the ceding of trust is not easy. As he observes, there are indications of "how problematic the proclamation of salvation was among the exiles" (p. 185). In essence, "they have no real confidence in Yahweh's sovereignty," a situation that necessitates a "confrontation between Yahweh's omnipotence and the people's unbelief" (p. 187).[93] However, that "the group of exiles who are willing to trust in Yahweh's plan of salvation is relatively small" (p. 197)—and likely to grow smaller on account of the unfulfilled promises of chs. 40–55—reflects how the reliability of God is never conclusively established. Indeed, beyond the issue of how difficult it is to trust in God, the evidence Laato presents can be used equally in support of the contention that the God of the Isaianic text is unreliable and possibly unjust. In the way that God is depicted as making promises that, contrary to their own content, by the end of the book remain unfulfilled, and that are subsequently continually pushed into the future, the lingering shadow of unreliability is never incontrovertibly eliminated from the divine character. Given this and the adoption of only a very mildly ironic reading stance, even as one appreciates the lyrical appeal of the poetry of consolation and divine promise,[94] it is thus possible to take a more sympathetic attitude to all those encoded in the text who, at whatever stage, deemed "the whole plan of salvation concerning Zion . . . as wishful thinking."[95] Consequently, it is also

92. This reinforces Laato's earlier comment that "the section 42:14–44:8 reveals to I R that the censure of the people is intended not to condemn them but to persuade them to put their trust in Yahweh and his plan of salvation" (p. 190).

93. One may posit that the depth of the crisis of trust in Yahweh, in part at least, gives rise to the elevated nature of the consolation and promises contained in chs. 40–55. However, an even deeper crisis of confidence in Yahweh may be assumed on the part of some of those who overcame their initial reservations and trusted, only to be let down, with unfulfilled hopes and expectations. As this dynamic develops, a sectarian impulse deepens; see further below.

94. Against this appreciative posture, Carroll argues that "the tendency to overrate Second Isaiah as a great prophet has added profundity to the obscurity of his work." Carroll also suggests that "it might be more accurate and more acute to see in his work evidence of the serious decline of Israelite prophecy" ("Second Isaiah and the Failure of Prophecy," 119).

95. Laato, *About Zion I Will Not Be Silent*, 191.

possible to affirm the assessment that "words of future consolation, however, cannot wholly soothe the pains of the present, nor do they totally
acquit God of the charge of injustice."[96]

6. The Coercive God of a Coercive Text?

Although it is true that "the Book of Consolation . . . abounds in haunt-
ingly beautiful passages expressing Yahweh's patient, unforgetting love
for his people,"[97] and may be intended, at one level, to persuade its hearers to believe in the promises it contains,[98] these dimensions should not
be completely divorced from more disturbing features of the text.

Without unreservedly endorsing the postmodern idea of the totalizing
nature of all texts with universal pretensions,[99] it is difficult to avoid the
conclusion that a strain of thought in Isa 40–55 tends in this coercive[100]
(as opposed to persuasive) direction, in which "the monotheistic emphasis" is "linked with the motif of creation"[101] (40:12–14, 25–26; 45:5, 12;
51:13).

96.   Laytner (*Arguing with God*, 83) in the context of a section entitled "Rabbinic
Responses to the Exile."

97.   George M. Soares-Prabhu, "Laughing at Idols: The Dark Side of Biblical
Monotheism (An Indian Reading of Isaiah 44:9–20)," in *Reading from this Place*.
Vol. 2, *Social Location and Biblical Interpretation in Global Perspective* (ed.
Fernando F. Segovia and Mary Ann Tolbert; Minneapolis: Fortress, 1995), 109–31
(128). On this dimension of the Isaianic text, see also Walter Brueggemann, *Cadences
of Home: Preaching among Exiles* (Louisville, Ky.: Westminster John Knox, 1997);
idem, *Deep Memory, Exuberant Hope*; idem, "Planned People/Planned Book," in
Broyles and Evans, eds., *Writing and Reading the Scroll of Isaiah*, 1:19–37. See also
Goldingay, *Isaiah*, 222–23.

98.   See Gitay, *Prophecy and Persuasion*; though, see further Goldingay, who
argues that rather than being persuasive, the text "shouts very loud" ("Isaiah 40–55
in the 1990s," 225).

99.   Lyotard, *The Postmodern Condition*, 81. The benefit of this analysis is that it
may sensitize readers to the way texts have often been used in exclusionary ways
and to support certain agendas related to power arrangements. Carlos Fuentes in *The
Years with Laura Diaz* has an exiled Spanish Republican, in the context of speaking
about the need "to diversify life" and "to pluralise the world," subversively observe,
"We have to give up the illusion of totality. The word says it all: there's only a slight
difference between the desire for totality and totalitarian reality" (p. 277).

100. See Rikki E. Watts, "Consolation or Confrontation? Isaiah 40–55 and the
Delay of the New Exodus," *TynBul* 41, no. 1 (1990): 31–59.

101. Laato, *About Zion I Will Not Be Silent*, 189. Laato asserts that "universalism also justifies the strong monotheistic pathos in the Book of Isaiah" (p. 208). On
monotheism, Klaus Koch writes: "[T]he ethical monotheism which the nineteenth
century celebrated as the great achievement of prophecy . . . emerges more clearly in

Texts broadly similar to these in theme and intention (Job 11:7–9; 25:2–6; 37:22–24) are deployed by Job's visitors in order to impress upon him the incommensurable nature of God. Indeed, God also uses the same logic at great rhetorical length (38:4–40:2), with the aim of brow-beating Job, who has the temerity to question divine justice, and of cowing him into submission (42:2–6). Both in Job and Isaiah, however, while the power of the divine is strongly accented, how this raw power is related to or serves the interests of justice is neither clarified nor explored.[102] Regarding the twin characteristics of divine nature spoken of in Ps 62:11–12, claims about the strength of God are rhetorically evident, but the love of God remains more uncertain. The divine voice in the conclusion to the book of Job never actually addresses Job's concern about the justice of God. In a somewhat disjointed way, Job is over-whelmed by God and then justified (Job 42:7), but never satisfactorily

Deutero-Isaiah than anywhere else" (*The Prophets: The Babylonian and Persian Periods* [London: SCM Press, 1983], 2:135). John Barton asserts that "monotheism finds its clearest expression in the Old Testament in the Isaianic corpus" ("Ethics in the Book of Isaiah," 77). See also Bernhard Lang, *Monotheism and the Prophetic Minority: An Essay in Biblical History and Sociology* (The Social World of Biblical Antiquity 1; Sheffield: Almond, 1983); Roy A. Rosenberg, "Yahweh Becomes King," *JBL* 85, no. 3 (1966): 297–307; Herbert Cohn, "From Monolatry to Mono-theism," *JBQ* 26 (1998): 124–26; Robert Gnuse, *No Other Gods: Emergent Monotheism in Israel* (JSOTSup 241; Sheffield: Sheffield Academic Press, 1997); Johannes C. de Moor, *The Rise of Yahwism: The Roots of Israelite Monotheism* (BETL 91; Louvain: Louvain University Press, 1990). From an African perspective, see T. L. J. Mafico, "The Divine Compound Name Yahweh Elohim and Israel's Monotheistic Polytheism," *Journal of Northwest Semitic Languages* 22, no. 1 (1996): 155–73.

102. Bruce Zuckerman notes how in certain instances force is given primacy over righteousness (*Job the Silent* [Oxford: Oxford University Press, 1991], 105, 112). Van Wolde also follows this line, noting that "immense power and violence form part of the creation itself" (*Mr and Mrs Job*, 121). According to her, part of the theological strategy of the book of Job is to demonstrate the marginal position of humanity in creation. This idea directs attention away from any suggestion that God acts unjustly. Yet if humanity is as marginalized in the scheme of things as sug-gested, there is something incongruous in the plot of the book deriving from an intense focus on the faith of one human being. The nature of the license God gives the Satan in the context of testing Job's faith raises questions about the trustworthi-ness of the character of God that are never completely settled. Suspicion and doubt linger. This point notwithstanding, van Wolde effectively decouples the concept of justice from that of power, on which see further below. Note, however, how Barbara Kingsolver has an African character say, "Don't try to make life a mathematics problem with yourself in the centre and everything coming out equal" (*The Poison-wood Bible*, 309).

answered. God apparently endorses, not the theology of the visitors, but the protest of Job, so long as in the end he toes the party line and acknowledges God. As Brueggemann observes in a discussion of presence and theodicy:

> Israel is given finally to theodicy, to the question of God's reliability, God's presence, God's willingness to be connected to Israel. The issue surfaces in many places, but of course most dramatically and powerfully in the book of Job. It is clear, moreover, that the resolution of the Joban question in 42:6 is fogged at best, perhaps a characteristic move. . . .[103]

Brueggemann terms this a "tradition of affirmation."[104] Similarly, while Isa 40–55 contains moving assertions of the love and concern of God (e.g. 41:8–14; 43:1–2; 49:15–18), recourse to the language of power suggests an undercurrent of coercive menace directed against those who continue to resist the rhetorical blandishments of God (40:27; 43:26; 45:9; 49:14; 50:11). If, as seems possible, this group that resists the appeals of the prophetic voice contains people who (like Job[105]) harbor genuine doubts about the justice of God in abandoning them to exile and suffering, it is doubtful whether a combination of vitriol directed against them and an appeal to the unsurpassable might of God in creation addresses their concerns. Even in the midst of the positive promissory rhetoric of Isa 40–55, questions linger concerning the nature of God. Some of those who do not accede to the rhetorical onslaught of Isa 40–55 (unlike Job in his narrative context) may be justified in so doing (as Job also would have been).

103. Walter Brueggemann, "Biblical Theology Appropriately Postmodern," in Bellis and Kaminsky, eds., *Jews, Christians, and the Theology of the Hebrew Scriptures*, 97–108 (103).
104. Brueggemann, "Biblical Theology Appropriately Postmodern," 103. On the behavior of God in Job 42:6 and Job's reaction, see also, as Brueggemann directs, Jack Miles, *God: A Biography* (New York: Knopf, 1995), 425 n. 324. Paul Ricoeur also contends that Job's questions in 42:1–6 are never answered ("Toward a Hermeneutic of the Idea of Revelation," in *Essays on Biblical Interpretation* [ed. Lewis S. Mudge; Philadelphia: Fortress, 1980], 73–118 [89]). The contention is shared by George Steiner ("Our Homeland, the Text," 10). For a more positive and understanding interpretation of the voice of God from the midst of the storm, see van Wolde, *Mr and Mrs Job*, 107–50.
105. Laytner also makes this connection (*Arguing with God*, 35). He argues that "Job, Lamentations, Deutero-Isaiah, and Ezekiel attempted, by various means" to address the "twofold threat" of doubts concerning God's omnipotence and justice raised by the experience of exile. He continues, "Job is not the only work to deal with the problems arising out of the exile. Lamentations, Deutero-Isaiah, and Ezekiel also attempt alternative theological interpretations" (p. 36).

These lingering doubts about the character of God are compounded further when one considers that the refrain "I will not give my glory to another" (וכבודי לאחר לא־אתן; 42:8; 48:11) suggests a divine participation in pride (in this case specifically monotheistic pride), a general trait the display of which in others necessitates being brought low (2:17).[106] Again without unreservedly agreeing with the thesis, it is difficult to deny to some degree what Schwartz terms "an unrelenting ideology of possessive monotheism,"[107] which invariably finds expression in pride and leads to a disturbing rhetoric, implicit in which is exclusion and the threat of violence.[108]

Soares-Prabhu addresses this theme in a stimulating article in which he reveals the dangerously limited religious understanding displayed in the Isaianic attack on idol worship in Babylon.[109] He concludes that "the nationalist monotheism of Second Isaiah is . . . a fundamentalist reaction"[110] to a crisis that encourages delusions of domination (as reflected

---

106. Geoffrey J. Aimers conceives the struggle between Job and God as essentially one centering on honor, with God asserting God's "honour as the one to whom allegiance is owed as the true guarantor of justice and only source of piety" ("The Rhetoric of Social Conscience in the Book of Job," *JSOT* 91 [2000]: 99–107 [106]).

107. Schwartz, *The Curse of Cain*, 75. For a critical review of Schwartz's proposal regarding the relationship between monotheism and violence, see Miroslav Volf, "Jehovah on Trial," *Christianity Today* 42 (1998): 32–35.

108. This rhetoric of power and violence found in the mouth of God, against those who do not succumb to the promises of Isa 40–55, in turn fuels the sectarian rhetoric directed against those who become skeptical of God when they return to Jerusalem but find that the earlier promises remain unfulfilled. Thus rhetoric attributed to the divine in Isa 40–55 plays its part in the deepening spiral of bitter sectarianism in chs. 56–66.

109. For a much more positive understanding of this attack, see Brueggemann, *Deep Memory, Exuberant Hope*, 11.

110. Soares-Prabhu, "Laughing at Idols," 129. In stressing the dangerous nationalism of Isa 40–55, Soares-Prabhu follows N. Snaith, "The Servant of the Lord in Deutero-Isaiah," in *Studies in Old Testament Prophecy* (ed. H. H. Rowley; Edinburgh: T. & T. Clark, 1950), 187–200. This thesis is expanded in H. Orlinsky and N. Snaith, *Studies on the Second Part of the Book of Isaiah* (VTSup14; Leiden: Brill, 1977), 97–117, 135–264. Fredrik Holmgren is also skeptical about benign universalist claims made for these chapters (*With Wings as Eagles*). See also D. E. Hollenberg ("Nationalism and 'The Nations' in Isaiah XL–LV," *VT* 19 [1969]: 21–36), especially for reference to studies to which the works of Snaith and Orlinsky are related (i.e. P. A. H. de Boer, *Second Isaiah's Message* [Leiden: Brill, 1956]; R. Martin-Achard, *A Light to the Nations* [Edinburgh: T. & T. Clark, 1962]). For Soares-Prabhu, if this material contains a universalist perspective, it is one of "a nationalist and fundamentalist tone," in which difference is not tolerated and

in the Isaianic use of exodus imagery), but that fails to engender "a genuine breakthrough to universalism."[111] With regard to the exodus imagery, one of the ways in which God entices Israel to opt for the divine-restoration program is to promise that something similar to what happened to Israel will happen to Babylon. In a disturbing way that is rooted in vengeance and finds expression in the imagery of female degradation, God effectually indicates that Babylon, depicted as a virgin daughter (47:1), will undergo experiences (47:2–10) comparable to those visited upon the women of Jerusalem (32:9–14).[112]

Thus doubts persist about the trustworthiness of the character of God. Jeremiah 49:11 may assert that orphans and widows can trust (בטח) God, but Isa 9:16 (ET v. 17) casts severe doubt on this assertion. As Miscall observes, the weaving together of different strands in the Isaianic corpus "produces a tapestry that is, at once, repulsive and attractive, horrible and fascinating."[113] The characterization of the divine is part of this tapestry and cannot be resolved convincingly in terms of reliability and trustworthiness.

---

destruction of the "other" implied ("Laughing at Idols," 129). This supports my view that once this dynamic is established and set loose, it also operates within an "elect" group/nation, fostering sectarianism. In a sequential reading this is what happens progressively in the book of Isaiah.

111.   Soares-Prabhu, "Laughing at Idols," 130. This corresponds to the danger implicit in exodus imagery. On this exclusivist tendency leading to lack of concern for and violence against those beyond the boundaries of the elect, viewed through the lens of holiness, see Brueggemann, "Vision for a New Church and a New Century Part II." I argue that Isa 58:6–10 erodes this ideology; see also Brueggemann, *Deep Memory Exuberant Hope*, 8, 38.

112.   See Miscall, *Isaiah*, 114–15. See also idem, "Isaiah: Dreams and Nightmares, Fantasy and Horror." In this article, Miscall argues that "although Isaiah 47 is explicitly against Lady Babylon . . . Daughter Zion lingers in the background. The ambiguity increases from verse 10 on. What is said to Lady Babylon about her past and threatened destruction in verses 10–15 is also said of Jerusalem in others parts of Isaiah. . . . This relates to another frequent element in horror tales, the brutality that is threatened and usually carried out against women. God takes the role of the monster" (p. 159). Conceivably, thus, both Babylonians and Israelites could, in the words of an eleventh-century poet-rabbi, say to God, "Let this sight come before You: young women, who put their trust in You, slaughtered in broad daylight, the fairest of women—their wombs slashed open and the afterbirth forced out from between their legs" (quoted in Laytner, *Arguing with God*, 143). On this topic see also M. Franzmann, "The City as Woman: The Case of Babylon in Isaiah 47," *ABR* 43 (1995): 1–19; J. Goldingay, "What Happens to Ms Babylon in Isaiah 47, Why, and Who Says So?," *TynBul* 47 (1996): 215–43.

113.   Miscall, "Isaiah: Dreams and Nightmares, Fantasy and Horror," 161.

7. The Confessions of God: Isaiah 40:1–2

נחמו נחמו עמי יאמר אלהיכם: דברו על־לב ירושלם וקראו אליה כי מלאה
צבאהכי נרצה עונה כי לקחה מיד יהוה כפלים בכל־חטאתיה:

Comfort, comfort my people, says your God; tenderly speak to Jerusalem
and call to her that her term of service is over, that her iniquity is
pardoned, that from Yahweh's hand she has received double for all her
sins.

The assessment that the Isaianic corpus reflects a hinterland of doubt
about the nature of the character of God, in conjunction with the argument that what is commonly known as Second Isaiah might, in addition
to its designation as the "Book of Consolation,"[114] also be termed the
"Book of Coercion," supports the contention that Isaiah contains emana-
tions from what has been called the dark side of God (e.g. Isa 45:7).[115] In
turn, this evaluation, with its constituent strands, legitimates more
nuanced and balanced readings of texts (e.g. 40:2; 54:7) that a majority
of scholars have traditionally interpreted on the assumption of the
goodness of the divine. It also therefore encourages and supports minority readings of these passages as a valid option worthy of consideration
for the way and to the extent they open interpretative possibilities linguistically and thematically congruent with the subtle nature of the text as a
whole. The readings are indicated by a consistently applied hermeneutical approach, in this case, a close-reading technique rooted in literary
theory.

These passages are examined briefly to illustrate how the refusal to
accept as a given the justice of God potentially changes Isa 40–55. The
change is from an offer of divine assistance one would be foolish to dis-
regard to, in part at least, an attempt at re-establishing divine credentials
of which one might justifiably be suspicious. Drawing attention to the

114. E.g. McKenzie, *Second Isaiah*, 16–17.
115. David M. Gunn, *The Fate of King Saul: An Interpretation of a Biblical Story*
(JSOTSup 14; Sheffield: JSOT Press, 1980), 131. Brueggemann speaks of "texts of
darkness," in which the "response of Yahweh . . . is disproportionate to any available
affront" (*Deep Memory, Exuberant Hope*, 81). William H. C. Propp argues for the
existence of a "semi-autonomous dark side" to the divine nature (*Exodus 1–18: A
New Translation with Introduction and Commentary* [AB 2; New York: Doubleday,
1999], 409). This idea of God possessing a dark side may be derived from Rudolph
Otto (*The Idea of the Holy* [trans. J. W. Harvey; Oxford: Oxford University Press,
1950], 31), who uses the phrase the "demonic divine" in association with divine
"violent ferment" (p. 17), and of God's actions being perceived as both "crazy"
(p. 26) and "bewildering" (p. 27).

way calling for faith "is an important stylistic feature in Deutero-Isaiah's preaching," Westermann observes that it was "uttered at a time when men were gradually turning away from God, gradually closing their minds to him, and gradually letting their faith grow cold."[116] They may have had better reason to turn away than has been widely acknowledged.

After the judgment oracle in 39:5–7, anticipating the exile to Babylon, 40:1–2 represents a rhetorical change of direction.[117] In 40:1–2, comfort rather than condemnation is the keynote of the initial prophetic announcement. God wants God's people to be comforted and Jerusalem spoken to tenderly, informing her that "her hard service has been completed, that her sin has been paid for" (40:2). Interestingly, the text adds "that she has received from the Lord's hand double (כפלים) for all her sins" (40:2).

With regard to this phrase, and in particular to the term כפלים[118] used within the passage, Calvin lays down the hermeneutical *ne plus ultra* line that has significantly influenced interpretation to the present. He argues: "Here the word *double* denotes 'large and abundant,'" but "it must not be imagined that the punishments were greater than the offences, or equal to them; for we ought to abhor the blasphemy of those who accuse God of cruelty, as if he inflicted on men excessively severe punishment."[119] Taking their cue from Calvin, but with a slightly different interpretative emphasis, other scholars nonetheless preserve the integrity of divine action by arguing that the cumulative effect of the threefold pattern of v. 2b indicates that God's punishment, in a sort of Goldilocks and the

---

116. Westermann, *Isaiah 40–66*, 34.

117. The rhetoric may also indicate an underlying historical referent. Thus Brueggemann, summing up a widely held historical-critical position, observes: "In 39:5–7, the prophet sounded an oracle to King Hezekiah anticipating Judah's exile into Babylon, which in due course occurred. As the book of Isaiah is arranged, there is a long silence after that oracle, a silence that lasts over 150 years" (*Isaiah 40–66*, 15).

118. Jan L. Koole speaks of "the striking dual form כפלים," thereby indicating its unusualness (*Isaiah*. Part 3, Vol. 1. *Isaiah 40–48* [Kampen: Kok Pharos, 1997], 54). For a helpful survey of the history of interpretation of vv. 1–2, and an introduction to the longer passage of which they are a part, see Koole, *Isaiah*. Part 3, Vol. 1, 44–55; see also Anthony Phillips, "Double for All Her Sins," *ZAW* 94 (1982): 130–32.

119. Calvin, *Commentary on the Book of the Prophet Isaiah*, 3:202–3. Along the same lines, though with a more tortured and convoluted logic that is finally not completely consistent, Delitzsch argues that the concept of "double punishment . . . is not to be pressed arithmetically, in which case God would appear over-righteous, and therefore unrighteous. Jerusalem has not suffered more than it deserved; but God's compassion now regards what His justice was forced to inflict on Jerusalem as super-abundant" (*Biblical Commentary on the Prophecies of Isaiah*, 2:135).

Three Bears theology,[120] is "just right" and therefore proportionate for the crime.[121]

One interpretation that Calvin labels "ingenious" but unsustainable is "that the Lord repays double favour for their [God's people's] sins."[122] The interpretation, though, is entertained by some exegetes, in part, at least, because of the way it permits the excessive generosity and graciousness of God to be emphasized.[123] By this hermeneutical maneuver, even more clear blue water is placed between the punishment/suffering of the people and the idea that God's involvement in and administering of punishment could have been conceived, at some level, as disproportionate.

Whatever differences may exist between these approaches, they all answer Koole's question as to "whether this double punishment is

120. Robert P. Carroll, on the nursery-rhyme theme, notes that "in preserving the freedom of God to be God some theologians have come perilously close to installing Humpty Dumpty ('a word means what I choose it to mean') as his prophet" (*When Prophecy Failed: Reactions and Responses to Failure in the Old Testament Prophetic Traditions* [London: SCM Press, 1979], 176). On the subject of textual polyvalence, which goes against the historicist's search for "the right answer," Carroll jibes, "Where meaning becomes indeterminate the spectre of Humpty Dumpty stalks all interpretation" (p. 216).

121. Supporters of this view include G. von Rad, "Kiplayim in Jes. 40:2 = 'Äquivalent?,'" *ZAW* 79 (1967): 80–82; Westermann, *Isaiah 40–66*, 36; Motyer, *Prophecy of Isaiah*, 299. Whybray allows that the term "may be a deliberate overstatement to drive home the point" or that it means "the right amount' (*Isaiah 40–66*, 49–50). Brueggemann, paying no special attention to the term in question, but commenting on v. 2b as a unit, notes that "Jerusalem has suffered enough to satisfy its affront to Yahweh" (*Isaiah 40–66*, 18). Oswalt observes that "Israel has suffered immensely for her sins," but makes sure that God cannot be accused of excess (*Book of Isaiah: Chapters 40–66*, 50).

122. Calvin, *Commentary on the Prophet Isaiah*, 3:202.

123. So Alexander, *Commentary on Isaiah*, 2:94–95. Edward J. Young interprets the first two points of comfort in v. 2b as reflecting "that the punishment meted out . . . is satisfactory," before pondering whether double "refers to punishment and suffering or whether it indicates blessing and mercy received from the Lord" (*The Book of Isaiah*, 3:23–24). He concludes the latter, citing one supporting text (Isa 61:7) in which the word כפלים does not appear (in this instance, the term משנה is used twice in the one verse) and another (Job 11:6) in which it is found in the mouth of one of Job's visitors as he defends the justice of God (on this, see further below). Without any discussion of the term כפלים, but clearly standing in this interpretative tradition, which accents the beneficence of God, Webb asks incredulously, "Could fifty, sixty, or seventy years of exile pay for rebellion that had gone on for scores of generations? Could it atone even for the sins of those directly affected, let alone for those of their ancestors?" (*Message of Isaiah*, 162).

consistent with God's justice" in the affirmative.[124] They also agree, either explicitly or implicitly, "that the expression 'double' should not be taken literally."[125] Against this trend, however, Knight states: "It is true that she [Israel] had suffered *double*." But he promptly retreats from this statement by proposing that "it *appeared* that she had made double payment for her past disloyalty." He adds: "But even if she were to suffer ten times as much as she had done, she could never pay for them [her sins] in any sense at all."[126] The probity of the divine is effectually placed beyond reproach by giving God carte blanche to do as God pleases.

In the context of a discussion of "the punishment by captivity of those who had not been responsible for the nation's sin,"[127] which raises the issue of the justice of God, Muilenburg contends in contradictory fashion that "the expression *double for all her sins* is characteristic Oriental exaggeration." He then immediately asserts that "God's punishment of Israel has been greater than she deserved."[128] Effectively addressing Muilenburg's concern about one generation paying the price for the wrongdoing of its predecessors, Phillips takes כפלים to mean that two generations have suffered, the latter on behalf of the former.[129] The strength of this reading is that it attempts to understand the term כפלים within its literary context by relating it to the theme (as found, e.g., in

124. Koole, *Isaiah*. Part 3, Vol. 1, 54.

125. Ibid., 55. McKenzie tends toward the literal, but with a historical perspective, in the way he takes double to refer to "the double penalty . . . of 587 B.C., in which the kingdom of Judah was overturned by the Babylonians and Jerusalem was destroyed and abandoned" (*Second Isaiah*, 16).

126. Knight, *Isaiah 40–55*, 9 (emphasis in original).

127. Muilenburg, *IB* 5:424 (the comment is actually made by Henry Sloane Coffin in the "Exposition" section). On this subject, Giovanni Garbini observes, "[N]ow the people, far from its native land, were experiencing the punishment without knowing exactly what their fathers had done wrong" (*History and Ideology in Ancient Israel*, 90). Garbini adds that "those born in the exile were beginning to feel themselves *victims unjustly punished* for a crime which others had committed" (emphasis added). According to Garbini, "this is the first manifestation of an attitude clearly expressed by Joel (4 [EVV 3]:19) when he speaks of Judah as 'innocent blood.'"

128. Muilenburg, *IB* 5:425.

129. Phillips, "Double for All Her Sins," 132. Ultimately, for Phillips, despite the acceptance that "Jerusalem *has* suffered 'double for all her sins' . . . the prophet makes an appeal to justice irrelevant" (emphasis in original), essentially because "it is through their vicarious suffering that the glorious future envisaged by the prophet is to be realized." However, as noted, the failure of the "glorious future" to materialize creates problems for the optimistic nature of this interpretation, one of which is that God cannot be completely absolved of the charge of excess.

Isa 53) of suffering for the sake of others. Again, however, God's integrity is protected.

Without displaying the same propensity to retreat from the theological implications of taking כפלים at linguistic face value, Watts states that "Jerusalem has received a full, even a *double* portion that atoned for *all her sins*,"[130] but he pursues the matter no further. Similarly, Beeby states that "Israel's time of service is ended, and they have already suffered twice as much as they should have,"[131] but he does not explicate the implications.

8. *The Lens of Literary Theory*

Literary theory helps clarify the underlying hermeneutical assumptions in the preceding interpretations and in identifying viable reading options that can be applied to the term כפלים. Discussing basic modes of interpretation, Aichele notes two primary ways of reading: the spiritual/modernist, which strives for unicity in reading and essentially governs the analyses surveyed above; and the literal/postmodern, which hosts ambiguity as inevitable.[132] Making a general comment, Carr notes that "postmodern streams of literary interpretation have already pointed out that all texts are multivalent to one extent or another, especially poetic and narrative texts found throughout much of the Bible."[133] Supporting this viewpoint, Eco, corroborating Jakobson, asserts that "the aesthetic [poetic] use of language is marked by the *ambiguity* and the *self-focusing character* of the messages articulated by it."[134] For Eco, "by ambiguity the message is rendered creative in relation to the acknowledged possibilities of the code" deployed in its interpretation.[135]

Thus, applied to the case at hand, "a literal translation will leave more reading options open than will a spiritual translation, which by its very nature seeks to clarify the source text."[136] The ambiguous nature of Isa 40:2b is underscored when it is remembered that, irrespective of methodological considerations, the term כפלים is less than straightforward

---

130. Watts, *Isaiah 34–66*, 80 (emphasis in original).

131. Beeby, *Canon and Mission*, 53.

132. Aichele, *Sign, Text, Scripture*, 48 (emphasis in original).

133. David Carr, "Untamable Text of an Untamable God," *Int* 54, no. 4 (2000): 347–62 (349).

134. Umberto Eco, *The Role of the Reader* (Bloomington: Indiana University Press, 1979), 90 (emphasis in original).

135. Ibid.

136. Aichele, *Sign, Text, Scripture*, 55.

and therefore does not lend itself to the type of closure sought for it.[137] Rather, given its limited usage in the Hebrew Bible[138] and its elusive quality, it properly functions to arrest the reader and at the very least to preclude too easy and glib an arrival at a coherent univocal reading of the verse. At most, with its undertone of disjunction, it destabilizes and decenters the predominant sense of 40:1–2 and intimates that even as God seeks to comfort, release, and forgive, concomitantly there lingers a sense that the divine has not always dealt fairly with the people.[139]

With the concentration above on the possibility of construing the divine character as periodically untrustworthy, acceptance of this sense of the word כפלים produces an entirely plausible reading that does justice to the subtlety of the text and the sensitivity of the issue.[140] Furthermore, the idea of God confessing to excess (see also the discussion of 54:7 below) or the perception that God has acted excessively (64:8–11 [ET vv. 9–12]) recurs within the book of Isaiah as a whole. So, in connection with 40:2, Oswalt asserts that "Israel has suffered immensely

---

137.   This is acknowledged by Oswalt, who concedes that "the exact sense of *kiplayim* here is not clear" (*Book of Isaiah: Chapters 40–66*, 43 n. 5). See also Koole, who ponders that "it remains unclear why the text does not use the common derivatives of שׁנה but the *striking dual form* כפלים" (*Isaiah*. Part 3, Vol. 1, 54 [emphasis added]).

138.   The כפל root occurs in Exod 26:9; 28:16; 39:9 (twice); Ezek 21:19 (ET v. 14); Job 41:5 (ET v. 4). The dual form, כפלים, in addition to Isa 40:2, is found only in Job 11:6, on which see below.

139.   As Goldingay honestly admits, "Precisely what that doubling means is not clear" (*Isaiah*, 224). Blenkinsopp, on the legitimacy of a literalist interpretation, notes that "if taken literally, the statement that Israel has paid double (*kiplayim*) for all its sins could raise serious questions about the evenhanded and equitable administration of justice by God" (*Isaiah 40–55: A New Translation with Introduction and Commentary* [AB 19A; New York: Doubleday, 2000], 181). Supportive of the idea that God is re-establishing divine credentials, Blenkinsopp argues that vv. 3–5 describe "a processional way . . . for the return of Yahveh to his people."

140.   Bringing together the ideas of ambiguity and the confession of God, in 52:3 and 52:5 the adverb חנם may be translated "for nothing," that is, "for no financial reward," or "for nothing," that is, "for no reason." Context suggests that the former may be more applicable in 52:3, but 52:5 is much more ambiguous, with the implication of the divine making confession if the latter is allowed. The sense of ambiguity and doubt about the character of God increases in light of the use of אפס in 52:4, in the phrase "and the Assyrian oppressed them [my people] for nothing." Surely Assyria attacked and oppressed them because God dispatched them (10:6), or is God suffering from selective-memory syndrome? With regard to the term חנם, van Wolde illustrates its ambiguous deployment in the opening of the book of Job and its importance in indicating the profound change that occurs in Job during the book (*Mr and Mrs Job*, 27–28, 139–41).

for her sins, but now it is complete; she need fear nothing more from God's hand."[141] But the same confidence is not shared by those who, presumably after trusting in promises such as those contained in 40:1–2, end up complaining, "Do not be angry, O God, beyond excess (עד־מאד) nor remember for ever (אל־לעד) iniquity" (64:8 [ET v. 9]). They poignantly conclude with the question, "Will you keep silent and afflict us beyond excess (עד־מאד)?" (64:11 [ET v. 12]).

The only other usage of the term כפלים in the Hebrew Bible is in Job 11:6, as Zophar, one of Job's visitors, responds to a Joban protest. The depth of Job's anguish is indicated by his complaint that irrespective of his guilt (רשע) or innocence/righteousness (צדק), and beyond them both, he is intensely aware of his existential affliction (10:15). The issue of his guilt or innocence before God is, to his mind, an irrelevancy, a reasonable observation to make given the propensity of Job's comforters and their theological successors to justify whatever God decides to do, and consequently to place the justice of the divine beyond question.

Against Job's position, Zophar wishes Job to experience a revelation of the double(כפלים)-sided nature of divine wisdom (חכמה; Job 11:6), a constituent dimension of which, to a mere human being, is the unfathomable nature of the deep things of God (11:7). This line of defense is similar to that implied in sections that Isa 40:1–2 introduces (e.g. 40:12–14, 25–26; 45:5, 7, 12; 51:12–13). However, whereas the use of כפלים in Job 11:6 constitutes part of a defense of the integrity of God, its use in Isa 40:2 is less dogmatically conclusive, containing at minimum a trace of doubt about the character of God and therefore creating a tension with the Isaianic strain, which speaks of the unknowability of God's ways from a human viewpoint. To interpret כפלים in Isa 40:2b in a fashion that presses for a harmonizing closure and a theological certainty the text does not permit is again to place oneself in the company of Job's visitors and to do violence to the richness of the text.

Brueggemann adds support to understanding כפלים in Isa 40:2b as containing an irreducible hint of concern about God's punishment of Jerusalem. He practices a hermeneutic of retrieval on a problematic text (1 Sam 15[142]) in which God authorizes the obliteration (חרם) of an enemy and acts with unfair inconsistency toward Saul. Brueggemann observes with regard to the term נחם, by which a divine change of mind is indicated, that it is "important to recognise that the same root word,

141.   Oswalt, *Book of Isaiah: Chapters 40–66*, 50.

142.   See Mark Wallace, *The Second Naiveté: Barth, Ricoeur, and the New Yale School* (Studies in American Biblical Hermeneutics 6; Macon, Ga.: Mercer University Press, 1990).

especially in 2 Isaiah, means 'comfort' (40:1; 49:13; 51:3)."[143] He continues, "I do not suggest that 'comfort' is the intent of the term here [1 Sam 15]. It is plausible, nonetheless, to imagine that the narrator and the hearers of the text would hear hints and traces of 'comfort' in this brutal narrative."[144] If a suggestion of comfort is detected in a text predominantly concerned with brutality, such as 1 Sam 15, then "hints and traces" of excess may be discerned in a text devoted primarily to the announcement of comfort, such as Isa 40:1–2. The use of כפלים legitimizes this interpretation in this context.

9. *The Confessions of God: Isaiah 54:6–7*

כי־כאשה עזובה ועצובת רוח קראך יהוה ואשת נעורים כי תמאס אמר
אלהיך: ברגע קטן עזבתיך וברחמים גדלים אקבצך:

> For Yahweh has called to you as to an abandoned wife hurt in spirit, as to the deserted wife of youth, your God says: for a fleeting instant I abandoned you, but with abundant compassion I will enfold you.

A comparable interpretative issue to that observed in Isa 40:2b, also with potentially detrimental implications for the character of God, is raised in 54:7–8. This issue is centered in God's statement that the divine self "abandoned" (עזב; 54:7)[145] God's wife (presumably Israel) and acted toward her in a "flood of anger" (בשצף קצף; 54:8). Calvin is troubled by the theological consequences of the anthropomorphic image of God "bailing out"[146] of the implied marriage covenant and has recourse to the language of "seeming" in order to avoid awkward questions. After stating that God "will not cast off or abandon his people," irrespective "of the treachery of men," or for that matter God's own "sort of admission of the fact," Calvin argues that "what the Prophet says in this passage must therefore refer to our feelings and to outward appearance, because we *seem* to be rejected by God when we do not perceive his presence and protection."[147]

This type of hermeneutic, with its emphasis on human misperception, is, as Brueggemann observes, a "common interpretive procedure" that is nonetheless "deeply problematic." He argues that

---

143. Brueggemann, *Deep Memory, Exuberant Hope*, 50.

144. Ibid., 50–51.

145. This term is also found in 54:6, עזב.

146. Brueggemann uses this term to describe the activity of 54:7–8 (*Isaiah 40–66*, 153).

147. Calvin, *Commentary on the Prophet Isaiah*, 4:140 (emphasis added).

It appeals to theological-dogmatic convictions nowhere grounded in the particular texts, but imposed upon the text in order to dismiss a reading that on the face of it is not in doubt. Moreover, if one explains away as "human and mistaken" such self-assertions [Isa 54:7–8] made by Yahweh, one is hard put to draw the line and treat with seriousness the textual self-disclosures of Yahweh that one prefers. It may be claimed that the dismissal of the assertion is "canonical," that is, read in relation to many other texts that say otherwise and are judged to be more central. Such a claim, however, is characteristically reductionist, and flattens the dialectic that, in my judgment, belongs properly to canonical reading.[148]

According to this valid assessment, Calvin's approach is less than adequate.

Other commentators also gear their interpretation to ensure that the behavior of the divine character may not be impugned. Motyer is disturbed by translations that he regards as "remarkably free"—but that are, in actuality, quite possible—for the way they make "the husband blameworthy."[149] Speaking of the rejected bride, from the outset Oswalt wants it irrefutably established that "the fault is all her own."[150] Webb, with disdain for the idea that there might be a relationship between message and medium, moves directly to what he takes the verses to mean in their broadest theological generality, without any discussion of the terms by which this is mediated.[151]

More sensitive to both the language of the text and the troubling questions concerning the nature of God to which it gives rise,[152] Hanson borrows the term *tensegrity* from the world of architecture in order to try to resolve perceived difficulties. He proposes that this concept offers the possibility of "the integration into one structure of dissimilar elements" in such a fashion that neither "homogeneity" nor "chaos" prevails, as a result of which "by the end of the chapter [54] . . . a sense of coherence has emerged from the *seeming* contradictions."[153] For Hanson, at "the

148. Brueggemann, *Deep Memory, Exuberant Hope*, 82. For a survey of how problematic texts have been dealt with, see pp. 81–84.
149. Motyer, *Prophecy of Isaiah*, 447.
150. Oswalt, *Book of Isaiah: Chapters 40–66*, 421.
151. Webb simply states, "[A]s the LORD then took her to be his bride, entering into a covenant with her at Mount Sinai, so he would take her again and renew his relationship with her" (*Message of Isaiah*, 216).
152. Paul D. Hanson ponders, "If God is the one who has brought on the catastrophe rather than some dark and evil agent, how can there be hope for release?" (*Isaiah 40–66*, 170). He concludes that "this is the terrifying form that theodicy takes in monotheistic religion."
153. Ibid., 169 (emphasis added). Note also how the phrase "*seeming contradictions*" (emphasis added) is used specifically with regard to 54:7–8, which Hanson views as "the heart of the chapter" (p. 171).

deepest level" this chapter is about transformation, and this "transformation must originate with God."[154] This conclusion implies the ultimate reliability of God, whatever initial reservations may have been entertained.

Westermann also recognizes that Isa 54 "is an exceptionally impressive example of Deutero-Isaiah's poetic art" in which a "perfect unity" is "achieved between poetry and proclamation."[155] He concurs that vv. 7–8 represent "the poem's climax," the epicenter of which indicates that "a change has come over God. He ceases from wrath, and again shows Israel mercy." He concludes with the assertion that "this makes everything all right again,"[156] thereby, like Hanson, implying no long-term criticism of God.

Thus, although both these critics are much more sensitive to the contours of the text, both in the final analysis protect the integrity of the divine. However, the rhetorical movement from abandonment, no matter how brief (ברגע קטן; 54:7), to compassion (רחמים; 54:7), no matter how extensive (גדלים; 54:7), and from angry momentary (רגע; 54:8) hiding to the promise of endless loving faithfulness (חסד עולם; 54:8) and compassion (רחם; 54:8), does not necessarily confer theological absolution on the divine. For some, quite legitimately, this rhetoric might not make "everything all right again." This group of wounded people, contra Hanson but consistent with my argument, may represent a source of transformation that is an alternative to God. Abused and abandoned women need not only look to their erstwhile husbands and partners as the sole origin of transformation in their lives.[157]

154. Ibid., 170.

155. Westermann, *Isaiah 40–66*, 270.

156. Ibid., 274.

157. Goldingay, after acknowledging that the whole image deployed in the chapter "would no longer work" in a modern Western culture, suggests that "the solution for a Western woman today who has had her husband walk out on her is to learn to be her own person, perhaps with the help of her sisters, and a man who has walked out in a fit of temper can by no means assume that he can walk back in. . . . Yahweh speaks as if it were a case of walking out in a fit of temper, though other passages have made clear that there were deeper problems than that" (*Isaiah*, 310–11). Significantly, one of those problems is Yahweh's use of power, "but Ms Jerusalem knows what it is like to be on the receiving end of that power. . . . The implication is that Ms Jerusalem has grounds for asking some hard questions before having her man back, and Yahweh is anticipating those questions" (p. 311). Furthermore, with regard to God's reassurance "I won't do it again": "Once more, a modern woman would have some reservations about such reassurances. This is exactly what abusive husbands say before resuming abuse."

Oswalt advises that "we should not be troubled over the idea of an angry God. The alternative is Aristotle's Unmoved Mover."[158] But in setting up this opposition, he is dealing in theological categories extrinsic to the world of the text. The innocence of God is assumed before the text is read, and interpretation is determined by this exterior assumption. Irrespective of type or intensity, divine anger is always justified. When the text, however, is entered to a significantly greater degree on its own terms, other interpretative possibilities become available. In this way the particularity of text is given priority over general theological assumption.[159] Sawyer undertakes this approach in relation to the presentation of Israel in terms of female imagery in chs. 49–66.[160] Sawyer's approach may be regarded as an analysis and explication of the implications of the time "when God, as it were, lost his temper."[161]

With specific reference to 54:1–10, Sawyer acknowledges that the woman "was partly to blame" but contests, on the grounds that her culpability "is insignificant beside the repeated references to her suffering," that the man "takes prime responsibility for the tragedy."[162] Attentive to the unfolding drama of the piece, he further discerns that "Yahweh, 'the Holy One of Israel . . . God of all the earth' (v. 5) is represented as behaving like a remorseful husband, pleading with his wife to trust him and take him back" in order "to convince her that he really loves her and that she can trust him."[163] In essence, God is apologizing to God's abandoned wife for wrongdoing on the part of the divine as "he sets aside all hardness and pomposity . . . and comes to her, on bended knee as it were, to plead with her to let bygones be bygones and start again."[164] Adhering to an open reading of the text, the credentials of the divine might not be found convincing nor God's appeal persuasive, and therefore rejection is possible and even understandable.

158. Oswalt, *Book of Isaiah: Chapters 40–66*, 421.

159. Ludwig Wittgenstein allies a "craving for generality" with a "contemptuous attitude towards the particular case" (*The Blue and Brown Books: Preliminary Studies for the "Philosophical Investigations"* [Oxford: Blackwell, 1969], 18). In this case the particularity of Isa 54 is severely downplayed in a sizeable section of interpretation to conform it to the generalized assumption of divine goodness.

160. John F. A. Sawyer, "Daughter of Zion and Servant of the Lord in Isaiah: A Comparison," *JSOT* 44 (1989): 89–107. Sawyer regards his piece as an attempt to correct what he perceives as the overemphasis in Christian interpretation on the servant imagery, especially in Isa 53.

161. Sawyer, *Isaiah*, 2:152.

162. Sawyer, "Daughter of Zion and Servant of the Lord," 94.

163. Ibid., 95–96.

164. Ibid., 96. F. Hecht argues that Yahweh apologies here ("Die Interpretasie van Jes. 54:7a," *NGTT* 4 [1963]: 117–19 [118]).

For Sawyer, the benefit of pursuing this type of reading strategy is that it uncovers unusual and arresting dimensions of the divine character.[165] This is also true for Brueggemann, who finds 54:7–8 "among the most remarkable in scripture" for the "astonishing" and "candid admission on the part of Yahweh . . . that Yahweh did indeed abandon Israel" in "a genuine . . . not apparent"[166] sense. Accentuating the peculiar nature of these verses, Brueggemann observes that they do not claim "that this abandonment is punishment or that wife-Israel has sinned," but rather that they intimate "Yahweh coming as close to an expression of regret or apology for exile as is possible." It is little wonder he suggests "that such a portrayal of Yahweh is awkward for 'high Christian theology' that will entertain no such dimension of Yahweh."[167] Tracy has proposed that a text "can become a classic for the reader only if the reader is willing to allow that present horizon [i.e. the present horizon of the reader] to be vexed, provoked, challenged by the claim to attention of the text itself."[168] This happens with respect to Isa 54 when the horizon of assumed divine probity is disturbed by the claims of vv. 7–8. In this way the text "speaks anew."[169]

Literary artistry erodes absolutist theological claims.[170] The irremediably allusive nature of art ensures that it stands in tension with the univocal tendency of dogmatic claims. As Brueggemann insists, supportive of this viewpoint, "In these verses . . . no blame is assigned to Israel as cause of the abandonment, though Yahweh says, 'In overflowing wrath.' From the text itself, such 'wrath' could as well be capriciousness on the part of Yahweh as righteous, warranted indignation."[171] Doubt

165.   Sawyer, "Daughter of Zion and Servant of the Lord," 96. Sawyer states, "If you find it hard to believe that such an image of Yahweh can really appear in scripture, then you need only look elsewhere in these remarkable chapters [49–66] to find evidence that it can."

166.   Brueggemann, *Isaiah 40–66*, 153.

167.   Ibid. This reading is reinforced in Brueggemann's *Deep Memory, Exuberant Hope*, where Brueggemann argues that "Yahweh has taken the disruptive actions" on the basis that "the two words ('abandon, hid') are straightforward and unambiguous. Yahweh did abandon" (pp. 79–80).

168.   David Tracy, *The Analogical Imagination: Christian Theology and the Culture of Pluralism* (London: SCM Press; New York: Crossroad, 1981), 105; see, in general, pp. 99–153.

169.   Ibid., 107. On this idea, see also Ernst Fuchs, *Hermeneutik* (Tübingen: Mohr, 1970), 249–56.

170.   As noted above, Westermann (*Isaiah 40–66*, 270) and Hanson (*Isaiah 40–66*, 169) recognize the carefully wrought design of Isa 54 but shy away from implications for the stability of the character of God.

171.   Brueggemann, *Deep Memory, Exuberant Hope*, 80.

about the trustworthiness of God is never completely expunged from the text. That both Isa 40:1–2 and 54:7–8 contain confessional elements indicative of dubious behavior on the part of God reinforces this sense of doubt. As Sawyer argues, intentionally linking chs. 54 and 40:

> The guilt of Zion, the reason why she suffered, is only fleetingly referred to in ch. 54, and nowhere else in the main story. The point is made there and in the opening verses of ch. 40, that her suffering is out of all proportion to her guilt ("she has received double for all her sins").[172]

Bearing this in mind properly affects interpretation and undermines the idea of questioning the sanity of anyone (of whatever era) who would even consider doubting or resisting the "comfort, comfort" of 40:1.

10. *Isaiah and the Conversion of God?*

Sawyer notes how, in the latter half of the book of Isaiah, imagery applied to God ranges from that of the warrior or king[173] to "feminine imagery of childbearing." In the latter, God is depicted as "a midwife assisting at the birth" of a new order, featuring "positive images of maternal warmth, contentment and fecundity to a degree unparalleled in biblical tradition."[174] Thus, in this portion of the Isaianic material, Yahweh is presented as both "like a judge or a king eager to demonstrate his power" and as a character who "empties himself of that exalted status."[175] Sawyer insists that "God's role in both is stressed."[176] This raises the question as to whether there is a discernible relationship between these dimensions of God's person or whether they simply alternate in a more random way.[177] At a deeper level, one may ask if the

172. Sawyer, "Daughter Zion and Servant of the Lord," 103. On this type of approach, see further Patricia Tull Willey, *Remember the Former Things: The Recollection of Previous Texts in Second Isaiah* (Atlanta: Scholars Press, 1997), esp. 229–61.

173. Sawyer, "Daughter Zion and Servant of the Lord," 106. This is termed "predominantly male imagery" rooted in the idea of God "imposing his authority on the world."

174. Ibid. On this theme, see also p. 98.

175. Ibid., 105. This second aspect of the divine character is termed "the almost kenotic love of Yahweh," further supporting the contention that the concept of kenosis plays a part in Isa 40–66. I have argued that kenosis has played a part with respect to 58:6–10.

176. Ibid., 106.

177. Miscall talks about how "Isaiah struggles mightily to hold . . . different worlds and . . . different gods together, whether in balance or in tension and contradiction" ("Isaiah: Dreams and Nightmares, Fantasy and Horror," 156).

interplay between these images of divine activity reflects a change in the character of God.

There is some critical warrant for proposing such a conversion or reification[178] of God in chs. 40–66. Koch sees in an early section of Deutero-Isaiah (42:8–13) "the first beginnings of a refashioning of the idea of God,"[179] while Garbini posits that it was "the encounter between Cyrus and 'Deutero-Isaiah' . . . which marked the transition from Yahweh Sabaoth as 'God of the armed bands' to being 'God of the universe.'"[180] Attentive to the perspective of the exiled group that Second Isaiah is addressing, Croatto argues that "the figure of Yahweh must appear worn out"[181] to this group, given its disenchantment "with its traditional God, who is responsible"[182] for its situation. In response to this situation, in which the ability to trust God is crucially important,[183] Croatto insists that "the first step is to remold the figure of Yahweh in such a way as to render the God of Israel's proposal for liberation credible."[184]

---

178.   For a contemporary example of this sort of theological rethinking in light of changed circumstances, see Jacques Pohier, *God in Fragments* (trans. John Bowden; London: SCM Press, 1985). This reflection follows Pohier's *Quand je dis Dieu* (Paris: Éditions du Seuil, 1977), which was subsequently condemned by the Vatican in 1979 and led to severe disciplinary sanctions being enacted against Pohier. In connection with the characterization of God in the prophetic literature, Kathleen M. O'Connor suggests a fragmented God in whose textual representation "language of divine tears offsets language of the divine punisher and wrathful judge" ("The Tears of God," 185). The way in which O'Connor accepts exile as the context for this struggling with the multifaceted nature of God supports the idea that it gave rise to divergent ideas about God that were not easily integrated or harmonized even within finally redacted single works.

179.   Koch, *The Prophets*, 2:125.

180.   Garbini, *History and Ideology in Ancient Israel*, 87. This particular transition does not imply a renunciation of violence.

181.   J. Severino Croatto, "Exegesis of Second Isaiah from the Perspective of the Oppressed: Paths for Reflection," in Segovia and Tolbert, eds., *Reading from this Place*, 2:219–36 (221).

182.   Ibid., 222.

183.   Croatto asks, "What can Yahweh do to win them [the people] back?" ("Exegesis of Second Isaiah," 222), a question made all the more difficult to answer given God's responsibility for their plight. Croatto proposes that the author "has to *convince* the addressees that it is Yahweh . . . who is both able and willing to save them" (emphasis in original), a task that "is by no means easy since the addressees believe that their God has forgotten them" (p. 223). More than this, according to Croatto, the addressees believe that Yahweh is the source of their predicament, a factor that exacerbates the difficulty of trusting God.

184.   Ibid., 224.

In exploring the issue more systematically, Lind perceives a disjunction between ways under God that are permissible for Cyrus and the way in which the servants of God are ideally called to live. These latter ways indicate the profoundest level of God's character and represent a renunciation of and therefore conversion from violence.[185] For Lind, the passages in which Cyrus appears describe him "as Yahweh's agent who exercises violent political power to achieve his purpose."[186] Ultimately, however, "Deutero-Isaiah is saying that the politics which tries to control by coercion is ineffective" and "not really divine." Consequently, "The exiles could not hold to the monotheism of Yahweh on the basis of ancient Near Eastern power politics."[187] Instead, grounded in their trust in Yahweh's ability to speak a word and bring it to fruition,[188] and shaped by the logic of the servant songs,[189] they are to "testify to the moral quality of the unity toward which Yahweh is leading the nations, and thus also to the moral quality of the unity of God."[190]

In this construal, the "servant poems are an essential part of Deutero-Isaiah's concept of monotheism, a monotheism which rejected the gods of power politics for the unicity of Yahweh who alone can provide continuity of community by the politics of creative word-event."[191] By attributing primary hermeneutical importance to these servant poems, Lind reifies the character of God to exclude all traces of coercion. On the basis of this analysis, he asserts that "a radically new political

185. See S. D. Snyman, "Trends in the History of Research on the Problem of Violence in the Old Testament," *Skrif en Kerk* 18, no. 1 (1997): 127–45; also, Dianne Bergant, "Violence and God: A Bible Study," *Missiology* 20, no. 1 (1992): 45–54.
186. Millard C. Lind, "Monotheism, Power, and Justice: A Study in Isaiah 40–55," *CBQ* 46 (1984): 432–46 (438–39). According to Lind, "As a monotheist, Deutero-Isaiah must relate Cyrus to Yahweh" (p. 438).
187. Ibid., 435.
188. Ibid., 436–37, in which Lind develops his theory of "word-event" or "word-deed." Against this credulous reading, however, Carroll pointedly observes: "It is ironic that so much of Second Isaiah's expectations failed to materialise, for he was the prophet who insisted that one mark of the superiority of his deity was that he could declare the future. . . . A god who cannot foretell the future is no god! So the followers of Second Isaiah were faced with the problematic of prophecy—how to explain why Yahweh's revelation of the future had not been confirmed by historical reality. Small wonder that the oracles in Is. lvi–lxvi contain so much accusation and vilification against the community" ("Second Isaiah and the Failure of Prophecy," 130).
189. Following Duhm's designation of these as Isa 42:1–7; 49:1–9a; 50:4–9a, 10–11; 52:13–53:12.
190. Lind, "Monotheism, Power, and Justice," 432–33.
191. Ibid., 442.

kingdom . . . will arise upon the chaos created by Cyrus," the foundation of which will be "the persuasion of Yahweh's word." In this "new world-wide community," furthermore, "all mankind will be one in their trust in his [Yahweh's] word-deed for continuity of community and in their voluntary commitment to his will."[192]

While interesting and attractive in several regards, Lind's thesis is finally too schematic and has no convincing explanation for why, if peace and persuasion are central to the divine character, God chooses the violence of Cyrus to achieve divine ends. On this subject, Lind's revealing comment is that "the creator God . . . can save as he chooses, though his methods may be paradoxical to the unity of his character."[193] In other words, God's renunciation of violence is neither total nor absolute. As Miscall observes in connection with 54:16, but with a more general provenance, "Divine remorse doesn't include a total and final renunciation of rage and violence."[194] Thus the tension between the different aspects of God's character "continues on throughout the rest of Isaiah."[195] Or in the general assessment of Coleridge, which may also be applied to this dimension of the Isaianic text:

> In its refusal to give mastery to any single voice, the Bible is an unusual master-narrative. It is also unusual in the way its narrative unfolds by way of huge dislocations, refusing any sense of the smooth connectedness that some find objectionable in certain kinds of narrative.[196]

11. *In Critical Dialogue with Croatto*

I now briefly place the results of this research in critical dialogue with the work of three scholars in order to assess how it might challenge,

---

192. Ibid., 437. In this proposal, the Isaianic new exodus and the process by which every knee shall bow and every tongue confess the Lordship of Yahweh (45:23) are envisaged as being conducted peacefully. Furthermore, in making persuasion and servant-oriented self-giving integral to "the moral quality of tôrâ-justice," human manifestations of these qualities become derivative of the divine nature; however, an expression of such qualities, especially as in Isa 58:6–10, may be understood as human in origin if coercive violence and the will to self-aggrandizing glory are not completely expunged from God's character.

193. Ibid., 441.

194. Miscall, "Isaiah: Dreams and Nightmares, Fantasy and Horror," 161.

195. Ibid., 164.

196. Mark Coleridge, "Life in the Crypt, or Why Bother with Biblical Studies?," *BibInt* 2, no. 2 (1994): 139–51 (148). Another way of putting this is to say, following Mikhail M. Bakhtin, that the Isaianic text, and more generally the biblical text, is irremediably polyphonic (*Problems of Dostoevsky's Poetics* [trans. R. W. Rotsel; Ann Arbor, Mich.: Ardis, 1973).

modify, and support their thinking. These scholars respectively represent the fields of biblical hermeneutics, doctrinal theology, and contemporary missiology.

For Croatto, reading is not a disinterested enterprise. Rather, reading has an explicit purpose, and that purpose is to assist and empower the oppressed in their struggle "for political and social liberation and hence economic liberation as well."[197] As part of this liberationist agenda, the liberative nature of God is assumed.[198] More than this, the impression is that divine endorsement is positively sought for a liberationist reading, as if anything less would necessitate a total rejection of the text. In concluding his essay on Second Isaiah, Croatto claims "to find in the text a profound harmony (not a simple parallelism or concordism) with reality itself," but significantly acknowledges that were this not the case, "a clash would have occurred with the reading from the perspective of the oppressed, and the text would have been put aside as irrelevant to the situation at hand."[199] This is what might be termed an all-duck-or-no-dinner approach in which "a *univocal* meaning"[200] containing no "anti-liberationist"[201] strain is sought.

It is difficult, however, to avoid the conclusion that this is a forced reading, determined by prior ideological commitments, in which, by happy coincidence, what is found is what is sought, and in which the alterity of the text is eliminated as a constitutive factor. Also writing from a liberationist perspective, Ceresko refers to "the ambiguity and elusiveness of the poetry"[202] in Isa 40–45. If, as demonstrated, these qualities pertain as much to the character of God rendered by that poetry, then Croatto's assessments, plus their hermeneutical basis, are difficult to sustain. Moreover, recognizing the plurivocity of the text, with its different ideological strands (some liberationist, others anti-liberationist), is not by definition antithetic to the liberationist "situation at hand," but in fact might assist in fostering a more focused, nuanced social analysis.

197. Croatto, "Exegesis and Second Isaiah," 236. For a broader explication of his hermeneutic, see further Croatto, *Biblical Hermeneutics*.

198. Croatto, "Exegesis and Second Isaiah," 226. Babylonian texts that honor Marduk are dismissed as myths representing "an ideological legitimation for the Babylonian Empire and its repression of other peoples," while nothing is said of similar tendencies in Israelite exodus imagery (223).

199. Ibid., 235.

200. Ibid., 226, where it is argued that "a term can be dense, suggestive, but not ambiguous from the point of view of the message."

201. Ibid., 235 (emphasis in original).

202. Anthony R. Ceresko, *Introduction to the Old Testament: A Liberation Perspective* (Maryknoll, N.Y.: Orbis; London: Chapman, 1992), 234.

It might also help in developing a more shrewd awareness of the realities confronting those who would seek justice.[203]

Even embracing the idea of God having a dark side, which manifests itself periodically in acts of excess and injustice, does not necessarily corrode the liberationist task. If the goal is *human* liberation, that the operation flows from the just nature of God and consequently receives divine sanction is not absolutely essential. Thus a degree of assent can be afforded Carroll's apposite comment that

> liberation theology's readings of the Bible need to be made much sharper in order to take into account the repeated biblical assertion of YHWH's authorship of evil and maintenance of injustice in the world. Whatever modernity may claim about structural evil in the community, biblical ideology identifies structural evil with the ways of YHWH.[204]

This is true even if Carroll tends to overstate his case.

12. *In Critical Dialogue with Soulen*

Soulen offers a stimulating study devoted to the renegotiation of the relationship between Christianity and the Jewish people, given their common grounding in the God of Israel. The study addresses Christianity's historically considerable supersessionist conceit[205] and raises a number of points about the nature of faith in a post-Holocaust, post-Christendom world.[206] Seriously taking issue with Christianity's traditional and virtually

---

203.   Pleins notes that in the final part of the book of Isaiah (chs. 40–66) it is the nation, and particularly the ruling elites, who are now taken as the poor (*Social Visions of the Hebrew Bible*). Acknowledging this reality has detrimental implications for Croatto's agenda. Yet, note how elsewhere Croatto is aware of and guards against this interpretation (*Isaías: La palabra profética y su relectura hermenéutica—La liberación es posible* [Buenos Aires: Lumen, 1994], 2:40–55).

204.   R. P. Carroll, "Blindsight and the Vision Thing: Blindness and Insight in the Book of Isaiah," in Broyles and Evans, eds., *Writing and Reading the Scroll of Isaiah*, 1:79–93 (83–84 n. 10).

205.   Kendall Soulen, *The God of Israel and Christian Theology* (Minneapolis: Fortress, 1996), x.

206.   In its post-Holocaust, anti-supersessionist orientation, Soulen's work may be placed in the context of Rosemary Radford Ruether, *Faith and Fratricide* (New York: Seabury, 1974); C. Thoma, *A Christian Theology of Judaism* (New York: Paulist, 1980); J. T. Pawlikowski, *Christ in the Light of the Christian–Jewish Dialogue* (New York: Paulist, 1982); Paul van Buren, *A Theology of the Jewish-Christian Reality* (3 vols.; San Francisco: Harper & Row, 1980–88); C. M. Williamson, *A Guest in the House of Israel: Post-Holocaust Church Theology* (Louisville, Ky.: Westminster John Knox, 1993).

exclusive emphasis on "the catastrophe of sin" and its Christological solution, Soulen argues that "Christians have commonly limited the notion of a divine economy to God's work as Redeemer" and therefore "can be said to have submitted the concept of divine economy to a consistent soteriological reduction."[207] As he notes, further pressing his case, "the antithesis of sin and redemption is not the central theme of the Hebrew Scriptures, nor is it an object of concern in its own right."[208] Making it so inevitably fails to do justice to the richness of the biblical vision[209] and dangerously perpetuates a model that "depicts carnal Israel's role in the economy of redemption as essentially transient by virtue of the spiritualizing and universalizing impetus of God's salvific will."[210]

Against this propensity to attribute paradigmatic importance to one theological category or problem and to state its resolution in a reductionist fashion, Soulen still acknowledges that "sin, evil, and oppression (and the corresponding need for redemption and liberation) are undeniable dimensions of God's history with Israel and the nations" (p. 112). Yet he proposes the "significance of an *economy of consummation*" (p. 110 [emphasis in original]) in which "God's history with Israel and the nations is oriented at every point towards God's eschatological reign of *shalom*, where God's work as Consummator will finally be fulfilled"

---

207. Soulen, *God of Israel and Christian Theology*, 111.

208. Ibid., 112.

209. Ibid., 109, where Soulen talks about the "limitations of the church's standard canonical narrative." He observes, "Traditionally, Christians have assumed that the hermeneutical complexity of the Christian Canon is sufficiently addressed by positing Jesus Christ as the ultimate unifying center of both parts of the Christian canon" (p. 113).

210. Ibid., 109 (subsequent bracketed references in the main text are to this source). Soulen writes, "Barth's theology of consummation embodies the logic of economic supersessionism as clearly as any in the history of the church. The incarnation brings Israel's history to a conclusion in principle, after which Israel's sole legitimate destiny is to be absorbed into the spiritual church. If nevertheless the Jewish people paradoxically survive the end of their own history, then this can only be ascribed to their blind rejection of the gospel" (pp. 92–93). Soulen adds, however, that "while Barth embraces the logic of economic supersessionism, he refuses to deduce from it punitive supersessionism, that is, the view that God has abrogated God's covenant with Israel on account of its unbelief. With an eloquence that has few parallels in Christian theology, Barth insists upon God's unbroken fidelity towards the Jews despite their disbelief in the gospel, a fidelity that will endure to the end of time. Yet the fact remains that, for Barth, Israel's continued existence is a mystery, an enigmatic testimony to God's unfathomable fidelity to human creation in the face of abysmal blindness and unbelief."

(p. 112; see also p. 151). According to this construal, "The hermeneutical center of the Scriptures is the God of Israel's eschatological reign, conceived as the final outcome of God's work as the One who consummates the human family in and through God's history with Israel and the nations." This center, however, does not stand in splendid isolation, for Soulen "suggests that the Christian canon possesses an irreducibly double focus" (p. 113). He contends that

> The hermeneutical center of the Apostolic Witness is "good news about the kingdom of God and the name of Jesus Christ" (Acts 8:12). These twin *foci* of the Christian canon are related like two concentric circles. The eschatological reign of the God of Israel provides the indispensable hermeneutical context for the center of Christian faith, namely, the gospel about God's kingdom and the name of Jesus Christ. (p. 113)

Consequently,

> liberation from powers that destroy is a matter of utmost urgency precisely because such powers threaten to cut humankind off from God's economy of consummation, where God's blessings are bestowed. In this sense, God's work as Redeemer confirms rather than supplants the centrality of God's work as Consummator in a Christian reading of the Scriptures. (p. 112)

If the coming reign of God is taken as having the establishment of a just social order (in keeping with, for example, the vision of Isa 65:17–25) as one of its constituent elements,[211] then there is much to affirm in this interpretation. This is true especially for the way Soulen's reading highlights the need for "solidarity with the human other" (p. 141), "Christian discipleship" necessarily taking "a cruciform shape" (p. 167), and "suffering love, to which Jew and Greek alike are called to be conformed" (p. 168), as central to the quest for justice. These statements accord well with what has been discerned with regard to Isa 58:6–10.

Soulen, however, is primarily a systematic or dogmatic theologian and consequently does not assess the implications of a "dark side" to the divine for his construction. In Soulen's account, God wills blessing for all creation (pp. 117–40) and if curse befalls creation it is as a result of "the human family" turning "its back on God's blessing" and doing "violence on the human other."[212] Thus God is absolved as the originator of curse and the attendant violence. Whatever blessing and justice exist in the world flow derivatively from and in emulation of the divine nature, which, in a way not supported by the biblical witness, is understood as not

---

211. Ibid., 141–42, where this is strongly implied.
212. Ibid., 142. On curse more generally, see pp. 141–55.

participating in the modalities of injustice and curse. Incorporating biblical acknowledgment of periodic divine excess and violence, and therefore curse, erodes the assurance of this construal and creates the possibility of understanding solidarity and justice, and therefore blessing, as having periodic human origin, perhaps finding expression in the face of perceived divine abandonment or abuse.

As a corrective to the way in which Christianity has minimized the importance of the Jews in God's plan of eschatological blessing, Soulen argues for the maintenance "of Israel's national privilege" (p. 168), noting that "Gentiles have used the standard [i.e. supersessionist] model to suppress recognition that God's blessing for creation can be accepted only in solidarity with Israel."[213] While there is an undeniable element of accuracy in Soulen's statement, in the sense that Israel, however that term is interpreted, is part of the human family, the concept of solidarity implied is peculiar in the way it gives automatic primacy to Israel. It thereby creates the possibility of an arrogant and aggressive strain in Israelite/Israeli/Jewish thought being encouraged and placed beyond reproach.[214]

Moreover, from a global missiological perspective, this analysis seems unnecessarily forced and shaped specifically by the prevailing North American context, and generally by theological considerations (e.g. guilt) of the Western Church. For theological reasons, an Asian, African, or Latin American might wonder why this solidarity with Israel need be presupposed as the *sole* avenue for availing of divine blessing. From a practical viewpoint, he or she might struggle to find ways to embody this solidarity.[215] This model thus curtails the sovereignty of God to effect blessing where God wills, offers no satisfactory theological explanation for the blessing a people may have experienced before it ever heard of Israel, and does not account for the way the Noaic covenant with all creation forms the broader context of the covenant with Israel.

213. Ibid., 154. At present Palestinians might wonder exactly what form that solidarity should take.

214. Ibid., 141, where to an extent Soulen recognizes that Jews can cut themselves off "from God's economies of mutual blessing" by seeking "to procure blessing on [their] own terms at the other's expense."

215. See Kosuke Koyama, *Mount Fuji and Mount Sinai: A Pilgrimage in Theology* (London: SCM Press, 1984). See also, Choan-Seng Song, *The Compassionate God: An Exercise in the Theology of Transposition* (London: SCM Press, 1982); idem, *Theology from the Womb of Asia* (London: SCM Press, 1988); and Choan-Seng Song's trilogy, *Jesus and the Reign of God, Jesus in the Power of the Spirit*, and *Jesus, the Crucified People* (Minneapolis: Fortress, 1993, 1994, and 1996). See also Kwesi A. Dickson, *Uncompleted Mission: Christianity and Exclusivism* (Maryknoll, N.Y.: Orbis, 1991).

Furthermore, in insistently defending the idea of Jewish identity,[216] to the extent that categorization as either Jew or Gentile becomes virtually an order of creation,[217] Soulen, in a way reminiscent of old jokes in which heaven is divided into sectors for the various denominations, comes close to implying that when the eschatological reign of God's *shalom* finally dawns, the old division of Jew and Gentile will still persist (one gets the impression Soulen might say "rightly"). By way of contrast to this strained position, occasions of genuine human solidarity, redolent of a search for authentic justice and rooted in kenotic acts (such as exemplified in Isa 58:6–10), should be construed as examples of realized eschatology in which barriers between human beings, including those between Jews and Gentiles, are properly dissolved. In this understanding, no *a priori* scheme explaining the relationship between Jews and Gentiles in the journey towards blessing and justice is presupposed. Instead, irrespective of where such events take place or who participates in them, the reign of God is conceived as having been made manifest precisely in the midst of common humanity.

13. *In Critical Dialogue with Cruchley-Jones*

In a thought-provoking study drawn from contemporary missiology, Cruchley-Jones likens the present context of the Western European Church to that of exile.[218] As the central problems for ancient Israel were "their disobedience and complacency in assuming they were forever in God's favour,"[219] so too the Western European Church has become complacently ecclesiocentric, "replacing the coming kingdom with the established church" (p. 202). He identifies exile as "the decommissioning

216.   Soulen warns that "discounting Jewish identity in favour of identity simply as a person or creature of God poses a great threat to Israel" (*God of Israel and Christian Theology*, 154). This assertion depends on Michael Wyschogrod (*The Body of Faith: God in the People Israel* [San Francisco: Harper & Row, 1989], 181–85).

217.   Soulen, *God of Israel and Christian Theology*, 154. Soulen does acknowledge that "human beings can say no to their 'supernatural' identities as Jews and Gentiles," but clearly this is not recommended.

218.   At present, this is not an uncommon analogy. See, e.g., Brueggemann, *Cadences of Home: Preaching among Exiles*; Erskine Clarke, ed., *Exilic Preaching: Testimony for Christian Exiles in an Increasingly Hostile Culture* (Harrisburg, Pa.: Trinity, 1998).

219.   Peter Cruchley-Jones, *Singing the Lord's Song in a Strange Land?* (Studies in the Intercultural History of Christianity 123; Frankfurt: Peter Lang, 2001), 202; see also pp. 42–44 (subsequent bracketed references in the main text are to this source).

of God's people" (p. 44) and poignantly poses the question as to whether there is still a role in mission for "not my people" (Hos. 1:9) (pp. 187–208). To this question Cruchley-Jones gives a qualified affirmative answer, on condition that the people live faithfully "in the dialectic 'My People—Not My People'" (p. 192). Assessing the positive dimension of the terrible disruption of exile, he contends that "exile is still the setting in which God's people discover what it means to be God's people and how to live as God's people, even as it flies in the face of the hegemony of Zion and Christendom" (p. 193).

While stressing the undoubted richness and pertinence of Cruchley-Jones's study (to which justice cannot be done by the brevity of these comments), two points in particular arise. The first is that for someone with such a questioning, creatively subversive agenda, Cruchley-Jones too readily accedes to the ideology of the biblical text in agreeing "that the cause of exile lay with the people" (p. 41). In a sense he thus aligns himself with the dominant voice in the text, which represents the interests of those who controlled the text's final composition: invariably a sector of the social, ecclesial, or political establishment.[220] Given Cruchley-Jones's avowal "to be alert to ecclesiocentrism"[221] and to develop a missiological understanding in tension with the officialdom of the Church (including, presumably, regnant interpretations of its texts), his proposal, so open to plurality and emphasizing the self-giving rather than domineering side of God, might have been better placed in the tradition and context of those encoded in the text who argued against the established viewpoint and traces of whose voices may still be found. For example, if "the wicked" of Isa 48:22 include those who oppose the ideology of power and restoration in vv. 17–21, Cruchley-Jones would surely be sympathetic to them.[222] Similarly, one assumes that he would

220. See Davies, *Scribes and Schools*. This type of analysis is clearly grounded in the Marxist insight that the ideas of the ruling elite become the ruling or dominant ideas in society. See Eagleton, *Marxism and Literary Criticism*, 5.

221. Cruchley-Jones, *Singing the Lord's Song in a Strange Land?*, 202.

222. Ibid., 49. Cruchley-Jones takes a positive attitude to the call of Jer 29; conceivably, some of those termed "wicked" in Isa 48:22 can be understood as living out of some sense of that call. The designation "wicked," without clarification of what exactly the wickedness consists, may be little more than a pejorative term directed against those who disagree with the speaker. Related to this subject, see how Yehoshua Amir relates how Rav Kook, chief rabbi of Jaffa in the early twentieth century, when confronted with the *halutz*, a group of Jewish "young pioneers bent on settling in the country and setting up there a new socialistic workers' society," called them "the wicked ones" because they "denied the 'divine idea of Israel'" ("Messianism and Zionism," in *Eschatology in the Bible and in Jewish and*

approve, against the obvious sense of the passage, that there was no one
to assist God in the bloody work of 63:1–6, as for him this type of God
should be rejected. Generally a more critical handling of the biblical text
would have been more in keeping with the tenor of the rest of the work.

The second point is in relationship to the term *Missio Dei*,[223] the heart
of which, in a way similar to Soulen, Cruchley-Jones identifies as the
intention of God "to bring to fulfilment his [God's] plan for creation"
(p. 44). In this enterprise, furthermore, God "seeks the participation of
others with [God]" (p. 44) to bring about justice for all. Any departure
from this ethical orientation functionally becomes an abdication of the
ecclesial or human role in the *Missio Dei* (pp. 191–93). God is thus
opposed to brokenness and injustice and, consequently for Cruchley-
Jones, God may be encountered among the suffering of the earth, displaying solidarity with them as the first step in bringing them healing and
restoration in the establishment of a just social order (pp. 176–86).
Among others, Cruchley-Jones appreciatively quotes Kvanig, who asserts
that the human scream "shows us where to look for God,"[224] and that:

> The scream of the starving child in Ethiopia, the pain in the schoolgirl's
> face as the bullet hits her, the despair of the mother in the intifada, they
> bear witness to the cruelty of people. . . . But they also show us the pain
> of God . . . and each scream is a scream heard in heaven, moving the
> world one step further to liberation.[225]

This is a powerful statement for contributing to a deeper understanding
of the wider ramifications of the category *Missio Dei*. It does not,
however, give due weight to the implications for the concept of God
periodically being identified as a violator of excess—something, as

Christian Tradition (ed. Henning Graf Reventlow; JSOTSup 243; Sheffield: Sheffield Academic Press, 1997], 13–30 [24]). However, while never renouncing this
view, Rav Kook experienced a challenge to it on account of the mutual respect that
developed between himself and these secular Zionists.

    223. In the modern era, this concept can be traced to the Willingen International
Missionary Conference of 1952. See Thomas, ed., *Classic Texts in Mission and
World Christianity*, 101–21. For comment on the conference, see Bosch, *Trans-
forming Mission*, 389–90.

    224. Helge S. Kvanig, "Theology of the Scream: The Violator and Violated in
the Biblical Tradition," *Ecumenical Review* 45, no. 3 (1993): 328–36 (334).

    225. Ibid., 334–35. This analysis is premised on the assumption that "the God of
the Israelites is not like human beings. His values were founded in justice and
righteousness" (p. 330). Interestingly, though, Kvanig proposes that through the
human scream "God is challenged to change and liberate" (p. 334). The results of
my study suggest that this change entails God turning away from God's violent,
abusive propensities.

noted, attested in the Isaianic corpus and more broadly in the biblical tradition. Such acknowledgment subverts the concept of *Missio Dei* as deployed by Cruchley-Jones (in keeping with other theologians), but the process of subversion creates space for a legitimate *missio humanitatis* devoted to the search for justice. In the type of terminology used by Cruchley-Jones, there is a necessary dialectic between the *Missio Dei* and the *missio humanitatis*.[226]

14. *Conclusion: The Nature of Metaphor*

Achebe, one of the foremost of Africa's postcolonial writers, correctly warns that "we must always remember that the extravagant attire which Metaphor wears to catch our eye is merely a ploy to engage our hearts and minds."[227] In other words, one of the functions of metaphor is to engender serious thought about the issue(s) to which it relates.[228] Applied to this discussion, the way God is metaphorically depicted, among other things, as an abusive, abandoning husband (Isa 54:6–8), invites radical reflection on the nature of God, in which the idea of divine trustworthiness is questioned as one dimension of that metaphor.

In a standard articulation of the relationship between the hope contained in Isa 40–55 and the disappointment reflected in 56–66, Clements notes that "Deutero-Isaiah . . . assured the exiles of Yahweh's sovereign power to bring them back to their homeland and to bring about a rebirth of the nation."[229] But "disappointment and despondency would be a wholly understandable reaction on their part" to the manifest failure of this "stirring message," which "had foretold supernatural blessing for the homecoming Jews."[230] I argue that trust in this God was never easy or straightforward, and that this conclusion is inextricably bound up with the poetic, imagistic, and metaphorical way the divine is portrayed. Had they listened attentively to the glowing preaching of Isaiah and pursued its implications, the exiles would have realized they were taking a risk in

---

226. Less inclusively, *missio hominis*. This may be related to Küng's idea of the *humanum*; see Hans Küng, *Global Responsibility: In Search of a New World Ethic* (London: SCM Press, 1991).

227. Achebe, *Home and Exile*, 16–17.

228. In a way that anticipates more fully developed reader-response approaches, C. H. Dodd talks of how a parable "arrests the hearer," with the ultimate purpose of teasing him or her "into active thought" (*The Parables of the Kingdom* [London: Nisbet, 1948], 16).

229. R. E. Clements, *God and Temple: The Idea of the Divine Presence in Ancient Israel* (Oxford: Blackwell, 1965), 108.

230. Ibid., 123.

trusting in this God. Perhaps some of them did conclude that the risk of trusting such a God was too great and decided to stay where they were. Given the subsequent narratological development in the book of Isaiah, perhaps they were right. Although, strictly speaking, the book of Isaiah may not be "a polyphonic chorus"[231] on account of the way voices opposed to the prophetic ideology are suppressed, the deployment of metaphor (especially in Isa 54) guarantees significant openness with regard to interpretative possibilities. In Thiselton's understanding of "open" and "closed" texts, closed texts "inform but ask nothing of the reader other than passive acceptance of information," while open texts "challenge, frustrate, surprise, or provoke . . . into active response."[232] In this scheme the Isaianic text is characteristically an example of the latter. Thus, while it may not exactly invite "active participation in the choral conversation,"[233] neither is "closure of [its] meanings"[234] possible.

Brueggemann proposes that "an alternative approach to these 'darkened' texts will need to move from a *metaphysical* to a *dramatic* approach to interpretation." For him, the propensity of "a conventional approach to Christian theology that posits a 'nature of God' . . . outside the text" functions as a way "to justify or explain away a text without facing its concrete claim seriously." Ultimately, "such an approach cannot take such texts with theological seriousness, because matters are settled on grounds other than the text and in other arenas."

With regard to the problematic God of Isa 54:6–8, Brueggemann thus contends that "when God asserts, 'For a brief moment I have abandoned you,' we have a God who abandons Israel for a brief moment. That is what Yahweh says, what Yahweh does, and who Yahweh is." He insists that:

> The character who has once uttered these lines and committed these acts remains always the character who has once uttered these lines and committed these acts. There is more to this character than these particular lines, but these lines become inescapably part of who this character is, no matter what other renderings, actions, and utterances may follow.[235]

231. Anthony C. Thiselton, "Communicative Action and Promise in Interdisciplinary, Biblical, and Theological Hermeneutics," in *The Promise of Hermeneutics* (ed. Roger Lundin, Clarence Walhout, and Anthony C. Thiselton; Grand Rapids, Mich.: Eerdmans; Cambridge: Paternoster, 1999), 133–239 (179).
232. Ibid., 153.
233. Ibid., 179.
234. Terrence W. Tilley, *The Evils of Theodicy* (Washington, D.C.: Georgetown University Press, 1991), 109.
235. Brueggemann, *Deep Memory, Exuberant Hope*, 84 (emphasis in preceding quotations appeared in original).

Once this literary mode of reading,[236] rooted in the idea of the biblical drama,[237] is applied, a sense of doubt lingers over the reliability and trustworthiness of God.[238] Lundin writes: "A contemporary hermeneutical theory informed by the Christian faith will be more concerned . . . with questions of trustworthy fidelity than with those of absolute certainty."[239] But close attention to the biblical text and the God encoded in it places even this welcome departure from the quest for dogmatic certitude under strain, particularly if "trustworthy fidelity" is taken to refer solely to God. As has been argued, God is occasionally presented as being less than trustworthy and reliable.[240] The comment of a modern exile that "perhaps the greatest loss is that trust is destroyed"[241] may with some justification be applied to the attitude of a section of Israelite society, as encoded in the Isaianic text, to their God. Acknowledgment of this possible reading legitimates an innovative human role in addressing issues (including that of the search for justice) that fall within the sphere of human activity and opens the possibility of humanity affecting the attitude of God in the divine–human dialectic.[242]

236.   David Robert Ord and Robert B. Coote draw the distinction between "steno language and tensive language." In the former "a stenographer takes down exactly what is said, without interpretation. . . . It is the kind of language in which every word is carefully defined and usually means only one thing. Tensive language, on the other hand, employs words in such a way as to generate tension. This is the language characteristic of the artistic community, the language of poetry, metaphor, and symbol" (*Is the Bible True? Understanding the Bible Today* [London: SCM Press, 1994], 35). Van Wolde speaks of "the ambiguity characteristic of poetry" (*Mr and Mrs Job*, 45).

237.   See also William Stacy Johnson, "Rethinking Theology: A Postmodern, Post-Holocaust, Post-Christendom Endeavour," *Int* 55, no. 1 (2001): 5–18.

238.   At the time of writing, a news story emerged in Britain of a miscarriage of justice that resulted in the unfair imprisonment of a man for 27 years (see the *Guardian Weekly* [15–21 February 2001]). Defending the justice system, one commentator argued that the correct verdict was arrived at eventually; perhaps so, but the time lag in arriving at the verdict ensures that doubt lingers over the reliability and trustworthiness of the system.

239.   Lundin, "Interpreting Orphans," 5.

240.   Yvonne Sherwood similarly speaks of "the horrors of an unpredictable deity" ("Of Fruit and Corpses and Wordplay Visions: Picturing Amos 8:1–3," *JSOT* 92 [2001]: 5–27 [15]).

241.   Janna Letts and Fiona Whythead, eds., *Captured Voices* (London: Indigo, 2000), 11.

242.   Phillips discusses how, during the exile, the human perception of the injustice of one generation paying for the wrongdoing of another led, as enshrined in Deuteronomic legislation, to the ruling out of anyone but the criminal being held

Writing of Melville's "love of metaphor" in connection with the novel *Moby-Dick*, Wood argues that this love leads Melville "marvellously astray, theologically," and that in consequence "his 'wandering' love of language breaks up his God."[243] Wood concludes:

> *Moby-Dick* represents the triumph of this atheism of metaphor. Or, perhaps, this polytheism of metaphor. For it is a book in which allegory explodes into a thousand metaphors; a book in which the Puritan habit of reading signs and seeing stable meanings behind them is mocked by an almost grotesque abundance of metaphor.[244]

While it may be overstating the case to suggest that these comments could apply to the book of Isaiah, the Isaianic text, even with its mono-theistic propensity, tends in this direction. Metaphor and poetic language generally destabilizes assurance of meaning, particularly with regard to the character of God.

---

liable for the crime. He argues that "since this resulted in a higher morality being attributed to human justice than divine[,] . . . ideas about the latter also had to alter" ("Double for All Her Sins," 131).

   243.   James Wood, "The All of the If," *New Republic* (March 1997): 29–36 (34).

   244.   Ibid.

Conclusion

THE PRIMACY OF JUSTICE

1. *Turning Away from God*

Brueggemann identifies Isa 1:4, within the opening condemnation of the people in the book of Isaiah, as containing "a massive, comprehensive catalogue of the full Old Testament inventory of vocabulary for sin." Brueggemann writes that "general terms" in the first half of the verse give way to "two strong, active verbs"[1] (עזב and נאץ) indicating "that Israel is fully turned against Yahweh."[2] Acknowledging that "the last line in verse 4 is a difficult phrase," Brueggemann nonetheless concludes that "in its place it seems to make a climactic claim that Israel has become completely alien (other) to Yahweh."[3] Effectually, the people have turned away from God, an overall charge explicated in the accusation that the people/nation "have forsaken (עזב[4]) the Lord," have "despised (נאץ) the Holy One of Israel,[5] and thus, in the phrase נזרו אחור, are utterly

---

1. Brueggemann, *Isaiah 1–39*, 15.
2. Ibid., 16. Kaiser (*Isaiah 1–12*, 18) finds v. 4b perplexing and suggests "that a later editor did not find the charges raised in the first half of the verse precise enough and expanded them with material from the Deuteronomistic repertory." See also W. L. Holladay, "The Crux in Isaiah 1:4–6," *VT* 33 (1983): 235–37.
3. Brueggemann, *Isaiah 1–39*, 16. Oswalt (*The Book of Isaiah: Chapters 1–39*, 88–89) notes that while the meaning of the final phrase is disputed, it constitutes abandonment of God.
4. It is interesting to chart the use of this term in the Isaianic corpus: in 58:2 it is posited that the people are like a nation (בגוי) that "did not forsake (לא עזב) its God. If 1:4 charges that the people have forsaken God, 54:7 reveals that it is also possible for God to forsake (עזב) the people. In 42:16, in a passage in which God is described as both "like a mighty man, like a warrior" (v. 13), and "like a woman in labor" (v. 14), God promises "I will not forsake (לא עזב) them." But this is insufficiently convincing to stop Zion lamenting in 49:14, "Yahweh has forsaken me (עזב)." Isaiah 17:9, in the broader context of a passage concerned with turning from idolatry (v. 8) on "that day" when people "will look to their maker . . . the Holy One of Israel" (v. 7), envisions the strong cities of Israel's enemies being "forsaken" (עזב) and left like a "deserted" (עזובה) wasteland.
5. Isaiah 5:24 envisages a fiery end for those who have rejected the law of the Lord almighty and who "have despised (נאץ) the word of the Holy One of Israel."

estranged from God. As noted, this phrase is problematical,[6] but the combination of זור[7] and אחור creates the impression that the people have become alienated from God through having turned their back or turned away from God, perhaps including through idolatry.[8] On the basis of their analyses, both Brueggemann and Oswalt infer that human capacity for just action independent of God is impossible,[9] an absolutized stance I have questioned and comment on further in this conclusion.

Isaiah 59:13, in the course of an anguished confession of sin,[10] also deploys the imagery of turning away from God, although expressed in different terminology. In this passage, those confessing their many offenses, sins, and iniquities (v. 12) present their behavior as "turning away (סוג[11])from our God," an act that is explicated in terms of "rebellion

Isaiah 52:5, in the ambiguous context of God's people having been taken away "for nothing" (חנם), speaks of God's name being "despised" (נאץ). Isaiah 60:14, presumably addressed to the faithful remnant who turn back to God, but couched in terms which have the potential to fuel ideas of nationalistic supremacy, promises that "all who despise you (נאץ) shall bow down at your feet."

6. The Hebrew may be translated literally as "they are completely estranged backwards."

7. Ezekiel 14:5, speaking of how the people are estranged from God through following idols, is the only other occurrence in the Hebrew Bible where the term is found in this form.

8. Oswalt (*The Book of Isaiah: Chapters 1–39*, 88) takes this position on the strength of the link to Ezek 14:5. Interestingly, in a way that from one perspective might be construed as ameliorating the sinfulness of the people, he writes: "Typically, they tried to keep both God and the gods. . . . For the most part, they did not consciously abandon God, but their attempt to keep both amounted to abandonment and was, in the eyes of the prophets, rebellion" (p. 89). The sense of turning away from God implied in 1:4 may be connected rhetorically to the "turning aside" (סור) from doing evil called for in 1:16. The wider rhetorical pattern of 1:16–17, as argued in Chapter 1, suggests that—accepting the intrinsically just nature of God—turning toward justice can be construed as turning toward God.

9. Brueggemann (*Isaiah 1–39*, 16) writes of "the disastrous future Israel generates for itself by its Yahweh-mocking conduct" and of how "the poet prepares us to watch while this beloved creature of Yahweh engages in self-destruction." Oswalt (*Book of Isaiah: Chapters 1–39*, 88) asserts more directly, "Righteousness is found only in the Lord and in those related to him. . . . The otherness of this God is distinctively moral. Thus to act immorally is a particular affront to him, and to forsake him is to be doomed to act immorally."

10. Brueggemann (*Isaiah 40–66*, 199) observes that "it is difficult to imagine a more wholesale admission of failure!" Oswalt (*Book of Isaiah: Chapters 40–66*, 524) notes that "this is all reminiscent of ch. 1. . . . Is nothing different?"

11. In the only other two uses of this term in Isaiah, 42:17 concludes a passage that seeks to entice those to whom it is addressed to "sing a new song to the Lord"

and denial of the Lord" (59:13). Here again Oswalt takes the opportunity to argue that human origination of justice is impossible. In a comparable statement to the one quoted above with regard to 1:4, he proposes that 59:13 illustrates that "whenever people try to live a lie, especially a big one, that we can be fully human without dependence on God, a false impression of reality is given. And when life is rooted in falsehood, justice and righteousness rapidly become an impossibility."[12] However, while the community of 59:13 acknowledges its "denial" (כחש) of God, Job 31:28 refuses to make any such concession. By way of contrast to the people's abject incapacity in Isa 59 to be able to do anything to engender "justice" (משפט) and "righteousness" (צדקה)—the word pair is found in Isa 59:9 and 14—Job 31 implies that Job has been an exemplar of justice, hospitality, and trust in God, and that only if the contrary had been the case could it have been alleged that he had "denied (כחש) God above" (31:28). Job himself, however, insists that this is not so, and that he has, as it were, fulfilled all righteousness, but has still suffered, a matter he wants addressed by God. In this instance, the last in which Job speaks in the book, contra Oswalt, the justice of God is impugned, while the capacity for just action to originate in humanity is maintained.

The conclusion that turning one's back on God, if neither entirely nor ultimately justified, is understandable in a sequential reading,[13] especially

---

(42:10). It threatens that "those who trust in idols . . . will be turned back (סוג) in utter shame." Isaiah 50:5, in strong contrast to the communal voice of 59:13, depicts a model character who has had his ears opened by the Lord, has not been rebellious, and has "not turned (לא סוג) back (אחור)." The conflict in this passage ends with the assertion, "This is what you shall receive from my hand: You will lie down in torment" (50:12). See also Zeph 1:6, where in the context of condemning idolatry, "those who turn back (סוג) from following after Yahweh and neither seek the Lord nor enquire of God" are warned that they will be punished. The condemnation and punishment of vv. 12–13 are couched in very Isaianic terms; ironically, in the broader sweep, Isa 59 is addressed to people who have at some level been seeking God out and are eager to know the Lord's ways (58:2).

12. Oswalt, *Book of Isaiah: Chapters 40–66*, 523.

13. Westermann (*Isaiah 40–66*, 344) proposes that Isa 59 is a response to the complaint that the arm of the Lord is too short to save. Given that this is also the issue at stake in 50:2, it is possible to construe that some (or perhaps the descendants of some) who allowed themselves to be rhetorically persuaded of God's salvific intention at that time now depressingly find themselves asking the same question again. As early as 3:10, the righteous are promised that "it will be well with them, for they will enjoy the fruit of their deeds." But the issue of righteous folk dying before this happens, according to one point of view, gives rise to the promissory rhetoric of "resurrection" in 26:19. Eventually those who continue to follow God, in

in light of the failure of the glowing promises of chs. 40–55 to come to
pass as predicted,[14] and the lingering sense that occasionally the divine
may be disproportionately harsh in the execution of judgment.[15] In relation to the character of God, thus, while Watts may attempt to argue that
the Yahweh of Isaiah's vision is a complex though finally integrated
entity,[16] I tend more toward Miscall's conclusion that the disparate,
mutually exclusionary, contradictory dimensions of the divine character
oscillate between each other and finally "can't be sorted out"[17] satisfactorily. God is an experienced reality of opposite poles in whom "The
Compassioner, the Loving God, stands over against the Divine Monster,
the Ogre."[18] As a consequence,

> The new creation of universal peace and worship is always troubled and
> ruined by the perpetual presence of the corpses. . . . The ultimate horror is
> the realization that "the monsters can always come again," that God's

a continuation of the confessional tone of ch. 59, dispiritedly call out, "Do not be
angry beyond measure" (64:8 [ET v. 9]), and, "Will you keep silent and punish us
beyond measure?" (64:11 [ET v. 12]).

14. As Carroll ("Second Isaiah and the Failure of Prophecy," 130) observes,
"Second Isaiah's test for the gods was simply: 'Tell us what is to come hereafter,
that we may know that you are gods' (xli 23). A god who cannot foretell the future is
no god! So the followers of Second Isaiah were faced with the problematic of
prophecy—how to explain why Yahweh's revelation of the future had not been
confirmed by historical reality. Small wonder that the oracles in Is. lvi–lxvi contain
so much accusation and vilification against the community." Along the same lines,
but from a broadly evangelical perspective, Goldingay ("Isaiah 40–55 in the 1990s,"
225) contends: "Isaiah 40–55 shouts very loud, and we have laid down and sur-
rendered. Yet a work that shouts loud may be suspected of susceptibility to
deconstruction. Of course the exposure of this susceptibility need not be a hostile
act, but the act of someone who appreciates the text, who more than anyone wants to
understand, and who wants the object of appreciation to be understood." Goldingay
further argues that reading through "rose-tinted spectacles" and thereby "attempting
to hide from ambiguities and uncertainties but not succeeding in hiding them from
the eyes of those who appreciate them" is ill-advised and dishonorable. This tends
in the direction of interpreting the book of Isaiah as what David M. Gunn terms
"serious entertainment" (*The Story of King David: Genre and Interpretation*
[JSOTSup 6; Sheffield: JSOT Press, 1978], 61). For a discussion and defense of the
failure of the promises to materialize, see H. G. M. Williamson, *Variations on a
Theme: King, Messiah, and Servant in the Book of Isaiah* (Carlisle: Paternoster,
1998), 189–202.

15. Poignantly expressed in the phrase עד־מאד in 64:8 and 11 (ET vv. 9 and 12).

16. Watts, "The Characterization of Yahweh in the Vision of Isaiah," 448–49.

17. Miscall, "Isaiah: Dreams and Nightmares, Fantasy and Horror," 165.

18. Ibid., 166.

righteous anger again turns to cosmic rage. Isaiah's book and world are located somewhere in the play between these dreams and nightmares, between fantasy and horror.[19]

More generally, therefore, the type of instability discerned in the characterization of the divine can be found throughout the Isaianic text as a whole. As a result, in both form and content, it does not readily lend itself to assured, certain, dogmatic readings. Something of this allusive, polyvalent orientation in the prophetic writings is encapsulated in Hosea's recording of the divine voice saying, "I spoke by the prophets, gave them many visions (חָזוֹן[20])and by the hand of the prophets producing comparisons/parables/similitudes (אֲדַמֶּה[21])"(Hos 12:11 [ET v. 10]). Amplifying this theme of similitude or comparison specifically in terms of metaphor, Landy recognizes that metaphors both "order the world" and "also disarrange it." He explains:

> Such disarrangement happens when metaphors become complex, contradictory, nested one inside the other, when they disrupt sentences, fragment the wholeness we construct. The poetry of Isaiah is characteristically extremely difficult, violent, dissociative; passages of great poetic virtuosity alternate with others of radical simplicity. Critics have devoted themselves to solving the problems of the text by assigning different sections or verses to different hands, by unravelling it. This, however, avoids the problem, and domesticates the prophet to our expectations. Prophetic language, according to this view, cannot be impossibly difficult. The

---

19. Ibid.

20. This is the word with which the book of Isaiah opens. Most commentators hold that the superscription of which it is a part refers to the entire book. See Wildberger, *Isaiah 1–12*, 2–3; Sweeney, *Isaiah 1–39*, 72. See also Childs, *Isaiah*, 11–12; John Goldingay, "Isaiah i 1 and ii 1," *VT* 48 (1998): 326–32; and Edgar W. Conrad, *Reading Isaiah* (OBT; Minneapolis: Fortress, 1991), 118, who argue not altogether convincingly for a narrower field of reference. Use of the term רבב with it in Hos 12:11 (ET v. 10) creates the impression of a vision being multiplied, and thus perhaps definitive meaning being successively reduced. This sense of meaning becoming blurred is also implied in the movement of the speech of God (דבר) being translated into prophetic vision: with the shift from one mode of communication to another, the possibility of slippage in meaning increases. The possibility of further confusion arises when prophetic vision is translated into prophetic speech/writing (inferred from the "hand of the prophets" producing similitudes and comparisons [דמה]).

21. This term is found in Isa 40:18, 25, and twice in 46:5 in stressing the incomparability of God. Despite this emphasis, however, the Isaianic corpus abounds in comparisons of God to numerous things. The term is also found in 10:7 and 14:24 in the context of the intentionality and planning of God. The only other occurrence in Isaiah is 1:9, in which thankful survivors argue that without divine assistance they would have become like Sodom and Gomorrah.

impossibility of the language, however, may express the impossibility of
communicating the vision, the twin exigencies of desire to speak, to
persuade, to heal, and the prohibition against doing so, and hence the
mystery from which and of which the prophet speaks. The poetry is then
anti-poetry, a making of a poetic world that decomposes.[22]

While this may be strongly and provocatively expressed, particularly
the intimation that the text may have a built-in propensity to decom-
position, it does underline the fraught nature of too close an alignment
with or, effectively, advocacy for, a specific aspect of the rhetoric of the
book.[23] It also exposes the way dogmatically conforming the text to a
particular theologically determined agenda distorts its poetic elusiveness
through an imposed reductionism and, at worst, turns the interpreter into
a figure like one of Job's visitors.[24]

2. A Farewell to Arms?

The way the text resists a simplistic "insider" identification with its
rhetoric may be illustrated with reference to the way פגע (59:16)
functions in a passage that at one level invites the acceptance of God
depicted as a violent warrior.[25] The Lord is portrayed as surveying Israel

22. Francis Landy, "Vision and Voice in Isaiah," *JSOT* 88 (2000): 19–36 (30).
Carroll ("Blindsight and the Vision Thing," 93) terms Isaiah "the strangest of
biblical texts," which as also "the most visionary . . . calls for the most visionary of
readings." See also Miscall, "Isaiah: The Labyrinth of Images." On the subject of
order/disorder, see M. Bal, "Metaphors he Lives By," *Semeia* 61 (1993): 185–207.
23. Walter Brueggemann ("Planned People/Planned Book") tends in this
direction, positing a clear choice between (1) the ways of Babylon, "which function
paradigmatically for every 'plan' that seeks to oppose and resist the intention of
Yahweh," and (2) the poetically mediated promises of God articulated through the
rhetoric of Second Isaiah, which are available only when Israel has "fully embraced
the intention of Yahweh" (p. 34). This stark dichotomy does not pay sufficient
attention to the way coercive, violent aspects of the Isaianic rhetoric and all the
rhetoric conveys about the complex, perplexing, problematic nature of God makes it
possible to legitimate turning away from God. In fairness, Brueggemann does
recognize, though, that it is necessary to "guard against any 'plan' that vetoes or
disregards human activity" (p. 27).
24. This company includes Oswalt ("Righteousness in Isaiah"), who reads the
book in an exceedingly harsh theological way that takes a dim view of humanity and
endorses the book's most judgmental strain. This approach is certainly able to host
and accept violent imagery as part of its theological scheme, which is ultimately
more profoundly negative about humanity than the text itself as a whole, or the
wider biblical account.
25. See Blenkinsopp, *Isaiah 56–66*, 197–98.

and consequently being displeased that there is no justice (59:15b).[26] Yahweh sees that there is no one doing justice and is wonderingly disturbed that there is no one to intercede/intervene/interpose on God's behalf to do the work of justice (59:16a).[27] So the divine pursues a lone course of action marked by widespread vengeance, zeal, and retribution, all carried out in an energetic, vigorous fashion (59:16b–19). The immediate, conventional, and perhaps obvious reading infers that the content of the type of justice lacking in 59:15b is explained in the violent-warrior imagery of the following verses.[28] In this interpretation, it is possible to understand the looked-for intervention of v. 16a as the human equivalent of the divine rage as manifested in vv. 16b–19. Thus an authorization of violence may be sought as justified human participation in the righteous retribution of God: this is apparently the kind of intervention encouraged and endorsed by the rhetoric of the passage.[29]

However, read against the use of פגע in 53:6 and 53:12, a different construal of intervention emerges in which the human role is to challenge God. In the context of this overall passage, the Lord lays the iniquity of a group upon one who does not deserve to be injured on its account or for its errors, but who nonetheless intercedes with God on its behalf. On the basis of the resonance produced by this intertextual reference, intervention is constituted by intercession with God in order to turn away divine

26. Oswalt ("Righteousness in Isaiah," 190–91) makes clear that doing right is beyond human capacity and must therefore be seen as a gift of God. This being the case, and presumably God knowing it, Oswalt raises the question why God should be displeased. Logically there are no grounds for divine displeasure in Oswalt's theologically bleak and rhetorically insensitive scheme. As Derrida pointedly notes, "[T]o be just or unjust and to exercise justice, I must be free and responsible for my actions, my behaviour, my thoughts, my decisions" ("Force of Law," 961).

27. Alexander, *Commentary on Isaiah*, 2:370–71.

28. Though Goldingay observes that 59:15b "stands in an ambiguous relationship to the prayer that preceded. It has both encouraging and worrying features" (*Isaiah*, 334).

29. So 64:4 (ET v. 5) suggests that God "meets" (פגע) those who work righteousness and remember God's ways (of violence?). Isaiah 47:3, in an oracle against Babylon, speaks of vengeance (נקם; as in 59:17) and God intervening for (i.e. sparing; פגע) no person. Brueggemann (*Isaiah 40–66*, 200–202) essentially follows this line of interpretation, although he does concede with regard to the warrior imagery that "the poet engages in rhetorical overkill." He does not go so far as to suggest that those who align themselves with this conception of God should engage in violence for justice and righteousness on behalf of the divine, although this may be the logic of his exposition. Oswalt (*Book of Isaiah: Chapters 40–66*, 527–28) identifies with the God of the text by viewing the divine violence as the efficacious way "sin" will be eliminated; therefore, the violence is supported.

anger, even at the risk that such an intervention may result in the unmerited absorption of God's rage. This nuance undermines the impulse to view human action as necessarily a replication of divine, and instead offers humanity a moderating, intercessory role in the face of the divine: if there had been someone or some group to intervene with God in 59:16, perhaps the divine rage would have been curtailed.[30]

This sense of humanity opposing the potentially indiscriminate excess of divine anger is accentuated if the concept of intervening is allowed to be illuminated by the idea of "standing in the breach"[31] (עמד בפרץ), a phrase in Ps 106:23 and Ezek 22:30 that underscores the human capacity for defusing divine wrath: in the former case God's anger is turned away because of the role Moses plays; in the latter it is not because no one like Moses can be found (Ezek 22:31). Indeed, rather than participating in divine destruction or seeking to justify destruction theologically, the occurrence of פרץ with גדר in Isa 58:12[32] intimates that repairing and restoring community are the proper work for human hands. Playing in the background of this discussion, the figure of Abraham arguing with God to avert the destruction of paradigmatically sinful Sodom and Gomorrah (Isa 1:9, 10; 13:19; Sodom is mentioned in isolation in 3:9) makes the whole idea of human beings standing up to God even more radical: they not only have an intercessory or even substitutionary role,[33] but also an authentically argumentative one.

---

30. In this interpretation, because God finds no one to intercede, God's enemies and foes (59:18) may also be taken to include those who consider themselves "insiders" with God. Consequently, divine violence can be understood as being visited on "insider" and "outsider" alike. As Westermann notes, the prophet "includes himself in the confession, a sign that the harsh confrontation between prophet and nation of the earlier period no longer obtained" (*Isaiah 40–66*, 349).

31. Delitzsch (*Biblical Commentary on the Prophecies of Isaiah*, 2:376–77) makes this connection in his comment that there was "no-one who . . . formed a wall against the impending ruin and covered the breach with his body." For him, intervention is on the one hand restraining corruption and on the other interceding with God for the corrupt.

32. The word pair is also found in Ezek 22:30 and 13:5.

33. John F. A. Sawyer outlines how some of most disturbing aspects of the imagery of Isa 63 have perhaps been moderated by being Christologically transposed ("The Gospel according to Isaiah," *ExpTim* 113, no. 2 [2001]: 39–43 [41]). With regard to mediaeval passion iconography, Sawyer writes that "the red garments of the wine-treader in Isaiah 63 are also quoted as a prefiguration of the sufferings of Christ drenched with his own blood. Indeed in some grotesque interpretations of the passage, going back to the patristic period, Christ the True Vine is the victim, crushed in the wine-press so that his blood flows out, like the juice of grapes, into a chalice placed beneath. Occasionally . . . the wooden frame of the wine-press is

Rather than endorsing the right of God to go berserk or, even worse, seeking to sanction religious violence as supposedly congruent with divine intention (God would have done it anyway if warriors on earth had not been willing to undertake the crusade/ jihad),[34] this reading begins to subvert the entire concept of the legitimacy of divine rage, while at the same time implicitly urging that as humanity pursues justice it must also expose, resist, confront, and oppose the God of violence.[35] In this way there is the prospect of ending "divine violence," which may also be called "sovereign violence."[36] This further supports the view that the lack of help given in the savagery of Isa 63:1–6[37] is to humanity's credit: this is precisely the type of God that should be rejected. As Knierim insists, "Violence, any violence, represents or participates in the destruction of peace and peaceful process. This must also be said with regard to the tension in the Bible between the God of war and the God of peace."[38] The latter must prevail and humanity has a role in ensuring that it does.

Hunter's proposal that the Song of Songs be understood as a form of poetic protest elucidates the line of interpretation here applied to the

designed to suggest a cross so that the connection between Isaiah 63 and the death of Christ on the Cross is highlighted. In some early sixteenth-century representations of the crucifixion, Christ's bleeding feet are shown trampling on grapes, and the inscription above his head reads *torcular calcavi solus* 'I trod the winepress alone' from Isaiah 63:3."

34. E.g., see James Reston Jr., *Warriors of God: Richard the Lionheart and Saladin in the Third Crusade* (London: Faber & Faber, 2001).

35. Related to the work of Clines, this approach agrees that justice "is a human problem" but maintains that there are also legitimate theological issues to be addressed that do not represent collapsing "the social problem into a theological one" ("Quarter Days Gone," 258). With regard to the book of Job, René Girard argues for the rejection of the God of violence ("Job as Failed Scapegoat," in *The Voice from the Whirlwind: Interpreting the Book of Job* [ed. Leo G. Perdue and W. Clark Gilpin; Nashville: Abingdon, 1992], 185–207). Clines warns that "the Reformers, like most traditional commentators, were unable to jettison the speeches of the friends—as the narrative logic demands—because they found too much congenial and conventional 'wisdom' in them" (*Interested Parties*, 169).

36. Derrida ("Force of Law," 979), citing Walter Benjamin, *Selected Writings*. Vol. 1, *1913–26* (ed. M. Bullock; Cambridge, Mass.: Belknap, 1996), 236–52. Derrida, commenting on Benjamin, speaks of "the annihilating violence of destructive law (*Rechtsvernichtend*), which is termed 'divine' (implicit meaning: Jewish, it seems to me)" (p. 981).

37. Westermann (*Isaiah 40–66*, 350) makes this connection, specifically to 63:5a, but in an uncritical way.

38. Knierim, *The Task of Old Testament Theology*, 120.

book of Isaiah, especially the way Hunter contends that it "protests by implication."[39] After talking about "the incredible descriptive richness which can only be attained by poetry," he continues:

> But as much as poetry provides this powerful vehicle of expression it can serve as the ultimate medium of illusiveness, which in its turn, serves as the ideal path of protest. Through this path the protest can be made without being outright and yet be teasing enough to be noticed. Poetry can protest without being offensive or having a fear of retaliation. The Song of Songs uses poetry because its message was sensitive but important and its author was sensible enough to be aware of the value of this ideal means of communication. The reader could draw associations from a context wherein the message of protest could be heard from the otherwise allusive language of poetry.[40]

While there are thus plausible reasons for turning away from God, a train of thought within the Isaianic corpus also encourages what could be termed wrestling with a problematic God in the context of seeking justice.[41] This is a theme upon which several conclusions can be drawn in

39. Jannie Hunter, "The Song of Protest: Reassessing the Song of Songs," *JSOT* 90 (2000): 109–24 (111).

40. Ibid., 117. The importance of the God-as-warrior motif in the Hebrew Bible implies the necessity to question its validity obliquely (see the discussions by Gerhard von Rad, *Holy War in Ancient Israel* [Grand Rapids: Eerdmans, 1991]; P. D. Miller, *The Divine Warrior in Early Israel* [Cambridge: Cambridge University Press, 1973]; Susan Niditch, *War in the Hebrew Bible: A Study in the Ethics of Violence* [Oxford: Oxford University Press, 1993]; T. Longman, III, and D. G. Reid, *God is a Warrior* [Grand Rapids: Eerdmans, 1995]). In the turn to hosting less vengeance-based and more servant-oriented, kenotic models of life and theology, skepticism and irony on the part of the final redactor or composer with regard to God's power as a warrior undermines the stability of the older convictions (though on occasions the violence of God is so exaggerated and disturbing that one recalls the quip made on the occasion of Henry Kissinger winning the Nobel Peace Prize: "Who needs irony?"). This is perhaps especially so if at one level of its final form the book of Isaiah is taken to be the poetic/dramatic reflection of an elite (so Watts, *Isaiah 1–33*, and idem, *Isaiah 34–66*) who, as Norman Cohn writes, were "[s]haken by events that seemed to call in question the very existence of an ordered world" and left "wrestling with a sense of utter disorientation and frustration" (*Cosmos, Chaos, and the World to Come: The Ancient Roots of Apocalyptic Faith* [New Haven: Yale University Press, 1993], 162). Perhaps the curious comment in Isa 28:21 to the effect that war is "strange" and "alien work" for God should be considered a precursor to a later subversion.

41. If the latter chapters of Isaiah represent a "democratization" of earlier themes, then in this case the ways of the servant become the ways of the servant community. See W. A. M. Beuken, "Servant and Herald of Good Tidings," in *The Book of Isaiah/Le livre d'Isaïe: Les oracles et leurs relectures unité et complexité de*

light of the study conducted of Isa 58:6–10 and the role it plays in the book of Isaiah as a whole, though particularly in the closing chapters.

3. *Justice and the Role of Isaiah 58:6–10*

If true that the Isaianic corpus is marked in one of its dimensions by judgment and confrontation, a characteristic present even in the work's most appealing and invitational section,[42] then it is also true that this tendency to division and dispute deepens and intensifies in the closing chapters,[43] eventually resulting in outright sectarianism.[44] In this conflicted world, no matter how the various groupings are identified from

l'ouvrage (ed. Jacques Vermeylen; BETL 81; Louvain: Louvain University Press, 1989), 411–42; idem, "The Main Theme of Trito-Isaiah 'The Servants of Yahweh,'" *JSOT* 47 (1990): 67–87; and Williamson, *Variations on a Theme*, 167–202. Edgar Conrad identifies "the advice of the messengers" with "the word of the servant" ("Messengers in Isaiah and the Twelve: Implications for Reading Prophetic Books," *JSOT* 91 [2000]: 83–97 [88]).

42. For example, see further Watts, "Consolation or Confrontation?," 35–40.

43. Westermann identifies how invective once addressed to those outside the nation has been appropriated and "directed against a section" within (*Isaiah 40–66*, 352). Commenting on this, Brueggemann observes that "in religious communities (the church!) some of the most extreme negative rhetoric occurs in internal disputes in which the most violent language is reserved for fellow members of the community. The rhetoric of ruthlessness often operates toward those closest at hand" (*Isaiah 40–66*, 201). Speaking of 57:1–13, Brueggemann notes "the deep and defining division in the community of emerging Judaism" (p. 175); of 59:1–21, he writes, "[T]he poem reflects the conflictual situation of the community of early Judaism and the readiness of the poet to enter into severe disputation with others in the community" (p. 194).

44. On this, see Joseph Blenkinsopp, "Interpretation and the Tendency to Sectarianism: An Aspect of Second Temple History," in *Jewish and Christian Self-Definition: Aspects of Judaism in the Graeco-Roman Period* (ed. E. P. Sanders with A. I. Baumgarten and Alan Mendelson; Philadelphia: Fortress, 1981), 2:1–26; idem, "A Jewish Sect of the Persian Period," *CBQ* 52 (1990): 5–20; idem, *A History of Prophecy in Israel* (rev. ed.; Louisville, Ky: Westminster John Knox, 1996), 181–222; idem, "The Social Roles of Prophets in Early Achaemenid Judah," *JSOT* 93 (2001): 39–58. See also A. Rofé, "Isaiah 64:1–4: Judean Sects in the Persian Period as Viewed by Trito-Isaiah," in *Biblical and Related Studies Presented to Samuel Iwry* (ed. A. Kort and S. Morschauser; Winona Lake: Eisenbrauns, 1985), 205–17; Shemaryahu Talmon, "The Emergence of Jewish Sectarianism in the Early Second Temple Period," in *King, Cult, and Calendar in Ancient Israel* (Leiden: Brill; Jerusalem: Magnes, 1986), 165–201; Hanson, *The Dawn of Apocalyptic*; Schramm, *The Opponents of Third Isaiah*. On the subject more generally, see Jack T. Sanders, *Schismatics, Sectarians, Dissidents, Deviants* (London: SCM Press, 1993).

the text,[45] or categorized in socio-theological orientation,[46] Isa 58:6–10 offers the potential for the worst excesses of sectarianism to be ameliorated as people of different outlook are offered the possibility to engage not in abstract theological castigation but in the praxis of just, community-enhancing activity.

Moreover, the tendency in sectarianism to self-righteously accept (and perhaps even will) the destruction of others (e.g. 66:17) is moderated by the implication discerned in 58:9 that those involved in the quest for justice will themselves endure suffering. This factor thus considerably reduces the opportunity to stand apart and gloat over the hardship of others. The radicality of 58:6–10, centered in the practice of hospitality, which breaks down barriers between people, creating, at its best, a space for people of divergent backgrounds and experiences to encounter one another,[47] thus stands in tension with the taunting tone of 65:13a: "My servants will eat, but you will go hungry; my servants will drink, but you will go thirsty."[48]

In this opposition between sectarianism and solidarity, the latter category, conceived in terms of Isa 58:6–10, is sufficiently broad to include those who harbor reservations about the character of the divine[49] but who are nevertheless committed to issues of justice.[50] Consequently

45. For example, "the servants of Yahweh" (65:8, 9, 13 [three times], 14, 15; 66:14); "those who tremble" (66:5).

46. For a survey of proposals in the history of interpretation, see Blenkinsopp, "A Jewish Sect of the Persian Period," 7 n. 6.

47. T. R. Hobbs warns about placing "matters of hospitality within modern ethical concerns for justice" ("Hospitality in the First Testament and the 'Teleological Fallacy,'" *JSOT* 95 [2001]: 3–30 [7]). Hobbs concludes that hospitality "had little to do with 'being kind to strangers' in the sense of philanthropy" (p. 29). Whatever the general truth of this assessment, Isa 58:6–10 does indeed make the connection between justice and hospitality and in its protokenotic inference has a depth of meaning beyond mere philanthropy.

48. Against this type of orientation and in support of the ethic of Isa 58, Waldemar Janzen argues that "hospitality is that dimension of the familial paradigm which ensures that pursuit of family shalom does not degenerate into in-group selfishness" (*Old Testament Ethics: A Paradigmatic Approach* [Louisville, Ky: Westminster John Knox, 1994], 44).

49. In the modern world, for one possible route to taking leave of God, see represented on this theme Don Cupitt, *Taking Leave of God* (London: SCM Press, 1980). For comment on Cupitt's work, see Scott Cowdell, *Atheist Priest? Don Cupitt and Christianity* (London: SCM Press, 1988); see also Stephen Ross White, *Don Cupitt and the Future of Christian Doctrine* (London: SCM Press, 1994).

50. In terms of the question posed by Cruchley-Jones, "Can '*not my people*' be in mission?" (*Singing the Lord's Song in a Strange Land?*, 187–208), and following

the primacy of justice is affirmed in the sense that it is possible to practice justice without necessarily in all regards embracing or acceding to
the God encoded in the book of Isaiah.

Thus despite biblical assertions of the order that God is "a father to the
fatherless and widow" (Ps 146:9), there are times when grounds emerge
to doubt the veracity of such claims: "They slay the widow . . . they
murder the fatherless" (Ps 94:6; see also Ps 82:3, 4, and perhaps most
poignantly the utter devastation of women and children depicted in the
book of Lamentations).[51] On such occasions, when some call out to God
to fulfill the role of avenger (Ps 94:1–6), Isa 58:6–10 encourages humanity in its calling to set free . . . break every yoke . . . share food . . . provide
shelter . . . clothe the naked and not turn away from fellow human beings,
thereby resisting the impulse expressed in Ps 109:9, 10.

The psalmist contends that "the heavens are Yahweh's, but the earth
God has given to human beings" (Ps 115:16), a sphere of activity in
which humanity is responsible for instituting and pursuing justice. As
van Wolde, commenting on Job 40–41, argues, "Justice has not been
woven as a pattern into the garment of the world, nor is God burdened
with its administration. It is an ideal that must be realized by human
beings within their society, through them and for them, and it cannot be
put to God's account."[52]

Part of the function of humanity is also, however, to contend with the
divine in order to attempt to ensure that vengeance is not excessive and
therefore unjust. Consequently, Isa 58:6–10 does not conform to the
predominant Isaianic view that quietism, reflecting an absolute trust in
the eventual intervention of God (a posture that ultimately eventuates in
an apocalyptic worldview), is the only or necessarily best stance to adopt
in the face of a disordered world.[53] The passage instead advocates

discussion, there is a role in the search for justice for those who perceive themselves
to have been rejected by God and indeed for those who have rejected God. Michael
Taylor, talking about important aspects of seeking justice in the world, observes that
"They are not peculiarly Christian and they are all the better for that, but they are
compatible and coherent with the Bible and Christian tradition" (*Poverty and
Christianity*, 118). Later, he affirms the notion of "consensus building between
various interested parties committed to the same cause" (p. 123), which is that of
justice.

51. See especially on this theme of Lamentations and the loss of children,
Linafelt, *Surviving Lamentations*, 35–61.

52. Van Wolde, *Mr and Mrs Job*, 129. Or as Barbara Kingsolver has a character
assert, "Don't expect God's protection in places beyond God's dominion" (*The
Poisonwood Bible*, 309).

53. Barton, "Ethics in the Book of Isaiah."

human-based action for a standard of justice that disavows acts of vengeance: whatever understanding of vengeance may be attributed to, desired from, or appropriate for the divine, the role of humanity is the search for justice through community.

There are also several other ways in which my interpretation of Isa 58:6–10 stands at variance with more prominent and recurring perspectives within the book of Isaiah. Against the view, which in part derives from royalist theology,[54] that Zion will be the prime location for encountering God and learning the ways of God (e.g. Isa 2:1–5; 33:20–24; 65:17–25),[55] Isa 58:6–10 offers a less centered vision in which God will be encountered anywhere[56] in the course of the struggle for justice.[57] In a related way, 58:6–10 does not participate in the new-exodus type of nationalistic ideology[58] that eventuates in dreams of a resurgent Israel becoming rich at the expense of the nations and being served by them (60:5–14; 61:5, 6).[59] Isaiah 58:6–10 is not invested in what might be

54. Pleins talks about "the royalist character of the Isaianic project" (*Social Visions of the Hebrew Bible*, 237). Further discussing the final form of the text, he discerns a "persistent royal hope" (p. 263) in its overall shaping.

55. See Jon D, Levenson, "The Jerusalem Temple in Devotional and Visionary Experience," in *Jewish Spirituality* (ed. Arthur Green; 2 vols.; London: SCM Press, 1985), 1:32–61. Levenson also makes the case that "the Temple was conceived as a microcosm, a miniature world" (*Creation and the Persistence of Evil: The Jewish Drama of Divine Omnipotence* [Princeton: Princeton University Press, 1988], 78–99 [86]), the destruction of which opened the possibility of encountering God elsewhere in the brokenness of a post-Temple world, when that ideal model had been shattered. See M. Lodahl, *Shekhinah Spirit: Divine Presence in Jewish and Christian Religion* (New York: Paulist, 1992); Webb, "Zion in Transformation"; Landy, "Strategies of Concentration and Diffusion." Pleins notes that "ultimately, Zion is to be the center where YHWH rules as king and prince" (*Social Visions of the Hebrew Bible*, 252).

56. Perhaps saying "Here am I" (Isa 58:9) even to those not directly seeking the divine, as indicated by 60:1. The theme of the presence, absence, and hiddenness of God would require a full-scale study in its own right; as a point of departure, see further Terrien, *The Elusive Presence*.

57. From a priestly point of view a similar decentering of Jerusalem may be construed from Mal 1:11.

58. Pleins observes that "books such as Isaiah and Ezekiel would appear to bring forth social visions rooted in intense nationalistic fervor" (*Social Visions of the Hebrew Bible*, 218). Reiterating this point, he argues that "the program of Isaiah is a decidedly nationalist political program" (p. 263). He also notes how "the exiled elite has forever transformed the ancient prophetic texts, turning them into a manifesto for their own nationalist agenda, now stamped with a divine imprimatur" (p. 267).

59. For biting comments on comparable ideological rhetoric in the book of Haggai, see Clines (*Interested Parties*, 46–75), where he talks in terms of a sector of the Jewish people promoting the idea of "a world dictator" who is going to

termed the "golden age" rhetorical claims of other Isaianic passages that have an overt messianic/ eschatological[60] orientation (e.g. 7:13–17; 9:2–7; 11:1–9),[61] that belie their coercive, even violent dimensions.[62]

---

inaugurate a new era (p. 72). Clines continues, however, that "even if the wealth of all the nations is going to come pouring into Jerusalem, no one expects it to end up in the pocket of Joe Citizen; turning the local shrine into Fort Knox is not everyone's idea of eschatological bliss." Clines (p. 74) is deeply critical of Hans Walter Wolff, who maintains that "what is being expressed here is not greed on Israel's part, or some sort of Jewish egoism" (*Haggai: A Commentary* [Minneapolis: Augsburg, 1988], 82). Clines also criticizes von Rad, who contends that "there is no question here of greed for gain" (Gerhard von Rad, *The Problem of the Hexateuch and Other Essays* [Edinburgh: Oliver & Boyd, 1966], 240).

60. On this subject, see further the collection of essays edited by Reventlow, *Eschatology in the Bible and in Jewish and Christian Tradition.*

61. On the influence of passages such as these (particularly Isa 11) in the broader construction of the book of Isaiah, see Marvin A. Sweeney, "The Reconceptualization of the Davidic Covenant in Isaiah," in *Studies in the Book of Isaiah: Festschrift Willem A. M. Beuken* (ed. J. Van Ruiten and M. Vervenne; BETL 132; Louvain: Louvain University Press, 1997), 41–61.

62. Related to this general discussion, the rhetoric of Isa 2:1–5, concluding with the exhortation "Come, O house of Jacob, let us walk in the light of the Lord" (v. 5), implies Israel following in what the nations have already started, a reading supported by Marvin A. Sweeney ("Micah's Debate with Isaiah," *JSOT* 93 [2001]: 111–24 [115]). This potentially positive evaluation of the nations is enhanced by interpreting the assertion in the related passage—"All the nations may walk in the name of their gods" (Mic 4:5a)—as generously hosting plurality and diversity without superiority or condemnation. This is the reading of Abraham Heschel, "No Religion is an Island," in *No Religion is an Island: Abraham Joshua Heschel and Interreligious Dialogue* (ed. Harold Kasimow and Byron L. Sherwin; Maryknoll, N.Y.: Orbis Books, 1991), 3–22 (19); and Schwartz, *The Curse of Cain*, 38. Miroslav Volf by contrast views the verse much more exclusively (*Exclusion and Embrace*, 198). As Sweeney ("Micah's Debate with Isaiah," 116) observes, "[T]he nations and Israel will enjoy an era of world peace under YHWH's worldwide sovereignty, but they will do so by going their separate ways religiously." But taken as a whole, Sweeney recognizes that Micah envisages Israel as "an independent state, ruled by a Davidic monarch, that will bring YHWH's punishment to the nations and stand at their centre" (p. 122). Similarly, Itumeleng J. Mosala regards the final hand shaping the book of Micah as producing "imperialist theology . . . more suited to the interests of a formerly powerful class whose pride has been hurt by exile than to a previously oppressed class whose real interests lie in the building of democratic structures to guarantee its protection and liberation" (*Biblical Hermeneutics and Black Theology in South Africa* [Grand Rapids: Eerdmans, 1989], 134). Finally, therefore, neither Micah nor Isaiah sustains a consistently positive view of the nations. J. Severino Croatto sees references to the nations as speaking exclusively about members of the diasporas within the nations ("The 'Nations' in the Salvific Oracles of Isaiah" [paper presented at the annual meeting of the SBL, San Francisco, 1997]. Writing of the

Instead this passage operates with a much more modest agenda, which is nonetheless of importance for how it contributes to articulating distinctive aspects of social justice within the Isaianic corpus. Rather than looking toward an idealized, utopian future (note how etymologically "utopia" literally means "nowhere"),[63] the rhetorical force of 58:6–10 is accented in such a way as to point to its contingent arrival in the midst of present social realities wherever action for justice is instigated (58:6) and radical hospitality practiced (58:7).[64] Thus the possibility of realized eschatology is accepted more than in other eschatologically oriented Isaianic texts, and it should be stressed that in this realization there is a role for those who have experienced the absence or injustice of God.[65] To the extent that 58:6–10 addresses issues such as hunger, thirst, and the provision of shelter, which humanity has the capacity if not the will to resolve, it is therefore talking about *realizable* eschatology.

In addition, Isa 58:6–10 helps begin a deconstructive redefinition of the much vaunted idea of universalism[66] in the book of Isaiah. The move

relationship between the colonial center and its margins in language reminiscent of Isa 2:1–5, Chinua Achebe cites Ama Ata Aidoo (*Our Sister Killjoy* [Reading, Mass.: Addison Wesley, 1997]) describing how "oppressed multitudes from the provinces rush to the imperial seat because that is where they know all salvation comes from" (*Home and Exile*, 94).

63. Classically, see Thomas More, *Utopia* (London: Penguin, 1965).

64. The orientation of this reading is akin to Dietrich Bonhoeffer, who in the course of explicating his idea of a religionless Christianity for a world come of age (popularized in John A. T. Robinson, *Honest to God* [London: SCM Press, 1963], esp. 29–44) speaks of how "before God and with God we live without God," in giving of ourselves in the interest of our neighbor (*Letters and Papers from Prison* [London: SCM Press, 1971], 360). Furthermore, in terms of Jürgen Moltmann (*Theology of Hope* [London: SCM Press, 1967], 70), who takes issue with the *futurum aeternum* concept, it affirms a role for humanity in "the realization of the eschatological *hope of justice*" (p. 329 [emphasis in original]).

65. The burden of this study is thus not with the necrology of the "God is dead" school of secular thought, but with where God is to be found in the world and by whom. See also Jacques Ellul, *Hope in Time of Abandonment* (New York: Seabury, 1972).

66. Bringing together the concepts of universality and justice, Achebe, in discussing the movement from colonialism to postcolonialism, suggests that now, "after a short period of dormancy and a little self-doubt about its erstwhile imperial mission, the West may be ready to resume its old domineering monologue in the world" (*Home and Exile*, 83). Further, faced with the world as it is, Achebe argues: "To suggest that the universal civilization is in place already is to be willfully blind to our present reality and, even worse, to trivialize the goal and hinder the materialization of a genuine universality in the future" (p. 91). Ultimately, for him, "enchanted

is away from the horizon of grand visionary schemes awaiting final consummation and toward a recognition of the *potentiality* for justice to be
sought by anyone, anywhere,[67] irrespective or indeed transgressive of
national boundaries,[68] through the enactment of measures congruent with
the type of activity indicated by the text.[69]

territories of universal wisdom" (p. 96) turn out to be one set of culturally conditioned values that masquerade as objectively universal, coercively seeking to impose
themselves on other cultures. Therefore he rejects this approach, arguing that "diversity is the engine of the evolution of living things, including living civilizations"
(p. 97). Related to this discussion, see David J. Krieger, who persuasively explains
the latent imperialistic dimension in the Western world by noting that "*both* Christian and Secular Humanist thought share the same basic structure, which may be
called *apologetic universalism*" (*The New Universalism: Foundations for a Global
Theology* [Maryknoll, N.Y.: Orbis, 1991], 4 [emphasis in original]). See also Lucien
Legrand, *Unity and Plurality: Mission in the Bible* (trans. Robert R. Barr; Maryknoll, N.Y.: Orbis, 1990). On how the Bible has been used to underwrite the colonial
agenda, see Michael Prior, *The Bible and Colonialism: A Moral Critique* (The
Biblical Seminar 48; Sheffield: Sheffield Academic Press, 1997).

    67. In a phrase relevant to this discussion, David Stern suggests that God
becomes "hopelessly entrapped in the pathos of human existence" once the divine
presence departs from the temple ("*Imitatio Hominis*: Anthropomorphism and the
Character(s) of God in Rabbinic Literature," *Prooftexts* 12 [1992]: 151–74 [159]).

    68. Pleins, along these lines, argues that "compassion to war refugees [even of
former enemies] is the concrete form of Israel's role in the international arena. . . . In
viewing both Isaiah and Genesis in their final form as works addressing the
postexilic situation, it is clear that there were thinkers, both prophetic and otherwise,
who saw Israel's survival to be intimately connected to a successful outbreak of
regional peace. . . . The ravages of war were to give way to intercommunal relief,
support, and rebuilding. This is a profound, if precarious vision" (*Social Visions of
the Hebrew Bible*, 233). Within this vision, Isa 58:6–10 plays its part. James
Muilenburg proposes that "even the enemy must be treated as a neighbor" (*The Way
of Israel: Biblical Faith and Ethics* [New York: Harper & Row, 1961], 70). Related
to this, in the contemporary context, the *Guardian Weekly* (14–20 February 2002)
reports how Israeli army reservists refusing to serve in occupied Palestinian territory
would not participate in actions intended "to rule, expel, destroy, blockade,
assassinate, starve and humiliate an entire people." In their way, these soldiers resist
the type of rhetoric, a strain of which exists in the book of Isaiah, that encourages the
subjugation and subordination of one people by and to another.

    69. This reading is consistent with a line of interpretation that eventuates in Matt
25:31–46, in which justice to the Jesus who comes in the guise of the stranger is
determinative of salvation. Similarly, Michael Prior argues that the "triumphalistic
and nationalistic" tone of Isa 61 is subverted by conflation with 58:6 (*Jesus the
Liberator: Nazareth Liberation Theology (Luke 4.16–30)* [The Biblical Seminar 26;
Sheffield: Sheffield Academic Press, 1995], 135). This results in the conclusion "that
God was not a chauvinistic nationalist—he could not be boxed in and domesticated"

4. Isaiah 58:6–10 and Derrida's Concept of Justice

Derrida offers a framework by which this construal may better be understood. He eschews and professes to keep a considerable distance from the idea of all horizons, "from the Kantian regulative idea or from the messianic advent." While such horizons, in "their conventional interpretation," are "both the opening and the limit that defines an infinite progress or a period of waiting[,] . . . justice, however unpresentable it may be, doesn't wait"[70] but demands an immediate response (p. 967).[71] Although for Derrida "a performative" act made to such a demand "cannot be just, in the sense of justice, except by founding itself on conventions and so on other anterior performatives . . . it *may* have an *avenir*, a 'to come' which," as he contends, "I rigorously distinguish from the future that can always reproduce the present" (p. 969).

In this way, the possibility of the conception and practice of justice is retained:

> Justice remains, is yet, to come, *à venir*, it has an, it is *à venir*, the very dimension of events irreducibly to come. It will always have it, this *à venir*, and always has. Perhaps it is for this reason that justice, insofar as it is not only a juridical or political concept, opens up for *l'avenir* the transformation, the recasting or refounding of law and politics. "Perhaps," one must always say perhaps for justice. There is an *avenir* for justice and there is no justice except to the degree that some event is possible which,

(p. 136). As Prior argues, "The core of Jesus' message is that the good news of Isaiah 61 . . . is transposed into good news for all who are oppressed" (p. 141). Reinforcing this assessment, Prior insists that "the liberation Jesus inaugurated in Nazareth was not a national liberation. It was a liberation for all" (p. 201). In this, as I propose, Jesus stands in line with the scope and implications of Isa 58:6–10. From a Palestinian perspective, Naim Ateek is particularly attuned to the way "the Bible is a record of dynamic, sometimes severe, tension, between nationalist and universalist conceptions of the deity" (*Justice, and Only Justice*, 92). He correctly observes that although Second Isaiah contains elements of the "universal and inclusive nature of God" (p. 96), it also includes a decidedly nationalistic dimension. For a good introduction to Palestinian theology, see Lance D. Laird, "Meeting Jesus Again in the First Place: Palestinian Christians and the Bible," *Int* 55, no. 4 (2001): 400–12.

70. Derrida, "Force of Law," 967. Subsequent bracketed references in the main text are to this source.

71. Derrida asserts that "the instant of decision is a madness, says Kierkegaard. This is particularly true of the instant of the just decision that must rend time and defy dialectics." Related to Isa 58:6–10, the decision to act for justice is indeed invested with madness in the way that it will lead to "crying for help" (58:9). This idea is underscored by Derrida's assertion that "there is no *justesse*, no justice, no responsibility except in exposing oneself to all risks, beyond certitude and good conscience" (p. 1025).

as event, exceeds calculation, rules, programs, anticipations and so forth. Justice as the experience of absolute alterity is unpresentable, but it is the chance of the event and the condition of history. No doubt an unrecognizable history, of course, for those who believe they know what they're talking about when they use this word, whether its a matter of social, ideological, political, juridical or some other history. (pp. 969–71; 970 is the French text)

Finally, for Derrida, "justice exceeds law and calculation" (p. 971) and while "the universalization of *droit* [law] is its very possibility," in the relationship between justice and law, justice insists on "the irreducible singularity of each situation" (p. 1023).

Working at the interface of this tension between the universal and the singular as it grows from the difference between law and justice, he has what he terms the "audacious thought" of the necessity for "a sort of justice without *droit*" (p. 1023).[72] Ultimately this is rooted in Derrida's explication of the idea that justice is undeconstructible. He argues that "justice in itself, if such a thing exists, outside or beyond law, is not deconstructible. No more than deconstruction itself, if such a thing exists. Deconstruction is justice" (p. 945).[73] As Caputo comments, "Deconstruction is possible only insofar as justice is undeconstructible, for justice is what deconstruction aims at, what it is about, what it *is*."[74] Further illuminating the implications of the nature of Derrida's concept of justice, Caputo underlines how it focuses sharply on "the call of singularity, i.e., justice, and allows us to see that justice is a matter of singularity not universality, of *kardia* not law-keeping" (pp. 194–95). According to this interpretation, in which "the time of justice and the time of singularity are the same" (pp. 202–3), Caputo observes that "the universal is insistently haunted by the ghost of its other" and thus "never quite fits, can never quite be fitted into the concrete" (p. 203), which is afforded primacy. Consequently, "[T]he projection of justice has to do with action, not making. It is a projection upon the possible, not the remodeling of the world according to a model" (p. 207).

72. In a related fashion, as Bob Dylan puts it in the song "Absolutely Sweet Marie," "But to live outside the law, you must be honest" (*Writings and Drawings* [London: Jonathan Cape, 1973], 217).

73. Laying out the steps of his thinking, Derrida notes, "1. The deconstructibility of law (*droit*), of legality, legitimacy or legitimation (for example) makes deconstruction possible. 2. The undeconstructibility of justice also makes deconstruction possible, indeed is inseparable from it. 3. The result: deconstruction takes place in the interval that separates the undeconstructibility of justice from the deconstructibility of *droit* (authority, legitimacy, and so on)."

74. Caputo, *Demythologizing Heidegger*, 193. Subsequent bracketed references in the main text are to this source.

5. *Liminality as a Function of Text*

Although sympathetic to liberationist themes, strictly speaking this book should not be considered as an example of liberation theology because it has not followed the liberationist methodology of affording experience (or praxis) primary status in interpretation and theology.[75] Instead it has focused primarily on the text itself, following the lead of Steiner who has argued that for a certain type of Jew "the text is home."[76] In a way that may be related to the nationalistic dimension in the book of Isaiah, which dreams of a return to the glory days of the temple and the subjugation of the nations to emergent Judaism's interests, Steiner suggests that "the Davidic and Solomonic Temple may have been an erratum, a misreading of the transcendent mobility of the text."[77] He continues:

> [T]he dialectical relations between an unhoused at-homeness in the text, between the dwelling-place of the script on the one hand (wherever in the world a Jew reads and meditates Torah *is* the true Israel), and the territorial mystery of the native ground, the promised strip of land on the other, divides Jewish consciousness. (p. 5 [emphasis in original])

Steiner further argues that "reading, textual exegesis, are an exile from action, from the existential innocence of *praxis*, even where the text is aiming at practical and political consequence. The reader is one who (day and night) is absent from action" (p. 5).

Aware of how exclusive preoccupation with the text—a virtual inhabitation of the text at the expense of all else—may be open to criticism on

---

75. See Gutiérrez, *A Theology of Liberation*, 6–11. More pithily, Carlos Mesters contends that "the common people are putting the Bible in its proper place, the place where God intended it to be. They are putting it in second place. Life takes first place!" ("Use of the Bible in Christian Communities of the Common People," in Gottwald and Horsley, eds., *The Bible and Liberation*, 3–16 [15]). For a helpful explanation of "the Three Levels of Liberation Theology," see Leonardo Boff and Clodovis Boff, *Introducing Liberation Theology* (Wellwood: Burns & Oates, 1987), 13. Recently, however, Protestant liberation theologians have been arguing for a more central role for the biblical text in the struggle for justice. On this, see Sherron Kay George, who asserts that "Protestant contextual theologians place greater emphasis on the primacy and normative role of the biblical text. While they seek liberation, they have concerns with *how* it is achieved, and consequently use the Bible to scrutinize both the tools of structural analysis and the methods of political liberation" ("From Liberation to Evangelization: New Latin American Hermeneutical Keys," *Int* 55, no. 4 [2001]: 367–77 [371]).

76. Steiner, "Our Homeland, the Text," 7.

77. Ibid., 5. Steiner contends that "the dwelling assigned, ascribed to Israel is the House of the Book," not the land. Subsequent bracketed references in the main text are to this source.

a number of accounts (p. 5),[78] Steiner asserts that, for some, dedication to the text is "the open secret of the Jewish genius and of its survival" (p. 7), poignantly observing that even so "that survival came within a breath of annihilation."[79] Consequently, "[W]hether they are seen as positive or negative, the 'textual' fabric, the interpretative practices of Judaism are ontologically and historically at the heart of Jewish identity" (p. 7).

Steiner, however, moves from a position of what might be termed textual absolutism when he acknowledges that "the incessant readings of the primary texts, the exegetic, disputatious, elaborative readings of these readings (the process is formally and pragmatically endless) . . . seek to elicit present application; they aim at the futurities always latent in the original act of revelation" (p. 7). He thereby indicates that the act of reading contains the seed of potential growth out from the text to engagement with the world, with the whole process rooted in what has been gained through initial struggle with the text. Moreover, consonant with my conviction in this book, grounded in findings related to Isa 58:6–10 in particular, Steiner is keenly aware that "nationalism is a sort of madness, a virulent infection edging the species towards mutual massacre" (p. 21). Significantly, he perceives that "between the claims of nationhood and universality," too close an integration with the former category, especially in its extreme nationalistic manifestations, precludes a "disinterested pursuit of justice" (p. 21). He continues, "Locked materially in a material homeland, the text may, in fact, lose its life-force, and its truth values may be betrayed" (p. 24). Steiner draws the conclusion:

> [H]uman beings must learn to be each other's guests on this small planet, even as they must learn to be guests of being itself and of the natural world. This is a truth humbly immediate, to our breath, to our skin, to the passing shadow we cast on a ground inconceivably more ancient than our visitation, and it is also a terribly abstract, morally and psychologically exigent truth. Man will have to learn it or he will be made extinct in suicidal waste and violence. (p. 24)

78. Steiner writes, "The 'textuality' of the Jewish condition, from the destruction of the Temple to the foundation of the state of Israel, can be seen, has been seen by Zionism, as one of tragic impotence." Further, Steiner outlines how Hegel viewed Jews as trapped in "an awesome pathology, a tragic, arrested stage in the advance of human consciousness" (p. 7) on account of their dedication to "Their Book," adherence to which Hegel regarded as a "desperate endeavour to keep the world at bay and to remain in God's neighbourhood" (p. 6).

79. Ibid., 5, where it is also noted that "the text was the instrument of exilic survival."

In its eschewal of the type of nationalism that feeds on the hope of the oppressed in their turn becoming akin to the oppressors, plus its call to self-giving solidarity and the practice of radical hospitality in the search for social justice, Isa 58:6–10 may, in its way, be construed as according with the direction of Steiner's thought.[80] Developing this idea of the text stimulating readers to a certain course of action and borrowing a term from social anthropology,[81] we can say that the text functions in a liminal way, encouraging readers to cross the threshold between text and world in a praxis marked by a new depth and creativity.[82] In this instance, Isa 58:6–10 lends itself to a liberationist orientation, but avoids the risk of "the existential innocence of *praxis*"[83] by implying that involvement in the search and struggle for justice will lead to crying out in pain. This warning is thus built into the process of continuing to reflect on praxis once the initial movement from text to activity encouraged and shaped by the text has been undertaken.[84]

80. The chief rabbi of the United Hebrew Congregations of the Commonwealth, Jonathan Sacks, in a New Year's message delivered in the wake of the events of 11 September 2001, broadcast on BBC and posted on the "Website of the Chief Rabbi," astutely observes: "I used to think that the greatest command in the Bible was 'You shall love your neighbour as yourself.' I was wrong. Only in one place does the Bible ask us to love our neighbour. In more than thirty places it commands us to love the stranger. . . . It isn't hard to love our neighbours because by and large our neighbours are people like us. What's tough is to love the stranger. . . . That's the real challenge. . . . Loving your neighbour is easy; loving the stranger is hard. But it's strangers who enlarge our world, who give us something we couldn't make on our own, who create the rich counterpoint of society with all its complex harmonies and chords. And that is something to welcome, not fear. At the end of his life Moses said: See I have set before you life and death, blessing and curse. Therefore choose life. Since last Tuesday, those words have become suddenly terrifying and fateful. In the coming year may God give us strength to choose life."

81. See Victor Turner, *The Ritual Process: Structure and Anti-structure* (Ithaca, N.Y.: Cornell University Press, 1969); idem, *The Anthropology of Performance* (New York: PAJ Publications, 1986). See also Bobby Alexander, *Victor Turner Revisited: Ritual as Social Change* (Atlanta: Scholars Press, 1991).

82. Magonet, affirming Proust's idea of works of art as "*thresholds*" (emphasis in original), argues that "those works of art which are most meaningful to us . . . are those which take us a certain way then leave us, having shown us a road" (*A Rabbi's Bible*, 35).

83. Steiner, "Our Homeland, the Text," 5.

84. This focus on the text is congruent with the shift within liberation theology itself to place greater emphasis on the Bible. As Boff observes, "The Roman Catholic Church has much to learn from the Protestant churches where love of the word of God is concerned" (*New Evangelization*, 47). Patrick and Scult trace the idea of the text as a spur to praxis back to "Aristotle's *exemplum*, which along with

In a related way, Carr proposes that "'synergy' is an image which can convey the dynamism and power of liberative encounter with Scripture."[85] Rejecting "a term like *application*," with its suggestion "that first you discover a truth in Scripture which only later you 'apply,'" he argues that "as opposed to one source of energy working alone, *synergy* is the interaction of different sources of energy to produce a force greater than mere addition would produce."[86] A text like 58:6–10 therefore has the potential to generate different energies for justice, and thus, while the text is important as a generative point, "the issue is not primarily focus on the Bible in itself but the Bible's potential as a life-giving resource for liberation."[87]

Ultimately, following Tracy, the world of the text directs us toward an extratextual reality.[88] Gunn and Fewell contend that the Hebrew Bible "shows us not merely patriarchy, élitism, and nationalism" but also "the fragility of these ideologies through irony and counter-voices," as a consequence of which, in texts of this provenance, the Bible

> may be uncovering a world in need of redemption and healing and a world-view much in need of change. This is the kind of reading that can transform us. If we realize that the world of the Bible is a broken world, that its people are human and therefore limited, that its social system is flawed, then we might start to see more clearly our own broken world, our own human limitations, and our own defective social systems. And who knows? Maybe we shall find ourselves called to be the agents of change.[89]

A text such as Isa 58:6–10, in a world which has the resources to address and rectify many of its most obvious and pressing scandals,[90] but lacks the political will to do so, may make its contribution, in circles where it is read, in helping to fill out the content and cost of becoming an agent of

the *enthymeme* can be seen as a central method of using language to move people to action" (*Rhetoric and Biblical Interpretation*, 47).

85. David Carr, "Synergy toward Life: A Paradigm for Liberative Christian Work with the Bible," *Quarterly Review* 10, no. 4 (1990): 40–55 (43).

86. Ibid. (emphasis in original).

87. Ibid.

88. David Tracy, "Metaphor and Religion: The Test Case of Christian Texts," in *On Metaphor* (ed. Sheldon Sacks; Chicago: University of Chicago Press, 1978), 89–104 (97–99).

89. David M. Gunn and Danna N. Fewell, *Narrative in the Hebrew Bible* (London: Oxford University Press, 1993), 204–5.

90. It is estimated that 33,000 children a day die of hunger and related causes in a world that has the capacity to feed itself many times over. More generally, see Neal, *The Just Demands of the Poor*.

change. Of course, such transformative action may be embarked upon without reference to any biblical text by people responding to obvious injustice and need in the world.

This study recognizes, furthermore, that the Bible as a whole, and even individual texts within the Bible, speak in a plurality of often contradictory voices, and that therefore, as Barr warns, it is difficult to use the Bible in a straightforward way in support of a particular agenda.[91] Certain texts, however, do carry weight and pose a challenge: in the way 58:6–10 represents a deepening of the concept of social justice within the book of Isaiah from what Derrida calls "Law" to "Justice," it can be taken as one such text.[92] Isaiah 1:16–17 is much more a call to act in accordance with law, whereas 58:6–10, especially in its protokenotic orientation, is much more a call to justice. This underscores my thesis that 58:6–10 represents a deepening of the concept of social justice within the book of Isaiah as drawn on a trajectory from 1:16–17. Conse-quently, while true that much of Isaiah reflects a conservative social ethos[93] that comes close to the dismissive attitude to the poor found in Jer 5:4, Isa 58:6–10 stands in genuine tension with this and redirects ethical thought in a more radical way.[94] More generally, comments and claims related to Isa 58:6–10 are made with the understanding that it is one text among a wide array of texts, but one which speaks in a particular voice.

Related to theology, this idea of the loss of a unifying principle[95] is encapsulated in comments—clearly influenced by postmodern thought— from Hodgson, who argues that "there is no triumphal march of God in history, no special history of salvation, but only a plurality of partial, fragmentary, ambiguous histories of freedom."[96] Interestingly, for all of his long-standing reservations about using the Bible to bring about social change,[97] Barr ends his recent critical survey of trends in Old Testament

91. Barr, *The Scope and Authority of the Bible*, 109.

92. Derrida insists "that justice exceeds law and calculation" ("Force of Law," 971).

93. Barr (*The Scope and Authority of the Bible*, 100), in addition to previous citations to this effect by Barton and so on.

94. For a model of biblical ethics that is better able to cope with the range of voices found in the Bible, see Tom Deidun, "The Bible and Christian Ethics," in *Christian Ethics: An Introduction* (ed. Bernard Hoose; London: Cassell, 1998), 3–46.

95. Mark Coleridge argues that the Bible has lost its role as "the grand legiti-mating and unifying narrative of Western culture" ("Life in the Crypt," 141).

96. Peter C. Hodgson, *God in History: Shapes of Freedom* (Nashville: Abingdon, 1989), 233.

97. See further Barr, *The Scope and Authority of the Bible*.

studies, in which some of the same concerns find expression,[98] by indicating that, for him,

> the "freedoms" being achieved in the postmodernist world . . . such as
> equality of status and opportunity do not count for so very much in a
> world where inequalities of wealth are increasing on a vast scale and
> where these inequalities are steadily eroding the reality of the democratic
> processes on which freedoms depend.[99]

This is a serious point well made, which may, as Barr indicates, necessitate for those interested a revaluation or coming back to Old Testament texts[100] for any contribution they might make in retaining and extending authentic freedom: in this enterprise, Isa 58:6–10 could be afforded a significant role.

With respect to the nature of postmodernism in general, among its several constituent strands, it displays tendencies both toward a teasing playfulness and a destructive negativity. West notes in this regard that "while plurality, ambiguity, partiality and particularity have created a space for the poor and marginalized to articulate and practice their own christianities, these same impulses have often led biblical scholars, theologians and other christian intellectuals into postmodern play or postmodern nihilism."[101] For West, thus, "postmodernism provides the negative moment, but it does not know how to dream."[102] However,

---

98. James Barr, *History and Ideology in the Old Testament: Biblical Studies at the End of a Millennium* (Oxford: Oxford University Press, 2000), 39 n. 22.

99. Ibid., 177. In a related way, Valentine Cunningham, discussing the fashion model Cindy Crawford's talk of feeling empowered in an MTV advertisement for her *Shape Your Body* workout video, acidly observes how "the language of power and empowering absorbed into a clichéd Californian solipsistic body-fetishizing rhetoric . . . laughably leaves the actual power structures of late capitalist marketplace economics—imperialist, exploitative of women—firmly in place" (*In the Reading Gaol*, 45).

100. Barr, *History and Ideology in the Old Testament*, 178.

101. Gerald O. West, "Reading the Bible and Doing Theology in the New South Africa," in Carroll R. et al., eds., *The Bible in Human Society*, 445–58 (449).

102. Ibid., 450. Also skeptical of the overall value of postmodernism, Achebe depicts the incongruity of an African (or anyone else from the margins of the world created by Western colonialism) enthusiastically embracing the postmodern condition when they and their people had not even experienced modernity. He writes, "Let us imagine a man who stumbles into an alien ritual in its closing stages when the devotees are winding down to a closing chorus of amens, and who immediately and enthusiastically takes up the singing with such loudness and gusto that the owners of the ritual stop their singing and turn, one and all, to look in wonder at this postmodernist stranger. Their wonder increases tenfold when they ask the visitor later what kind of modernism his people had had, and it transpires that neither he nor his

while "the play of pluralism or the abyss of meaninglessness are the constant companions of most postmodern intellectuals . . . they are not the only choices."[103] As West argues, "[P]ostmodernism, through an interface with liberation . . . hermeneutics, provides an opportunity for socially engaged intellectuals 'to do theology with' the poor and marginalized."[104]

According to West, new approaches to the Bible and theology[105] have created "cracks in 'orthodox' hegemony" of such significance that "longing for 'the good old days' will not be enough to keep" such approaches at bay.[106] Along similar lines, Coleridge contends that "it is possible to understand the whole of Scripture as testimony to a people's persistently unsuccessful mourning of the *mirabilia Dei*, and therefore as an elaborate and by no means morbid fantasy."[107] Then, in an overtly postmodernist way, playing on how with a change of spelling "Scripture becomes S*crypt*ure," with "a crypt at its heart," Coleridge writes: "Exegesis as fantasy may turn morbid, and it will if we live and work in an anachronistic world where things are presumed to be as they once were, as if the Bible still functioned in our society as the kind of masternarrative it once was."[108] Returning to the idea of the text as an occasion of synergistic liminality,[109] Coleridge proposes that if study of the Bible

people had ever heard the word modernism" (*Home and Exile*, 82). Of such people, Achebe concludes, "[O]ne tends to be rather impatient with one's colleagues, from Africa and other dispossessed places, who don't seem to know the score. Or, worse, who do but choose the fleshpots" (p. 84). For a fine novelistic presentation of this sort of phenomena, see Rukun Advani's *Beethoven among the Cows* (Delhi: Ravi Dayal, 1995), in which Lavatri Alltheorie, one of the novel's characters, is described as a "post-modern theoretician, boa deconstructor, discourse analyst, post-structuralist critic, feminist historian of subalternity, colonialism and gender" who lectures white students on "the semiology of Deconstruction and the Deconstruction of semiology" (pp. 145–46).

103. West, "Reading the Bible," 450.

104. Ibid., 449.

105. Ibid., 445–48.

106. Ibid., 449.

107. Coleridge, "Life in the Crypt," 145.

108. Ibid.

109. This is significantly different from the conceptualization of Childs, for whom the text itself is where God is encountered. On this see Roy A. Harrisville, "What I Believe My Old Schoolmate is Up To," in *Theological Exegesis: Essays in Honor of Brevard S. Childs* (ed. Christopher R. Seitz and Kathryn Greene-McCreight; Grand Rapids, Mich., and Cambridge, England: Eerdmans, 1999), 7–25 (16, 18, 22, 25). However, observe that when the text itself raises theologically difficult or sensitive issues, particularly concerning the character of God, the idea of the "rule of faith" becomes operative and functionally takes primacy over the

is reduced to "a radically privatised discourse . . . the crypt would become a tomb." More generatively and hopefully, "The fantasy may also prove creative, but only if the moment of mourning is allowed to become a moment of discovery, if the crypt is allowed to become a womb."[110]

In keeping with the thrust of such analyses, I have endeavored to be serious in theological creativity[111] rather than defensive,[112] and missiologically authentic rather than conformed to extant ecclesial models.[113]

---

problematic specificity of the text. On this see Brueggemann, *Deep Memory, Exuberant Hope*, 81–89; on the subject generally, see David Lyle Jeffrey, *People of the Book: Christian Identity and Literary Culture* (Grand Rapids: Eerdmans, with the Institute for Advanced Christian Studies, 1996).

110.   Coleridge, "Life in the Crypt," 145. Similarly, Brueggemann outlines how "Old Testament theology, if it is not reductive or coercive, may be an invitation that could keep the academic discipline from being turned in upon itself, preoccupied with greater and greater intensity on issues that matter less and less" (*Deep Memory, Exuberant Hope*, 119). On the matter of morbidity, Achebe (*Home and Exile*, 80), in a way germane to this discussion, cites Antonio Gramsci, *Prison Notebooks*: "The old is dying and the new cannot be born; in this interregnum there arises a great diversity of morbid symptoms."

111.   For a good summary of what is meant by creative, see Taylor, *Poverty and Christianity*, 95–121.

112.   The general posture of more conservative scholars; whatever criticisms may be leveled against liberation theology, in its various strands it undeniably takes seriously the injustice and brokenness of the world. By contrast, Carl Trueman speaks with some pride about how evangelicals have been "remarkably successful in the last sixty years, at least within the sphere of academia, where evangelicals have made their mark particularly in the field of biblical studies" ("The Future of Evangelical Scholarship: A British Perspective," in Trueman, Gray, and Blomberg, eds., *Solid Ground*, 291–309 [303–4]), but the state of the world does not even merit a mention. Great emphasis is placed on the Church and the Academy, but in a disappointing and dispiriting way their relationship to the broader category of the world in which they are irremediably located is not acknowledged, much less explored. In fairness, in a companion piece Craig Blomberg recognizes the concept of the kingdom or reign of God extending to both Church and world, significantly without the Church necessarily being given priority over the world ("The Past, Present, and Future of American Evangelical Scholarship," in Trueman, Gray, and Blomberg, eds., *Solid Ground*, 310–19 [316]). Colin Gunton, from an evangelical position, insists that "theology is not theology if it does not in some way shape the life of the Christian community and through that the life of the world" ("Trinity and Trustworthiness," 284). Isaiah 58, in its protokenotic embrace of pain theology, which has been so little adopted, leaves few, if any, theological traditions unchallenged.

113.   David Bosch insists that "ecclesiology . . . does not precede missiology" (*Transforming Mission*, 372). Thus mission is not about perpetuating and replicating patterns of Church prescriptively derived from the biblical text (what might be called

At the same time, I have tried to recognize the value of being "Appropriately Postmodern."[114] I have therefore sought to adhere to Brueggemann's insight that "the practitioner of Old Testament theology must move between a credulous fideism and a knowing, suspicious skepticism, wherein the former does not pay sufficient attention to the *problematic* of the witness, and the latter is *tone deaf* to the core claim of the witness."[115] Oscillations between these dimensions, in my case, have pertained to the search for social justice.

Consequently, I have not assumed the innocence or justice of God but have incorporated into my discussion textual evidence of the idea that the divine on occasions acts disproportionately or abusively.[116] As a result, the role of humanity in the continuing search for justice in the world may be affirmed.[117] As a result, the role of humanity in the continuing search for justice in the world may be affirmed. But not in the manner of the Enlightenment thinkers, who had conviction that they could translate "the Christian vision of a heavenly city into a future earthly utopia." Thus, "they called upon their contemporaries to forget about 'God' and put their hope in a blessed future in which would be realized that happiness which is everybody's right and which 'God' has never been able to

the "application" or "adaptation" model) but engaging transformatively with context, assisted by dialogue with the text (what might be called the "incarnational" model). On these models and their missiological development and significance, see Aylward Shorter, *African Christian Theology* (Maryknoll, N.Y.: Orbis, 1986); and idem, *Toward a Theology of Inculturation* (Maryknoll, N.Y.: Orbis, 1988).

114. This phrase is borrowed from Brueggemann, "Biblical Theology Appropriately Postmodern."

115. Brueggemann, *Deep Memory, Exuberant Hope*, 121 (emphasis in original). Similarly, Brueggemann argues that "Christian theology of the Hebrew Scriptures cannot afford innocent affirmation because neither text nor life is like that" ("Biblical Theology Appropriately Postmodern," 104).

116. Brueggemann contends that "the Only One of Israel is not innocently 'omnipotent, omnipresent, and omniscient,' as too much Christian theology has insisted, but is a God present with and absent from, a God to be praised in full adoration and assaulted as an abuser" ("Biblical Theology Appropriately Postmodern," 104). How these aspects are to be held together is, though, problematical. With regard to the "omni" trio of divine attributes, as Dorothee Sölle perceives, "[A]ll three statements about the absoluteness of God—his omnipotence, omniscience, omnipresence—all three 'omnis' express a fatal imperialistic tendency in theology" (*Thinking about God*, 189).

117. See further Taylor, *Poverty and Christianity*; idem, *Not Angels but Agencies: The Ecumenical Response to Poverty—A Primer* (London: SCM Press; Geneva: WCC Publications, 1995); also, Hans Küng, *A Global Ethic for Global Politics and Economics* (London: SCM Press, 1997).

provide.[118] Rather, the hope for humanity is better captured by the tone and sentiments of the Angolan independence leader Agostinho Neto. Well aware of the massive imperial forces ranged against his embryonic nation as it attempted to create a more just and humane future for its citizens, Neto still maintained that "hope is ourselves—our children travelling towards a faith that feeds life."[119]

6. *Finally . . . Come the Poets*[120]

I recognize the appeal in the book of Isaiah of the type of poetry that speaks grandly of the eschatologically oriented occasion:

> . . . once in a lifetime
> The longed-for tidal wave
> of justice can rise up,
> And hope and history rhyme[121]

But I also acknowledge that at one level poetry, even when talking about the often privileged Isaianic corpus, is a "wretched rage for order . . . an eddy of semantic scruples / in an unstructurable sea." Despite the poet's "grandiloquent and deprecating" posture, "his talk of justice" therefore often remains "the rhetorical device / of an etiolated emperor."[122]

In their different styles and tones, both Mahon and Heaney intimate the limitations of poetry in a broken world. Mahon envisages how "somewhere beyond the scorched gable and the / burnt-out buses" the poet practices his "dying art . . . far from his people," before tellingly accentuating the disjunction between poet and world with the lines "and

118. Lesslie Newbigin, *The Other Side of 1984: Questions for the Churches* (Geneva: WCC Publications, 1983), 3.

119. Quoted in *Sound Bites: Quotes for Our Times*, compiled by the New Internationalist (Oxford: New Internationalist, 1997), 51. See also Basil Davidson, *Let Freedom Come: Africa in Modern History* (Boston: Little, Brown, 1978); idem, *The Search for Africa: History, Culture, Politics* (New York: Random House, 1994). For a moving novelistic portrayal of human beings persisting in the quest for social justice, see Kingsolver, *Poisonwood Bible*. In keeping with the tenor of Neto's quotation, Derek Mahon writes, "The ideal future / Shines out of our better nature, / Dimly visible from afar" ("The Sea in Winter," 113).

120. The subheading comes via Walt Whitman and plays on the title of Walter Bruggemann, *Finally Comes the Poet: Daring Speech for Proclamation* (Minneapolis: Fortress, 1989).

121. Seamus Heaney, *The Cure at Troy: A Version of Sophocles's "Philoctetes"* (London: Faber & Faber in association with Field Day, 1990), 77.

122. Mahon, "Rage for Order," in *Poems, 1962–1978*, 44.

the fitful glare of his high window is as / nothing to our scattered glass."[123] Heaney, with a studied degree of self-effacement, confesses,

Human beings suffer,
They torture one another,
They get hurt and get hard.
No poem or play or song
Can fully right a wrong
Inflicted and endured.[124]

Yet both also make claims for the importance of poetry. Heaney, after the implication of that "fully" has had time to sink in, in exhortation writes like the drum major of hope, encouraging the reader:

. . . hope for a great sea-change
On the far side of revenge.
Believe that further shore
Is reachable from here.
Believe in miracle[125]

He ends with the redolently Isaianic image of a new world coming into being with "outcry and the birth-cry / Of new life at its term."[126] Mahon, by way of contrast, warns that whatever reservations might exist about the worth of poetry and the poet in society, "it cannot be / long till" those who in revolutionary fervor "tear down / to build up with a desperate love" will "have need of his / desperate ironies."[127]

It is clear that many of the promissory passages related to the theme of justice in the book of Isaiah are never realized in the world of the text.[128] Given that these instances and the text as a whole cannot be conformed to any one dogmatic scheme, except by vast reductionism, I have tried to negotiate between the tendencies to excessive cynicism and undue hope, demonstrated in the poems by Mahon and Heaney. I have sought, following Brueggemann's analysis of the present state of Old Testament theology,[129] to signal a willingness in all modesty to play a small part in attempting to direct "the academic community away from self-preoccupied triviality that is such a waste, the ecclesial communities away from

123.   Ibid.
124.   Heaney, *Cure at Troy*, 77.
125.   Ibid.
126.   Ibid., 78.
127.   Mahon, "Rage for Order," in *Poems, 1962–1978*, 44.
128.   The ultimate example of, in this case, ironically conceived liminality in the book of Isaiah?
129.   Brueggemann, *Deep Memory, Exuberant Hope*, 111–22.

excessive certitude that is idolatry, and the civic community away from brutality rooted in autonomy."[130] My aim has been to provoke thought and encourage action for justice: justice for the poor, justice for creation, signs of the new heavens and the new earth.

130. Ibid., 122.

BIBLIOGRAPHY

Abrams, M. H. "The Deconstructive Angel." *Critical Inquiry* 3 (1977): 425–32.

Achebe, Chinua. *Home and Exile*. Oxford: Oxford University Press, 2000.

—"An Image of Africa: Racism in Conrad's *Heart of Darkness*." Pages 251–62 in *Heart of Darkness: An Authoritative Text, Background, and Source Criticism*, by Joseph Conrad. Edited by Robert Kimbrough. 3d ed. New York: Norton, 1988.

Advani, Rukun. *Beethoven among the Cows*. Delhi: Ravi Dayal, 1995.

Aichele, George. *Sign, Text, Scripture: Semiotics and the Bible*. Interventions 1. Sheffield: Sheffield Academic Press, 1997.

Aichele, George, et al. *The Postmodern Bible: The Bible and Culture Collective*. New Haven: Yale University Press, 1995.

Aidoo, Ama Ata. *Our Sister Killjoy*. Reading, Mass.: Addison Wesley, 1997.

Aimers, Geoffrey J. "The Rhetoric of Social Conscience in the Book of Job." *JSOT* 91 (2000): 99–107.

Alexander, T. Desmond. "The Old Testament View of Life after Death." Pages 120–33 in Trueman, Gray, and Blomberg, eds., *Solid Ground*.

Alexander, Bobby. *Victor Turner Revisited: Ritual as Social Change*. Atlanta: Scholars Press, 1991.

Alexander, Joseph Addison. *Commentary on Isaiah.*. Grand Rapids: Kregel Classics, 1992 (1867).

Amir, Yehoshua. "Messianism and Zionism." Pages 13–30 in *Eschatology in the Bible and in Jewish and Christian Tradition*. Edited by G. H. Reventlow. JSOTSup 243. Sheffield: Sheffield Academic Press, 1997.

Anderson, Bernhard W. "Exodus and Covenant in Second Isaiah and Prophetic Tradition." Pages 339–60 in *Magnalia Dei: The Mighty Acts of God*. Edited by Frank Moore Cross, Werner E. Lemke, and Patrick D. Miller Jr. New York: Doubleday, 1976.

—"Exodus Typology in Second Isaiah." Pages 177–95 in Anderson and Harrelson, eds., *Israel's Prophetic Heritage*.

Anderson, Bernhard W., and Walter Harrelson, eds. *Israel's Prophetic Heritage: Essays in Honor of James Muilenburg*. London: SCM Press, 1962.

Anderson, Robert T. "Was Isaiah a Scribe?" *JBL* 79 (1960): 57–58.

Ashcroft, Bill, Gareth Griffiths, and Helen Tiffin, eds. *Post-colonial Studies: The Key Concepts*. London: Routledge, 2000.

—*The Post-colonial Studies Reader*. London: Routledge, 1995.

Ateek, Naim. *Justice, and Only Justice: A Palestinian Theology of Liberation*. Maryknoll, N.Y.: Orbis, 1989.

Austin, J. L. *How to do Things with Words*. London: Oxford University Press, 1963.

Bair, Deirdre. *Samuel Beckett: A Biography*. London: Picador/Pan, 1980.

Bakhtin, Mikhail M. *Problems of Dostoevsky's Poetics*. Translated by R. W. Rotsel. Ann Arbor, Mich.: Ardis Press, 1973.

Bal, Mieke. "Metaphors he Lives By." *Semeia* 61 (1993): 185–207.

—*Narratology: Introduction to the Theory of Narrative*. Translated by Christine von Boheemen. Toronto: University of Toronto Press, 1985.

—*On Meaning-Making*. Sonoma, Calif.: Polebridge, 1994.

—*On Story-Telling*. Sonoma, Calif.: Polebridge, 1991.

Balasuriya, Tissa. *The Eucharist and Human Liberation*. Maryknoll, N.Y.: Orbis, 1979.

Balentine, Samuel E. *The Hidden God: The Hiding of the Face of God in the Old Testament*. Oxford: Oxford University Press, 1983.

Baltzer, Klaus. *Deutero-Isaiah*. Hermeneia. Minneapolis: Fortress, 2001.

Barr, James. *History and Ideology in the Old Testament: Biblical Studies at the End of a Millennium*. Oxford: Oxford University Press, 2000.

—*The Scope and Authority of the Bible*. Xpress Reprints. London: SCM Bookroom, 1993.

—*The Semantics of Biblical Language*. Oxford: Oxford University Press, 1961.

Barstad, Hans. *The Myth of the Empty Land: A Study in the History and Archaeology of Judah during the "Exilic" Period*. Oslo: Scandinavian University Press, 1996.

Barthes, Roland. *Image–Music–Text*. Edited and translated by Stephen Heath. London: Fontana Press, 1977.

—*The Semiotic Challenge*. Translated by Richard Howard Blackwell. Oxford: Blackwell, 1988.

Barton, John. "History and Rhetoric in the Prophets." Pages 51–64 in *The Bible as Rhetoric: Studies in Biblical Persuasion and Credibility*. Edited by Martin Warner. London: Routledge, 1990.

—*Isaiah 1–39*. OTG. Sheffield: Sheffield Academic Press, 1995.

—*Reading the Old Testament: Method in Biblical Study*. 2d ed. London: Darton, Longman & Todd, 1996.

Bashford, Bruce. "The Rhetorical Method in Literary Criticism." *Philosophy and Rhetoric* 9 (1976): 133–46.

—"Ethics in the Book of Isaiah." Pages 67–77 in vol. 1 of Broyles and Evans, eds., *Writing and Reading the Scroll of Isaiah*.

Battles, F. L. "God was Accommodating Himself to Human Capacity." *Int* 31 (1977): 19–38.

Baxter, A. G. "What Did Calvin Teach about Accommodation?" *Evangel* 6, no. 1 (1988): 20–22.

Beeby, H. Daniel. *Canon and Mission*. Harrisburg, Pa.: Trinity, 1999.

—"A Missional Approach to Renewed Interpretation." Pages 268–83 in *Renewing Biblical Interpretation*. Edited by Craig Bartholomew, Colin Greene, and Karl Möller. Carlisle: Paternoster; Grand Rapids: Zondervan, 2000.

Begrich, Joachim. "Das priesterliche Heilsorakel." *ZAW* 52 (1934): 81–92.

Bellis, Alice Ogden, and Joel S. Kaminsky, eds. *Jews, Christians, and the Theology of the Hebrew Scriptures*. Atlanta: Society of Biblical Literature, 2000.

Belsey, Catherine. "Literature, History, Politics." Pages 400–10 in Lodge, ed., *Modern Criticism and Theory*.

Benin, S. D. "The 'Cunning of God' and Divine Accommodation." *Journal of the History of Ideas* 45 (1984): 179–91.

Benjamin, Walter *Selected Writings*. Vol. 1. *1913–26*. Edited by M. Bullock; Cambridge, Mass.: Belknap, 1996.

Bennington, Geoffrey, and Jacques Derrida, eds. *Jacques Derrida*. Chicago: University of Chicago Press, 1993.

Bergant, Dianne. "Violence and God: A Bible Study." *Missiology* 20, no. 1 (1992): 45–54.

Berquist, Jon L. *Judaism in Persia's Shadow: A Social and Historical Approach.* Minneapolis: Fortress, 1995.

Beuken, W. A. M. "Isaiah 28: Is it Only Schismatics that Drink Heavily? Beyond the Synchronic versus Diachronic Controversy." Pages 15–38 in de Moor, ed., *Synchronic or Diachronic?.*

—"The Main Theme of Trito-Isaiah 'The Servants of Yahweh.'" *JSOT* 47 (1990): 67–87.

—"Servant and Herald of Good Tidings." Pages 411–42 in Vermeylen, ed., *The Book of Isaiah/Le Livre D'Isaïe.*

Birkeland, H. "The Beliefs in Resurrection of the Dead in the Old Testament." *VT* 3 (1950–51): 60–78.

Bitzer, Lloyd F. "The Rhetorical Situation." *Philosophy and Rhetoric* 1 (1968): 1–14.

Black, Edwin. *IBM and the Holocaust: The Strategic Alliance between Nazi Germany and America's Most Powerful Corporation.* New York: Crown, 2001.

Blenkinsopp, Joseph. *A History of Prophecy in Israel.* Rev. ed. Louisville, Ky.: Westminster John Knox, 1996.

—"Interpretation and the Tendency to Sectarianism: An Aspect of Second Temple History." Pages 1–26 in *Jewish and Christian Self-Definition: Aspects of Judaism in the Graeco-Roman Period.* Edited by E. P. Sanders. Vol. 2. Philadelphia: Fortress, 1981.

—*Isaiah 1–39.* AB 19. New York: Doubleday, 2000.

—*Isaiah 40–55: A New Translation with Introduction and Commentary.* AB 19A. New York: Doubleday, 2000.

—*Isaiah 56–66.* AB 19B. New York: Doubleday, 2003.

—"A Jewish Sect of the Persian Period." *CBQ* 52 (1990): 5–20.

—"Second Isaiah—Prophet of Universalism." *JSOT* 41 (1988): 83–103.

—"The Social Roles of Prophets in Early Achaemenid Judah." *JSOT* 93 (2001): 39–58.

—*Wisdom and Law in the Old Testament: The Ordering of Life in Israel and Early Judaism.* Oxford Bible Series. Oxford: Oxford University Press, 1995.

Bloch-Smith, Elizabeth. *Judahite Burial Practices and Beliefs about the Dead.* JSOTSup 123. Sheffield: JSOT Press, 1992.

Blomberg, Craig. "The Past, Present, and Future of American Evangelical Scholarship." Pages 310–19 in Trueman, Gray, and Blomberg, eds., *Solid Ground.*

Blumenthal, David R. *Facing the Abusing God: A Theology of Protest.* Louisville, Ky.: Westminster John Knox, 1993.

Boer, P. A. H. de. *Second Isaiah's Message.* Leiden: Brill, 1956.

Boff, Leonardo. "Christianity with an Authentic Face: Reflections on the Future of the Church in Latin America." Pages 152–67 in *Hans Küng: New Horizons for Faith and Thought.* Edited by Karl-Josef Kuschel and Hermann Häring. Translated by John Bowden. London: SCM Press, 1993.

—*New Evangelization: Good News to the Poor.* Translated by Robert R. Barr. Maryknoll, N.Y.: Orbis, 1991.

Boff, Leonardo, and Clodovis Boff. *Introducing Liberation Theology.* Wellwood: Burns & Oates, 1987.

Bonhoeffer, Dietrich. *Letters and Papers from Prison.* London: SCM Press, 1971.

Booth, Wayne C. *The Rhetoric of Fiction.* 2d ed. Chicago: University of Chicago Press, 1983.

—*A Rhetoric of Irony.* Chicago: University of Chicago Press, 1975.

Bosch, David. *Transforming Mission: Paradigm Shifts in the Theology of Mission.* Maryknoll, N.Y.: Orbis, 1991.

Bovati, Pietro. "Le langage juridique du prophète Isaïe." Pages 177–96 in Vermeylen, ed., *The Book of Isaiah/Le Livre D'Isaïe*.

—*Re-establishing Justice: Legal Terms, Concepts, and Procedures in the Hebrew Bible*. Translated by Michael J. Smith. JSOTSup 105. Sheffield: JSOT Press, 1994.

Bowen, Murray. *Family Therapy in Clinical Practice*. New York: Aronson, 1978.

Boyarin, D. *Intertextuality and the Reading of Midrash*. Bloomington: Indiana University Press, 1990.

Braybrooke, Marcus, ed., *Stepping Stones to a Global Ethic*. London: SCM Press, 1992.

Brinton, Alan. "Situation in the Theory of Rhetoric." *Philosophy and Rhetoric* 14 (1981): 234–48.

Brock, B. L., and Robert L. Scott. *Methods of Rhetorical Criticism: A Twentieth-Century Perspective*. 2d ed. Detroit: Wayne State University Press, 1980.

Brown, W. P. "The So-Called Refrain in Isaiah 5:25–30 and 9:7–10:4." *CBQ* 52 (1990): 432–43.

Broyles, C. C., and C. A. Evans, eds. *Writing and Reading the Scroll of Isaiah: Studies of an Interpretive Tradition*. 2 vols. VTSup 70.1–2. Leiden: Brill, 1997.

Brueggemann, Walter. "Biblical Authority: A Personal Reflection." Pages 5–31 in *Struggling with Scripture*. Edited by Walter Brueggemann, William C. Placher, and Brian K. Blount. Louisville, Ky.: Westminster John Knox, 2002.

—"Biblical Theology Appropriately Postmodern." Pages 97–108 in Bellis and Kaminsky, eds., *Jews, Christians, and the Theology of the Hebrew Scriptures*.

—*Cadences of Home: Preaching among Exiles*. Louisville, Ky.: Westminster John Knox, 1997.

—*Deep Memory, Exuberant Hope*. Minneapolis: Fortress, 2000.

—*Finally Comes the Poet: Daring Speech for Proclamation*. Minneapolis: Fortress, 1989.

—"Five Strong Readings of the Book of Isaiah." Pages 87–104 in M. D. Carroll R. et al., eds., *The Bible in Human Society*.

—*Hopeful Imagination: Prophetic Voices in Exile*. Philadelphia: Fortress, 1986.

—*Interpretation and Obedience: From Faithful Reading to Faithful Living*. Minneapolis: Fortress, 1991.

—*Isaiah 1–39*. WBC. Louisville, Ky.: Westminster John Knox, 1998.

—*Isaiah 40–66*. WBC. Louisville, Ky.: Westminster John Knox, 1998.

—"Jeremiah: Intense Criticism/Thin Interpretation." *Int* 42 (1988): 268–80.

—*The Message of the Psalms: A Theological Commentary*. Minneapolis: Augsburg, 1989.

—"The Need for Neighbor." *The Other Side* (July–August 2003): 32–36.

—*Old Testament Theology: Essays on Structure, Theme, and Text*. Edited by Patrick D. Miller. Minneapolis: Fortress, 1992.

—"Planned People/Planned Book?" Pages 19–37 in vol. 1 of Broyles and Evans, eds., *Writing and Reading the Scroll of Isaiah*.

—*Theology of the Old Testament: Testimony, Dispute, Advocacy*. Minneapolis: Fortress, 1997.

—*The Threat of Life: Sermons on Pain, Power, and Weakness*. Edited by Charles L. Campbell. Minneapolis: Fortress, 1996.

—"The Uninflected *Therefore* of Hosea 4:13." Pages 231–49 in vol. 1 of Segovia and Tolbert, eds, *Reading from this Place*.

—*Using God's Resources Wisely: Isaiah and Urban Possibility*. Louisville, Ky.: Westminster John Knox, 1993.

—"Vision for a New Church and a New Century Part I: Homework Against Scarcity." *Union Seminary Quarterly Review* 54, nos. 1–2 (2000): 21–39.

—"Vision for a New Church and a New Century Part II: Holiness Become Generosity." *Union Seminary Quarterly Review* 54, nos. 1–2 (2000): 45–64.

Bryan, M. S. "The Threat to the Reputation of YHWH: The Portrayal of the Divine Character in the Book of Ezekiel." Ph.D. diss., University of Sheffield, 1992.

Bundell, Kevan. *Forgotten Farmers: Small Farmers, Trade, and Sustainable Agriculture*. London: Christian Aid, 2002.

Calvin, John. *Commentary on the Book of the Prophet Isaiah*. 4 vols. Edinburgh: Calvin Translation Society, 1850–53.

Caputo, John D. *Demythologizing Heidegger*. Bloomington: Indiana University Press, 1993.

—*More Radical Hermeneutics: On Not Knowing Who We Are*. Bloomington: Indiana University Press, 2000.

—*The Prayers and Tears of Jacques Derrida: Religion without Religion*. Bloomington: Indiana University Press, 1997.

Carr, David M. "Reading Isaiah from Beginning (Isaiah 1) to End (Isaiah 65–66): Multiple Modern Possibilities." Pages 188–218 in Melugin and Sweeney, eds., *New Visions of Isaiah*.

—"Synergy toward Life: A Paradigm for Liberative Christian Work with the Bible." *Quarterly Review* 10, no. 4 (1990): 40–55.

—"Untamable Text of an Untamable God." *Int* 54, no. 4 (2000): 347–62.

Carroll, Robert P. "Blindsight and the Vision Thing: Blindnesss and Insight in the Book of Isaiah." Pages 79–93 in vol. 1 of Broyles and Evans, eds., *Writing and Reading the Scroll of Isaiah*.

—"Clio and Canons: In Search of a Cultural Poetics of the Hebrew Bible." *BibInt* 5, no. 4 (1997): 300–23.

—"Poets Not Prophets." *JSOT* 27 (1983): 25–31.

—"Second Isaiah and the Failure of Prophecy." *Studia Theologica* 32 (1978): 119–31.

—*When Prophecy Failed: Reactions and Responses to Failure in the Old Testament Prophetic Traditions*. London: SCM Press, 1979.

Carroll R., M. Daniel, David J. A. Clines, and Philip R. Davies, eds. *The Bible in Human Society: Essays in Honour of John Rogerson*. JSOTSup 200. Sheffield: Sheffield Academic Press, 1995.

Ceresko, Anthony R. *Introduction to the Old Testament: A Liberation Perspective*. Maryknoll, N.Y.: Orbis; London: Geoffrey Chapman, 1992.

Cheyne, T. K. *Introduction to the Book of Isaiah*. London: Adam & Charles Black, 1895.

Childs, Brevard S. *Introduction to the Old Testament as Scripture*. Minneapolis: Fortress, 1979.

—*Isaiah*. Louisville, Ky.: Westminster John Knox, 2001.

Chomsky, Noam. *The Culture of Terrorism*. Boston: South End Press, 1988.

—*Necessary Illusions: Thought Control in Democratic Societies*. Boston: South End Press, 1989.

—*On Power and Ideology: The Managua Lectures*. Boston: South End Press, 1987.

—*Profit over People: Neoliberalism and Global Order*. New York: Seven Stories, 1999.

—*Year 501: The Conquest Continues*. Boston: South End Press, 1993.

Clarke, Erskine, ed. *Exilic Preaching: Testimony for Christian Exiles in an Increasingly Hostile Culture*. Harrisburg, Pa.: Trinity, 1998.

Clements, R. E. *God and Temple: The Idea of the Divine Presence in Ancient Israel.* Oxford: Blackwell, 1965.

—"Isaiah: A Book without an Ending." *JSOT* 97 (2002): 109–26.

—*Isaiah 1–39.* NCB. Grand Rapids: Eerdmans, 1980.

—"The Prophecies of Isaiah and the Fall of Jerusalem in 587 B.C." *VT* 30 (1980): 421–36.

Clifford, Richard. *Fair Spoken and Persuading: An Interpretation of Second Isaiah.* New York: Paulist, 1984.

Clines, David J. A. *Interested Parties: The Ideology of Writers and Readers of the Hebrew Bible.* JSOTSup 205. Sheffield: Sheffield Academic Press, 1995.

—"Possibilities and Priorities of Biblical Interpretation in an International Perspective." *BibInt* 1, no. 1 (1993): 67–87.

—"Quarter Days Gone: Job 24 and the Absence of God." Pages 242–58 in Linafelt and Beal, eds., *God in the Fray.*

Clines, David J. A., David M. Gunn, and Alan J. Hauser, eds. *Art and Meaning: Rhetoric in Biblical Literature.* JSOTSup 19. Sheffield: JSOT Press, 1982.

Coggins, Richard J. "Do We Still Need Deutero-Isaiah?" *JSOT* 81 (1998): 72–92.

Coggins, R., A. Phillips, and M. Knibb, eds. *Israel's Prophetic Tradition: Essays in Honour of Peter R. Ackroyd.* Cambridge: Cambridge University Press, 1982.

Cohn, Herbert. "From Monolatry to Monotheism." *Jewish Bible Quarterly* 26 (1998): 124–26.

Cohn, Norman. *Cosmos, Chaos, and the World to Come: The Ancient Roots of Apocalyptic Faith.* New Haven: Yale University Press, 1993.

Coleridge, Mark. "Life in the Crypt, or Why Bother with Biblical Studies?" *BibInt* 2, no. 2 (1994): 139–51.

Collier, Peter, and Helga Geyer-Ryan, eds. *Literary Theory Today.* Cambridge, Mass.: Polity, 1990.

Conley, Thomas. *Rhetoric in the European Tradition.* White Plains, N.Y.: Longman, 1990.

Conrad, Edgar W. "The Community as King in Second Isaiah." Pages 99–111 in *Understanding the Word: Essays in Honor of Bernhard W. Anderson.* Edited by James T. Butler, Edgar W. Conrad, and Ben C. Ollenburger. JSOTSup 37. Sheffield: JSOT Press, 1985.

—*Fear Not Warrior: A Study of 'al tira' Pericopes in the Hebrew Scriptures.* Brown Judaic Studies 75. Chicago: Scholars Press, 1985.

—"Messengers in Isaiah and the Twelve: Implications for Reading Prophetic Books." *JSOT* 91 (2000): 83–97.

—*Reading Isaiah.* OBT. Minneapolis: Fortress, 1991.

—"The Royal Narratives and the Structure of the Book of Isaiah." *JSOT* 41 (1988): 67–81.

—"Yehoshua Gitay: 'What is *He* Doing?' " *JSOT* 27 (2002): 237–41.

Coote, Robert B., and Mary P. Coote. *Power, Politics, and the Making of the Bible.* Minneapolis: Fortress, 1990.

Cowdell, Scott. *Atheist Priest? Don Cupitt and Christianity.* London: SCM Press, 1988.

Crenshaw, James L. "Introduction: The Shift from Theodicy to Anthropodicy." Pages 1–16 in idem, ed., *Theodicy in the Old Testament.*

—*A Whirlpool of Torment: God as Oppressive Presence.* OBT. Philadelphia: Fortress, 1984.

—ed. *Theodicy in the Old Testament.* Issues in Religion and Theology 4. Philadelphia: Fortress; London: SPCK, 1983.

Croatto, J. Severino. *Biblical Hermeneutics: Toward a Theory of Reading as the Production of Meaning.* Translated by Robert R. Barr. Maryknoll, N.Y.: Orbis, 1987.

—"The Debt in Nehemiah's Social Reform." Pages 39–59 in *Subversive Scriptures: Revolutionary Readings of the Christian Bible in Latin America.* Edited by Leif E. Vaage. Valley Forge, Pa.: Trinity, 1997.

—"Exegesis of Second Isaiah from the Perspective of the Oppressed: Paths for Reflection." Pages 219–36 in vol. 2 of Segovia and Tolbert, eds., *Reading from this Place.*

—*Exodus: A Hermeneutics of Freedom.* Rev. ed. Maryknoll, N.Y.: Orbis, 1981.

—*Imaginar El Futuro: Estructura retórica y querigma del Tercer Isais—Isaías 56–66.* Buenos Aires: Lumen, 2001.

—*Isaías: La Palabra Profética y su relectura hermenéutica—La Liberación es Posible.* Vol. 2, *40–55.* Buenos Aires: Lumen, 1994.

—"The 'Nations' in the Salvific Oracles of Isaiah." Paper presented at the annual meeting of the Society of Biblical Literature, San Francisco, 1997.

—"The Socio-historical and Hermeneutical Relevance of the Exodus." Pages 125–33 in *Exodus: A Lasting Paradigm.* Edited by Bas Van Iersel and Anton Weiler. Edinburgh: T. & T. Clark, 1987.

Cruchley-Jones, Peter. *Singing the Lord's Song in a Strange Land?* Studies in the Intercultural History of Christianity 123. Frankfurt: Peter Lang, 2001.

Cunningham, Valentine. *In the Reading Gaol: Postmodernity, Texts, and History.* Oxford: Blackwell, 1994.

Cupitt, Don. *Taking Leave of God.* London: SCM Press, 1980.

Darr, Katherine Pfisterer. *Isaiah's Vision and the Family of God.* LCBI. Louisville, Ky.: Westminster John Knox, 1994.

Davidson, Basil. *Let Freedom Come: Africa in Modern History.* Boston: Little, Brown, 1978.

—*The Search for Africa: History, Culture, Politics.* New York: Random House, 1994.

Davie, Donald. "Personification." *Essays in Criticism* 31, no. 2 (1981): 91–104.

Davies, Andrew. *Double Standards in Isaiah: Re-evaluating Prophetic Ethics and Divine Justice.* Leiden: Brill, 2000.

Davies, Eryl W. *Prophecy and Ethics: Isaiah and the Ethical Tradition of Israel.* JSOTSup 16. Sheffield: JSOT Press, 1981.

Davies, Philip R. *Scribes and Schools: The Canonization of the Hebrew Scriptures.* Louisville, Ky.: Westminster John Knox, 1998.

Deidun, Tom. "The Bible and Christian Ethics." Pages 3–46 in *Christian Ethics: An Introduction.* Edited by Bernard Hoose. London: Cassell, 1998.

Delitzsch, Franz. *Biblical Commentary on the Prophecies of Isaiah.* 2 vols. Edinburgh: T. & T. Clark, 1910.

Derrida, Jacques. *Aporias.* Stanford, Calif.: Stanford University Press, 1993.

—"Force of Law: The 'Mystical Foundations of Authority.'" *Cardozo Law Review* 11 (July/August 1990): 920–1045.

—*Limited Inc.* Edited by Gerald Graff. Translated by Samuel Weber and Jeffrey Mehlman. Evanston, Ill.: Northwestern University Press, 1988.

—*Margins of Philosophy.* Translated by Alan Bass. Chicago: University of Chicago Press, 1982.

—*Of Grammatology*. Translated by Gayatri Chakravorty Spivack. Baltimore: The Johns Hopkins University Press, 1976.

—*Politics of Friendship*. Translated by George Collins. London: Verso, 1997.

—*Positions*. Translated by Alan Bass. Chicago: University of Chicago Press, 1981.

—*Speech and Phenomena*. Translated by David B. Allison. Evanston, Ill.: Northwestern University Press, 1973.

Dick, Michael Brennan. "Prophetic *Poiesis* and the Verbal Icon." *CBQ* 46 (1984): 226–46.

Dickson, Kwesi A. *Uncompleted Mission: Christianity and Exclusivism*. Maryknoll, N.Y.: Orbis, 1991.

Dodd, C. H. *Integral Spirituality: Resources for Community, Peace, Justice, and the Earth*. Maryknoll, N.Y.: Orbis, 1990.

—*The Parables of the Kingdom*. London: Nisbet, 1948.

Dorr, Donal. *Integral Spirituality: Resources for Community, Peace, Justice, and the Earth* (Maryknoll, N.Y.: Orbis, 1990).

Douglas, Mary, and Aaron Wildavsky. *Risk and Culture*. Berkeley: University of California Press, 1982.

Douglas-Klotz, Neil. "Midrash and Postmodern Inquiry: Suggestions toward a Hermeneutics of Indeterminacy." *Currents in Research: Biblical Studies* 7 (1999): 181–93.

Douthwaite, Richard. *The Growth Illusion: How Economic Growth has Enriched the Few, Impoverished the Many, and Endangered the Planet*. Devon: Resurgence, 1992.

Dowey, E. A. *The Knowledge of God in Calvin's Theology*. New York: Columbia University Press, 1952.

Duchrow, Ulrich. *Property for People, Not for Profit: Alternatives to the Global Tyranny of Capital*. London: Zed Books, 2004.

Duhm, B. *Das Buch Jesaja*. 5th ed., Handkommentar zum Alten Testament 3.1. Göttingen: Vandenhoeck & Ruprecht, 1968 (1892).

Dylan, Bob. *Writings and Drawings*. London: Jonathan Cape, 1973.

Eagleton, Terry. "Capitalism, Modernism, and Postmodernism." Pages 385–98 in Lodge, ed., *Modern Criticism and Theory*.

—*Literary Theory: An Introduction*. Minneapolis: University of Minnesota Press, 1983.

—*Marxism and Literary Criticism*. London: Routledge, 2002.

Eco, Umberto. *The Role of the Reader*. Bloomington: Indiana University Press, 1979.

Eichrodt, Walther. *Ezekiel: A Commentary*. OTL. London: SCM Press, 1970.

Eissfeldt, Otto. "The Promises of Grace to David in Isaiah 55:1–5." Pages 196–207 in Anderson and Harrelson, eds., *Israel's Prophetic Heritage*.

Ellis, John M. *Against Deconstruction*. Princeton: Princeton University Press, 1989.

Ellis, Marc H. *Unholy Alliance: Religion and Atrocity in Our Time*. London: SCM Press, 1997.

Ellul, Jacques. *Hope in Time of Abandonment*. New York: Seabury, 1972.

Eslinger, Lyle. "Ezekiel 20 and the Metaphor of Historical Teleology: Concepts of Biblical History." *JSOT* 81 (1998): 93–125.

Evans, Alice Frazer, Robert A. Evans, and William Bean Kennedy, eds. *Pedagogies for the Non-Poor*. Maryknoll, N.Y.: Orbis, 1987.

Fanon, Frantz. *The Wretched of the Earth*. Translated by Constance Farrington. New York: Grove Press, 1963.

Fensham, F. Charles. "Widow, Orphan, and the Poor in Ancient Near Eastern Legal and Wisdom Literature." *JNES* 21 (1962): 129–39.

Fichtner, J. "Jesaja unter den Weisen." *TLZ* 74 (1949): cols. 75–80.

Fiddes, P. *The Creative Suffering of God.* Oxford: Oxford University Press, 1988.

Fohrer, G. "Jesaja 1 als Zusammenfassung der Verkündigung Jesajas." *ZAW* 74 (1962): 251–68.

Foucault, Michael. *Language, Counter-Memory, Practice: Selected Essays and Interviews.* Edited and with an Introduction by Donald F. Bouchard. Translated by Donald F. Bouchard and Sherry Simon. Oxford: Blackwell, 1977.

Franzmann, M. "The City as Woman: The Case of Babylon in Isaiah 47." *ABR* 43 (1995): 1–19.

Freire, Paulo, *Education for Critical Consciousness.* New York: Continuum, 1994.

—*Pedagogy of the Oppressed.* New York: Continuum, 1992.

Frey, Christopher. "The Impact of the Biblical Idea of Justice on Present Discussions of Social Justice." Pages 91–104 in Reventlow and Hoffman, eds., *Justice and Righteousness.*

Frolov, Serge. "Returning the Ticket: God and his Prophet in the Book of Jonah." *JSOT* 86 (1999): 85–105.

Frye, Northrop. *The Double Vision: Language and Meaning in Religion.* Toronto: United Church Publishing, 1991.

Fuchs, Ernst. *Hermeneutik.* Tübingen: Mohr, 1970.

Fuentes, Carlos. *The Years with Laura Díaz.* London: Bloomsbury, 2001.

Gadamer, Hans-Georg. *Truth and Method.* Translated by Garrett Barden and John Cumming. London: Sheed & Ward, 1975. First published 1960 as *Wahrheit und Methode.* Tübingen: J. C. B. Mohr.

Gammie, J. G. *Holiness in Israel.* OBT. Minneapolis: Fortress, 1989.

Garbini, Giovanni. *History and Ideology in Ancient Israel.* Repr. Xpress Reprints. London: SCM Press, 1997.

Geller, Stephen A. "Were the Prophets Poets?" *Prooftexts* 3 (1983): 211–21.

George, Sherron Kay. "From Liberation to Evangelization: New Latin American Hermeneutical Keys." *Int* 55, no. 4 (2001): 367–77.

George, Susan. *A Fate Worse than Debt.* London: Penguin, 1988.

Girard, René. "Job as Failed Scapegoat." Pages 185–207 in Perdue and Gilpin, eds., *The Voice from the Whirlwind.*

Gitay, Yehoshua. *Isaiah and his Audience: The Structure and Meaning of Isaiah 1–12.* Assen: Van Gorcum, 1991.

—*Prophecy and Persuasion: A Study of Isaiah 40–48.* FTL 14. Bonn: Linguistica Biblica, 1981.

—"Prophetic Criticism—'What are they Doing?': The Case of Isaiah—A Methodological Assessment." *JSOT* 96 (2001): 101–27.

—"Reflections on the Study of the Prophetic Discourse: The Question of Isaiah 1:2–20." *VT* 33 (1983): 207–21.

Glicksberg, Charles S. *The Ironic Vision in Modern Literature.* The Hague: Martinus Nijhoff, 1969.

Gnuse, Robert. *No Other Gods: Emergent Monotheism in Israel.* JSOTSup 241. Sheffield: Sheffield Academic Press, 1997.

Goldingay, John. "How Far Do Readers Make Sense? Interpreting Biblical Narrative." Pages 172–89 in Trueman, Gray, and Blomberg, eds., *Solid Ground.*

—*Isaiah.* NIBCOT. Peabody, Mass.: Hendrickson; Carlisle: Paternoster, 2001.

—"Isaiah i 1 and ii 1." *VT* 48 (1998): 326–32.

—"Isaiah 40–55 in the 1990s: Among Other Things, Deconstructing, Mystifying, Intertextual, Socio-critical, and Hearer-Involving." *BibInt* 5, no. 3 (1997): 225–46.

—*Theological Diversity and the Authority of the Old Testament.* Carlisle: Paternoster, 1995.

—"What Happens to Ms Babylon in Isaiah 47, Why, and Who Says So?" *TynBul* 47 (1996): 215–43.

Good, Edwin M. *Irony in the Old Testament.* Philadelphia: Westminster, 1965.

Gordis, Robert. *The Book of God and Man: A Study of Job.* Chicago: University of Chicago Press, 1965.

—*Poets, Prophets, and Sages: Essays in Biblical Interpretation.* Bloomington: Indiana University Press, 1971.

Gossai, Hemchand. *Justice, Righteousness, and the Social Critique of the Eighth-Century Prophets.* New York: Peter Lang, 1993.

Gottwald, Norman K. "Tragedy and Comedy in the Latter Prophets." *Semeia* 32 (1984): 83–96.

Gottwald, Norman K., and Richard A. Horsley, eds. *The Bible and Liberation: Political and Social Hermeneutics.* Rev. ed. Maryknoll, N.Y.: Orbis; London: SPCK, 1993.

Gowan, Donald E. "Wealth and Poverty in the Old Testament: The Case of the Widow, the Orphan, and the Sojourner." *Int* 41 (1987): 341–53.

Grabbe, Lester L., ed. *Leading Captivity Captive: The Exile as History and Ideology.* JSOTSup 278. Sheffield: Sheffield Academic Press, 1998.

Graff, Gerald. *Literature against Itself: Literary Ideas in Modern Society.* Chicago: University of Chicago Press, 1979.

Gray, George Buchanan. *A Critical and Exegetical Commentary on the Book of Isaiah.* 2 vols. Edinburgh: T. & T. Clark, 1912.

Gray, Mark. "Amnon: A Chip Off the Old Block? Rhetorical Strategy in 2 Samuel 13:7–15, the Rape of Tamar, and the Humiliation of the Poor." *JSOT* 77 (1998): 39–54.

—"La búsqueda de justicia con reconciliación: La rhetórica de Isaías 58, 6–10." *Revista Bíblica* 65, nos. 1–2 (2003): 41–62.

—Review of Peter D. Miscall, *Isaiah 34–35: A Nightmare/A Dream. Themelios* 25, no. 2 (2000): 71–72.

Green, Garrett. *Theology, Hermeneutics, and Imagination: The Crisis of Interpretation at the End of Modernity.* Cambridge: Cambridge University Press, 2000.

Greenblatt, Stephen. "Resonance and Wonder." Pages 74–90 in Collier and Geyer-Ryan, eds., *Literary Theory Today.*

Groothuis, Douglas. *Truth Decay: Defending Christianity against the Challenges of Postmodernism.* Downers Grove, Ill.: InterVarsity, 2000.

Gross, Jan T. *Neighbors: The Destruction of the Jewish Community at Jedwabne, Poland.* Princeton: Princeton University Press, 2001.

Groves, Joseph W. *Actualization and Interpretation in the Old Testament.* Atlanta: Scholars Press, 1987.

Gunn, David M. *The Fate of King Saul: An Interpretation of a Biblical Story.* JSOTSup 14. Sheffield: JSOT Press, 1980.

—"New Directions in the Study of Biblical Hebrew Narrative." *JSOT* 39 (1987): 65–75.

—*The Story of King David: Genre and Interpretation.* JSOTSup 6. Sheffield: JSOT Press, 1978.

Gunn, David M., and Danna N. Fewell. *Narrative in the Hebrew Bible.* London: Oxford University Press, 1993.

Gunton, Colin. "Trinity and Trustworthiness." Pages 275–84 in Helm and Trueman, eds., *The Trustworthiness of God.*

Gutiérrez, Gustavo. "Option for the Poor." Pages 22–37 in *Systematic Theology: Perspectives from Liberation Theology.* Edited by Jon Sobrino and Ignacio Ellacuria. London: SCM Press, 1996.

—*The Power of the Poor in History.* London: SCM Press, 1983.

—"A Preferential Option for the Poor." Pages 193–95 in *Classic Texts in Mission and World Christianity.* Edited by Norman E. Thomas. American Society of Missiology Series 20. Maryknoll, N.Y.: Orbis, 1995 (Also published as *Readings in World Mission.* London: SPCK, 1995.)

—*A Theology of Liberation: History, Politics, and Salvation.* Translated and edited by Sister Caridad Inda and John Eagleson. London: SCM Press, 1974.

—*We Drink from Our Own Wells: The Spiritual Journey of a People.* London: SCM Press, 1984.

Habel, Norman C. *The Book of Job: A Commentary.* OTL. London: SCM Press, 1985.

Habermas, Jürgen. *The Philosophical Discourse of Modernity: Twelve Lectures.* Translated by Frederick Lawrence. Cambridge, Mass.: Polity, 1987.

Handelman, Susan. *The Slayers of Moses: Emergence of Rabbinic Interpretation in Modern Literary Theory.* Albany, N.Y.: SUNY Press, 1982.

Hanson, Paul D. *The Dawn of Apocalyptic: The Historical and Sociological Roots of Jewish Apocalyptic Eschatology.* Philadelphia: Fortress, 1975.

—*Isaiah 40–66.* Interpretation. Louisville, Ky.: John Knox, 1995.

Harris, R. Laird, Gleason L. Archer Jr., and Bruce K. Waltke, eds. *Theological Wordbook of the Old Testament.* 2 vols. Chicago: Moody Press, 1980.

Harrisville, Roy A. "What I Believe My Old Schoolmate is Up To." Pages 7–25 in *Theological Exegesis: Essays in Honor of Brevard S. Childs.* Edited by Christopher R. Seitz and Kathryn Greene-McCreight. Grand Rapids: Eerdmans, 1999.

Hart, Kevin. *The Trespass of the Sign: Deconstruction, Theology, and Philosophy.* Cambridge: Cambridge University Press, 1989.

Hartman, G. H. "The Struggle for the Text." Pages 3–18 in *Midrash and Literature.* Edited by G. H. Hartman and S. Budick. New Haven: Yale University Press, 1986.

Heaney, Seamus. *The Cure at Troy: A Version of Sophocles's "Philoctetes."* London: Faber & Faber in association with Field Day, 1990.

Hecht, F. "Die Interpretasie van Jes. 54:7a." *NGTT* 4 (1963): 117–19.

Helm, Paul, and Carl Trueman, eds., *The Trustworthiness of God: Perspectives on the Nature of Scripture.* Leicester: Apollos, 2002.

Hendel, Ronald S. "The Social Origins of the Aniconic Tradition." *CBQ* 50 (1988): 365–82.

Heschel, Abraham J. *The Prophets.* 2 vols. New York: Harper & Row, 1962.

—"No Religion is an Island." Pages 3–22 in *No Religion is an Island: Abraham Joshua Heschel and Interreligious Dialogue.* Edited by Harold Kasimow and Byron L. Sherwin. Maryknoll, N.Y.: Orbis, 1991.

Hirsch, David. *The Deconstruction of Literature: Criticism after Auschwitz.* Providence, R.I.: Brown University Press, 1991.

Hirsch, E. D. Jr. *Validity in Interpretation.* New Haven: Yale University Press, 1967.

Hobbs, T. R. "Hospitality in the First Testament and the 'Teleological Fallacy.'" *JSOT* 95 (2001): 3–30.

Hodgson, Peter C. *God in History: Shapes of Freedom.* Nashville: Abingdon, 1989.

Hoffmann, Hans Werner. *Die Intention der Verkündigung Jesajas.* BZAW 136; Berlin: de Gruyter, 1974.

Holladay, W. L. "The Crux in Isaiah 1:4–6." *VT* 33 (1983): 235–37.

—"Isaiah 3:10–11: An Archaic Wisdom Passage." *VT* 18 (1968): 481–87.

Hollenberg, D. E. "Nationalism and 'the Nations' in Isaiah XL–LV." *VT* 19 (1969): 21–36.

Holmgren, Fredrick. *With Wings as Eagles: Isaiah 40/50—An Interpretation.* Chappaqua, N.Y.: Biblical Scholars Press, 1973.

Hoppe, Leslie J. "Isaiah 58:1–12." *BTB* 13 (1983): 44–47.

Horner, Winifred Bryan. *The Present State of Scholarship in Historical and Contemporary Rhetoric.* Columbia: University of Missouri Press, 1990.

Houston, Walter. "Tragedy in the Courts of the Lord: A Socio-literary Reading of the Death of Nadab and Abihu." *JSOT* 90 (2000): 31–39.

Huddleston, Trevor. *Naught for Your Comfort.* Glasgow: Collins, 1956.

Hunter, A. Vanlier. *Seek the Lord! A Study of the Meaning and Function of the Exhortations in Amos, Hosea, Isaiah, Micah, and Zephaniah.* Baltimore: St. Mary's Seminary and University, 1982.

Hunter, Jannie. "The Song of Protest: Reassessing the Song of Songs." *JSOT* 90 (2000): 109–24.

Irvine, S. A. "The Isaianic Denkschrift: Reconsidering an Old Hypothesis." *ZAW* 104 (1992): 216–31.

Ishiguro, Kazuo. *Remains of the Day.* London: Faber & Faber, 1989.

Jablès, Edmond. *The Book of Margins.* Translated by R. Waldrop. Chicago: University of Chicago Press, 1993.

Jackson, Ben. *Poverty and the Planet: A Question of Survival.* World Development Movement. Harmondsworth: Penguin, 1990.

Jameson, Fredric. "The Politics of Theory: Ideological Positions in the Postmodernism Debate." Pages 373–83 in Lodge, ed., *Modern Criticism and Theory.*

Janzen, Waldemar. *Old Testament Ethics: A Paradigmatic Approach.* Louisville, Ky.: Westminster John Knox, 1994.

Jeanrond, Werner. *Theological Hermeneutics: Development and Significance.* London: SCM Press, 1991.

Jeffrey, David Lyle. *People of the Book: Christian Identity and Literary Culture.* Grand Rapids: Eerdmans, with the Institute for Advanced Christian Studies, 1996.

Jenkins, David. *Market Whys and Human Wherefores: Thinking Again about Markets, Politics, and People.* London: Continuum, 2000.

Jobling, David. "Globalization in Biblical Studies/Biblical Studies in Globalization." *BibInt* 1, no. 1 (1993): 96–110.

—"Writing the Wrongs of the World: The Deconstruction of the Biblical Text in the Context of Liberation Theologies." *Semeia* 51 (1990): 81–118.

Johnson, Barbara. "The Surprise of Otherness: A Note on the Wartime Writings of Paul de Man." Pages 13–22 in Collier and Geyer-Ryan, eds., *Literary Theory Today.*

Johnson, William Stacy. "Rethinking Theology: A Postmodern, Post-Holocaust, Post-Christendom Endeavour." *Int* 55 (January 2001): 5–18.

Kaiser, Otto. *Isaiah 1–12: A Commentary.* Translated by John Bowden. 1983. OTL. 2d ed., London: SCM Press, 1996.

—*Isaiah 13–39.* Translated by R. A. Wilson. OTL. London: SCM Press, 1974.

Karpin, Michael, and Ina Friedman. *Murder in the Name of God: The Plot to Kill Yitzhak Rabin.* London: Granta, 1999.

Katz, Ronald C. *The Structure of Ancient Arguments: Rhetoric and its Near Eastern Origin.* New York: Shapolsky/Steinmatzky, 1977.

Kierkegaard, Søren. *Fear and Trembling.* Translated by Walter Lowrie. New York: Anchor Books, 1954.

Kim, Kirsteen. "Missiology as Global Conversation of (Contextual) Theologies." Research paper, Queen's Foundation, Birmingham, England, October 2002.

Kingsolver, Barbara. *The Poisonwood Bible—A Novel.* New York: Harper Perennial, 1999.

Kissane, Edward J. *The Book of Isaiah.* 2 vols. Dublin: Richview Press, 1941–43.

Knierim, Rolf P. *The Task of Old Testament Theology: Substance, Method, and Cases.* Grand Rapids: Eerdmans, 1995.

Knight, George A. F. *Isaiah 56–66: The New Israel.* ITC. Grand Rapids: Eerdmans; Edinburgh: Handsel, 1985.

Knox, Norman. "On the Classification of Irony." *Modern Philology* 70 (1972): 53–62.

Koch, Klaus. "Origin and Effect of Social Critique of the Pre-exilic Prophets." *Bangalore Theological Forum* 11 (1979): 91–108.

—*The Prophets: The Assyrian Period.* 2 vols. London: SCM Press, 1982.

—*The Prophets: The Babylonian and Persian Periods.* Vol. 2. London: SCM Press, 1983.

Kohrs Campbell, Karlyn, and Kathleen Hall Jamieson, eds. *Form and Genre: Shaping Rhetorical Action.* Falls Church, Va.: Speech Communication Association, 1976.

Koole, Jan L. *Isaiah.* Part 3, Vol. 1, *Isaiah 40–48.* Kampen: Kok Pharos, 1997.

Kosmala, H. "Form and Structure of Isaiah 58." *ASTI* 5 (1967): 69–81.

Koyama, Kosuke. *Mount Fuji and Mount Sinai: A Pilgrimage in Theology.* London: SCM Press, 1984.

Krieger, David J. *The New Universalism: Foundations for a Global Theology.* Maryknoll, N.Y.: Orbis, 1991.

Kristeva, Julia. *Desire in Language: A Semiotic Approach to Literature and Art.* Edited by Leon S. Roudiez. New York: Columbia University Press, 1980.

Küng, Hans. *A Global Ethic for Global Politics and Economics.* London: SCM Press, 1997.

—*Global Responsibility: In Search of a New World Ethic.* London: SCM Press, 1991.

Kvanig, Helge S. "Theology of the Scream: The Violator and Violated in the Biblical Tradition." *Ecumenical Review* 45 (July 1993): 328–36.

Laato, Antti. *About Zion I Will Not Be Silent: The Book of Isaiah as an Ideological Unity.* CB 44. Stockholm: Almqvist & Wiksell, 1998.

—"The Composition of Isaiah 40–55." *JBL* 109 (1990): 207–28.

Labahn, Antje. "The Delay of Salvation within Deutero-Isaiah." *JSOT* 85 (1999): 71–84.

Labuschange, C. B. *The Incomparability of Yahweh in the Old Testament.* Leiden: Brill, 1966.

Laird, Lance D. "Meeting Jesus Again in the First Place: Palestinian Christians and the Bible." *Int* 55, no. 4 (2001): 400–12.

Lamb, M. L. *Solidarity with Victims: Toward a Theology of Social Transformation.* New York: Crossroad, 1982.

Landy, Francis. "Strategies of Concentration and Diffusion in Isaiah 6." *BibInt* 7, no. 1 (1999): 58–86.

—"Vision and Voice in Isaiah." *JSOT* 88 (2000): 19–36.

Lang, B. *Monotheism and the Prophetic Minority: An Essay in Biblical History and Sociology.* The Social World of Biblical Antiquity 1. Sheffield: Almond, 1983.

—"Prophetie, prophetische Zeichenhandlung und Politik in Israel." *TQ* 161 (1981): 273–80.

—"Street Theatre, Raising the Dead, and the Zoroastrian Connection in Ezekiel's Prophecy." Pages 297–316 in *Ezekiel and His Book*. Edited by Johan Lust. BETL 74. Louvain: Peeters, 1986.

Lasine, Stuart. "Bird's-Eye and Worm's-Eye Views of Justice in the Book of Job." *JSOT* 42 (1988): 29–53.

Lawrence, D. H. *Phoenix II: Uncollected, Unpublished, and Other Prose Work by D. H. Lawrence*. Edited by Warren Roberts and Harry T. Moore. London: Heinemann, 1968.

—*Selected Literary Criticism*. Edited by Anthony Beal. London: Heinemann, 1956.

—*Studies in Classic American Literature*. London: Penguin in association with William Heinemann, 1971 (1923).

Laytner, Anson. *Arguing with God: A Jewish Tradition*. Northvale, N.J.: Aronson, 1990.

Leclerc, Thomas L. *Yahweh is Exalted in Justice: Solidarity and Conflict in Isaiah*. Minneapolis: Fortress, 2001.

Lee, Nancy C. "Genocide's Lament: Moses, Pharaoh's Daughter, and the Former Yugoslavia." Pages 66–82 in Linafelt and Beal, eds., *God in the Fray*.

Legrand, Lucien. *Unity and Plurality: Mission in the Bible*. Translated by Robert R. Barr. Maryknoll, N.Y.: Orbis, 1990.

Letts, Janna, and Fiona Whythead, eds. *Captured Voices*. London: Indigo, 2000.

Levenson, Jon D. *Creation and the Persistence of Evil: The Jewish Drama of Divine Omnipotence*. Princeton: Princeton University Press, 1988.

—*The Death and Resurrection of the Beloved Son: The Transformation of Child Sacrifice in Judaism and Christianity*. New Haven: Yale University Press, 1993.

—*The Hebrew Bible, the Old Testament, and Historical Criticism: Jews and Christians in Biblical Studies*. Louisville, Ky.: Westminster John Knox, 1993.

—"The Jerusalem Temple in Devotional and Visionary Experience." Pages 32–61 in vol. 1 of *Jewish Spirituality*. Edited by Arthur Green. 2 vols. London: SCM Press, 1985.

Linafelt, Tod. *Surviving Lamentations: Catastrophe, Lament, and Protest in the Afterlife of a Biblical Book*. Chicago: University of Chicago Press, 2000.

—"Taking Women: Readers/Responses/Responsibility in Samuel." Pages 99–113 in *Reading between Texts: Intertextuality and the Hebrew Bible*. Edited by Danna Nolan Fewell. LCBI. Louisville, Ky.: Westminster John Knox, 1992

—"The Undecidability of ברך in the Prologue to Job and Beyond." *BibInt* 4, no. 2 (1996): 154–72.

Linafelt, Tod, and Timothy K. Beal, eds. *God in the Fray: A Tribute to Walter Brueggemann*. Minneapolis: Fortress, 1998.

Lind, Michael. *Vietnam: The Necessary War*. New York: Free Press, 2000.

Lind, Millard C. "Monotheism, Power, and Justice: A Study in Isaiah 40–55." *CBQ* 46 (1984): 432–46.

Lindsay, Hal. *The Late Great Planet Earth*. Grand Rapids: Zondervan, 1970.

Lindström, Fredrik. *Suffering and Sin: Interpretations of Illness in the Individual Complaint Psalms*. Stockholm: Almqvist & Wiksell, 1994.

Locke, Jason W. "The Wrath of God in the Book of Isaiah." *Restoration Quarterly* 35, no. 4 (1993): 221–33.

Lodahl, M. *Shekhinah Spirit: Divine Presence in Jewish and Christian Religion*. New York: Paulist, 1992.

Lodge, David, ed. *Modern Criticism and Theory: A Reader*. London: Longman, 1988.

Lohfink, N. "The Present and Eternity: Time in Qoheleth," *Theology Digest* 34 (1987): 236–40

Longman, T., III, and D. G. Reid. *God is a Warrior.* Grand Rapids: Eerdmans, 1995.

Lüdemann, Gerd. *Heretics: The Other Side of Early Christianity.* London: SCM Press, 1996.

—*The Unholy in Holy Scripture: The Dark Side of the Bible.* London: SCM Press, 1996.

Lundin, Roger. "Interpreting Orphans: Hermeneutics in the Cartesian Tradition." Pages 1–64 in Lundin, Walhout, and Thiselton, eds., *The Promise of Hermeneutics.*

—ed. *Disciplining Hermeneutics: Interpretation in Christian Perspective.* Grand Rapids: Eerdmans; Leicester: Apollos, 1997.

Lundin, Roger, Clarence Walhout, and Anthony C. Thiselton, eds. *The Promise of Hermeneutics.* Grand Rapids: Eerdmans; Cambridge: Paternoster, 1999.

Lurje, M. *Studien zur Geschichte der wirtschaftlichen und sozialen Verhältnisse in israelitisch-jüdischen Exil.* BZAW 45. Giessen: Töpelmann, 1927.

Lyotard, Jean-François. *The Differend: Phrases in Dispute.* Translated by Georges Van Den Abbeele. Manchester: Manchester University Press, 1988.

—*The Postmodern Condition: A Report on Knowledge.* Translated by Geoff Bennington and Brian Massumi. Theory and History of Literature 10. Minneapolis: University of Minnesota Press, 1999.

Macherey, Pierre. *A Theory of Literary Production.* Translated by Geoffrey Wall. London: Routledge & Kegan Paul, 1978.

Mackie, Robert, ed. *Literacy and Revolution: The Pedagogy of Paulo Freire.* New York: Continuum, 1981.

Mafico, T. L. J. "The Divine Compound Name Yahweh Elohim and Israel's Monotheistic Polytheism." *Journal of Northwest Semitic Languages* 22, no. 1 (1996): 155–73.

Magonet, Jonathan. *A Rabbi's Bible.* London: SCM Press, 1991.

Mahon, Derek. "The Sea in Winter." Page 111 in idem, *Poems, 1962–1978.*

—"Beyond Howth Head." Page 52 in idem, *Poems, 1962–1978.*

—*Poems, 1962–1978.* Oxford: Oxford University Press, 1979.

—"Rage for Order." Page 44 in idem, *Poems, 1962–1978.*

Mailloux, Steven. *Reception Histories: Rhetoric, Pragmatism, and American Cultural Politics.* Ithaca, N.Y.: Cornell University Press, 1998.

—*Rhetorical Power.* Ithaca, N.Y.: Cornell University Press, 1989.

Man, Paul de, "Semiology and Rhetoric." Pages 121–40 in *Textual Strategies: Perspectives in Post-structuralist Criticism.* Edited by Josué V. Harari. London: Methuen, 1980.

Martin-Achard, R. *A Light to the Nations.* Edinburgh: T. & T. Clark, 1962.

Marty, Martin. "America's Iconic Book." Pages 1–23 in *Humanizing America's Iconic Book.* Edited by Gene M. Tucker and Douglas A. Knight. Chico, Calif.: Scholars Press, 1982.

McDonagh, Sean. *The Greening of the Church.* Maryknoll, N.Y.: Orbis; London: Geoffrey Chapman, 1990.

McGrath, Alister E. *The Genesis of Doctrine: A Study in the Foundation of Doctrinal Criticism.* Grand Rapids: Eerdmans, 1990.

McKeating, Henry *Ezekiel.* OTG. Sheffield: Sheffield Academic Press, 1993.

McKenzie, John L. *Second Isaiah: Introduction, Translation, and Notes.* AB 20. Garden City, N.Y.: Doubleday, 1968.

Melugin, Roy F. "Figurative Speech and the Reading of Isaiah 1 as Scripture." Pages 282–305 in Melugin and Sweeney, eds., *New Visions of Isaiah.*

—"Isaiah in the Worshipping Community." Pages 244–64 in *Worship and the Hebrew Bible: Essays in Honour of John T. Willis*. Edited by Matt Patrick Graham, Rick R. Marrs, and Steven L. McKenzie. Sheffield: Sheffield Academic Press, 1999.

Melugin, Roy F., and Marvin A. Sweeney, eds. *New Visions of Isaiah*. JSOTSup 214. Sheffield: Sheffield Academic Press, 1996.

Mesters, Carlos. *Defenseless Flower: A New Reading of the Bible*. Translated by Francis McDonagh. Maryknoll, N.Y.: Orbis; London: Catholic Institute for International Relations, 1989.

—"The Use of the Bible among the Common People." Pages 78–92 in *Ministry by the People: Theological Education by Extension*. Edited by F. Ross Kinsler. Geneva: WCC Publications; Maryknoll, N.Y.: Orbis, 1983.

—"Use of the Bible in Christian Communities of the Common People." Pages 3–16 in Gottwald and Horsley, eds., *The Bible and Liberation*.

Mettinger, Tryggve N. D. "The God of Job: Avenger, Tyrant, or Victor?" Pages 39–49 in Perdue and Gilpin, eds., *The Voice from the Whirlwind*.

Meynet, Roland. *Rhetorical Analysis*. JSOTSup 256. Sheffield: Sheffield Academic Press, 1998.

Michel, D. "Zur Eigenart Tritojesajas." *Theologica Viatorum* 10 (1965–66): 213–30.

Miles, Jack. *God: A Biography*. New York: Knopf, 1995.

Millar, J. Gary. *Now Choose Life: Theology and Ethics in Deuteronomy*. Leicester: Apollos, 1998.

Miller, Patrick D. *The Divine Warrior in Early Israel*. Cambridge: Cambridge University Press, 1973.

—"Prayer and Divine Action." Pages 211–32 in Linafelt and Beal, eds., *God in the Fray*.

—*They Cried to the Lord: The Form and Theology of Biblical Prayer*. Minneapolis: Fortress, 1994.

Milton, J. "Paradise Lost." In *The Portable Milton*. Edited by Douglas Bush. Harmondsworth: Penguin, 1977.

Miscall, Peter D. *Isaiah*. Readings: A New Biblical Commentary. Sheffield: JSOT Press, 1993.

—*Isaiah 34–35: A Nightmare/A Dream*. JSOTSup 281. Sheffield: Sheffield Academic Press, 1999.

—"Isaiah: Dreams and Nightmares, Fantasy and Horror." *Journal of the Fantastic in the Arts* 8 (1997): 151–69.

—"Isaiah: The Labyrinth of Images." *Semeia* 54 (1991): 103–21.

Moltmann, Jürgen. *Theology of Hope*. London: SCM Press, 1967.

Monbiot, George. *The Age of Consent: A Manifesto for a New World Order*. London: Flamingo, 2003.

Moor, Johannes C. de, *The Rise of Yahwism: The Roots of Israelite Monotheism*. BETL 91. Louvain: Louvain University Press, 1990.

—ed. *Synchronic or Diachronic? A Debate on Method in Old Testament Exegesis*. Leiden: Brill, 1995.

Moore-Lappé, Frances, et al. *World Hunger—Twelve Myths*. London: Earthscan, 1998.

More, Thomas. *Utopia*. London: Penguin, 1965.

Mosala, Itumeleng J. *Biblical Hermeneutics and Black Theology in South Africa*. Grand Rapids: Eerdmans, 1989.

Motyer, Alec. *The Prophecy of Isaiah*. Leicester: InterVarsity, 1993.

Muecke, Douglas C. *The Compass of Irony*. London: Methuen, 1969.

—*Irony*. London: Methuen, 1970.

Muilenburg, James. "The Book of Isaiah, Chapters 40–66." Pages 381–773 in vol. 5 of *The Interpreter's Bible*. Edited by G. A. Buttrick et al. 12 vols. New York: Abingdon-Cokesbury, 1951–57.

—*The Way of Israel: Biblical Faith and Ethics*. New York: Harper & Row, 1961.

Müller, Karl, et al., eds. *Dictionary of Mission: Theology, History, Perspectives*. Maryknoll, N.Y.: Orbis, 1999.

Murray, Robert. "Prophecy and Cult." Pages 200–16 in Coggins, Phillips, and Knibb, eds., *Israel's Prophetic Tradition*.

Nakanose, Shigeyuki. *Josiah's Passover: Sociology and the Liberating Bible*. Maryknoll, N.Y.: Orbis, 1993.

Neal, Marie Augusta. *The Just Demands of the Poor: Essays in Socio-Theology*. New York: Paulist, 1987.

Neely, A. "Mission as Kenosis: Implications for Our Times." *Princeton Seminary Bulletin* 10, no. 3 (1989): 202–22.

Newbigin, Lesslie. *The Other Side of 1984: Questions for the Churches*. Geneva: WCC Publications, 1983.

Niditch, Susan. *War in the Hebrew Bible: A Study in the Ethics of Violence*. Oxford: Oxford University Press, 1993.

Noll, K. L. "Is there a Text in this Tradition? Readers' Response and the Taming of Samuel's God." *JSOT* 83 (1999): 31–51.

Norris, Christopher. *Deconstruction*. Rev. ed. London: Routledge, 2002.

Nürnberger, Klaus. *Prosperity, Poverty, and Pollution: Managing the Approaching Crisis*. Pietermaritzburg, South Africa: Cluster; London: Zed Books, 1999.

O'Connell, Robert H. *Concentricity and Continuity: The Literary Structure of Isaiah*. JSOTSup 188. Sheffield: Sheffield Academic Press, 1994.

O'Connor, Kathleen M. *Lamentations and the Tears of the World*. Maryknoll, N.Y.: Orbis, 2002.

—"The Tears of God and Divine Character in Jeremiah 2–9." Pages 172–85 in Linafelt and Beal, eds., *God in the Fray*

Ord, David Robert, and Robert B. Coote. *Is the Bible True? Understanding the Bible Today*. London: SCM Press, 1994.

Orlinsky, H., and N. H. Snaith, eds. *Studies on the Second Part of the Book of Isaiah*. VTSup 14. Leiden: Brill, 1977.

Orwell, George. *Homage to Catalonia*. Harmondsworth: Penguin, 1977 (1938).

Oswalt, J. N. *The Book of Isaiah: Chapters 1–39*. NICOT. Grand Rapids: Eerdmans, 1986.

—*The Book of Isaiah: Chapters 40–66*. NICOT. Grand Rapids: Eerdmans, 1998.

—"Righteousness in Isaiah: A Study of the Function of Chapters 56–66 in the Present Structure of the Book." Pages 177–91 in vol. 1 of Broyles and Evans, eds., *Writing and Reading the Scroll of Isaiah*.

Otto, Rudolph. *The Idea of the Holy*. Translated by J. W. Harvey. Oxford: Oxford University Press, 1950.

Packer, James. "Hermeneutics and Biblical Authority." Pages 137–54 in Trueman, Gray, and Blomberg, eds., *Solid Ground*.

Patrick, Dale. *The Rhetoric of Revelation in the Hebrew Bible*. OBT. Minneapolis: Fortress, 1999.

Patrick, Dale, and Allen Scult. *Rhetoric and Biblical Interpretation*. JSOTSup 82. Sheffield: Almond, 1990.

Patte, Daniel. *Ethics of Biblical Interpretation: A Reevaluation.* Louisville, Ky.: Westminster John Knox, 1995.

Paul, Shalom M. "Polysensuous Polyvalency in Poetic Parallelism." Pages 147–63 in *Sha'arei Talmon Studies in the Bible, Qumran, and the Ancient Near East: Presented to Shemaryahu Talmon.* Edited by Michael Fishbane and Emanuel Tov with the assistance of Weston W. Fields. Winona Lake, Ind.: Eisenbrauns, 1992.

Pauritsch, K. *Die neue Gemeinde: Gott sammelt Ausgestossene und Arme (Jesaia 56–66).* AnBib 47. Rome: Biblical Institute Press, 1971.

Pawlikowski, J. T. *Christ in the Light of the Christian–Jewish Dialogue.* New York: Paulist, 1982.

Perdue, Leo G. *The Collapse of History.* OBT. Minneapolis: Fortress, 1994.

Perdue, Leo G., and W. Clark Gilpin, eds. *The Voice from the Whirlwind: Interpreting the Book of Job.* Nashville: Abingdon, 1992.

Pfeiffer, Robert. "The Dual Origin of Hebrew Monotheism." *JBL* 46 (1927): 193–206.

Phillips, Anthony. "Double for All Her Sins." *ZAW* 94 (1982): 130–32.

—"Prophecy and Law." Pages 217–32 in Coggins, Phillips, and Knibb, eds., *Israel's Prophetic Tradition.*

Pitstock, Catherine. *After Writing: On the Liturgical Consummation of Philosophy.* Oxford: Blackwell, 1998.

Pleins, J. David. "Poverty in the Social World of the Wise." *JSOT* 37 (1987): 61–78.

—*Social Visions of the Hebrew Bible: A Theological Introduction.* Louisville, Ky.: Westminster John Knox, 2001.

Plett, Heinrich. *Einführung in die rhetorische Textanalyse.* 3d ed. Hamburg: Buske, 1975.

—*Rhetorik der Affekte: Englische Wirkungsästhetik im Zeitalter der Renaissance.* Tübingen: M. Niemeyer, 1975.

Plöger, Otto. *Theocracy and Eschatology.* Oxford: Blackwell, 1968.

Pohier, Jacques. *God in Fragments.* Translated by John Bowden. London: SCM Press, 1985.

—*Quand je dis Dieu.* Paris: Éditions du Seuil, 1977.

Polan, Gregory. *In the Ways of Justice toward Salvation: A Rhetorical Analysis of Isaiah 56–59.* American University Studies, ser. 7, vol. 13. New York: Peter Lang, 1986.

Prior, Michael. *The Bible and Colonialism: A Moral Critique.* The Biblical Seminar 48. Sheffield: Sheffield Academic Press, 1997.

—*Jesus the Liberator: Nazareth Liberation Theology (Luke 4.16–30).* The Biblical Seminar 26. Sheffield: Sheffield Academic Press, 1995.

Pritchard, J. B., ed. *Ancient Near Eastern Texts.* 3d ed. Princeton: Princeton University Press, 1969.

Procksch, O. *Jesaja I: Kapitel 1–39 übersetzt und erklärt.* KAT 9. Leipzig: Deichert, 1930.

Propp, William H. C. *Exodus 1–18: A New Translation with Introduction and Commentary.* AB 2. New York: Doubleday, 1999.

Quayson, Ato. *Postcolonialism: Theory, Practice, or Process?* Cambridge, Mass.: Polity, 2000.

Rabinowitz, Isaac. "Pre-modern Jewish Study of Rhetoric: An Introductory Bibliography." *Rhetorica* 3 (1985): 137–44.

Reed, W. L. *Dialogues of the Word: The Bible as Literature according to Bakhtin.* New York: Oxford University Press, 1993.

Reid, Loren D. "The Perils of Rhetoric Criticism." *The Quarterly Journal of Speech* 30 (1944): 416–22.

Renaud, B. "La critique prophetique de l'attitude d'Israel face aux nations: Quelques jalons." *Concilium* 220 (1988): 43–53.

Rendtorff, Rolf. *Canon and Theology: Overtures to an Old Testament Theology.* OBT. Minneapolis: Fortress, 1993.

Reston, James, Jr. *Warriors of God: Richard the Lionheart and Saladin in the Third Crusade.* London: Faber & Faber, 2001.

Reventlow, Henning Graf, and Yair Hoffman, eds. *Justice and Righteousness: Biblical Themes and their Influence.* JSOTSup 137. Sheffield: JSOT Press, 1992.

Richard, L. *Christ: The Self-Emptying of God.* New York: Paulist, 1997.

Ricoeur, Paul. "Biblical Hermeneutics." *Semeia* 4 (1975): 23–148.

—*Hermeneutics and the Human Sciences.* Edited and translated by John B. Thompson. Cambridge: Cambridge University Press, 1998.

—*Interpretation Theory: Discourse and the Surplus of Meaning.* Fort Worth: Texas Christian University Press, 1976.

—*A Ricoeur Reader: Reflection and Imagination.* Edited by Mario Valdés. New York: Harvester-Wheatsheaf, 1991.

—"Toward a Hermeneutic of the Idea of Revelation." Pages 73–118 in *Essays on Biblical Interpretation.* Edited by Lewis S. Mudge. Philadelphia: Fortress, 1980.

Rignell, L. G. "Isaiah Chapter 1: Some Exegetical Remarks with Special Reference to the Relationship between the Text and the Book of Deuteronomy." *Studia Theologica* 11 (1958): 140–58.

Robinson, John A. T. *Honest to God.* London: SCM Press, 1963.

Rodd, Cyril S. *Glimpses of a Strange Land: Studies in Old Testament Ethics.* Edinburgh: T. & T. Clark, 2001.

Rodney, Walter. *How Europe Underdeveloped Africa.* Washington, D.C.: Howard University Press, 1982.

Rodriquez, Maria Arlinda, and Heloise da Cunha. "Living with the Poor in Brazil." Pages 216–25 in *Trends in Mission toward the Third Millennium.* Edited by William Jenkinson and Helene O'Sullivan. Maryknoll, N.Y.: Orbis, 1993.

Rofé, A. "Isaiah 64:1–4: Judean Sects in the Persian Period as Viewed by Trito-Isaiah." Pages 205–17 in *Biblical and Related Studies Presented to Samuel Iwry.* Edited by A. Kort and S. Morschauser. Winona Lake, Ind.: Eisenbrauns, 1985.

Romero, Oscar. *Voice of the Voiceless.* Translated by Donald Walsh. Maryknoll, N.Y.: Orbis, 1985.

Rosenberg, Roy A. "Yahweh Becomes King." *JBL* 85, no. 3 (1966): 297–307.

Roy, Arundhati. *The Chequebook and the Cruise-Missile.* London: Harper Perennial, 2004.

Ruether, Rosemary Radford. *Faith and Fratricide.* New York: Seabury, 1974.

Said, Edward W. *Beginnings, Intention, and Method.* New York: Columbia University Press, 1975.

—*Culture and Imperialism.* New York: Knopf, 1993.

—*The World, the Text, and the Critic.* London: Faber & Faber, 1984.

Sanders, Jack T. *Schismatics, Sectarians, Dissidents, Deviants.* London: SCM Press, 1993.

Sauer, Georg. "Die Umkehrforderung in der Verkündigung Jesajas." Pages 277–95 in *Wort-Gebot-Glaube: Beiträge zur Theologie des Alten Testaments.* Edited by Hans Joachim Stoebe et al. Zürich: Zwingli Verlag, 1970.

Sawyer, John F. A. "'Blessed Be My People Egypt' (Isaiah 19.25): The Context and Meaning of a Remarkable Passage." Pages 57–71 in *A Word in Season: Essays in Honour of William McKane*. Edited by J. D. Martin and P. R. Davies. JSOTSup 42. Sheffield: JSOT Press, 1986.
—"A Change of Emphasis in the Study of the Prophets." Pages 233–49 in Coggins, Phillips, and Knibb, eds., *Israel's Prophetic Tradition*.
—"Daughter of Zion and Servant of the Lord in Isaiah: A Comparison." *JSOT* 44 (1989): 89–107.
—*The Fifth Gospel: Isaiah in the History of Christianity*. Cambridge: Cambridge University Press, 1996.
—"The Gospel according to Isaiah." *ExpTim* 113, no. 2 (2001): 39–43.
—"Hebrew Words for the Resurrection of the Dead." *VT* 13 (1973): 218–34.
—*Isaiah*. 2 vols. The Daily Study Bible. Edinburgh: St. Andrews Press; Philadelphia: Westminster, 1984.
Schökel, Luis Alonso. *A Manual of Hermeneutics*. The Biblical Seminar 54. Sheffield: Sheffield Academic Press, 1998.
Scholes, Robert. *Textual Power: Literary Theory and the Teaching of English*. New Haven: Yale University Press, 1985.
Schneidau, Herbert N. "Biblical Narrative and Modern Consciousness." Pages 132–50 in *The Bible and the Narrative Tradition*. Edited by Frank McConnell. New York: Oxford University Press, 1986.
Schramm, Brooks. *The Opponents of Third Isaiah: Reconstructing the Cultic History of the Restoration*. JSOTSup 193. Sheffield: Sheffield Academic Press, 1995.
Schreiter, Robert J. *Reconciliation: Mission and Ministry in a Changing Social Order*. Maryknoll, N.Y.: Orbis; Cambridge, Mass.: Boston Theological Institute, 1992.
Schüssler Fiorenza, Elisabeth. *Bread Not Stone: The Challenge of Feminist Biblical Interpretation*. Boston: Beacon, 1984.
—*Rhetoric and Ethic: The Politics of Biblical Studies*. Minneapolis: Fortress, 1999.
Schwartz, Regina M. *The Curse of Cain: The Violent Legacy of Monotheism*. Chicago: University of Chicago Press, 1997.
Scott, James, ed. *Exile: Old Testament, Jewish, and Christian Conceptions*. Leiden: Brill, 1997.
Scott, R. B. Y. "The Book of Isaiah, Chapters 1–39." Pages 151–381 in vol. 5 of *The Interpreter's Bible*. Edited by G. A. Buttrick et al. 12 vols. New York: Abingdon-Cokesbury, 1951–57.
Scott, Robert L. "On Viewing Rhetoric as Epistemic." *Central States Speech Journal* 18 (1967): 9–17.
Searle, John R. *Speech Acts: An Essay in the Philosophy of Language*. Cambridge: Cambridge University Press, 1972.
Segovia, Fernando F. "In the Wake of Liberation: Postcolonial and Diasporic Criticisms." Pages 91–111 in *Los caminos inexhauribles de la palabra: Las relecturas creativas en la Biblia y de la Biblia*. Edited by Guillermo Hansen. Buenos Aires: Lumen, 2000.
Segovia, Fernando F., and Mary Ann Tolbert, eds. *Reading from this Place*. Vol. 1, *Social Location and Biblical Interpretation in the United States*. Minneapolis: Fortress, 1995.
—*Reading from this Place*. Vol. 2, *Social Location and Biblical Interpretation in Global Perspective*. Minneapolis: Fortress, 1995.
Seitz, Christopher R. *Isaiah 1–39*. Interpretation. Louisville, Ky.: John Knox, 1993.

—"Isaiah 1–66: Making Sense of the Whole." Pages 105–26 in *Reading and Preaching the Book of Isaiah*. Edited by Christopher R. Seitz. Philadelphia: Fortress, 1988.

—*Word without End: The Old Testament as Abiding Theological Witness*. Grand Rapids: Eerdmans, 1998.

—*Zion's Final Destiny: The Development of the Book of Isaiah. A Reassessment of Isaiah 36–39*. Minneapolis: Fortress, 1991.

Semler, Johann Salomo. *Vorbereitung zur theologischen Hermeneutik*. 4 vols. Halle: Carl Hermann Hemmerde, 1760–69.

Shelley, P. "A Defence of Poetry." Pages 23–59 in *Peacock's Four Ages of Poetry, Shelley's Defence of Poetry, Browning's Essay on Shelley*. Edited by H. F. B. Brett-Smith. Oxford: Blackwell, 1972.

Sherwood, Yvonne. " 'Darke Texts Needs Notes': On Prophetic Prophecy, John Donne, and the Baroque." *JSOT* 100 (2002): 47–74.

—"Of Fruit and Corpses and Wordplay Visions: Picturing Amos 8:1–3." *JSOT* 92 (2001): 5–27.

Shorter, Aylward. *African Christian Theology*. Maryknoll, N.Y.: Orbis, 1986.

—*Toward a Theology of Inculturation*. Maryknoll, N.Y.: Orbis, 1988.

Sillars, M. O. "Persistent Problems in Rhetorical Criticism." Pages 69–88 in *Rhetoric and Communication: Studies in the University of Illinois Tradition*. Edited by J. Blankenship and H. G. Stelzner. Urbana: University of Illinois Press, 1976.

Skinner, J. *The Book of the Prophet Isaiah*. 2 vols. CB. Cambridge: Cambridge University Press, 1900.

Slotki, Israel W. *Isaiah*. London: Soncino, 1949.

Smith, Daniel. *Religion of the Landless: The Social Context of the Babylonian Exile*. Philadelphia: Fortress, 1989.

Smith, George Adam. *The Book of Isaiah*. 2 vols. Rev. ed., London: Hodder & Stoughton, 1927.

Smith, P. A. *Rhetoric and Redaction in Trito-Isaiah: The Structure, Growth, and Authorship of Isaiah 56–66*. Leiden: Brill, 1995.

Smith-Christopher, Daniel L. *A Biblical Theology of Exile*. OBT. Minneapolis: Fortress, 2002.

Snaith, N. H. "Isaiah 40–66: A Study of the Teaching of the Second Isaiah and its Consequences." Pages 139–46 in *Studies on the Second Part of the Book of Isaiah*. Edited by H. Orlinsky and N. H. Snaith. VTSup 14. Leiden: Brill, 1977.

—"The Servant of the Lord in Deutero-Isaiah." Pages 187–200 in *Studies in Old Testament Prophecy*. Edited by H. H. Rowley. Edinburgh: T. & T. Clark, 1950.

Snyman, S. D. "Trends in the History of Research on the Problem of Violence in the Old Testament." *Skrif en Kerk* 18, no. 1 (1997): 127–45.

Soares-Prabhu, George M. "Laughing at Idols: The Dark Side of Biblical Monotheism (An Indian Reading of Isaiah 44:9–20)." Pages 109–31 in vol. 2 of Segovia and Tolbert, eds., *Reading from this Place*.

Sölle, Dorothee. *Thinking about God: An Introduction to Theology*. London: SCM Press; Philadelphia: Trinity, 1990.

Song, Choan-Seng. *The Compassionate God: An Exercise in the Theology of Transposition*. London: SCM Press, 1982.

—*Jesus and the Reign of God*. Minneapolis: Fortress, 1993.

—*Jesus in the Power of the Spirit*. Minneapolis: Fortress, 1994.

—*Jesus, the Crucified People*. Minneapolis: Fortress, 1996.

—*Theology from the Womb of Asia*. London: SCM Press, 1988.

Soulen, Kendall. *The God of Israel and Christian Theology*. Minneapolis: Fortress, 1996.

Stacey, David. *Isaiah 1–39*. Epworth Commentaries. London: Epworth, 1993.

Steiner, George. "Our Homeland, the Text." *Salmagundi* 6 (winter–spring 1985): 4–25.

Stenning, J. F., ed. and trans. *The Targum of Isaiah*. Oxford: Clarendon, 1949.

Stern, David. "*Imitatio Hominis*: Anthropomorphism and the Character(s) of God in Rabbinic Literature." *Prooftexts* 12 (1992): 151–74.

Stroupe, Nibs, and Inez Fleming. *While we Run this Race: Confronting the Power of Racism in a Southern Church*. New York: Orbis, 1995.

Sugirtharajah, R. S. *The Bible and the Third World: Precolonial, Colonial, and Postcolonial Encounters*. Cambridge: Cambridge University Press, 2001.

—ed. *The Postcolonial Bible*. Bible and Postcolonialism 1. Sheffield: Sheffield Academic Press, 1998.

Sweeney, Marvin A. "The Book of Isaiah in Recent Research." *Currents in Research: Biblical Studies* 1 (1993): 141–62.

—"Formation and Form in Prophetic Literature." Pages 113–26 in *Old Testament Interpretation: Past, Present, and Future. Essays in Honor of Gene M. Tucker*. Edited by James Luther Mays, David L. Petersen, and Kent Harold Richards. Nashville: Abingdon, 1995.

—*Isaiah 1–4 and the Post-exilic Understanding of the Isaianic Tradition*. BZAW 171. Berlin: de Gruyter, 1988.

—*Isaiah 1–39*. Forms of Old Testament Literature 16. Grand Rapids: Eerdmans, 1996.

—"Micah's Debate with Isaiah." *JSOT* 93 (2001): 111–24.

—"The Reconceptualization of the Davidic Covenant in Isaiah." Pages 41–61 in *Studies in the Book of Isaiah: Festschrift Willem A. M. Beuken*. Edited by J. Van Ruiten and M. Vervenne. BETL 132. Louvain: Louvain University Press, 1997.

Talmon, Shemaryahu. *King, Cult, and Calendar in Ancient Israel*. Leiden: Brill; Jerusalem: Magnes, 1986.

Tamarkin Reis, Pamela. "Hagar Requited." *JSOT* 87 (2000): 75–109.

Tate, Marvin E. "The Book of Isaiah in Recent Study." Pages 22–56 in *Forming Prophetic Literature*. Edited by James W. Watts and Paul R. House. JSOTSup 235. Sheffield: Sheffield Academic Press, 1996.

Taylor, Mark C. *Altarity*. Chicago: University of Chicago Press, 1987.

—*Erring: A Postmodern A/theology*. Chicago: University of Chicago Press, 1984.

Taylor, Michael. *Not Angels but Agencies: The Ecumenical Response to Poverty. A Primer*. London: SCM Press; Geneva: WCC Publications, 1995.

—*Poverty and Christianity*. London: SCM Press, 2000.

Terrien, Samuel, *The Elusive Presence: Toward a New Biblical Theology*. New York: Harper & Row, 1978.

Thiselton, Anthony C.. "Communicative Action and Promise in Interdisciplinary, Biblical, and Theological Hermeneutics." Pages 133–239 in Lundin, Walhout, and Thiselton, eds., *The Promise of Hermeneutics*.

Thoma, C. *A Christian Theology of Judaism*. New York: Paulist, 1980.

Thomas, Norman E., ed. *Classic Texts in Mission and World Christianity*. American Society of Missiology Series 20. Maryknoll, N.Y.: Orbis, 1995. Also published as *Readings in World Mission*. London: SPCK, 1995.

Tilley, Terrence W. *The Evils of Theodicy*. Washington, D.C · Georgetown University Press, 1991.

Toombs, Lawrence E. "The Psalms." Pages 253–303 in *The Interpreter's One-Volume Commentary on the Bible*. Edited by Charles M. Laymon. Nashville: Abingdon, 1971.

Tracy, David. *The Analogical Imagination: Christian Theology and the Culture of Pluralism.* London: SCM Press; New York: Crossroad, 1981.

—"Metaphor and Religion: The Test Case of Christian Texts." Pages 89–104 in *On Metaphor.* Edited by Sheldon Sacks. Chicago: University of Chicago Press, 1978.

Trible, Phyllis. *Rhetorical Criticism: Context, Method, and the Book of Jonah.* Minneapolis: Fortress, 1994.

Trueman, Carl R.. "The Future of Evangelical Scholarship: A British Perspective." Pages 291–309 in Trueman, Gray, and Blomberg, eds., *Solid Ground.*

Trueman, Carl R., Tony J. Gray, and Craig L. Blomberg, eds. *Solid Ground: Twenty-five Years of Evangelical Theology.* Leicester: Apollos, 2000.

Tucker, Gene M., David L. Petersen, and Robert R. Wilson, eds. *Canon, Theology, and Old Testament Interpretation: Essays in Honor of Brevard Childs.* Philadelphia: Fortress, 1988.

Turner, Victor. *The Anthropology of Performance.* New York: PAJ Publications, 1986.

—*The Ritual Process: Structure and Anti-Structure.* Ithaca, N.Y.: Cornell University Press, 1969.

Van Buren, Paul. *A Theology of the Jewish–Christian Reality.* 3 vols. San Francisco: Harper & Row, 1980–88.

Van Dyke Parunak, H. "Oral Typesetting: Some Uses of Biblical Structure." *Biblica* 62 (1981): 153–68.

—"Transitional Techniques in the Bible." *JBL* 102 (1983): 525–48.

Van Houten, Christiana. *The Alien in Israelite Law.* JSOTSup 107. Sheffield: JSOT Press, 1991.

Van Leeuwen, R. C. "Wealth and Poverty: System and Contradiction in Proverbs." *Hebrew Studies* 33 (1992): 25–36.

Van Wolde, Ellen. *Mr and Mrs Job.* London: SCM Press, 1997.

Vanhoozer, Kevin J. *Is there a Meaning in this Text? The Bible, the Reader, and the Morality of Literary Knowledge.* Leicester: Apollos, 2001.

Vermeylen, Jacques, ed. *The Book of Isaiah/Le livre d'Isaïe: Les oracles et leurs relectures unité et complexité de l'ouvrage.* BETL 81. Louvain: Louvain University Press, 1989.

Vickers, Brian. *In Defence of Rhetoric.* Oxford: Clarendon, 1988.

Virgili, Fabrice. *La France "Virile": Des Femmes Tondues à la Libération.* Paris: Editions Payot, 2000.

Vogels, W. "Egypte mon Peuple: L'Universalisme d'Isa 19:16–25." *Bib* 57 (1976): 494–515.

Volf, Miroslav. *Exclusion and Embrace: A Theological Exploration of Identity, Otherness, and Reconciliation.* Nashville: Abingdon, 1996.

—"Jehovah on Trial." *Christianity Today* (27 April 1998): 32–35.

Von Rad, G. *Holy War in Ancient Israel.* Grand Rapids: Eerdmans, 1991.

—"Kiplayim in Jes. 40: 2 = 'Äquivalent?'" *ZAW* 79 (1967): 80–82.

—*The Problem of the Hexateuch and Other Essays.* Edinburgh: Oliver & Boyd, 1966.

Wallace, Mark. *The Second Naiveté: Barth, Ricoeur, and the New Yale School.* Studies in American Biblical Hermeneutics 6. Macon, Ga.: Mercer University Press, 1990.

Ward, Graham. *Barth, Derrida, and the Language of Theology.* Cambridge: Cambridge University Press, 1995.

Watson, Duane F., and Alan J. Hauser. *Rhetorical Criticism of the Bible: A Comprehensive Bibliography with Notes on History and Method.* Biblical Interpretation 4. Leiden: Brill, 1994.

Watson, Francis. *Text, Church, and World.* Edinburgh: T. & T. Clark, 1994.

Watts, John D. W. "The Characterization of Yahweh in the Vision of Isaiah." *Review and Expositor* 83 (1986): 439–50.

—*Isaiah 1–33.* WBC 24. Waco, Tex.: Word Books, 1985.

—*Isaiah 34–66.* WBC 25. Waco, Tex.: Word Books, 1987.

Watts, Rikki E. "Consolation or Confrontation? Isaiah 40–55 and the Delay of the New Exodus." *TynBul* 41, no. 1 (1990): 31–59.

Webb, B. G. *The Message of Isaiah.* BST. Leicester: InterVarsity, 1996.

—"Zion in Transformation: A Literary Approach." Pages 65–84 in *The Bible in Three Dimensions.* Edited by David J. A. Clines, S. E. Fowl, and S. E. Porter. JSOTSup 87. Sheffield: Sheffield Academic Press, 1990.

Weinfeld, Moshe. "Justice and Righteousness." Pages 228–46 in Reventlow and Hoffman, eds., *Justice and Righteousness.*

West, Gerald O. "Kairos 2000: Moving beyond Church Theology." *Journal of Theology for Southern Africa* 108 (2001): 55–78.

—"Reading the Bible and Doing Theology in the New South Africa." Pages 445–58 in M. D. Carroll R. et al., eds., *The Bible in Human Society.*

Westermann, Claus. *Genesis 12–36: A Commentary.* Minneapolis: Augsburg, 1985.

—*Isaiah 40–66: A Commentary.* Translated by David M. G. Stalker. OTL. London: SCM Press, 1969.

—*Roots of Wisdom: The Oldest Proverbs of Israel and Other Peoples.* Louisville, Ky.: Westminster John Knox, 1995.

Whedbee, J. W. *Isaiah and Wisdom.* Nashville: Abingdon, 1971.

White, Stephen Ross. *Don Cupitt and the Future of Christian Doctrine.* London: SCM Press, 1994.

Whybray, R. N. *The Good Life in the Old Testament.* London: T. & T. Clark, 2002.

—*Isaiah 40–66.* NCBC. Grand Rapids: Eerdmans; London: Marshall, Morgan & Scott, 1975.

—"Prophecy and Wisdom." Pages 181–99 in Coggins, Phillips, and Knibb, eds., *Israel's Prophetic Tradition.*

Widyapranawa, S. H. *The Lord is Saviour: Faith in National Crisis. A Commentary on the Book of Isaiah.* ITC. Grand Rapids: Eerdmans, 1990.

Wildberger, Hans. *Isaiah 1–12.* Translated by Thomas H. Trapp. Continental Commentary. Minneapolis: Fortress, 1991.

Willey, Patricia Tull. *Remember the Former Things: The Recollection of Previous Texts in Second Isaiah.* Atlanta: Scholars Press, 1997.

Williams, James G. "The Social Location of Israelite Prophecy." *JAAR* 37 (1969): 153–65.

Williams, P. J. "Lying Spirits Sent by God? The Case of Micaiah's Prophecy." Pages 58–66 in Helm and Trueman, eds., *The Trustworthiness of God.*

Williamson, C. M. *A Guest in the House of Israel: Post-Holocaust Church Theology.* Louisville, Ky.: Westminster John Knox, 1993.

Williamson, H. G. M. *The Book Called Isaiah: Deutero-Isaiah's Role in Composition and Redaction.* Oxford: Clarendon, 1994.

—"Isaiah and the Wise." Pages 133–41 in *Wisdom in Ancient Israel: Essays in Honour of J. A. Emerton.* Edited by John Day, Robert P. Gordon, and H. G. M. Williamson. Cambridge: Cambridge University Press, 1995.

—"Synchronic and Diachronic in Isaian Perspective." Pages 211–26 in de Moor, ed., *Synchronic or Diachronic?.*

—*Variations on a Theme: King, Messiah, and Servant in the Book of Isaiah.* Carlisle: Paternoster, 1998.

Wilner, Eleanor. *Sarah's Choice.* Chicago: University of Chicago Press, 1989.

Wilson, Robert R. *Prophecy and Society in Ancient Israel.* Philadelphia: Fortress, 1980.

Wimsatt, W. K., Jr., with M. C. Beardsley. *The Verbal Icon: Studies in the Meaning of Poetry.* London: Methuen, 1970 (1954).

Winkle, Dwight W. van. "An Inclusive Authoritative Text in Exclusive Communities." Pages 423–40 in vol. 1 of Broyles and Evans, eds., *Writing and Reading the Scroll of Isaiah.*

Wittgenstein, Ludwig. *The Blue and Brown Books: Preliminary Studies for the "Philosophical Investigations."* Oxford: Blackwell, 1969.

Wolff, Hans Walter. *Haggai: A Commentary.* Minneapolis: Augsburg, 1988.

Wolterstorff, Nicholas. *Divine Discourse: Philosophical Reflections on the Claim that God Speaks.* Cambridge: Cambridge University Press, 1993.

Wood, James. "The All of the If." *New Republic* (March 1997): 29–36.

World Trade Organisation (WTO). *Agreement Establishing the World Trade Organization.* Geneva: World Trade Organisation Information and Media Relations Divisions, 1995.

Wright, Christopher J. H. *Living as the People of God: The Relevance of Old Testament Ethics.* Leicester: InterVarsity, 1983.

Wright, D. F. "Accommodation and Barbarity in John Calvin's Old Testament Commentaries." Pages 413–27 in *Understanding Poets and Prophets: Essays in Honour of George Wishart Anderson.* Edited by A. Graeme Auld. JSOTSup 152. Sheffield: JSOT Press, 1993.

Wyschogrod, Michael. *The Body of Faith: God in the People Israel.* San Francisco: Harper & Row, 1989.

Young, Edward J. *The Book of Isaiah.* 3 vols. NICOT. Grand Rapids: Eerdmans, 1964–72.

Zuckerman, Bruce. *Job the Silent.* Oxford: Oxford University Press, 1991.

INDEX OF AUTHORS